# SERMONS
## on GOSPEL
# THEMES

# SERMONS
## *on* GOSPEL
# THEMES

Addressing the Bible's Dual Themes
of Justification and Sanctification

## CHARLES G. FINNEY

ANEKO
PRESS

We love hearing from our readers. Please contact us
at www.anekopress.com/questions-comments with
any questions, comments, or suggestions.

*Sermons on Gospel Themes*
© 2021 by Aneko Press
All rights reserved. First edition 1876.
Updated edition copyright 2021.

*Cover Design: Jonathan Lewis*
*Editor: Paul Miller*

Aneko Press
www.anekopress.com
Aneko Press, Life Sentence Publishing, and our logos are trademarks of
Life Sentence Publishing, Inc.
203 E. Birch Street
P.O. Box 652
Abbotsford, WI 54405
**RELIGION / Christian Living / Spiritual Growth**
Paperback ISBN: 978-1-62245-770-0
Paperback ISBN (Amazon): 978-1-62245-830-1
eBook ISBN: 978-1-62245-771-7
10   9   8   7   6   5   4   3   2   1
Available where books are sold

# Contents

Oberlin College

# Preface

These sermons were preached by President Charles Finney at Oberlin College during the years 1845-1861, and were reported from his lips by myself. In taking these reports, I aimed to give the points of the sermons and all the important statements word for word, to always retain the substance of thought, and especially to seize upon the illustrations and present their essential points. Taken down in a type of shorthand, they were later written out, and in every case read to Charles Finney in his study for any corrections he might desire, and for his endorsement. Consequently, these reports truthfully present the great doctrines preached and, in good measure it is believed, the method and manner of his preaching.

Few preachers in any age have surpassed Charles Finney in clear and well-defined views of conscience and of man's moral convictions. Few have been more fully at home in the domain of law and government. Few have learned more of the spiritual life from experience and from observation. Not many have distinguished the true from the false more closely or have been more skillful in putting their points clearly and prudently. Therefore, these sermons under God were full of spiritual power. They are given to the public in this form in the hope that at least a measure of the same wholesome saving power may never fail to bless the reader.

—Henry Cowles

# Chapter 1

# God's Love for a Sinning World

For God so loved the world, that he gave his only begotten Son, that whosoever believeth in him should not perish, but have everlasting life.
—John 3:16

Sin is the most expensive thing in the universe. Nothing else can cost so much. Pardoned or unpardoned, its cost is infinitely great. Pardoned, the cost falls primarily on the great atoning Substitute; unpardoned, it must fall on the head of the guilty sinner.

The existence of sin is a fact everywhere experienced and everywhere observed. There is sin everywhere in the human race, and it is a dreadful plague. Sin is the violation of an infinitely important law – a law designed and adapted to secure the highest good of the universe. Obedience to this law is naturally essential to the good of all. Without obedience, there could be no blessedness – even in heaven.

As sin is a violation of a most important law, it cannot be treated lightly. No government can afford to treat disobedience as a trifle, inasmuch as everything – the entire welfare of the government and of all the governed – depends upon obedience. The necessity of guarding law and of punishing disobedience is in proportion to the value of the interests at stake.

The law of God will not be dishonored by anything He will do. It has been dishonored by the disobedience of man, so there is even more need that God should stand by it to retrieve its honor. The utmost dishonor is done to law by disowning, disobeying, and despising it. Sinning man has done all this. This law is not only good, but it is intrinsically necessary to the happiness of the governed. Therefore, it becomes of all things most necessary that the Lawgiver should vindicate His law. He must do so by all means.

Consequently, sin has involved God's government in a vast expense. Either the law must be executed at the expense of the well-being of the whole race, or God must submit to allow the worst results of disrespect to His law – results that in some form must involve a vast expense.

For example, take any human government. Suppose the righteous and necessary laws that it imposes are disowned and dishonored. In such a case, the violated law must be honored by the execution of its penalty, or something else not less expensive, and probably much more so, must be endured. Transgression must cost happiness somewhere, and in a vast amount.

In the case of God's government, it has been deemed advisable to provide a substitute – one who would answer the purpose of saving the sinner, and also of honoring the law. This being determined, the next great question was how such an expense will be met.

The Bible informs us how the question was in fact decided. It was to be by a voluntary enrollment or donation. Call it what you will, it was a voluntary offering. Who will be in charge of this? Who will begin where so much is to be raised? Who will make the first sacrifice? Who will take the first step in a project so vast?

The Bible tells us. It began with the Infinite Father. He made the first great donation. He gave His only begotten Son. Having begun with this, having given Him first, He freely gives all else that the demands of the case can require. First He gave His Son to make the atonement due to law. Then He gave and sent His Holy Spirit to take charge of this work. The Son on His part consented to stand as the representative of sinners so that He could honor the law by suffering in their place. He poured out His blood. He made a whole life of suffering a free donation on the altar. He did not withhold His face from being spit upon, nor His back from being beaten. He did not hide from the utmost abuse that wicked men could heap on Him. The Holy Spirit also devotes Himself to the most self-denying efforts unceasingly in order to accomplish the great object.

It would have been a very quick method for God to have turned over His hand upon the wicked of the human race and quickly send them all down to hell, as He once did when certain angels *kept not their first estate* (Jude 1:6). Rebellion broke out in heaven. God did not let it continue long around His lofty throne. However, in the case of man, He changed His course. He did not send them all to hell, but devised a vast scheme of measures to gain people's souls back to obedience and heaven that involved the most amazing self-denials and self-sacrifices.

For whom was this great donation made? *God so loved the world* (John 3:16), which means the whole race of mankind. The "world" in this connection cannot mean any specific part only, but the whole race. Not only the Bible, but the nature of the case shows that the atonement must have been made for the whole world. For clearly, if it had not been made for the entire human race, no person of the race could ever know that it was made for himself, and therefore no one could believe on Christ in the sense of receiving by faith the blessings of the atonement. There would be complete uncertainty as to the people included in the limited provisions that we now believe to be made, and the entire donation would fail through the impossibility of rational faith for its reception.

Suppose a will is made by a rich man that leaves certain property to certain unknown people, described only by the name of "the elect." They are not described otherwise than by this term, and all agree that although the maker of the will had specific individuals in mind, he left no description of them that either the persons themselves, the courts, nor any living mortal can understand. Such a will is of necessity altogether null and void. No living person can make a claim under such a will, and it would not be any better if these elect were described as residents of a specific town. Since it does not include all the residents of that town, and does not define which of them specifically, all is lost. Everyone has an equal claim and no one has any specific claim, and so no one can inherit.

If the atonement had been made in this way, no living person would have any valid reason for believing himself to be one of the elect prior to his reception of the gospel. Therefore, he would have no authority to believe and receive its blessings by faith. In fact, the atonement must be entirely void based upon this supposition – unless a special revelation is made to the people for whom it is intended.

As the case is, however, the very fact that a person belongs to the race of Adam – the fact that he is human, born of a woman, is all-sufficient. It brings him within the limits. He is one of the world for whom God gave His Son, that whosoever would believe in Him might not perish, but would have everlasting life.

The inner motive in the mind of God for this great gift was love – love to the world. God so loved the world that He gave His Son to die for it. God loved the universe also, but this gift of His Son came from love to our world. True in this great act, He took effort to provide for the interests of the universe. He was careful to do nothing that could in the least let down the sacredness of His law. Most carefully did He intend to guard against misunderstanding as to His regard for His law and for the high interests of obedience and happiness in His moral universe. He meant once and for all to do away with the danger lest any moral agent would be tempted to undervalue the moral law.

It was not only from love to souls, but it was also from respect to the spirit of the law of His own eternal reason that He gave up His Son to die. The purpose to give up His Son originated in this. The law of His own reason must be honored and held sacred. He can do nothing inconsistent with its spirit. He must do everything possible to prevent the commission of sin and to secure the confidence and love of His subjects. So sacred did He hold these great objects that He would sooner baptize His Son in His own blood than endanger the good of the universe. Beyond a question, it was love and regard for the highest good of the universe that led Him to sacrifice His own beloved Son.

> The inner motive in the mind of God for this great gift was love – love to the world.

Let us next carefully consider the nature of this love. The text lays special stress on this: *God so loved*. His love was of such a nature and was so wonderful and so distinct in its character that it led Him to give up His only Son to die. More is evidently implied in this expression than simply its greatness. It is most distinct in its character.

Unless we understand this, we will be in danger of falling into the strange mistake of the Universalists, who are forever talking about God's love for sinners, but whose notions of the nature of this love never lead to repentance or to holiness. They seem to think of this love as simply good nature, and they conceive of God only as a very good-natured being whom no one needs to fear. Such ideas have not the least influence toward holiness, but the very opposite. It is only when we come to understand what this love is in its nature that we feel its moral power promoting holiness.

It may be reasonably asked that if God so loved the world, with a love characterized by greatness and by greatness only, why did He not save all the world without sacrificing His Son? This question suffices to show us that there is deep meaning in this word "so," and it should cause us to carefully study its meaning.

1. This love in its nature is not complacency. It is not a delight in the character of the human race. This could not be, for there was nothing loveable in their character. For God to have loved such a race complacently would have been infinitely disgraceful to Himself.

2. It was not mere emotion or feeling. It was not a blind impulse, though many seem to think it was. It seems to be often supposed that God acted as people do when they are carried away by strong emotion. But there could be no virtue in this. A man might give away all he is worth under such a blind impulse of feeling and yet be no more virtuous. In saying this, though, we do not exclude all emotion from the love of kindness, nor from God's love for a lost world. He had emotion, but not emotion only. Indeed, the Bible everywhere teaches us that God's love for mankind, lost in his sins, was paternal. It was the love of a father for his offspring – in this case, for a rebellious, defiant, prodigal offspring. In this love, there must of course blend the deepest compassion.

3. On the part of Christ, considered as Mediator, this love was paternal. He is not ashamed to call them brethren (Hebrews 2:11). In one point of view, He is acting for brethren, and in another, for children. The Father gave Him up for this work, and of course He sympathizes in the love appropriate to its relationship.

4. This love must be entirely unselfish, for He had nothing to hope or to fear – no profit to make out of His children if they would be saved. Indeed, it is impossible to imagine God as being selfish since His love embraces all creatures and all interests according to their real value. No doubt He took delight in saving our race. Why should He not? It is a great salvation in every sense, and it greatly increases the joy of heaven. It will greatly affect the glory and the blessedness of the Infinite God. He will eternally respect Himself for love so unselfish. He knows also that all His holy creatures will eternally respect Him for this work and for the love that gave it birth. Let it also be said, though, that He knew they would not respect Him for this great work unless they would see that He did it for the good of sinners.

> Because He loved all impartially, with no respect of persons, therefore He loved each one in particular.

5. This love was zealous, not that coldhearted state of mind that some imagine. It was not merely a concept, but it was a love that was deep, zealous, earnest, and burning in His soul as a fire that nothing can quench.

6. The sacrifice was a most self-denying one. Did it cost the Father nothing to give up His own beloved Son to suffer and to die such a death? If this is not self-denial, what is? Is it not the noblest self-denial for God to give up His Son to so much suffering? The universe could never have the idea of great self-denial if it were not for such an example.

7. This love was distinct because it was universal, and it was also universal because it was distinct. God loved each sinner in particular, and therefore He loved all. Because He loved all impartially, with no respect of persons, therefore He loved each one in particular.

8. This was a most patient love. It is rare to find a parent who so loves his child as to never be impatient. Let me go around and ask how many of you parents can say that you love all your children so well, with so much love, and with love so wisely ruling your heart and actions that you have never felt impatient toward any of them – so that you can take them in your arms under the greatest provocations and love them still, love them out of their sins, and love them into repentance and into the spirit of family? Of which of your children can you say that you never upset that child, that if you were to meet him in heaven, you could say that you never caused that child to be distressed? I have often heard parents say, "I love my children, but oh, how my patience fails me!" And after the dear ones are dead, you may hear their bitter moans: "How could I have caused my child so much stumbling and so much sin?"

God never provokes us. He is never impatient. His love is so deep and so great that He is always patient.

Sometimes when parents have unfortunate children, poor objects of compassion, they can bear with anything from them; but when their children are very bad, they seem to feel that they are quite excused for being impatient. In God's case, He does not have unfortunate children, but those who are intensely wicked, intelligently wicked. But oh, His amazing patience! He is so set upon their good, so desirous of their highest well-being, that no matter how they abuse Him, He sets himself to bless them still and to win them by the tears and blood and death of His Son in their place!

9. This is a jealous love, not in a bad sense, but in a good sense – in the sense of being exceedingly careful lest anything should occur to injure those He loves. It is like that of a husband and wife who truly love each other and are jealous with ever-wakeful jealousy over each other's welfare, seeking always to do all they can to promote each other's true interests.

This offering is already made – made in good faith. It was not just promised, but it was actually made. The promise, given long before, has been fulfilled. The Son has come, He has died and has made the ransom, and He lives to offer it – a prepared salvation to all who will embrace it.

The Son of God did not die to appease vengeance, as some seem to understand it, but He died under the demands of the law. The law had been dishonored by its violation, so Christ undertook to honor it by giving up to its demands His suffering life and atoning death. It was not to appease a vindictive spirit in God, but to secure the highest good of the universe in a dispensation of mercy.

Since this atonement has been made, all people in the human race have a right to it. It is open to everyone who will embrace it. Though Jesus still remains the Father's Son, by gracious right He belongs in an important sense to the human race – to everyone, so that every sinner has an interest in His blood if he will only come humbly forward and claim it. God sent His Son to be the Savior of the world – of whomsoever would believe and accept this great salvation.

God gives His Spirit to apply this salvation to us. He comes to each person's door and knocks, to gain admittance if He can, and to show each sinner that he may now have salvation. Oh, what a labor of love this is!

If this salvation is to be received, it must be received by faith. This is the only possible way. God's rule over sinners is moral, not physical, because the sinner is himself a moral and not a physical agent. Therefore, God can influence us in no way unless we will give Him our confidence. He never can save us by merely taking us away to some place called heaven – as if a change of place would change the voluntary heart. There can, therefore, be no possible way to be saved except by simple faith.

Do not mistake and suppose that embracing the gospel is simply to believe these historical facts without truly receiving Christ as your Savior. If this had been the plan, then Christ would have only needed to come down and die, and then go back to heaven and quietly wait to see who would believe the facts. But how different is the real case! Now Christ comes down to fill the soul with His own life and love. Repentant sinners hear and believe the truth concerning Jesus, and then receive Christ into the soul to live and reign there supreme and forever.

Many people make a mistake on this point, saying, "If I believe the facts as a matter of history, it is enough." No! No! This is not it by any means. *With the heart man believeth unto righteousness* (Romans 10:10). The atonement was indeed made to provide the way so that Jesus could come down to human hearts and draw them into union and sympathy with Himself, so that God could let down the arms of His love and embrace sinners, and so that law and government would not be dishonored by such tokens of friendship shown by God toward sinners. But the atonement will by no means save sinners only as it prepares the way for them to come into sympathy and fellowship of heart with God.

Now Jesus comes to each sinner's door and knocks. Listen! What is that? Why this knocking? Why did He not go away and stay in heaven, if that were the system, until people would simply believe the historical facts and be baptized, as some suppose, for salvation. But now, see how He comes down and tells the sinner what He has done, reveals all His love, and tells him how holy and sacred it is – so sacred that He can by no means act without reference to the holiness of His law and the purity of His government. Thus impressing on the heart the most deep and enlarged ideas of His holiness and purity, He enforces the need of deep repentance and the sacred duty of renouncing all sin.

## Remarks

1. The Bible teaches that sinners may forfeit their birthright and put themselves beyond the reach of mercy. I recently mentioned in a sermon the obvious necessity that God should guard Himself against the abuses of His love. The circumstances are such as to create the greatest danger of such abuse, and therefore He must make sinners know that they may not abuse His love, and cannot do so with impunity.

2. Under the gospel, sinners are in circumstances of the greatest possible responsibility. They are in the utmost danger of trampling down beneath their feet the very Son of God (Hebrews 10:29). *Come,* they say, *let us kill Him, and the inheritance shall be ours* (Mark 12:7). When God sends forth, last of all, His own beloved Son, what do they do? They add to all their other sins and rebellions the highest insult to this glorious Son! Suppose something similar to this were done under a human government. A case of rebellion occurs in some of the provinces. The king sends his own son, not with an army to cut them down quick in their rebellion, but gently, meekly, and patiently he goes among them, explaining the laws of the kingdom and exhorting them to obedience. What do they do in that case? With one consent, they unite to seize him and put him to death!

Maybe you deny the application of this and ask me, "Who murdered the Son of God? Were they not Jews?" Yes, and have you sinners had no part in this murder? Has not your treatment of Jesus Christ shown that you are most fully in sympathy with the ancient Jews in their murder of the Son of God? If you had been there, would anyone have shouted louder than you, "Away with Him! Crucify Him! Crucify Him!"? Have you not always said, *Depart from us; for we desire not the knowledge of thy ways* (Job 21:14)?

3. It was said of Christ that although He was rich, He became poor so that we through His poverty might be rich (2 Corinthians 8:9). How remarkably true this is! Our redemption cost Christ His life. It found Him rich, but made Him poor. It found us infinitely poor, but made us rich – even to all the wealth of heaven. However, no one can partake of these riches until they will each accept them for himself in the legitimate way. They must be received on the terms proposed, or the offer passes completely away and you are left poorer even than if no such treasures had ever been laid at your feet.

Many people seem to entirely misunderstand this case. They do not seem to believe what God says, but keep saying, "If, if, if there only were any salvation for me; if there were only an atonement provided for the pardon of my sins." This was one of the last things that was cleared up in my mind before I fully committed my soul to trust God. I had been studying the atonement. I saw its philosophical relevance. I saw what it demanded of the sinner, but it irritated me, and I said, "If I should become a Christian, how could I know what God would do with me?" Under this irritation, I said foolish and bitter things against Christ – until my own soul was horrified at its own wickedness, and I said, "I will make all things right with Christ if this is possible."

> Our redemption cost Christ His life. It found Him rich, but made Him poor. It found us infinitely poor, but made us rich.

In this way, many people advance upon the encouragements of the gospel as if it were only a possibility or an experiment. They take each forward step most carefully, with fear and trembling, as if there were the utmost doubt whether there could be any mercy for them. This is how it was with me. I was on my way to my office when the thought entered my mind: "What are you waiting for? You do not need to make this so difficult. All is done already. You only have to consent to the proposition. Give your heart right up to it at once. This is all."

And so it is. All Christians and sinners should understand that the whole plan is complete. They should understand that the whole of Christ – His character, His work, His atoning death, and His ever-living intercession – belongs to each and every person and simply needs to be accepted. There is a full ocean of it. There it is. You can just as well take it as not. It is as if you stood parched with thirst on the shore of an ocean of soft, pure water. You are welcome to drink, and you do not need to fear that you might exhaust that ocean or starve anyone else by drinking yourself. You do not need to feel that you are not made free to drink from that ocean of waters. You are invited and urged to drink, and to drink abundantly!

This ocean supplies all your need. You do not need to have in yourself the attributes of Jesus Christ, for His attributes become practically yours for all possible use. As the Scriptures say, He is of God made unto us wisdom, righteousness, sanctification, and redemption (1 Corinthians 1:30). What do you need? Wisdom? Here it is. Righteousness? Here it is. Sanctification? Here you have it. It is all in Christ. Can you possibly think of anything needful for your moral purity or your usefulness that is not here in Christ? Nothing. All is provided here.

Therefore, you do not need to say, "I will go and pray and try," as the hymn says:

> I'll go to Jesus though my sin
> Hath like a mountain rose,
> Perhaps He will admit my plea;
> Perhaps will hear my prayer.[1]

There is no need of any "perhaps." The doors are always open, like the doors of Broadway Tabernacle in New York that were made to swing open and fasten themselves open so that they could not swing back and close down upon the crowds of people thronging to pass through.

---

1    This is from a hymn by Edmund Jones that begins with "Come, humble sinner."

In the same way, the door of salvation is always open. It is fastened open, and no one can shut it – not even the pope, the devil, or any angel from heaven or from hell. There it stands, swung open and the passage wide open for every sinner of our race to enter if he will.

Sin is the most expensive thing in the universe. Are you well aware, sinner, what a price has been paid for you so that you can be redeemed and made an heir of God and of heaven? Oh, what an expensive business it is for you to indulge in sin!

What an enormous tax the government of God has paid to redeem this land from its ruin! Talk about the tax of Great Britain and of all other nations added together – it is all nothing compared to the sin-tax of God's government – that dreadful sin-tax! Think how much is kept in motion to save sinners! The Son of God was sent down, angels are sent as ministering spirits to the heirs of salvation (Hebrews 1:14), missionaries are sent, and Christians labor, pray, and weep in deep and anxious concern – all to seek and save the lost.

What an extraordinary, enormous tax is levied upon the benevolence of the universe to put away sin and to save the sinner! If the cost could be computed in solid gold, it would be a solid globe of itself! What an display of toil and cost from angels, Jesus Christ, the divine Spirit, and living men. Shame on sinners who hold on to sin despite all these benevolent efforts to save them, who instead of being ashamed of sin will say, "Let God pay off this tax! Who cares! Let the missionaries labor. Let pious women work their very fingers off to raise funds to keep all this human machinery in motion. It does not matter. What is all this to me? I have loved my pleasures, and I will pursue them!" What a callous heart this is!

Sinners can very well afford to make sacrifices to save their fellow sinners. Paul could do so for his fellow sinners. He felt that he had done his part toward making sinners, and now he wanted to do his part in converting them back to God. But look over there – that young man thinks he cannot afford to be a minister because he is afraid he will not be well supported. Does he not owe something to the grace that saved his soul from hell? Has he not some sacrifices to make since Jesus has made so many for him? Does he not have some sacrifices to make for those Christians, too, who were in Christ before him and who prayed and suffered and toiled for his soul's salvation? As to his danger of lacking bread in the Lord's work, let him trust his Great Master.

Let me also say that churches may be in great fault for not comfortably supporting their pastors. Let them know that God will assuredly starve them if they starve their ministers. Their own souls and the souls of their children will be as barren as death if they selfishly starve those whom God in His providence sends to feed them with the bread of life.

How much it costs to rid society of certain forms of sin, such as slavery, for example! How much has been expended already, and how much more yet remains to be expended before this bitter evil and curse and sin will be rooted from our land! This is part of God's great enterprise, and He will press it on to its completion. Yet at what an amazing cost! How many lives and how much agony it costs to get rid of this one sin!

Woe to those who make gain from the sins of men! Just think of the bartender – tempting people while God is trying to dissuade them from rushing on in the ways of sin and death! Think of the guilt of those who set themselves in array against God in this way! Christ has to contend with bartenders who are doing all they can to hinder His work.

Our subject richly illustrates the nature of sin as mere selfishness. It does not care how much sin costs Jesus Christ, how much it costs the church, how much it strains the benevolent sympathies and the self-sacrificing labors of all the good in earth or heaven. The sinner does not care about that. The sinner loves self-indulgence and will have it while he can. How many of you have cost your family members and friends countless tears and trouble to get you back from your ways of sin? Are you not ashamed when so much has been done for you, yet you cannot be persuaded to give up your sins and turn to God and holiness?

The whole effort on the part of God for mankind is one of suffering and self-denial. Beginning with the sacrifice of His own beloved Son, it is carried on with ever-renewed sacrifices and toilsome labors at a considerable and tremendous expense. Just think how long a time these efforts have continued already. Consider how many tears poured out like water it has cost, how much pain in many forms this enterprise has caused and cost – and yes, that very sin that you hold on to and keep close to your heart! God may well hate it when He sees how much it costs, and He will say, *O do not that abominable thing that I hate* (Jeremiah 44:4).

Yet God is not unhappy in these self-denials. So great is His joy in the results that He considers all the suffering but comparatively little, even as earthly parents enjoy the efforts they make to bless their children. Parents will almost work their very hands off for their children. Mothers sit up at night to sew until they reel with fatigue and blindness, but if you were to see their toil, you would often also see their joy, so intensely do they love their children.

Such is the labor, the joy, and the self-denial of the Father, the Son, and the Holy Spirit in their great work for human salvation. They are often grieved that so many will refuse to be saved. Toiling on in a common sympathy, there is nothing, within reasonable limits, that they will not do or suffer to accomplish their great work. It is wonderful to think how all creation also sympathizes in this work and its necessary sufferings. Go back to the scene of Christ's sufferings. Could the sun in the heavens look down unmoved on such a scene? No, for the sun could not even behold it, but veiled its face from the sight! All nature seemed to put on her robes of deepest mourning. The scene was too much for even inanimate nature to bear. The sun turned its back and could not look down on such a spectacle!

> He knew perfectly what it would cost Him to redeem sinners, and He knew that the result would amply justify all the cost.

The subject strongly illustrates the worth of the soul. Do you think that God would have done all this if He had had those low views on this subject that sinners usually have?

Martyrs and saints enjoy their sufferings, filling up in themselves what is lacking of the sufferings of Christ – not in the actual atonement, but in the subordinate parts of the work to be done. It is the nature of true religion to love self-denial.

The results will fully justify all the expense. God had well counted the cost before He began. Long before He formed a moral universe, He knew perfectly what it would cost Him to redeem sinners, and He knew that the result would amply justify all the cost. He knew that a wonder of mercy would be performed – that the suffering demanded of Christ, as great as it was, would be endured. He knew that infinitely glorious results would accumulate from this. He looked down the track of time into the distant ages where, as the cycles of time rolled along, there could be seen the joys of redeemed saints who are singing their songs and striking their harps anew with the everlasting song through the long, long, long eternity of their blessedness.

Was not this enough for the heart of infinite love to enjoy? What do you think of it, Christian? Maybe you now say, "I am ashamed to ask to be forgiven. How can I bear to receive such mercy! It is the price of blood, and how can I accept it? How can I make Jesus so much expense?"

You are right in saying that you have cost Him much expense, but the expense has been cheerfully met. The pain has all been endured and will not need to be endured again. It will not cost any more if you accept than if you decline. Moreover, let it be considered that Jesus Christ has not acted unwisely. He did not pay too much for the soul's redemption. He did not pay any more than the interests of God's government demanded and the worth of the soul would justify.

When you come to see Him face to face and tell Him what you think of it, when you are some thousands of years older than you are now, will you not adore that wisdom that manages this plan and the infinite love in which it had its birth? What will you then say of that amazing condescension that brought down Jesus to your rescue! Christian, have you not often poured out your soul before your Savior in acknowledgment of what you have cost Him, and then there seemed to be a kind of lifting up as if the very bottom of your soul were to rise and you wanted to pour out your whole heart to Him? If anyone had seen you, they would have wondered what had happened to you that had so melted your soul in gratitude and love.

Sinners, will you sell your birthright? How much will you take for it? How much will you take for your interest in Christ? For how much will you sell your soul? Would you sell your Christ? Of old they sold Him for thirty pieces of silver, and ever since then, the heavens have been raining tears of blood on our guilty world. If you were to be asked by the devil to name the price for which you would sell your soul, what would be the price named?

Lorenzo Dow once met a man as he was riding along a solitary road to fulfil an appointment, and he said to him, "Friend, have you ever prayed?"

"No."

"How much will you take to never pray for the rest of your life?"

"One dollar."

Dow paid the man a dollar and rode on. The man put the money in his pocket and went on – thinking. The more he thought, the worse he felt. He said, "I have sold my soul for one dollar! It must be that I have met the devil! Nobody else would tempt me so. With all my soul, I must repent or be damned forever!"

How often have you bargained to sell your Savior for less than thirty pieces of silver, or for the smallest trifle?

Finally, God wants volunteers to help on this great work. God has given Himself, He has given His Son, and He has sent His Spirit, but more laborers are still needed. What will you give? Paul said, *I bear in my body the marks of the Lord Jesus* (Galatians 6:17). Do you aspire to such an honor? What will you do? What will you suffer? Do not say that you have nothing to give. You can give yourself – your eyes, your ears, your hands, your mind, your heart, your all. Surely nothing you have is too sacred and too good to be devoted to such a work upon such a call! How many young men and young women are ready to go? Let your heart leap up and cry, *Here am I; send me* (Isaiah 6:8).

# Chapter 2

# In Trusting in the Mercy of God

I trust in the mercy of God forever and ever.
—Psalm 52:8

In dealing with this subject, I will discuss the following points:

I.    What mercy is

II.   What is implied in trusting in the mercy of the Lord forever

III.  The conditions on which we may safely trust in God's mercy

IV.   Several mistakes that are made on this subject

## I. What mercy is

1. Mercy as an attribute of God is not to be confounded with mere goodness. This mistake is often made. You will see at once that it is a mistake if you consider that mercy is directly opposed to justice, while justice is one of the natural and legitimate developments of goodness. Goodness may demand the exercise of justice; indeed, it often does. However, to say that mercy demands the exercise of justice is to use the word without meaning. Mercy asks for justice to be set aside. Of

course, mercy and goodness stand in very different relations to justice, and they are very different attributes.

2. Mercy is an arrangement to pardon the guilty. Its exercise consists in arresting and setting aside the penalty of law when that penalty has been incurred by transgression. It is, as has been said, directly opposed to justice. Justice treats every individual according to what he deserves; mercy treats the criminal very differently from how he deserves to be treated. What one deserves is never the rule by which mercy is guided, although it is precisely the rule of justice.

3. Mercy is exercised only where there is guilt. It always presupposes guilt. The penalty of the law must have been previously incurred, or else there can be no room for mercy.

4. Mercy can be exercised no farther than one deserves punishment. It may continue its exercise just as long as punishment is deserved, but no longer. It can go just as far as one's transgressions deserve, but no farther. If great punishment is deserved, great mercy can be shown. If endless punishment is due, then there is opportunity for infinite mercy to be shown, but not otherwise.

## II. What is implied in trusting in the mercy of the Lord forever

1. Trusting in mercy implies a conviction of guilt. No one can properly be said to trust in the mercy of God unless they have committed crimes and are conscious of this fact. Justice protects the innocent, and they may safely appeal to it for defense or remedy. But for the guilty, nothing remains but to trust in mercy. Trusting in mercy always implies a deep, heartfelt conviction of personal guilt.

2. Trust in mercy always implies that we have no hope on the obligation of justice. If we had anything to expect from justice, we would not look to mercy. The human heart is too proud to throw itself upon mercy while it presumes itself to have a valid claim to favor on the obligation of justice. Even more, to appeal to mercy when we could rightfully appeal to justice is never demanded either by God's law or the gospel, nor can it be in harmony with our relations to God's government. In fact, the thing is impossible in the very nature of the mind.

> Justice treats every individual according to what he deserves; mercy treats the criminal very differently from how he deserves to be treated.

3. To trust in mercy implies a proper understanding of what mercy is. Many people fail on this point because they confuse mercy with mere goodness, or with grace, which is considered as mere favor to the undeserving. Grace may be shown where there is no mercy, as the term "mercy" is applied to the pardon of crime. We all know that God shows favor, or grace, in the general sense to all the wicked on earth. *He makes His sun to rise on the evil and on the good, and sends rain on the just and on the unjust* (Matthew 5:45). However, to trust in this general favor shown to the wicked while on trial here is not trusting in the mercy of God. We never trust in mercy until we really understand what it is – pardon for the crimes of the guilty.

4. To trust in God's mercy implies a belief that He is merciful. We could not trust Him if we did not have such a belief. This belief must always

lie at the foundation of real trust. Indeed, so naturally does this belief produce that richness of the soul and resting upon God that we call trust, that in the New Testament sense it commonly includes both. Faith, or belief, includes a wholehearted commitment of the soul to God, and a sincere trust in Him.

5. To *trust in the mercy of God forever and ever* implies a conviction of deserving endless punishment. Mercy corresponds with the punishment that is deserved, and it can go no farther in its nature. It is rational to rely upon the exercise of mercy for as long as we deserve punishment, but no longer. A prisoner under a three years' sentence to a state prison may ask for the exercise of mercy in the form of pardon for that amount of time, but he will not ask for a pardon for ten years when he needs it only for three, or he will not ask for a pardon after his three years' term has expired. This principle is perfectly obvious. Where the deserving of punishment ceases, there mercy, along with our trust in mercy, also ceases. As long as the deserving of punishment continues, so may mercy, along with our trust in its exercise. When, therefore, the psalmist trusts in the mercy of God forever, he renounces all hope of ever being received to favor based upon the obligation of justice.

6. Trusting in mercy implies a cessation from all excuses and excuse-making. The moment you trust in mercy, you give up all apologies and excuses at once and entirely, for these imply a reliance upon God's justice. An excuse or apology is nothing more or less than an appeal to justice – a plea designed to justify our conduct. Trusting in mercy forever implies that we have ceased from all excuses forever.

Accordingly, a person on trial before a civil court, as long as he tries to justify himself and offer excuses, appeals to justice; but if he goes before the court and pleads guilty, offering no justification or excuse whatsoever, he throws himself upon the clemency of the court. This is quite another thing from self-justification. It sometimes happens that in the same trial, the accused party tries both measures. He first attempts his own defense, but finding this vain, he shifts his position, confesses his crime and poor judgment, and throws himself upon the mercy of the court.

It is always understood that when someone pleads guilty, he stops making excuses and appeals only to mercy. It is the same in any private matter with my neighbor. If I justify myself fully, I certainly have no confession to make, but if I am aware of having done him wrong, I freely confess my wrong and appeal to mercy. Self-justification stands directly against confession.

This is also how it is in parental discipline. If your child passionately justifies himself, he makes no appeal to mercy. But the moment he throws himself into your arms with tears and says, "I was wrong," he stops making excuses and trusts himself to mercy.

It is the same in the government of God. Trust in mercy is a final giving up of all reliance upon justice. You have no more excuses; you make none.

## III. The conditions on which we may safely trust in God's mercy

1. Public justice must be appeased. Its demands must be satisfied. God is a great public judge, sustaining infinitely responsible relations to the moral universe. He must be careful what He does.

Perhaps no measure of government is more delicate and difficult in its actions than the exercise of mercy. It is a most critical point. There is eminent danger of making the impression that mercy would trample down law. The very thing that mercy does is to set aside the execution of the penalty of law. The danger is that this might seem to set aside the law itself. The great problem is how the law can retain its full majesty when the execution of its penalty is entirely withdrawn. This is always a difficult and delicate matter.

In human governments, we often see great firmness exercised by the judge. During the scenes of the American Revolution, Washington was earnestly entreated to pardon British Major John André. The latter was eminently an amiable, lovely man, and his case excited a deep sympathy in the American army. Numerous and urgent petitions were made to Washington on his behalf, but Washington could not yield. They pleaded with him to see André, hoping that a personal interview might touch his heart, but Washington refused even to see him. He dared not trust his own feelings. He felt that this was a great crisis and that a nation's welfare was in peril. Hence his stern, unyielding decision. It was not that he lacked compassion of soul, for he had a heart to feel. Under the circumstances, though, he knew too well that no opportunity must be given to the indulgence of his tender sympathies. He dared not gratify these feelings lest a nation's ruin would be the penalty.

Such cases have often occurred in human governments – when every feeling of the soul is on the side of mercy and strong demands are made for leniency, but justice forbids.

Often in family government, the parent has an agonizing trial. He would sooner bear the pain himself than to inflict it upon his son, but interests that could be of great importance are at stake, and they must not be put in peril by the indulgence of his compassions.

If the exercise of mercy in such cases is difficult, how much more so in the government of God? Therefore, the first condition of the exercise of mercy is that something must be done to meet the demands of public justice. It is absolutely indispensable that law be sustained. No matter how much God may be inclined to pardon, yet He is too good to exercise mercy on any such conditions or under any such circumstances that will impair the dignity of His law, throw out a license to sin, and open the very floodgates of iniquity. God can never do this, and He knows He never should.

> Certainly no sinner has the least reason to hope for mercy until he repents.

On this point it only needs to be said now that this difficulty is completely removed by the atonement of Christ.

2. A second condition is that we repent. Certainly no sinner has the least reason to hope for mercy until he repents. Will God pardon the sinner who remains in his rebellion? Never. To do so would be most unjust in God and most ruinous to the universe. It would be virtually proclaiming that sin is just a triviality, that God does not care how set in wickedness the sinner's heart is, and that God will accept the most rebellious and unhumbled heart. Before God can do this, He must cease to be holy.

3. We must confess our sins. *He that covereth his sins shall not prosper: but whoso confesseth and forsaketh them shall have mercy* (Proverbs 28:13). God sustains such relations to the moral universe that He cannot forgive without the sinner's confession. He must have the sinner's testimony against himself and in favor of law and obedience.

Suppose a man convicted and sentenced to be hung petitions the governor for pardon, but is too proud to confess, at least in public. He says, "May it please your Honor, between you and me, I am willing to say that I committed that crime alleged against me, but you must not ask me to make this confession before the world. You will have some regard to my feelings and to the feelings of my numerous and very respectable friends. Before the world, therefore, I will continue to deny the crime. I trust, however, that you will suitably consider all the circumstances and grant me a pardon."

"Pardon you, you wretch!" the governor would say. "Pardon you when you are condemning the whole court and jury of injustice, and the witnesses of falsehood? Pardon you while you set yourself against the whole administration of justice in the state? Never! Never! You are too proud to take your own place and appear in your own character. How can I rely on you to be a good citizen? How can I expect you to be anything better than a bold evildoer?"

Let it be understood, then, that before we can trust in the mercy of God, we must really repent and make our confession as public as we have made our crime.

Now suppose that someone is convicted and seeks to be pardoned, but will not confess at all. He says to the governor, "I have no crimes to confess. I have done nothing particularly wrong. The reason I have acted as I have is that I have a desperately wicked heart. I cannot repent and never could. I don't know how it happens that I commit murder so easily. It seems to be second nature to me to kill my neighbor. I can't help it. I am told that you are very good and very merciful. They even say that you are love itself, and I believe it. Certainly, then, you will grant me a pardon. It will be so easy for you to do, and it would be so horrible for me to be hung. You know I have done only a little wrong, and that was only because I could not help it. You certainly cannot insist upon my making any confession. You would not have me hung because I don't repent. You certainly are too kind to do any such thing."

"I don't thank you for your good opinion of me," the angry reply must be. "The law will take its course. Your path is to the gallows."

Do you see that sinner over there? Hear him mock God in his prayer: "I trust in the mercy of God, for God is love."

Do you repent? "I don't know about repentance. That is not the question. God is love. God is too good to send people to hell. Those who think that He ever sends anyone to hell are wrong and they slander God."

Too good! Too good! Do you say that God is so good that He will forgive whether the sinner repents or not; too good to hold the reins of His government firmly; too good to secure the best interests of His vast kingdom? Sinner, the god you think of is a being of your own crazy imagination. Your god is not the God who built the prison of despair for hardened sinners. Your god is not the God who rules the universe by righteous law and also governs the human race on a gospel system that magnifies that law and makes it honorable.

4. We must really make restitution as far as lies in our power. You may see the bearing of this in the case of a highway robber. He has robbed a traveler of ten thousand dollars and is sentenced to the state prison for life. He petitions for pardon. He is very sorry for his crime. He will make any confession that can be asked, no matter how public; but will he make restitution? No, not he. He needs that money himself. He is so patriotic that he might give up half of it to the government. He is so generous that he is ready to make a donation of five thousand dollars for the public good! He is ready to donate a large sum of money to charitable causes – but whose money? Where is his justice to the person he has robbed? Will this reprobate consecrate to the public what he has torn from his neighbor and put it into the treasury of the government? No! Such a gift would burn right through the chest. What would you think if the government would tolerate such an act? You would abhor their wretched corruption.

Look at that man of the world. His whole business career is a course of overreaching. He cunningly slips his hands into his neighbor's pockets and fills up his own. His habit is to sell things for more than they are worth and buy them for less. He knows how to monopolize and make high prices, and then sell out his accumulated stocks. His mind is forever working to manage and make good bargains.

But this man at last must prepare to meet God, so he turns to his money to make it answer all things. He has a large gift for God. Maybe he will build a church or send a missionary – something at least big enough to buy a pardon for a life about which his conscience is not very easy. Yes, he has a splendid bribe for God – but will God take it? Never! God burns with indignation at the thought. Does God want your price of blood – those gains of oppression? Go and give them back to the suffering poor whose cries have gone up to God against you. How shameful to think of taking from your brother and giving some of it to God! You are not merely robbing Peter to pay Paul, but you are robbing man to pay God! The pardon of your soul is not bought in that way!

5. Another condition is that you really reform. Suppose there is a villain in our neighborhood who has become the terror of the entire region. He has already murdered a dozen defenseless women and children. He burns down our houses by night, plunders and robs during the day, and talks every day about his crimes at which every ear tingles. No one feels safe for a moment. He is a bold and bloody villain. At last he is arrested, and we all breathe more easily. Peace is restored.

However, this criminal, having received the sentence of death, petitions for pardon. He professes no repentance whatsoever, and does not even make a promise to try to change, yet the governor is about to give him a free pardon. If he does so, who will not say, "He should be hung up himself by the neck until he is dead"?

But what does that sinner say? "I trust in the great mercy of God. I have nothing to fear." Does he reform? No. What good can the mercy of God do for him if he does not change?

6. You must go the whole length in justifying the law and its penalty. Observe that convicted criminal. He does not believe that government has any right to take life for any crime. He constantly complains about the justice of such a proceeding, and on this ground insists that he must have a pardon. Will he get it? Will the governor take a position that is clearly opposed to the very law and constitution that he has sworn to

uphold? Will he repress the law to save one criminal, or even a thousand criminals? Not if he has the spirit of a ruler in his heart. If that guilty man wants mercy from the execution, he must admit the right of the law and of the penalty, or else he puts himself against the law and cannot be trusted in the community.

Now hear that sinner. He has much to say against his well-deserved sentence and against the justice of eternal punishment. He denounces the laws of God as cruelly and unrighteously severe. Sinner, do you think God can forgive you while you pursue such a course? He would as soon repeal His law and vacate His throne. You make it impossible for God to forgive you.

7. No sinner can be a proper object of mercy who is not entirely submissive to all those measures of the government that have brought him to conviction. Suppose a criminal would plead that there had been a conspiracy to catch and arrest him, that witnesses had been bribed to give false testimony, that the judge had charged the jury falsely, or that the jury had given an unrighteous verdict. Could he hope by such false allegations to obtain a pardon? Not at all. Such a person cannot be trusted to sustain law and order in a community under any government, human or divine.

Listen to that sinner complain and criticize. "Why," he asks, "did God allow sin and temptation to enter this world at all? Why does God let the sinner live at all to face a doom so dreadful? Why does God stop the sinner's path by His providence and cut him down in his sins?" Yet this very sinner talks about trusting in God's mercy, while the entire time he is accusing God of being an infinite tyrant and of seeking to crush the helpless, unfortunate sinner!

What do these complaints mean? What are they but the uplifted voice of a guilty rebel condemning his Maker for doing good and showing mercy to His own rebellious creatures? It only takes a moment to see that the temptation complained of is simply that which is good being placed before a moral agent to melt his heart by love. Yet the sinner criticizes this and pours out his complaints against God.

Be assured that unless you are willing to go the full length of justifying all that God does, He can never pardon you. God has no option to pardon a self-justifying rebel. The interests of myriads of moral beings forbid His doing so. When you will take the position most fully of justifying God and condemning yourself, you place yourself where mercy can reach you, and then it surely will – and not before.

8. You must accept most warmly the plan of salvation. This plan is based on the assumption that we deserve everlasting death and that if we are to be saved, it must be by sovereign grace and mercy. Nothing can save except mercy – mercy that meets the helpless sinner in the dust as the sinner, without an excuse or an apology, gives to God all the glory and takes to himself all the guilt and shame. There is hope for you, sinner, in embracing this plan with all your heart.

**Nothing can save except mercy.**

## IV. Several mistakes that are made on this subject

1. Many people really trust in justice instead of in mercy. They say, "God is just. God will not do me any injustice. I intend to do as well as I can, and then I can safely leave myself in the hands of a just God." It is true that God will not do you any injustice. You never need to fear that. But how terrible if God would give you strict justice! How fearful if you get no mercy! If God does not show you infinite mercy, then as certain as it is that you are a sinner, you are forever lost! Trusting in God's justice is a fatal rock. The sinner who can do it calmly has never seen God's law and his own heart. The psalmist did not say that he trusted in the justice of God forever and ever, but the psalmist said that he trusted in the mercy of God.

2. Many people professedly trust in the mercy of God without fulfilling the conditions on which mercy can be shown. They may hold on in such trusting until they die, but no longer.

3. Sinners do not consider that God cannot do away with their necessity to fulfil these conditions. He has no right to do so. The conditions spring out of the very constitution of His government, from His very nature, and must therefore be strictly fulfilled. God would sooner send

the whole race, even the whole universe, to hell rather than dispense with their fulfillment. If God were to set aside these conditions and forgive a sinner who was still unhumbled, unrepentant, and unbelieving, He would upset His throne, unsettle the moral universe, and kindle another hell in His own arms.

4. Many people are defeating their own salvation by self-justification. Pleas that excuse self and criticisms that accuse God are both alike and stand fatally in the way of pardon. Since the world began, no sinner has found mercy in this condition.

5. Many people pretend to trust in mercy who still profess to be punished for their sins as they go along. They claim to hope for salvation through mercy, yet they say that they are punished for all their sins in this life. Two more absurd and self-contradictory things were never put together – punished as much as they deserve here, yet saved through mercy! Why don't they plainly say that they will be saved after death through justice? Surely if they are punished as much as they deserve as they go through this life, justice will ask no more after death.

6. People who plead for the letter of mercy often really rely upon justice. The deep conviction of sin and what they really deserve does not sink into their souls until they realize what mercy is and until they feel that they can rely on nothing else.

7. Some people are covering up their sins, yet dream of going to heaven. Do they think they can hide those sins from the Omniscient Eye? Do they think to cover their sins and yet still prosper, despite God's dreadful word (Proverbs 28:13)?

8. We cannot reasonably ask for mercy beyond our acknowledged and felt guilt, and those who suppose that they can are making a fatal mistake. Without a deep conviction of conscious guilt, we cannot be honest and in earnest in pleading for mercy. Listen to that person pray who thinks that sin is not a big matter and that it does not deserve much punishment: "O Lord, I need a little mercy, only a little. My sins

have been few and of small account. Grant me, Lord, exemption from the brief and slight punishment that my few errors and mistakes may have deserved."

Listen to the Universalist pray: "O Lord, You know that I have been punished for my sins as I have gone through life. I have had a fit of sickness and various pains and losses, nearly or quite enough, You know, to punish all the sins I have committed. Now, therefore, I pray that You will give me salvation through Your great mercy." How astonishing that some people should hold such nonsense! How can a Universalist pray at all? What should they pray for? Not for pardon, for on their principles they have a valid claim to be exempt from punishment on the basis of justice, just as the criminal has who has served out his sentence in the state's prison.

The only rational prayer that can be made by them is that God will do them justice and let them go since they have already been punished enough. But why should they pray for this? God may be trusted to act in justice without their praying for it. I don't wonder that Universalists only pray a little. What do they have to pray for? Their daily bread? That is fine, but they do not need to pray for the mercy of God, for they believe that they suffer all that they deserve. That is a pleasing delusion that is flattering enough to human pride, but it is strange for rational minds, and it is terribly damaging!

> If we ask for only a little mercy, we will get none at all. If we are to get anything, we must ask for great blessings.

Restoration takes basically the same ground, but leaves a part of the penalty to be worked out in purgatory, claiming salvation on the ground of justice and not mercy. Mercy can have no place in any system of Universalism.[2] Every form of this system displays God in robes of justice – inflexible, fearful justice. These people say that they trust in the mercy of God, but what have they done with the gospel and with all that the Bible says about free pardon to the guilty? They have thrown it out of the Bible, and what have they given us instead? Only justice and punishment enough for sin in this world, or at least in a few years of purgatory. They believe that sin is a trivial matter, that God's governing

---

2    Universalism was a common belief in Finney's day. It teaches that all people will eventually be saved.

is a mere farce, that God is a liar, and that hell is just something imaginary to scare people. What is all this but such dire blasphemy as ever came from hell?

If we ask for only a little mercy, we will get none at all. This may seem strange, but it is nevertheless true. If we are to get anything, we must ask for great blessings. Suppose a man deserved to be hung, yet asks for only a little favor. Can he be forgiven? No. He must confess the whole of his guilt in its full and terrible form, and must show that he feels it in his very soul.

Sinner, you must come and confess your whole guilt as it is, or you will have no mercy. Come and get down, low, lower, infinitely low before God, and find mercy there. Hear the Universalist. All he can say at first is, "I thank God for a thousand things," but he begins to doubt whether this is quite enough. Maybe he needs a little more punishment than he has endured in this life. He sees a little more guilt, so he prays that God would let him off from ten years of deserved punishment in hell. If he sees a little more guilt, he asks for a reprieve from so much more punishment.

However, if truth flashes upon his soul and he sees his own heart and life in the light of God's law, he gets down lower and lower, as low as he can, and pours out his prayer that God would save him from that eternal hell that he deserves. He cries out, "Can God forgive so great a sinner?" Yes, and so much more readily the more you humble yourself and realize your need to ask for much mercy. Only come down and take such a position so God can meet you. Remember the prodigal son and that father running, falling on his neck, weeping, welcoming, and forgiving (Luke 15:11-32)! Oh, how that father's heart gushed with tenderness!

It is not the greatness of your sins, but the pride of your heart that keeps you from salvation. It is not anything in your past life, but it is your present state of mind that makes your salvation impossible. Think about that.

You do not need to wait to use any methods with God to persuade Him to save you. He is using means with you to persuade you to be saved. You act as if God could hardly be moved by any possible pleas and submissions to exercise mercy. Oh, you do not see how His great heart beats with compassion and presses the streams of mercy forth in all directions, pouring the river of the waters of life at your very feet, and creating such a pressure of appeal to your heart that you have to brace yourself against it to prevent yourself from being persuaded to repent. Do you see how God would gladly persuade you and break your heart in repentance so that He can bring you to where He can reach you with forgiving mercy and where He can come and bless you without resigning His very throne?

To deny that you deserve endless punishment is to render your salvation completely impossible. God can never forgive you on this basis because you are trying to be saved based upon justice. You could not make your damnation any more certain if you were to murder every person you meet. You tie up the hands of mercy and will not let mercy pluck you from the jaws of death.

> You see clearly why all people are not saved. Not because God is not willing to save everyone, but because they defeat the efforts God makes to save them.

It is as if your house were on fire, and you grab your loaded rifle to shoot down everyone who comes with a bucket to help you. You stand your ground amid the raging fire until you sink beneath the flames. Who can help you? Yet that is what the person is doing who is trying to make his family believe Universalism. It is as if he would shoot his rifle at the very heart of mercy every time she comes in view. He seems determined to drive off mercy, and for this purpose he gathers all the weapons of Universalism and throws himself into the citadel of this refuge of lies!

Oh, what a work of death this is! He seems determined that mercy will not reach him or his family, and mercy cannot come. See how mercy bends from heaven. God smiles in love while mercy weeps in compassion, bends from the very clouds, and holds out the pierced hand of the Crucified One. But the Universalist says, "No! I don't deserve the punishment. Away with the insult of a pardon offered through mere mercy!" What can be more fatal, more damning, and more ruinous to the soul?

You see very clearly why all people are not saved. It is not because God is not willing to save everyone, but it is because they defeat the efforts God makes to save them. They pursue every possible hideout and scheme, they resist conviction of guilt, and they resist every call of mercy. What is wrong with these people? What are they doing? Has God come down in His hot wrath and vengeance to cause them to rally to oppose Him with all their might?

No, but He has only come in mercy. They are fighting against His mercy, and not just against His righteous retributions of vengeance. If this were His dreadful arm of vengeance, you would quickly bow down or break beneath its blow. But if you would realize it, you would see that God's mercy comes in its soft whispers. It comes to win your heart, and what are you doing? You join yourselves together to resist its calls. You invent a thousand excuses. You run together to talk, and you talk away all serious thought. You run to some atheist or Universalist to find relief for your uneasy conscience.

Oh, sinner, this cannot do you any good. You run away from God, but why? What is the matter? Is God pouring down the floods of His great wrath? No, but mercy has come and would gladly gather you under her outspread wings where storms of wrath can never come. But no – the sinner pleads against it. The sinner criticizes, runs, fights, and resists the angel of mercy and throws down the waters of life from his lips.

Sinner, this scene is to end soon. The time is short. God will soon come. Death shakes his dart. That young man is sick; hear his groans. Are you going to die, my young friend? Are you ready? "I don't know. I am in great pain. Oh, how can I live so? How can I die? I can't take care of this now. It is too late – too late!"

Indeed, young man, you are in weakness now. God's finger has touched you. If I could only tell you some of the deathbed scenes that I have witnessed! If I could make you see them and hear the deep wailings of unutterable agony as the soul quivered and shuddered and desired to shrink away into annihilation from the awful eye – and was swept down swiftly to hell!

Those are the very people who ran away from mercy! Mercy could not reach them, but death can. Death seizes its victim. He drags the frightened, shrieking soul to the gateway of hell. See how that soul cringes and groans – what an unearthly groan – and he is gone! The sentence of execution has gone out, and there is no reprieve. That sinner did not want mercy when he could have had it, and now he cannot have it when he desires it. It is all over now.

Dying sinner, you can just as well have mercy today as not have it. All your past sins are no obstacle at all if you only repent and take the offered pardon. Your God offers you life. *As I live, saith the Lord God, I have no pleasure in the death of the wicked; but that the wicked turn from his way and live: turn ye, turn ye from your evil ways; for why will ye die?* (Ezekiel 33:11). Why will you reject such offered life? Will you still continue in your ways?

*Be astonished, O ye heavens* (Jeremiah 2:12). Indeed, if there was ever anything that filled the universe with astonishment, it is the sinner's rejection of mercy. Angels were astonished when they saw the Son of God made flesh, and when they saw Him nailed to a tree. How much more now to see the guilty sinner doomed to hell, yet rejecting offered pardon! They see that sinner putting it off and still delaying and delaying still, until the last curtain falls and the great bell tolls the awful ringing of the sinner's eternal death! Where is that sinner? Follow him. Down he goes, weeping and wailing along the sides of the pit. He reaches his own final home. He is in his own place now and forevermore! Mercy followed him to the very edge of the precipice, but could follow no longer. She has done her part.

What if a spirit from glory would come and speak to you for five minutes – a relative, maybe your mother; what would she say? What if a spirit from that world of despair would come and speak to you and tell you about the awful realities of that prison house? Would he tell you that the preacher has been telling you lies? Would he tell you not to be frightened by these made-up tales of horror? No, for the half has not been told you, and it never can be. Oh, how he would hold on to you and beg you to help him if he could only *flee from the wrath to come* (Matthew 3:7)!

# Chapter 3

# The Wages of Sin

The wages of sin is death.
—Romans 6:23

The death here spoken of is that which is due as the disciplinary measure of God's law.

In presenting the subject of our text, I must:

I.   Illustrate the nature of sin

II.  Specify some of the attributes of the penal sanctions of God's law

III. Show what this penalty must be

## I. Illustrate the nature of sin

I. An illustration will give us the best practical view of the nature of sin. You only have to imagine a government established to secure the highest well-being of the governed, and of the ruling authorities also. Suppose that the head of this government uses all his attributes in this enterprise – all his wealth, all his time, all his energies – to achieve the lofty goal of the highest general good. For this purpose, he enacts the best possible laws – laws that, if obeyed, will secure the highest good of

35

both subject and prince. He then takes care to set up adequate penalties, or else all his care and wisdom must be for nothing. He devotes all that he has and all that he is to the interests of his government without reserve or decrease.

However, some of his subjects refuse to sympathize with this movement. They say, "Charity begins at home," and they want themselves taken care of first. Basically, they are completely selfish. It is easy to see what this would be in a human government. The person who does this becomes the common enemy of the government and of all its subjects. This is sin.

This illustrates precisely the case of the sinner. Sin is selfishness. It sets up a selfish end, and uses selfish means to reach it. In respect to both its end and its means, it is absolutely opposed to **Each sinner maintains** God and to all the ends of general happiness that **that his own will** He seeks to secure. It denies God's rights and **should be the law.** discards God's interests. Each sinner maintains that his own will should be the law. The interest he sets himself to secure is entirely opposed to that proposed by God in His government.

All law must have punishment. Without consequences, it would only be advice. It is therefore essential to the distinctive and inherent nature of law that it have punishment. These punishments promise reward for obedience, and they also threaten penalty for disobedience. They vindicate the honor of the violated law.

These punishments may be either natural or governmental. Often both forms exist in other governments than the divine. Natural penalties are those evil consequences that naturally result without any direct interference of government to punish. Therefore, in all governments, the disrespect of its friends falls as a natural penalty on transgressors. They are the natural enemies of all good subjects.

In the divine government, sorrow of conscience and remorse fall into this class, and indeed many other things that are naturally the result of obedience on the one hand and of disobedience on the other.

There should also be governmental consequences. Every governor should make known his displeasure against the violation of his laws. To leave the whole question of obedience to mere natural consequences is obviously unjust to society. Inasmuch as governments are established to sustain law and secure obedience, they are bound to put forth their utmost energies in this work.

Another related instrument of government under some circumstances is that which we call discipline. One object of discipline is to go before the pain of penalty and force unwilling eyes to open to see that law has a government to back it up and that the sinner has a terrible penalty to fear. Being known and observed by people before they have broken the law, while as yet they have not seen or felt the fearfulness of penalty, it is designed to admonish them – to make them think and consider. Thus its special object is the good of the subject on whom it falls and of those who may witness its penalties being carried out. It does not propose to sustain the dignity of law by severe punishment. This belongs exclusively to the area of penalty. Discipline, therefore, is not punishment in the sense of visiting crime with deserved punishment, but aims to deter the subject of law from violating its precepts.

Disciplinary measures could scarcely exist under a government of pure law because such a government cannot defer inflicting the penalty. Discipline presupposes a state of suspended penalty; therefore, corrective measures must be broadly distinguished from disciplinary measures.

We are sinners, and therefore have little occasion now to dwell on the profitable features of God's government. We can have no claim to benefit under law, being completely prevented by our sin. We have everything to do with the features of punishment, however. I will therefore proceed to discuss some of this.

## II. We must specify some of the attributes of the disciplinary measures of God's law

God has given us reason. This affirms intuitively and irresistibly all the great truths of moral government. There are certain attributes that we know must belong to the moral law, such as intrinsic justice. The penalty should threaten no more and no less than is just. Justice must be an attribute of God's law, or else the whole universe must inevitably condemn it.

Intrinsic justice means and implies that the penalty should be equal to the obligation violated. The guilt of sin consists in its being a violation of obligation. The fault must be in proportion to the magnitude of the obligation violated, and consequently the penalty must be measured by this obligation.

Governmental justice is another attribute. This feature of law seeks to provide security against transgression. Law is not governmentally just unless its penalty is so measured as to provide the highest security against sin that the nature of the case allows. Suppose under any government that the punishment of law is insignificant and is not at all proportioned to the end to be secured. Such a government is unjust to itself and to the interests it is committed to maintain. Therefore, a good government must be governmentally just, providing in the severity of its penalties and in the certainty of those penalties being carried out the highest security that its law will be obeyed.

Corrective punishments should be worthy of the end aimed at by the law and by its author. Government is only a means to an end, with the proposed end being universal obedience and its consequent happiness. If law is indispensable for obtaining this end, its penalty should be structured accordingly.

The penalty, then, should be assigned according to the importance of the precept. If the specific law is of fundamental importance – of such importance that disobedience to it undermines the very existence of all government – then it should be guarded by the greatest and most solemn penalties. The penalties attached to its violation should be of the highest order.

The penalty should make an adequate expression of the lawgiver's views of the value of the end he proposes to secure by law, as well as of his views of the sacredness of his law and of the intrinsic guilt of disobedience. A penalty aims to bring forth the heart of the lawgiver – to show the earnestness of his desire to maintain the right, and to secure that order and well-being that depend on obedience. In the greatness of the penalty, the lawgiver brings forth his heart and pours the whole influence of his character upon his subjects.

The object of executing the penalty is precisely the same. It is not to exact revenge, as some seem to think, but is to act on the subjects of government with influences toward obedience. It has the same general object as the law itself has.

Corrective penalties should be an adequate expression of the lawgiver's regard for the public good and of his interest in it. In the law, he gave some expression; in the penalty, he gave still more. In the law, we see the object in view and have a manifestation of regard for the public interests; in the penalty, we have a measure of this regard, showing us how great it is. For example, suppose a human law were to punish murder with just a slight penalty. Under the pretense of being very tenderhearted, the lawgiver punishes this crime of murder with a fine of five dollars! Would this show that he greatly loved his subjects and highly valued their life and interests? Far from it. You cannot believe that a legislator has done his duty unless he shows how much he values human life, and unless he attaches a penalty proportionate in some good degree with the end to be secured.

One word as to the sentence of capital punishment in human governments. There is a difference of opinion as to which is most effective – solitary confinement for life, or death. Leaving this question without remark, I have to say that no one ever doubted that the murderer deserves to die. If some punishment other than death is to be preferred, it is not by any means because the murderer does not deserve death. No one can doubt this for a moment. It is one of the unalterable principles of righteousness that if a person sacrifices the interest of another, he sacrifices his own – an eye for an eye and life for life. *Whoso sheddeth man's blood, by man shall his blood be shed: for in the image of God made he man* (Genesis 9:6).

We cannot but affirm that no government places sufficient emphasis on the protection of human life unless it guards this trust with its highest penalties. Where life and all its vital interests are at stake, there the penalty should be as great and serious as is possible.

Moral means have two sides to their sensibility: hope and fear, and to these you can address the hope of good and the dread of evil. I am now speaking of the penalty. This is addressed only to fear.

I have said in substance that a penalty should adequately assert and vindicate the rightful authority of the lawgiver. It should also provide, if possible, an adequate rebuke of sin, and it should be based on a just appreciation of its nature. God's moral government embraces the whole intelligent universe and stretches with its vast results onward through eternity. Therefore, the sweep and breadth of its interests are absolutely unlimited, and consequently the penalties of its law, being set to vindicate the authority of this government and to sustain these immeasurable interests, should be beyond measure dreadful.

If anything beyond and more dreadful than the threatened penalty could be conceived, all minds would say, "This is not enough." With any just views of the relations and the guilt of sin, they could not be satisfied unless the penalty is the greatest that could be conceived. Sin is so vile, so harmful, so terribly destructive, and so far-sweeping in its ruin, that moral agents could not feel that enough is done as long as more could be done.

## III. What is the penalty of God's moral law?

Our text answers that *the wages of sin is death*. This certainly is not physical death, for both saints and animals die, neither of whom can be receiving the wages of sin. Besides, this would be no penalty if, after it is carried out, people went immediately to heaven. Such a penalty, considered as the wages of sin, would only be an insult to God's government.

> Sin is so vile, so harmful, so terribly destructive, and so far-sweeping in its ruin, that moral agents could not feel that enough is done as long as more could be done.

This cannot be spiritual death, for this is nothing else than a state of entire disobedience to the law. You cannot well conceive anything more absurd than to punish a person for disobedience by subjecting him to perpetual disobedience – an effort to sustain the law by dooming such offenders to perpetually violate the law – and nothing more.

This death is, though, endless misery, corresponding to the death penalty in human governments. Everybody knows what this is. It separates the criminal from society forever. It excludes him at once and completely from all the privileges of the government, and hands him over to hopeless ruin. Nothing more dreadful can be inflicted. It is the extreme penalty, fearful beyond any other that is possible for man to inflict. There can be no doubt that death as spoken of in our text is intended to correspond to the death penalty in human governments.

*For the wages of sin is death; but the gift of God is eternal life through Jesus Christ our Lord* (Romans 6:23). You will also observe that in our text *the gift of God* that is *eternal life through Jesus Christ our Lord* is directly contrasted with death, *the wages of sin*. This fact may throw light on the question respecting the nature of this death. We must look for the antithesis of *eternal life*.

This eternal life is not merely an eternal existence. Eternal life never means merely an eternal existence in any place where it is used in Scripture, but it does mean a state of eternal blessedness, implying eternal holiness as its foundation. The use of the term "life" in Scripture in the sense of real life – a life worth living (that is, real and rich enjoyment) – is so common as to supersede the necessity of special proof. The penalty of death is therefore the opposite of eternal life – it is eternal misery.

I must say a few words now regarding the objections raised against this doctrine of eternal punishment. All the objections I have ever heard amount only to this – that it is unjust. They may be expressed in somewhat various phraseology, but this is the only idea that is involved.

1. It is claimed to be unjust because "life is so short." How strangely people talk! Do they think that life is so short that people do not have time to sin enough to deserve eternal death? Do they forget that one sin incurs the penalty due for sinning? How many sins does it take to make one transgression of the law of God? People often talk as if they suppose it must require a great many, as if a person must commit a great many murders before he has committed the crime of murder enough to fall under the sentence of the court! What! Will a person come before the court and plead that although he has certainly broken the law, yet he has not lived long enough and has not broken the law enough times to incur its penalty? What court on earth ever recognized such a plea as proving anything else other than the foolishness and guilt of the one who made it?

2. It is also urged that "Man is so small, so very insignificant a being, that he cannot possibly commit an infinite sin." What does this objection

mean? Does it mean that sin is an act of creation and is to be measured therefore by the magnitude of that something that it creates? This would be an exceedingly wild idea of the nature of sin.

Does the objection mean that people cannot violate an obligation of infinite strength? That meaning is simply false, as everybody must know. Does he imply that the guilt of sin is not to be measured by the obligation violated? Then he does not know what he says, or else he wickedly denies known truth.

What! Do some say that man is so little that he cannot commit much sin? Is this the way we reason in similar cases? Suppose your child disobeys you. He is very much smaller than you are, but do you therefore exonerate him from blame? Is this a reason that nullifies his guilt? Can no sin be committed by inferiors against their superior? Have sensible people always been mistaken in supposing that the younger and smaller are sometimes under obligations to obey the older and the greater?

Suppose you strike the judge. Suppose you insult or attempt to assassinate the king. Is this a very small crime almost too excusable to be deemed a crime at all because you are in a lower position and he in a higher?

You say, "I am so little, so very insignificant! How can I deserve so great a punishment?" Do you reason that way in any other case except regarding your own sins against God? Never.

3. Some people say, "Sin is not an infinite evil." This language is uncertain. Does it mean that sin would not work infinite harm if allowed to continue indefinitely? This is false, for if only one soul were ruined by it, the harm accumulating from it would be infinite.

Does it mean that sin is not an infinite evil as seen in its present results and relations? Suppose we agree with this. It proves nothing to our purpose, for it may be true that the sum total of evil results from each single sin will not all be brought out in any duration less than eternity. How, then, can you measure the evil of sin by what you see today?

But there are still other considerations to show that the penalty of the law must be infinite. Sin is an infinite natural evil. It is so in the sense that there are no bounds to the natural evil it would introduce if not governmentally restrained. If sin were to ruin only one soul, there could be no limit set to the evil that would thus result.

Sin involves infinite guilt because it is a violation of infinite obligation. It is important here to notice a common mistake that grows out of confusion of ideas about the basis of obligation. Mistakes result from this in regard to what constitutes the guilt of sin. I might show here that when you misunderstand the basis of obligation, you will almost of necessity misunderstand the nature and extent of sin and guilt.

Let us return to our previous illustration. Here is a government that is wisely framed to secure the highest good of the governed and of all concerned. From where comes the obligation to obey? Certainly it comes from the intrinsic value of the end that is sought. But how broad is this obligation to obey? In other words, what is its true measure? I answer that it exactly equals the value of the end that the government seeks to secure and that obedience will secure, but that sin will destroy. By this measure of God, the penalty must be graduated. The lawgiver must determine by this how much punishment he must attach to his law in order to meet the demands of justice and benevolence.

God's law aims to secure the highest universal good. Its main and ultimate end is not, strictly speaking, to secure supreme homage to God, but rather to secure the highest good of all intelligent moral beings – God and all His creatures. If you see it in this way, you will see that the intrinsic value of the end to be sought is the real ground of obligation to obey the precept. Having estimated the value of this end, you have the value and strength of the obligation.

This is plainly infinite in the sense of being unlimited. In this sense, we affirm obligation to be without limit. The very reason why we affirm any obligation at all is that the law is good and is the necessary means of the highest good of the universe. Therefore, the reason why we affirm any penalty at all compels us to affirm the justice and necessity of an infinite penalty. We see that intrinsic justice must demand an infinite penalty for the same reason that it demands any penalty whatsoever. If any penalty is just, it is just because law secures a certain good. If this good aimed at by the law is unlimited in extent, so must be the penalty. Governmental justice thus requires endless punishment, or else it provides no sufficient guaranty for the public good.

The law not only is designed to secure infinite good, but it tends to secure it. Its tendencies are focused on the purpose; therefore, its penalty should be infinite. The law is not just to the interests it both aims and tends to secure unless it arms itself with infinite sanctions.

Nothing less than infinite penalty can be an adequate expression of God's view of the value of the great end on which His heart is set. When people talk about eternal death being too great a penalty for sin, what do they think of God's efforts to restrain sin all over the moral universe? What do they think of the death of His well-beloved Son? Do they suppose it is possible that God could give an adequate or corresponding expression to His hatred of sin by any penalty that is less than endless?

Nothing less could give an adequate expression to His regard for the authority of law. How fearful the results and how shocking the very idea that God would fail to make an adequate expression of His regard for the sacredness of that law that underlies the entire well-being of all His vast kingdom! You would insist that He should regard the violation of His law as Universalists do. How surely He would bring down an avalanche of ruin on all His intelligent creatures if He were to yield to your demands! If He were to affix anything less than endless penalty to His law, what holy being could trust the administration of His government? His regard for the public good forbids His attaching a light or finite penalty to His law. He loves His subjects too well.

**If He were to affix anything less than endless penalty to His law, what holy being could trust the administration of His government?**

Some people have strange notions of the way in which a ruler should express his regard for his subjects. They would have him so tenderhearted toward the guilty that they would receive his complete sympathy and favor. They would allow him perhaps to fine a murderer a few dollars, but not much more, if anything. The poor murderer's wife and children are so precious that you must not take away much of his money, and as regarding his liberty or his life – neither of these should be thought of.

What! Do you not know that human nature is very frail and corrupt, and therefore you should deal very lightly with penalties for murder? Maybe they would say that you may punish the murderer by keeping him awake one night – just one, but no more, and that God may let a guilty person's conscience disturb him about to this extent for the crime of murder! The Universalists do tell us that they will allow the Most High God to give a person a conscience that will trouble him a little if he commits murder – a little, maybe, for the first and maybe the second offense, but they are not accustomed to notice the fact that under this penalty of a troubling conscience, the more a man sins, the less he has to suffer. Under the operation of this descending scale, it will soon happen that a murderer would not get as much penalty as the loss of one night's sleep. These are the ideas that people reach when they stay clear of the affirmations of an upright reason and of God's revealing Word.

Speaking now to those who have a moral sense to affirm the right, as well as eyes to see the operation of law, I know you cannot deny the logical necessity of the death penalty for the moral law of God. There is a logical connection to every one of these propositions that you cannot escape.

No penalty less than infinite and endless can be an adequate expression of God's displeasure against sin and of His determination to resist and punish it. The penalty should continue as long as there are subjects to be affected by it – as long as there is need of any demonstration of God's feelings and governmental course toward sin.

Nothing less is the greatest that God can inflict, for He certainly can inflict an endless and infinite punishment. If, therefore, the exigency demands the greatest penalty He can inflict, then the penalty must be banishment from God, and endless death.

I must now remark that the gospel everywhere promotes the same. It holds that by the deeds of the law no flesh can be justified before God (Romans 3:20). Indeed, it not only affirms this, but it builds its entire system of atonement and grace upon this foundation. It constantly affirms that there is no such thing as paying the debt and canceling obligation, but that the sinner's only relief is forgiveness through redeeming blood.

So if the penalty is not endless death, what is it? Is it temporary suffering? Then how long does it last? When does it end? Has any sinner ever got through it – served out his time and been taken to heaven? We do not have even one testimony to prove such a case, but we have the solemn testimony of Jesus Christ to prove that there never can be such a case. He tells us that there can be no passing from hell to heaven or from heaven to hell. A great gulf is fixed between them over which no one will ever pass (Luke 16:26). You may pass from earth to heaven or from earth to hell, but these two states of the future world are wide extremes, and no person or angel will pass the gulf that divides them.

I ask what the penalty is, and you reply that it is only the natural consequences of sin as developed in a troubled conscience. It follows, then, that the more someone sins, the less he is punished, until it amounts to an infinitesimal quantity of punishment for which the sinner cares just nothing at all. Who can believe this? Under this system, if a person fears punishment, all he must do is throw himself into sin with more will and energy. He will then have the comfort of thinking that he can very soon get over all his uneasy feelings and get beyond any penalty whatsoever! Do you believe this is God's only punishment for sin? You cannot believe it.

Universalists always confuse discipline with punishment. They overlook this fundamental distinction and think that everything that people suffer here in this world is only punishment. However, it is hardly punishment at all, but is mainly disciplinary. They ask what good it will do a sinner to send him to an endless hell. Is not God perfectly benevolent, and if so, how can He have any other intent than to do the sinner all the good He can?

**Discipline, while the person was on earth, mainly sought his personal good.**

I answer that punishment is not designed to do good to that sinner who is punished. Rather, the punishment looks to accomplish good that is outside the one being punished and that accomplishes far greater good. Discipline, while the person was on earth, mainly sought his personal good; penalty looks to other results. If you ask whether God intends to do good to the universal public by penalty, I answer yes – that is precisely what He intends to do.

Under human governments, the penalty may aim in part to reform. So far, it is discipline. But the death penalty, after all delay is past and the fatal blow comes, aims not to reform. It is not discipline, but is only penalty. The guilty person is laid on the great public altar and is made a sacrifice for the public good. The intention is to make a fearful, dreadful impression on the public mind about the evil of transgression and the fearfulness of its consequences. Discipline looks not as much to the support of law as to the recovery of the offender. The day of judgment has nothing to do with reclaiming the lost sinner. That and all its issues are purely punitive, or disciplinary. It is strange that these obvious facts are often overlooked.

There is yet another consideration that is often disregarded – that underlying any safe disbursement of discipline, there must be a moral law, sustained by sufficient and fearful sanctions, to preserve the law-giver's authority and sustain the majesty and honor of his government. It would not be safe to trust a system of discipline, and indeed it could not be expected to take hold of the ruined with much force if it were not sustained by a system of law and penalty. This punishment given to the unconverted sinner must stand forever – an appalling fact that shows that justice is realized, the law is vindicated, and God is honored – and to make an enduring and dreadful impression of the evil of sin and of God's eternal hostility against it.

## Remarks

We hear many criticisms against future punishment. We would not be surprised at this except for the fact that the gospel advocates this truth and then proposes a remedy. One would naturally suppose that the mind would retreat from those fearful conclusions to which it is pressed when the relations of mere laws are contemplated, but when the gospel intervenes to save, then it becomes exceedingly strange that people would admit the reality of the gospel and yet reject the law and its penalties.

They talk of grace, but what do they mean by grace? When people deny the fact of sin, there is no room or occasion for grace in the gospel. To those who formally admit the fact of sin while essentially denying its sinfulness, grace is only a name. What right do people have to claim that they respect the gospel if they reject the punishments of the law of God and labor to disprove their reality? They make it only a farce – or at least a system of restitution for unreasonably severe laws under the legal system. Let not those who so dismiss the law assume that they honor God by applauding His gospel!

The representations of the Bible in regard to the final doom of the wicked are very remarkable. Spiritual truths are revealed by natural objects such as the gates and walls of the new Jerusalem to present the splendors and glories of the heavenly state. A spiritual telescope is put into our hands, and we are permitted to point it toward the glorious city *whose builder and maker is God* (Hebrews 11:10). We may survey its inner sanctuary, where the worshipping hosts praise God without ceasing. We see their flowing robes of white, the palms of victory in their hands, the beaming joy of their faces, and the expressions of divine joy in their souls.

This is heaven portrayed in symbolism. Who supposes that this is intended as hyperbole? Who criticizes these representations as extravagant in speech, as if designed to overrate the case or to raise unwarrantable expectations? No one believes this. No one ever brings this accusation against what the Bible says about heaven. What is the purpose in using this figurative method of representation? Beyond question, the purpose is to give the best possible idea of the facts.

Then we have the other side. The veil is lifted, and you come to the very verge of hell to see what is there. Whereas on the one hand all was glorious, on the other all is fearful and full of horrors. There is a bottomless pit. A deathless soul is cast into it. It sinks and sinks and sinks, going down into that dreadful pit that knows no bottom, weeping and wailing as it descends, and you hear its groans as they echo and reecho from the sides of that dread cavern of woe!

Here is another image. You have a *lake of fire and brimstone* (Revelation 20:10), and you see lost sinners thrown into its waves of rolling fire. They land upon its burning shore and gnaw their tongues for pain. There *their worm dieth not, and the fire is not quenched* (Mark 9:44). Not one drop of water can reach them to cool their tongues as they are *tormented in that flame* (Luke 16:24).

What do you think of this? Has God said these things to frighten our poor souls? Did He intend to play on our fears for His own amusement? Can you think so? No. Does it not rather grieve His heart that He must build such a hell and must plunge therein the sinners who will not honor His law and who will not embrace salvation from sinning through His grace? The waves of death roll darkly under the eye of the holy and compassionate One! He has no pleasure in the death of the sinner (Ezekiel 33:11), but He must sustain His throne and save His loyal subjects if He can.

Turn to another scene. Here is a deathbed. Did you ever see a sinner die? Can you describe the scene? Was it a friend, a relative, someone very dear to your heart? How long was he dying? Did it seem to you that the agony of death would never end? When my last child died, the struggle was long. It was dreadfully protracted and agonizing! Twenty-four hours in the agonies of fading nature! It made me sick. I could not watch it! But suppose it had continued until now. I would long since have died myself under the anguish and nervous exhaustion of witnessing such a scene. So would all our friends. Who could survive to the final end of such an awful death? Who would not cry out, "Oh, God, cut it short; cut it short in mercy!"

When my wife died, her death struggles were long and heartrending. If you had been there, you would have cried mightily to God, "Cut it short! Oh, cut it short and relieve this dreadful agony!" But suppose it had continued on and on all day and night – day after day, through its slow-moving hours, and night after night – long nights, as if there could be no morning.

> God wants us to understand what a terrible thing sin is and what fearful punishment it deserves.

The figure of our text supposes eternal dying. Let us imagine such a case. Suppose it would actually occur in some dear circle of sympathizing friends. A poor man cannot die! He lingers in the agony of death for a month, a year, five years, ten years – until all his friends are broken down and fall into their graves under the insupportable horror of the scene; yet still the poor man cannot die! He outlives one generation, and then another and another. One hundred years he is dying in mortal agony, yet he comes no nearer to the end! What would you think of such a scene? It would be an illustration – just a feeble illustration of the terrible second death!

God wants us to understand what a terrible thing sin is and what fearful punishment it deserves. He would willingly show us by such examples how terrible the doom of the determined sinner must be. Did you ever see a sinner die? Did you not cry out, "Surely the curse of

God has fallen heavily on this world!"? This is only a weak example of that heavier curse that comes in the second death!

The text affirms that death is *the wages of sin*. It is just what sin deserves. Labor earns wages and creates a rightful claim to such payment. In the same way, people earn wages when they sin. They become entitled to their pay. God considers Himself obligated to give them their well-deserved wages.

As I have often said, I would not say one word in this direction to distress your souls if there were no hope and no mercy possible. Would I torment you before the time? God forbid! Would I hold out the awful penalty before you and tell you there is no hope? No. I say these things to make you feel the need of escaping for your life.

Think of this: *the wages of sin is death*! God wants to erect a monument that will proclaim to all the universe: "Stand in awe and sin not!" God desires people, when they see this, to say, "What a dreadful thing sin is!" People are inclined to exclaim, "How horrible the penalty!" They are too likely to overlook the horrible sin and the deserved punishment of sin!

When God lays a sinner on his deathbed before our eyes, He invites us to look at the penalty of sin. There he lies agonizing, groaning, quivering, and racked with pain, yet he lives, and lives on. Suppose he lives on in this dying conditions for a day, a week, a month, a year, a dozen years, a century, a thousand years, a thousand ages, and still he lives on, dying perpetually yet never dead. Finally, the universe passes away. The heavens are rolled together as a scroll, and what then? There lies that sufferer still. He looks up and cries out, "How long? How long?" Like the ringing of eternal death, the answer comes down to him, "Eternally! Eternally!" Another cycle of eternal ages rolls on, and again he dares to ask, "How long?" Again the answer calls back, "Eternally! Eternally!" Oh, how this fearful answer comes thundering down through all the realms of agony and despair!

We are informed that in the final consummation of earthly scenes, *the judgment shall sit* (Daniel 7:26) and the books will be opened (Revelation 20:12). We will be there, and what is more, we will be there to close up our account with our Lord and receive what is due to us.

Which will you have on that final settlement day? The wages of sin?

Do you say, "Give me my wages. I will not be indebted to Christ"? Sinner, you will have them. God will pay you without fail and without keeping back from you anything that you are owed. He has made all the necessary arrangements and has your wages ready. But take care what you do! Look again before you take your final leap. The curtain will soon fall and all hope will have perished. Where then will I be? Where will you be? Will you be on the right hand or on the left (Matthew 25:31-46)?

The Bible places hell in the sight of heaven. The smoke of their torment as it rises up forever and ever is in full view from the heights of the heavenly city. You adore and worship God there, but as you cast your eye far off toward where the rich man lay, you see what it costs to sin. Not one drop of water can go there to cool their burning tongues, and therefore the smoke of their torment rises and rises forevermore. Take care what you do today!

Suppose you are looking into a vast crater where the surges of molten lava boil and roll up, and roll and swell, and continually spew forth huge amounts of lava to flood the plains below. I once stood in sight of Etna and looked down into its awful mouth. I could not refrain from crying out, "Tremendous! Tremendous!" I believe that was an image of hell.

**Sinner, you can still escape this fearful doom. This is the reason why God has revealed hell in His faithful Word.**

Sinner, think of hell and of you being cast into it. The lake of fire pours forth its volumes of smoke and flame forever, never ceasing, never exhausted. Upon that spectacle the universe can look and read, *The wages of sin is death.* Keep yourself from sin since this is the fate of the unpardoned sinner! Think what a demonstration this is in the government of God! What an exhibition this is of His holy justice and of His inflexible purpose to sustain the interests of holiness and happiness in all His vast dominions! Is not this worthy of God and of the sacredness of His great design of moral government?

Sinner, you can still escape this fearful doom. This is the reason why God has revealed hell in His faithful Word. Will this revelation to you be in vain, and worse than in vain?

What would you think if this whole congregation were pushed by some resistless force right up to the very brink of hell – but just as it seemed that we are all to be pushed over the dreadful edge, an angel rushes in, shouting as with seraphic trump, "Salvation is possible! Glory to God, glory to God, glory to God!"

You cry aloud, "Is it possible?"

"Yes, yes," he cries. "Let me take you up in my broad, loving arms and carry you to the feet of Jesus, for He is mighty and willing to save!

Is all this mere talk? No, for even if I could wet my lips with the dews of heaven and bathe my tongue in its founts of eloquence, I could not even then describe the realities.

Oh, Christians, are you trying to figure out how to get a little more property or more possessions, yet neglecting souls? Beware that you do not ruin souls that can never live again! Do you say that you thought they knew it all? They reply to you, "I did not think you believed a word of it yourselves. You did not act as if you did. Are you going to heaven? Well, I am going down to hell! There is no help for me now. You will sometimes think of me then, as you will see the smoke of my suffering rising up darkly across the glorious heavens. After I have been there a long, long time, you will sometimes think that I, who once lived by your side, am there. You cannot pray for me then, but you will remember that once you could have warned me and might have saved me."

I think that if there could be any bitterness in heaven, it would enter through such an avenue and spoil your happiness there!

# Chapter 4

# The Savior Lifted Up, and the Look of Faith

As Moses lifted up the serpent in the wilderness, even
so must the Son of Man be lifted up: that whosoever
believeth in him should not perish, but have eternal life.
—John 3:14-15

And I, if I be lifted up from the earth, will draw all men unto
me. (This he said, signifying what death he should die.)
—John 12:32-33

In order to make this subject plain, I will read the passage referred to:

And the LORD sent fiery serpents among the people,
and they bit the people; and much people of Israel died.
Therefore the people came to Moses, and said, We have
sinned, for we have spoken against the LORD, and against
thee; pray unto the LORD, that he take away the serpents
from us. And Moses prayed for the people. And the LORD
said unto Moses, Make thee a fiery serpent, and set it upon
a pole: and it shall come to pass, that every one that is bitten, when he looketh upon it, shall live. And Moses made a

serpent of brass, and put it upon a pole, and it came to pass, that if a serpent had bitten any man, when he beheld the serpent of brass, he lived.
—Numbers 21:6-9

This is the passage to which Christ alluded in the text. The object in both cases was to save people from perishing. The bite of the serpent, its influence being unchecked, is the death of the body. The effects of sin, unpardoned and uncleansed from the heart, are the ruin of the soul. Christ is lifted up so that sinners who believe in Him may not perish, but may have eternal life (John 3:16).

In such a connection, to perish cannot mean annihilation, for it must be the opposite of eternal life, and this is plainly much more than eternal existence. It must be eternal happiness – real life in the sense of wonderful enjoyment, and the counterpart of this, eternal misery, is presented under the term "perish." It is common in the Scriptures to find a state of endless misery contrasted with one of endless happiness.

We can observe two points of analogy between the brass serpent and Christ.

1. Christ must be lifted up as the serpent was in the wilderness. From the passage quoted above out of John 12, it is plain that this refers to His being raised up from the earth upon His cross at His crucifixion.

2. Christ must be held up as a remedy for sin, even as the brass serpent was held up as a remedy for a poison. It is not uncommon in the Bible to see sin represented as a disease or malady. For this malady, Christ had healing power. He professed to be able to forgive sin and to cleanse the soul from its moral pollution. He continually claimed to have this power, and He encouraged people to rely upon Him and to turn to Him to avail themselves of it. In all His personal instructions, He was careful to explain Himself as having this power and as being able to provide a remedy for sin.

In this respect, the serpent of brass was a type of Christ. Whoever looked upon this serpent was healed. Christ does not just heal from punishment, for to this the analogy of healing is less applicable – but He especially heals from sinning. He heals the heart from sin. He heals the soul and restores it to health. So it was said by the announcing angel: *Thou shalt call his name Jesus, for he shall save his people from their sins* (Matthew 1:21). His power avails to cleanse and purify the soul.

Both Christ and the serpent were lifted up as a remedy, and let it be especially noted that they were lifted up as a full and adequate remedy. The ancient Hebrews, bitten by fiery serpents, were not to mix up concoctions of their own devising to help with the cure. It was all-sufficient for them to look up to the remedy that God provided. God wanted them to understand that the healing was entirely His own work. The serpent on a pole was the only external object connected with their cure. They were to look to this, and in this most simple way, only by an expecting look that was indicative of simple faith, they received their cure.

Christ is to be lifted up as a present remedy. So was the serpent. The cure that was worked then was present and immediate. It involved no delay. This brass serpent was God's appointed remedy, and Christ is a remedy appointed of God, sent down from heaven for this specific purpose. It was indeed very wonderful that God would appoint a brass serpent for such a purpose – such a remedy for such a malady. It is no less wonderful that Christ was lifted up in agony and blood as a remedy for both the punishment and the heart-power of sin.

> Jesus Christ must now be lifted up from the pulpit as one crucified for the sins of men.

The brass serpent was a divinely certified remedy. It was not a remedy mixed together as thousands are with fancy-sounding names and fiery testimonials, but it was a remedy prepared and brought forth by God Himself, under His own testimony of its plentiful healing virtues.

So was Christ. The Father testifies to the perfect adequacy of Jesus Christ as a remedy for sin. Jesus Christ must now be lifted up from the pulpit as one crucified for the sins of men. His great power to save lay in His atoning death. He must not only be lifted up from the pulpit, but this display of His person and work must be endorsed, and not contradicted, by the experience of those who behold Him.

Suppose that in Moses' time many who looked at the brass serpent were seen to be still dying. Who could have believed the unqualified declaration of Moses that *every one that is bitten, when he looketh upon it, shall live*? It is the same here in the gospel and its witnesses. Undoubtedly the Hebrews had before their eyes many living witnesses who had been bitten and yet bore the scars of those wounds, but who, by looking, had been healed. Every such case would go to confirm the faith of the people in God's Word and in His own power to save. So Christ must be represented in His fullness, and this representation should be powerfully endorsed by the experience of His friends. Christ represents Himself as one ready and willing to save. This, therefore, is what is to be shown. This must be sustained by the testimony of His living witnesses.

The first point of analogy is the lifting up of the object to be looked upon, and the second is this very looking itself. People looked upon the serpent, expecting divine power to heal them. Even those ancient people in that comparatively dark age understood that the serpent was only a type, and not the very cause in itself of salvation.

There is something very remarkable in the relation of faith to healing. For example, take the case of the woman who had an issue of blood (Matthew 9:20-22; Luke 8:43-48). She had heard something about Jesus, and somehow had caught the idea that if she could just touch the hem of His garment, she would be made whole. She forced her way through the crowd – pale, trembling, and faint with weakness. If you had seen her, you would have wondered what this poor dying invalid was trying to do.

She knew what she was trying to do. At last, unnoticed by all, she reached the spot where the Holy One stood. She put forth her feeble hand and touched His garment. Suddenly He turned and asked, "*Who touched me?* Somebody touched Me. Who was it?" The disciples, astonished at such a question asked under such circumstances, replied, "The multitude crowds You on every side, and dozens of people are touching You every hour. Why, then, do You ask, *Who touched me?*

The fact was that somebody had touched Him with faith to be healed thereby, and He knew that the healing virtue had gone forth from Himself to some believing heart. How beautiful an illustration this is of simple faith, and how wonderful the connection between the faith and the healing!

In the same way, the Hebrews received that wonderful healing power by simply looking toward the brass serpent. No doubt this was a great mystery to them, yet it was nonetheless a fact. Let them look, for looking brings the cure, although not one of them can explain how the healing virtue comes. So we are really to look to Christ, and in looking, we receive the healing power. It does not matter how little we understand how the looking operates to give us the remedy for sin.

Looking to Jesus implies that we look away from ourselves. There is to be no mixing up of phony medicines along with the great remedy. Such a course is always sure to fail. Thousands fail in just this way. They forever try to be healed partly by their own empty, self-willed works, as well as partly by Jesus Christ. There must be no looking to man or to any of man's efforts or help. All dependence must be on Christ alone. As this is true in reference to pardon, so it is also true in reference to sanctification. This is done by faith in Christ. It is only through and by faith that you get that divine influence – the Spirit of God – that sanctifies the soul. It was this faith in action that was the power that healed the Hebrews in the wilderness.

> There must be no looking to man or to any of man's efforts or help. All dependence must be on Christ alone.

Looking to Christ implies looking away from ourselves in the sense of not relying at all on our own works for the cure desired – not even on works of faith. The looking is toward Christ alone as our all-prevalent, all-sufficient, and ever-present remedy.

There is a constant tendency in Christians to depend on their own works and efforts and not on simple faith in Christ. The woman with the issue of blood seems to have toiled many years to find relief before she came to Christ. She had no doubt tried everybody's prescriptions and also strained the capacity of her own ingenuity to its utmost, but all was of no avail. At last she heard of Jesus. He was said to do many wonderful works. She said within herself, *This must be the promised Messiah who is to bear our sicknesses and heal all the maladies of men. O let me rush to Him, for if I may but touch the hem of His garment, I will be made whole.* She did not stop to philosophize upon the manner of the cure. She did not lean on anyone's philosophy, and she had none of her own. She simply said, "I have heard of One who is mighty to save, and I flee to Him."

It is the same way in being healed of our sins. Despairing of all help in ourselves or in any other name than Christ's, and assured there is virtue in Him to work the cure, we expect it of Him and we go to Him to obtain it.

Several times within the last few years, people have come to me with the question, "Can I somehow be saved from my sins – actually saved, so as not to fall again into the same sins and under the same temptations?"

I have answered, "Have you ever tried looking to Jesus?"

"Oh, yes," they said.

"But did you expect to actually be saved from sin by looking to Jesus, and to be filled with faith, love, and holiness?"

"No; I did not expect that."

Now suppose someone had looked at the brass serpent for the purpose of speculation. He has no faith in what God says about being cured by looking, but he is inclined to try it. He will look a little and watch his feelings to see how it affects him. He does not believe God's Word, but since he is not absolutely sure that it is not true, he will agree to try it. This is not at all "looking" in the sense of our text. This would not have cured the bitten Israelite, nor can it heal the poor sinner. There is no faith in it.

**Sinners must look to Christ with both desire and intent to be saved.**

Sinners must look to Christ with both desire and intent to be saved. Salvation is the object for which they look. Suppose someone had looked toward the brass serpent, but without any willingness or purpose to be cured. This could do him no good. Nor can it do sinners any good to think of Christ in any way other than as a Savior, and a Savior for their own sins.

Sinners must look to Christ as a remedy for all sin. To want to make some exception that keeps some sins but agrees to abandon others indicates blatant rebellion of heart, and this can never be accepted by the All-Seeing One. There cannot be honesty in the heart that proposes to itself to seek deliverance from sin only in part.

Sinners can look to Christ at once, without the least delay. They do not need to wait until they are almost dead under some final disease. For the bitten Israelite, it was of no use to wait and delay looking to the serpent until he found himself in the grip of death. He might have said, "I am clearly wounded, but it is not swollen much yet. I do not feel the poison spreading through my system. I cannot look yet, for my case is not yet desperate enough. I could not hope to excite the compassion of the Lord in my present condition, and therefore I must wait." There was no need of such delay then, nor is there any more need or use for it in the sinner's case now.

We must look to Christ for blessings promised – not to works, but to faith. It is curious to see how many mistakes are made on this point. Many people want there to be great mental agony, long fasting, many bitter tears, and strong crying for mercy before deliverance can be looked for. They do not seem to think that all these manifestations of grief and distress are not of the slightest help because they are not simple faith, nor any part of faith, nor indeed any help toward faith. They are not needed at all for the sake of acting on the sympathies of the Savior.

It is all as if under the plague of serpents in the wilderness, people had set their minds at work to put together phony remedies – with creams and ointments and bandages and pills. All this treatment could avail nothing. There was only one effective cure, and if someone were only bitten and knew it, this would be the only preparatory step necessary to his looking as directed for his cure.

It is the same in the case of the sinner. If someone is a sinner and knows it, this is all he needs in order to go to Jesus. It is all of no avail to try to put together various prescriptions and to mix up remedies of his own devising to add to the great Remedy that God has provided. Yet there is a constant tendency in religious efforts toward this very thing – toward fixing up and relying upon an indefinite multitude and variety of spiritually false remedies.

See that sinner over there. See how he toils and agonizes. He would compass heaven and earth to work out his own salvation in his own way, to his own credit, and by his own works. See how he worries himself in the multitude of his own plans and ideas! He commonly finds himself in the deep mire of despair before he arrives at simple faith. Sadly he cries, "There can be no hope for me! My soul is lost!"

At last, the gleam of a thought breaks through the thick darkness of his mind: "Possibly Jesus can help me! If He can, then I will live, but not otherwise, for certainly there is no help for me except in Him." There he is in his despair. He is bowed in weariness of soul and is worn out with his vain efforts to help himself in other ways.

He now turns to help from above. "There is nothing else I can do except cast myself, in all my hopelessness, completely upon Jesus Christ. Will He receive me? Maybe He will, and that is enough for me to know." He thinks about it a little more: "Maybe, yes, maybe He will. I think He will, for they tell me He has done so for other sinners. I think He will. Yes, I know He will – and here is my guilty heart! I will trust Him. Yes, *though He slay me, yet I will trust in him*" (Job 13:15).

Have any of you experienced anything like that? "Maybe He will acknowledge my plea. Maybe He will hear my prayer."

This is as far as the sinner can dare to go at first, but soon you hear him crying out: "He says He will. I must believe Him!" Then faith gets hold of him and rests on promised faithfulness. Before he realizes it, his soul is *like the chariots of Amminadab* (Song of Solomon 6:12), and he finds his heart full of peace and joy as someone who is on the borders of heaven.

## Remarks

1. When it is said in John 12:32 that *I, if I be lifted up from the earth, will draw all men unto me*, the language is indeed general in form, but cannot be understood as strictly general without being brought into conflict with Bible truth and known facts. It is indeed a common manner of speaking to signify a great multitude. I will draw great numbers – a *great multitude, which no man could number* (Revelation 7:9). There is nothing here in the context, or in the subject, to require the strictly universal interpretation.

2. This method of the brass serpent was no doubt designed to test the faith of the Israelites. God often put their faith to the test, and often adapted His methods to educate their faith – to draw it out and develop it. He did many things to prove them, and He did so again in this case. They had sinned. Fiery serpents came among them, and many Israelites were poisoned and were dying on every hand. God said, "Make a brass serpent and set it upon a pole, and then raise it high before the eyes of

all the people. Now let the sufferers look on this serpent, and they will live." This put their faith to the test.

3. It is conceivable that many people perished through mere unbelief, although the provisions for their salvation were most abundant. "We look at a serpent of brass," they might say scornfully, "as if there were not impostors enough among the people, but Moses must give us yet another!" Maybe some people begin to think about the matter. They say, We will much sooner trust our tried physicians than these old wives' fables. What philosophical connection can anyone see between looking upon a piece of brass and being healed of a serpent's bite?"

Many people talk like this about the gospel. They wonder how any healing power can result from gospel faith. They hear some people say they are healed, and that they know the healing power has gone to their very soul. They say, "I looked to Jesus, and I was healed and made whole from that very hour." However, they consider all this as mere fanatical delusion. They can see none of their philosophy in it. But is this fanaticism? Is it any more strange than that a person bitten by a poisonous serpent would be healed at God's command by looking at a brass serpent?

> Many people stumble at the simplicity of the gospel.

4. Many people stumble at the simplicity of the gospel. They want something more complex! They want to see through it. They will not trust what they cannot explain. It is on this basis that many people stumble at the doctrine of sanctification by faith in Christ. It is so simple that their philosophy cannot see through it. However, the analogy provided in our text is complete. People are to look to Jesus so that they may not perish, but may have eternal life (John 3:15), and who does not know that eternal life involves entire sanctification?

5. The natural man always seeks for some way of salvation that will be altogether believable to himself. He wants to work out some form of self-righteousness, and he is not concerned about trusting in Christ alone. It does not seem to him natural or philosophical.

6. There is a startling and most alarming state of things in many churches: there is almost no Christ in their experience. It is most evident that He holds an exceedingly small space in the hearts of many who profess to follow Jesus. So far from knowing what salvation is as something to be attained by simply believing in Christ, they can only give you an experience of this sort. If you ask one of these people how he became a Christian, the answer is often, "I just made up my mind to serve the Lord."

"Is that all?"

"That's all."

"Do you know what it is to receive eternal life by simply looking to Jesus?"

"I don't think I understand that."

"Then you are not a Christian."

Christianity, from beginning to end, is received from Christ by simple faith. In this way, and only in this way, does the pardon of sin come to the soul, and only in this way can come that peace of God that passes all understanding and that lives in the soul with faith and love. In this way, sanctification comes through faith in Christ.

What, then, will we think of that religion that leaves Christ out of view? Many are looking for some wonderful sign or token, not understanding that it is by faith that they are to be brought completely into fellowship with Christ and into participation with His own life. By faith, Christ unites them to Himself. Faith working by love draws them into living union with His own moral being. All this is done by simply looking to Christ in faith.

When the brass serpent was up, many people no doubt perished because they would not accept and act upon such a simple remedy. Many people perished because they did not and would not realize their danger. If they saw people cured, they would say, "We don't believe it was done by the brass serpent on the pole. Those people were not much poisoned, so would not have died anyway." They assumed that those who ascribed their cure to the power of God were mistaken.

Many also perished from delay. They waited to see whether they were in danger of dying. They continued to wait until they were so sick and weak that they could only lie down and die.

Now in regard to the gospel. Some people are occupied with other matters that they consider more important, and of course they must delay. Many are influenced by others' opinions. They hear many stories. Such a person looked, yet lost his life. Another man did not look, yet was saved. People have different opinions about their professedly Christian neighbors, and this causes many to stumble. They hear that some people set out strong for Christianity, but seem to fail. They looked up as they thought about these things, but all in vain. Maybe it was so because they might have looked without real faith.

Some will philosophize until they make themselves believe it is all a delusion to look. They think they see many people who pretend to look and seem to look who do not find healing. Who can believe where there are so many stumbling blocks?

We can imagine that these discouraging appearances drove some people into despair in the wilderness, and certainly we see that the same causes produce these effects here in the case of sinners. Some people think they have committed the unpardonable sin. They class themselves among *those who were once enlightened* (Hebrews 6:4), knowing that for them *there remains no more sacrifice for sins, but a certain looking for of judgment and fiery indignation* (Hebrews 10:26-27). Some are sure that it is too late for them now. Their heart is as hard as stone. All is dark and as desolate as the grave. Look at him over there; his very look is that of a lost soul! Some of you might now be reasoning and disbelieving in this very way!

Many neglected to look because they thought they were getting better. They thought they saw some change of symptoms and some improvement. It is the same with sinners; they feel better after attending a church service, and if they show any improvement, they believe they are undoubtedly doing well.

Many of the ancient Hebrews may have refused to look because they had no good hope and were indeed full of doubts. If you had been there, you would have found a great variety of conflicting views – often even between brothers and sisters, fathers and mothers, and parents and children. Some ridiculed others; some were mad; some would not believe no matter what. Some sinners who should be seeking Christ today are deterred by reasons fully as frivolous and foolish as these.

It is easy for us to see the analogy between the manner of looking and the reasons for not looking at the brass serpent and to Christ the Savior. I do not need to push the analogy into its precise particulars any further, but the question for you all now is: Do you really believe that *as Moses lifted up the serpent in the wilderness, even so must the Son of man be lifted up: that whosoever believeth in him should not perish, but have eternal life*? Do you understand the simple remedy of faith?

Perhaps you ask what they were to believe. They were to believe that if they really looked at the brass serpent on the pole, they would certainly experience the needed healing. It was God's certified remedy, and they were to regard it as such.

What are you now to believe? You are to believe that Christ is the great antitype of that serpent lifted up in the wilderness, and that you are to receive from Him by simple faith all the blessings of a full and free salvation. Do you understand what is meant by simple faith? Do you ask, "What? Can I, a sinner, just focus my eye in simple faith on Jesus? Who can do this? Can I? How can it be that I should have this privilege?"

I see here today some whom I saw last fall in the meetings when you were inquiring more about the gospel and God's truth. What have you been doing since then? Have you been trying to work yourselves into some specific state of mind? Do you intensely wish that you could only feel a certain way according to some ideal you have in your mind? Do you understand that you are really to look by faith? Let this look of faith be to you as the touch of the poor woman with an issue of blood was to her dying body (Mark 5:24-34), believing that if you look in simple trust, Jesus will surely receive you and give you His divine love, peace, life, and light, and really make them flow through your whole moral being.

Do you believe it? No; don't you see that you do not believe it? Oh, but you say, "It is a great mystery!" I am not going to explain it, nor will I pretend that I can do so any more than I can explain how that woman was healed by touching the hem of the Savior's garment. The touch in this case and the looking in that case are only the means, the method, by which the power is to be received. The manner in which God operates is a thing of small consequence to us. Let us be satisfied that we know what we must do to secure the work of His divine Spirit in *all things that pertain unto life and godliness* (2 Peter 1:3-4).

> When we see any need, Christ is there to be received by faith alone – and His promises leave no need unprovided for.

You have doubtless had confused ideas of the way of salvation. You might you have been contriving and speculating and working based upon your own feelings. Now you pray, and having prayed, you say, "Now let me watch and see if this prayer has given me salvation!" This method is similar to if the Hebrew people, when bitten by serpents and commanded to look to the serpent of brass, would have gone about to apply here a bandage, there an ointment, and then an examination, all the time losing sight of just that one thing that God told them would infallibly cure them.

Oh, why would people forget, and why would they not understand, that all good needed by us comes from God through simple faith? When we see any need, Christ is there to be received by faith alone – and His promises leave no need unprovided for.

Now if this is the way of salvation, how astonishing that sinners would look every other way except toward Christ, and would put forth every other type of effort except the effort to look at once in simple faith to their Savior! How often we see them discouraged and confounded, working so hard and so completely in vain! It is no wonder that they would be so greatly misled.

Go around among the churches and ask if they ever expected to be saved from sin in this world. They do not expect to be saved from sin in this world, but they expect to be saved at death! If Christ has been quite unsuccessful in His efforts to sanctify your soul during your life, do you think He will send death on in time to help the work through? Can you believe this?

As long as Christians deny the glorious doctrine of sanctification by faith in Christ, both present sanctification and sanctification according to each person's faith (Matthew 9:29), it cannot be expected that they will teach sinners with simple clarity how to look to Christ in simple faith for pardon. Knowing so little of the power of faith in their own experience, how can they teach others effectively, or even truthfully? Thus, with the blind leading the blind, it is no wonder that both are found together where the Bible proverb represents both the leaders and the led as ending their mutual relations by both falling into the ditch (Matthew 15:14).

There seems to be no remedy for such a finality except for professing Christians to become the light of the world, and toward this end, to learn the meaning and to know the experience of simple faith. Once they learn faith, they will experience its transforming power and will be able to teach others the way of life.

## Chapter 5

# The Excuses of Sinners Condemn God

Wilt thou also disannul my judgment? Wilt thou condemn me, that thou mayest be righteous?
—Job 40:8

Although Job had generally spoken correctly of God, yet in his great anguish and distress under his severe trials, he had said some things that were hasty and abusive. The Lord rebuked him for these things. This rebuke is contained in our context of Job 40:1-8:

> Moreover the LORD answered Job, and said, Shall he that contendeth with the Almighty instruct Him? He that reproveth God, let him answer it.

> Then Job answered the LORD, and said, Behold I am vile; what shall I answer thee? I will lay my hand upon my mouth. Once have I spoken, but I will not answer; yea twice; but I will proceed no further.

> Then answered the LORD unto Job out of the whirlwind, and said, Gird up thy loins now like a man; I will demand of thee, and declare thou unto me. Wilt thou also disannul

my judgment? Wilt thou condemn me, that thou mayest be righteous?

It is not, however, my object to discuss the original purpose and connection of these words, but rather to consider their present application to the case of sinners. In pursuing this object, I will:

I.   Show that every excuse for sin condemns God

II.  Consider some of these excuses in detail

III. Show that excuses for sin add insult to injury

## I. Every excuse for sin condemns God

This will be apparent if we consider the following:

1. Nothing can be sin for which there is a justifiable excuse. This is entirely self-evident. It therefore needs neither explanation nor proof.

2. If God condemns that for which there is a good excuse, He must be wrong. This also is self-evident. If God condemns that which we have good reason for doing, no intelligence in the universe can justify Him.

3. God condemns all sin. He condemns it completely and will not allow the least defense or excuse for it. Therefore, either there is no excuse for it, or God is wrong.

4. Consequently, every excuse for sin lays blame upon God and practically accuses Him of tyranny. Whoever pleads an excuse for sin, therefore, blames God.

## II. We will consider some of these excuses and see whether the principles I have laid down are not just and true.

**1. Inability.** No excuse is more common. It is echoed and reechoed over every Christian land, and it is handed down age after age, never to be forgotten. Without shame, it is proclaimed that people cannot do what God requires of them.

Let us examine this and see what it amounts to. It is said that God requires what people cannot do. Does He know that people cannot do it? Most certainly. Therefore, He has no apology for requiring it, and the demand is most unreasonable. Human reason can never justify it. It is a natural impossibility.

But again, upon what penalty does God require what people cannot do? The threatened penalty is eternal death! Yes, eternal death, according to the views of those who plead inability as an excuse. God requires me, with the threat of eternal death, to do that which He knows I cannot do. This certainly condemns God in the worst sense. You might just as well directly accuse God of being an infinite tyrant.

Moreover, it is not for us to say whether on these conditions we will or will not accuse God of infinite tyranny, for we cannot help it. The law of our reason demands it.

Therefore, those who plant themselves upon these grounds accuse God of infinite tyranny. Sinner, it might be that when you promote the excuse of inability, you have not much considered that you are really accusing God of infinite tyranny. And you, Christian, who make this dogma of inability a part of your "orthodox" creed, may have little noticed its blasphemous bearings against the character of God; however, your failure to notice it does not change the fact. The unrighteous accusation is included in the very doctrine of inability, and it cannot be explained out of it.

I have indicated that this accusation is most truly blasphemous against God. Far be it from God to do any such thing! Will God require natural impossibilities, and proclaim eternal death upon people for not doing what they have no natural power to do? Never! Yet good people and bad people agree together to accuse God of doing this very thing, and of not just doing so once or twice, but consistently, through all ages, with all people, from the beginning to the end of time!

This is horrible! Nothing in all the government of God ever so insulted and abused Him! Nothing was ever more blasphemous and false! God says that His *commandments are not grievous* (1 John 5:3), but you, by this excuse of inability, proclaim that God's words are false. You declare that His commands are not only grievous, but are even naturally impossible! Listen! What does the Lord Jesus say? *My yoke is easy, and my burden is light* (Matthew 11:30). Do you deny this? Do you rise up in the very face of His words and say, "Lord, Your yoke is so difficult that no one can possibly endure it. Your burden is so heavy that no one can ever bear it"? Is not this contradicting and blaspheming Him who cannot lie (Titus 1:2)?

However, you take the ground that no one can obey the law of God. As the Presbyterian Confession of Faith says, "No man is able, either by himself, or by any grace received in this life, perfectly to keep the commandments of God; but doth daily break them in thought, word, and deed." Observe that this affirms not only that no one is naturally able to keep God's commands, but also that no one is able to do it "by any grace received in this life," thus making this declaration a libel on the gospel, as well as a clear misrepresentation of the law, of its Author, and of man's relations to both. It is only moderate language to call this assertion from the Confession of Faith a libel. If there is a lie either in hell or out of hell, this is a lie, or God is an infinite tyrant. If reason is allowed to speak at all, it is impossible for it to say less or otherwise than this. And has not God established the reason of man for the very purpose of taking notice of the righteousness of all His ways?

Let God be true, even though every man be proved a liar (Romans 3:4). In the present case, the remarkable fact that no one can appease his own conscience and convince himself that he is truly unable to keep the law shows that man lies – not God.

**2. Lack of time.** Suppose I tell one of my sons, "Go and do this duty or the punishment will be that you will be whipped to death."

He replies, "Father, I cannot possibly do it, for I do not have time. I must be doing that other business that you told me to do. Besides, if

I had nothing else to do, I could not possibly do this new business in the time you allow."

Now if this statement is the truth, and I knew it when I gave him the command, then I am a tyrant. There is no evading this charge. My conduct toward my son would be downright tyranny.

Therefore, if God really requires of you what you do not have time to do, He is infinitely to blame, for He surely knows how little time you have, and it is undeniable that He enforces His demands with most terrible penalties. What! Is God so unconcerned about justice, so thoughtless of the well-being of His creatures, that He can amuse Himself with red-hot thunderbolts and hurl them, despite justice and goodness, among His unfortunate creatures? Never! Never! This is not true; it is only the false assumption that the sinner makes when he pleads as his excuse that he does not have time to do what God demands of him.

> Therefore, if God really requires of you what you do not have time to do, He is infinitely to blame.

Let me ask you, sinner, how much time will it take you to do the first great duty that God requires – that is, to give Him your heart? How long will this take? How long do you need to make up your mind to serve and love God? Do you not know that this, when done, will be done in one moment of time? How long do you need to take to persuade yourself to do it?

Your meaning then may be this: "Lord, it takes me so long to make up my mind to serve You that it seems as if I will never have enough time for this. Even my entire life seems almost too short for me to bring my mind to this unwelcome decision." Is this your meaning, sinner?

Let us look at all sides of the subject. Suppose I say to my son, "Do this now, Son," and he replies, "I can't, Father, for I must do that other thing you told me to do." Does God do this with us? No. God only requires the duty of each moment in its time. That is all. He only asks us to use faithfully all the power He has given us – nothing more. He only requires that we do the best we can.

When He specifies the amount of love that will please Him, He does not say, "You shall love the Lord your God with the powers of an angel, with the burning heart of a seraph." No, but only *with all thy heart* (Matthew 22:37) – this is all. It is an infinitely ridiculous plea of the sinner that he cannot do as well as he can – that he cannot love God with all his own heart, soul, mind, and strength. "You will do the best that you are able to do," God says to the sinner. The sinner responds, "I am not able to do that." Oh, what foolish nonsense!

You complain that God is unreasonable. The truth is that God is the most reasonable of all beings. He only asks that we would use each moment for Him, in work or in rest, whichever is most for His glory. He only requires that we would do all we can to serve Him with the time, talents, and strength that He has given to us.

Some mother says, "How can I be religious? I have to take care of all my children." Indeed! Can't you get time to serve God? What does God require of you? Does He demand that you must forsake and neglect your children? No, indeed. He asks you to take care of your children – to take good care of them and to do it all for God. He says to you, "Those are My children," and He puts them into your hands, saying, "Take care of them for Me, and I will give you your wages."

Will it require more time to take care of your children for God than to take care of them for yourself? You now say, "I cannot be religious, for I must be up in the morning and get my breakfast." How much longer will it take you to get your breakfast ready to please God than to do the same to please yourself? How much more time must you have to do your duties for God than to do them selfishly?

What then do you mean by this excuse? The fact is that all these excuses show that the person making such excuses is delusional – not insane, but delusional. What does God require that is so great that you would be unable to do it for lack of time? Only this – that you would do it all for God. People who make this excuse seem to have completely overlooked the real nature of Christianity and of the requirements that God places upon them.

So it is with the excuse of inability. The sinner says, "I am unable." Unable to do what? Just do what you can do, for God never requires anything beyond this. Unless, therefore, you suppose that God requires more of you than you can do, your excuse is false, and even ridiculous. If, on the other hand you do not suppose this, then, if your excuse were true, it would show God to be unjust.

As I mentioned, when people use this excuse of having no time to be Christlike, they completely overlook or misrepresent the true idea of Christianity. The farmer pleads, "I can't be holy; I can't serve God, for I must sow my wheat." Well, sow your wheat – but do it for the Lord. But you say you have so much to do! Then do it all for the Lord. Another person says that he cannot follow Christ because he must study his lesson. Well, study, but do it for the Lord, and this will be pleasing to God.

The person who would neglect to sow his wheat or neglect to study because he wants to follow Jesus is crazy. He distorts the plainest things in the worst way. If you are to be holy, you must be industrious. The farmer must sow his wheat, and the student must study his lesson. An idle person can no more be Christian than the devil can be.

This idea that people cannot be Christian because they have some business to do is complete nonsense. It completely overlooks the great truth that God never forbids us from doing the appropriate business of life, but only requires that we should do it all for Him. If God did require us to serve Him in such a way that would compel us to neglect the practical duties of life, it would be truly a difficult situation. However, the whole truth is that He requires us to do precisely these duties, to do them all honestly and faithfully for Him,

> God never forbids us from doing the appropriate business of life, but only requires that we should do it all for Him.

and to do them in the best possible manner. Let the farmer take care of his farm, and see that he does it well, and above all, do it for God. It is God's farm, and the heart of every farmer is God's heart; therefore, let the farm be tilled for God, and the heart be devoted to Him alone.

**3. A sinful nature.** What is this sinful nature that some people blame for their sin? Do you mean by it that every ability and even the very essence of your character were poisoned and made sinful in Adam, and came down in this polluted state by inheritance to you? Do you mean that you were so born in sin that the substance of your being is completely saturated with it, and that all the powers of your being are themselves sin? Do you believe this?

I admit that if this were true, it would be a difficult case – very difficult indeed! Until the laws of my reason are changed, it would compel me to speak out openly and say, "Lord, this is a difficult case, that

You would make my nature itself a sinner, and then charge the guilt of its sin upon me!" I would not be able to help saying this. The deep echoings of my inner being would proclaim it without ceasing, and the breaking of ten thousand thunderbolts over my head would not deter me from thinking and saying so. The reason that God has given me would forever affirm it.

But the belief is an utter absurdity, for what is sin? God answers: *Sin is the transgression of the law* (1 John 3:4). You now contend that your nature is itself a breach of the law of God, and that it has always been a breach of God's law, from Adam to the day of your birth. You say that the stream of this sin came down in the veins and blood of your race – and who made it so? Who created the veins and blood of man? From whose hand sprang this physical and mental constitution? Was man his own creator? Did sin do a part of the work in creating your physical and your mental constitution? Do you believe any such thing? No; you credit your nature and its original capabilities to God, and therefore, you accuse Him of being guilty for being the author of your sinful nature.

> The fact is that sin can never consist in having a nature, nor in what nature is, but only and alone in the bad use that we make of our nature.

What a strange thing this is! If man is at fault for his sinful nature, why not condemn man for having blue or brown eyes? The fact is that sin can never consist in having a nature, nor in what nature is, but only and alone in the bad use that we make of our nature. This is all. Our Maker will never find fault with us for what He Himself has done or made. He will not condemn us if we will only make a proper use of our powers – of our intellect, our sensibility, and our will. He never holds us responsible for our original nature. If you will observe, you will find that God has given no law specifying what sort of nature and inherent powers we should have. He has given no law on these points, the transgression of which, if given, might somewhat resemble the definition of sin. But now, since there is no law about nature, nature cannot be a transgression.

Let me say here that if God were to make a law specifying what nature or constitution a person must have, it could not possibly be anything other than unjust and absurd because man's nature is not a proper subject for legislation, precept, and penalty since it lies entirely outside the bounds of voluntary action, or of any action of man at all.

Yet thousands of people have held the belief that sin consists largely in having a sinful nature. Yes, through long ages of past history, serious theologians have sincerely taught this dreadful dogma. It has resounded from pulpits and has been stereotyped for the press, and people have never seemed to grow tired of glorifying this dogma as the surest test of sound orthodoxy! Orthodoxy! There was never a more infamous libel on God! It would be difficult to name another belief that more sharply outrages common sense. It is nonsense – absurd and utter nonsense! It is even worse than nonsense! Think what harm it has caused! Think how it has maligned the law, the government, and the character of God! Think how it has filled the mouths of sinners with excuses from the day of its birth to this hour!

I do not mean to imply that the people who have held this belief have knowingly insulted God with it. I do not imply that they have been aware of the impious and even blasphemous aspect of this belief upon God. I am happy to think that some at least have done all this harm in ignorance. However, the fault and the wrong have not been any less because of the honest ignorance in which they were done.

**4. Sinners, in self-excuse, say they are willing to be Christians.** They are willing, they say, to be sanctified. Oh yes, they are very willing, but there is some great difficulty lying further back, or something else. They might not know just where it is, but it is somewhere, and it will not let them become Christians.

The fact is that if we are really willing, there is nothing more that we can do. To be willing is all we have to do morally in the case, and it is all we can do. However, the excuse as it is in the sinner's mouth maintains that God requires of us what is naturally impossible. It assumes that God requires of us something more than to be willing, and this, of course, is an impossibility for us.

If I will to move my muscles, and no motion follows, I have done all I can do; there is a difficulty beyond my reach, and I am not to blame for it. In the same way, if I were to will to serve God, and absolutely no effect would follow, I have done my utmost, and God can never demand anything more. In fact, to will is the very thing that God does require. *If there be first a willing mind, it is accepted* (2 Corinthians 8:12).

Tell me, parent, if you had told your child to do anything, and you saw him exerting himself to the utmost, would you ask anything more? If you would see a parent demanding and enforcing of a child more than he could possibly do, no matter how willing the child was, would you not denounce that parent as a tyrant? Certainly you would.

This excuse is completely false, for no sinner is willing to be any better than he actually is. If the will is right, all is right, and generally, the state of the will is the measure of one's moral character. Therefore, those people who plead that they are willing to be Christians while still remaining in their sins talk mere nonsense.

**5. Sinners say they are waiting God's time.** A lady in Philadelphia had been in great distress of mind for many years. On calling to see her, I asked, "What does God require of you? What is your situation?"

"Oh," she said, "God waited on me a long time before I began to seek Him at all, and now I must wait for Him as long as He did for me. That is what my minister tells me. You see, therefore, that I am waiting in great distress for God to be ready to receive me."

Now what is the real meaning of this? It comes to this, that God urges me to duty, but is not ready for me to do it. He tells me to come to the gospel feast, and I am ready, but He is not ready to let me in.

Does this not place all the blame upon God? Could anything do so more completely than this does? The sinner says, "I am ready and willing and waiting, but God is not yet ready for me to stop sinning. His hour has not yet come."

When I first began to preach, I found this idea almost universal. Often after urging people to duty, I have been confronted with people saying, "What? You place all the blame upon the sinner!"

"Yes, indeed I do," would be my reply.

An old lady once met me after preaching and exclaimed, "What! You direct people to get religion themselves! You tell them to repent themselves? You don't mean this, do you?"

"Indeed I do," I said.

She had been teaching for many years that the sinner's main duty is to wait for God's good time.

**6. Sinners make the excuse that their circumstances are very unusual.** "I know my duty well enough, but my circumstances are so unusual." Does not God understand your circumstances? Has not His providence been involved in making them what they are? If so, then you are throwing blame upon God. You say, "O Lord, You are a hard master, for You have never made any allowance for my circumstances."

But what, sinner, do you really mean in making this excuse? Do you mean that your circumstances are so unusual that God should excuse you from becoming a follower of Jesus, at least for now? If you do not mean as much as this, why do you make your circumstances your excuse at all? If you do mean this, then you are just as much mistaken as you can be, for God requires you, despite your circumstances, to abandon your sin. If your circumstances are now so unusual that you cannot serve God in them, you must abandon them or lose your soul. If they do allow you to serve God in them, then do so at once.

> If your circumstances are now so unusual that you cannot serve God in them, you must abandon them or lose your soul.

But you say, "I cannot get out of my circumstances." I reply that you can. You can get out of the wickedness of them, for if it is necessary in order to serve God, you can change them, and if not, you can repent and serve God in them.

**7. The sinner's next excuse is that his temperament is unusual.** "Oh," he says, "I am very nervous," or "My temperament is very sluggish; I seem to have no discernment." Now what does God require? Does He require of you another or a different sense from your own, or does He require only that you would use what you have according to the law of love?

However, this is the way it is with many people who make excuses. One person claims to have too little excitement, and another too much – so neither person can possibly repent and serve God! A woman came to me and pleaded that she was naturally too excitable and dared not trust herself, and therefore could not repent. Another person claims to have the opposite trouble of being too unemotional and hardly ever shedding a tear, and therefore could make nothing out of Christianity even if he would try. But does God require you to shed more tears than you are naturally able to shed, or does He only require that you should serve Him? Certainly this is all He requires.

Serve Him with the very powers He has given you. If your nerves are excitable, come and lay those quivering emotions into the hands of God. Pour out that emotion into the heart of God; this is all that He requires. I know how to sympathize with that woman, for I know much about an earnest affection – but does God require feeling and excitement, or only a complete consecration of all our powers to Himself?

**8. Another person gives the excuse that his health is so poor that he cannot go to Christian meetings, and therefore cannot be godly.** Well, what does God require? Does He require that

> God is infinitely the most reasonable being who ever existed.

you should go to all the meetings, day or night, whether you have the necessary health for it or not? Definitely not. If you are not able to go to the meetings, you can still give God your heart. If you cannot go in bad weather, be assured that God is infinitely the most reasonable being who ever existed. He makes all due allowance for every circumstance.

Does He not know all your weakness? Indeed He does. Do you suppose that He visits you when you are sick and denounces you for not being able to go to a meeting, or for not attempting to do so when unable, and for not doing everything when you are sick that you can do when healthy? No, not He, but He visits you as a Father. He comes to pour out the deepest compassions of His heart in kindness and in love, and why would you not respond to His loving-kindness?

He comes to you and says, "Give Me your heart, My child."

Now you reply, "I have no heart."

Then He has nothing to ask of you. He knows you have a heart, and He knows, too, that He has done enough to draw your heart in love and gratitude to Himself. He asks, "What can you find in all My interactions with you that is grievous?" If nothing, why do you bring forward excuses for sin that accuse and condemn God?

**9. Another excuse is like this: "My heart is so hard that I cannot feel anything."** This is very common, both among professors and non-professors of Christianity. In reality, it is only another form of the excuse of inability. In fact, all the sinner's excuses amount only to this: "I am unable. I cannot do what God requires." If the excuse of a hard heart is any excuse at all, it must be on the basis of actual inability.

But what is hardness of heart? Do you mean that you have such great lack of emotion that you do not have any feelings, or that you have no power to will or to act right? On this point, it should be considered that the emotions are completely involuntary. They go and come according to circumstances, and therefore are never required by the law of God, and are not, properly speaking, either Christianity itself or any part of it. Therefore, if by a hard heart you mean you have little emotion or feeling, this is not relevant to the subject. God asks you to yield your will and consecrate your desires to Him, and He asks this whether you have any feeling or not.

Real hardness of heart, in the Bible use of the phrase, means stubbornness of will. In a child, a hard heart means a will set in fixed stubbornness against following his parent's instructions and commands. The child may have either much or little emotion in connection with this. His emotions may be intense and thoroughly excited, or they may be dormant – yet the stubborn will may be there in either case.

The hardness of heart of which God complains in the sinner is precisely of this type. The sinner clings to his self-indulgence and will not relinquish it, and then complains of hardness of heart. What would you think of a child who, when required to do a most reasonable thing, would give the same kind of excuse? "My heart is so hard, I can't do it. My will is so set to have my own way that I cannot possibly yield to my father's authority."

This complaint is extremely common. Many sinners make this excuse who have been often warned, have often been prayed with and wept over, and who have often felt the conviction of sin. Does someone who makes this excuse really mean that he finds his will so stubborn that he cannot make up his mind to surrender to God's claims? Does he mean this, and does he really intend to announce his own disgrace?

Suppose you go to the demons in hell, and proclaim to them the gospel of God and the need to surrender to Him, and they would reply, "Oh, my heart is so hard, I can't." What would they mean by this? They would mean that they are so obstinate and their wills are so set in sin that they cannot for a moment consider the thought of repentance. This would be their meaning, and if the sinner tells the truth about himself and uses language correctly, he must mean the same. Oh, how he adds insult to injury by this declaration!

Suppose a child would say, "I cannot find it in my heart to love my father and my mother. My heart is so hard toward them that I can never love them. I can feel pleasure only in talking back to them and rejecting their authority." What an excuse this is! Does not this heap insult upon wrong?

Suppose a murderer were arraigned before the court, and before he was sentenced, he was permitted to speak and tell any reason as to why sentence should not be passed. Suppose he would stand up and say, "May it please the court, my heart for a long time has been as hard as a millstone. I have murdered so many men, and have been doing this for so long, that I can kill a man without the least misgiving of conscience. Indeed, I have such an unquenchable thirst for blood that I cannot help murdering whenever I have a good opportunity. In fact, my heart is so hard that I find I like this kind of work as much as any other."

Well, how long will the court listen to such a plea? The judge would exclaim, "Stop! Stop right there, you wretched villain! We will hear no more of your plea! Sheriff, bring in a gallows and hang the man within these very walls of justice, for I will not leave the bench until I see him dead! He will murder us all here in this house if he can!"

Now what will we think of the sinner who says the same thing? "O God," he says, "my heart is so hard that I can never love You! I hate You so sincerely that I will never decide to surrender my heart to You in love and willing submission."

Sinners, many of you have made this same plea: "My heart is so hard, I can't repent. I can't love and serve God." Go write it down. Proclaim it to the universe. Make your boast of being so hard-hearted that no pleading from God can ever move you. I think that if you were to make such an excuse, you would not be half through before the whole universe would chase you from their presence and from the face of these heavens until you would cry out for some rocks or mountains to hide you from their scathing rebukes! Their voice of indignation would rise up and ring along the arch of heaven like the roar of ten thousand tornadoes, and would overwhelm you with unutterable confusion and shame!

What! Do you insult and revile the Lord! Do you condemn that very God who has watched over you in unspeakable love, who has fanned you with His gentle breezes during your sickness, and who has fed you at His own table – even as you would not thank Him or even notice His providing hand?

Then when the sympathy of your Christian friends has caused them to plead with you to repent, and when they have made you a special subject of their prayers; when angels have wept over you, and unseen spirits have lifted their warning voices in your pathway to hell – you turn up your face of brass toward the Lord and tell Him that your heart is so hard that you cannot repent, and that you do not care whether you ever do or not! You seize a spear and plunge it into the heart of the Crucified One, and then cry out, "I cannot be sorry. My heart is hard as a stone! I don't care, and I will not repent!" What a wretch you are, sinner, if this is your plea!

But what does your plea amount to? Only this – that your heart is fully set to do evil. The sacred writer has revealed your case most clearly: *Because sentence against an evil work is not executed speedily, therefore the heart of the sons of men is fully set in them to do evil* (Ecclesiastes 8:11). You stand before the Lord in this foolish, blasphemous attitude – fully set in your heart to do evil.

**10. Another form of the same plea is, "My heart is so wicked that I can't."** Some people do not hesitate to declare this wickedness of heart. What do they mean by it? Do they mean that they are so hardened in sin and so desperately wicked that they will not bow to God? This is the only proper sense of their language, and this is the precise truth.

Since you bring this forward as your excuse, sinner, your intent must be to accuse God of this wickedness of heart. You might be trying to do this covertly, but you are really implying that God is involved in creating that wicked heart! That is it, and this is all of it. You would feel no interest in the excuse, and you would never say it, except for this unspoken implication that God is at fault for your wicked heart. This is merely the plea of inability, coupled with its twin sister, original sin, coming down in the created blood and veins of the human race under accusation of the Creator's responsibility.

**11. Another similar excuse is, "My heart is so deceitful."** Suppose someone would make this excuse for deceiving his neighbor: "I can't help cheating you. I can't help lying to you and hurting you. My heart is so deceitful!" Would anyone in his right mind ever suppose that this could be an apology or excuse for doing wrong? Never. Of course, unless the sinner intends in this excuse to set forth his own guilt and condemn himself, he must intend it as some sort of justification. If so, he is really trying to cast the blame upon God. This is usually the intention. He does not sincerely intend to confess his own sin, but he is trying to place the guilt of his deceitful heart upon God.

**12. Another person uses the excuse, "I have tried to become a Christian. I have done all I can do. I have tried often, earnestly, and for a long time."** You have tried, you say, to be a Christian. What is being a Christian? It is giving your heart to God. What is giving your heart to God? It is devoting your voluntary powers to Him. It is ceasing to live for yourself and instead living for God. This is being a Christian – the state you profess to have been trying to attain.

> What is giving your heart to God? It is devoting your voluntary powers to Him.

No excuse is more common than this. What is legitimately implied by saying that you are trying to be a Christian? A willingness to do your duty is always implied – that the heart, the will, is right already, and the trying refers only to the outward efforts – for there is no sense whatsoever in a person saying that he is trying to do what he has no intention or will to do. The very statement implies that his will is not only in favor of, but is thoroughly committed to and is really in earnest of, attaining the end chosen.

Consequently, they must mean that if someone tries to be a Christian, his heart is obedient to God, and his trying must refer to his outward action. These things, then, are so connected with the will that they follow by a law of necessity unless the connection is broken. When this takes place, no sin accompanies our failure to secure the outward act. God does not hold us responsible.

Therefore, the sinner should mean by this excuse, "I have obeyed God for a long time. I have had a right heart, and I have sincerely tried to achieve such external action as agrees with Christian character." If this is true, you have done your duty. But do you intend to affirm all this? No. Then what do you mean?

Suppose I would say to my son, "Do this; do it my son. Why have you not done it?"

"Oh," he says, "Father, I have tried."

However, he does not mean that he has ever intended to do it or that he has ever made up his mind to obey me. He only means, "I have been willing to try. I made up my mind to try to be willing. I have brought myself to be willing to try to will to do it!" That is all he means by that.

You say, "I have tried to get true religion." What is true religion that you could not get it? How did you fail? You have probably been trying in this way: God has said, "Give Me your heart," and you turned around and asked God to do it Himself, or maybe you simply waited for Him to do it. He commanded you to repent, and you have tried to get Him to repent for you. He said, "Believe the gospel," and you have only been thinking of trying to get Him to believe for you.

It is no wonder that you have tried for a long time in vain. How could it be otherwise? You have not been trying to do what God commanded you to do, but you have been trying to get God to change His system of moral government and put Himself in your place to do Himself the duty He requires from you. What a miserable corruption this is!

Now as to this whole excuse of having tried to be a Christian, what is the use of it? You will easily see its use when you properly realize that it is completely false when understood as you intend it, and that it is an unfair accusation against the character of God.

You say, "Lord, I know I can't. I have tried all I can, and I know I cannot become a Christian. I am willing to get true religion, but I do not seem able to do so.

Who, then, is to blame? Not yourself, according to your statement of your situation. Where, then, is the blame? Let me ask what would be said in the distant regions of the universe if you would say there that you have tried with all your heart to love and serve God, but you can't. They would never believe such an accusation against their own infinite Father! Of course, they will pronounce your doom as you deserve!

**13. Another excuse is that it will do no good to try.** What do you mean by this? Do you mean that God will not pay well for service done for Him? Do you mean that He will not forgive you if you repent? Do you think (as some do) that you have sinned away your day of grace?

Well, suppose you have. Is this any reason why you should continue in sin? Do you not believe that God is good and that He will forgive you if the good of the universe permits? Most certainly. Is the impossibility of His forgiving you, then, any reason why you should continue in sin forever, and forever be angry against a God of infinite goodness?

You believe Him to be compassionate and forgiving. Should you not then say that you will at least stop sinning against such a God? You can say with the man who dreamed that he was just then going to hell, as he was parting from his brother, who was going then to heaven, as his dream had it, "I am going down to hell, but I want you to tell God from me that I am greatly obliged to Him for ten thousand mercies that I never deserved. He has never done me the least injustice. Give Him my thanks for all the unmerited good He has done to me."

At this point he awoke and found himself bathed in tears of repentance and gratitude to his Father in heaven. If people would only act as reasonably as that man dreamed, it would be noble and right. If, when they think that they have sinned away the day of grace, they would say, "I know God is good. I will at least send Him my thanks. He has done me no injustice" – if they would take this course, they might at least have the satisfaction of feeling that it is a reasonable and a proper one in their circumstances. Sinner, will you do this?

**14. Another person gives the excuse, "I have offered to give my heart to Christ, but He won't receive me. I have no evidence that He receives me or ever will."** In the last inquiry meeting, a young woman told me that she had offered to give her heart to the Lord, but He would not receive her. This was accusing Jesus directly of lying, for He has said,

*Him that cometh to me, I will in no wise cast out* (John 6:37). You say, I came and offered myself, and He would not receive me. Jesus Christ says, *Behold I stand at the door and knock: if any man* – not if some certain people or some favored person, but – *if any man hear my voice, and open the door, I will come in to him* (Revelation 3:20).

Yet when you offered Him your heart, did He turn you away? Did He say, "Away sinner! Go away!"? No, sinner. He never did that – never. He has said that He never would do it. His own words are, *Him that cometh unto me, I will in no wise cast out.* Jesus said, *He that seeketh, findeth: to him that knocketh, it shall be opened* (Matthew 7:8).

But you say, "I have sought Him, and I did not find Him." Do you mean to insinuate that Jesus Christ is a liar? Have you accused Him to His very face? Do you make your solemn affirmation, "Lord, I did seek You. I knocked at Your gate, but in vain"? Do you intend to bring this excuse of yours as a solemn charge of falsehood against Jesus Christ and against God? This will be a serious business with you before it is done with.

**15. Someone else says, "There is no salvation for me."** Do you mean that Christ has made no atonement for you? The Bible says that He tasted death for everyone (Hebrews 2:9). It is declared that *God so loved the world, that he gave his only begotten Son, that whosoever believeth in him should not perish, but have everlasting life* (John 3:16). And do you now claim that there is no salvation provided and possible for you? Are you mourning all the way down to hell because you cannot possibly have salvation? When the cup of salvation is placed to your lips, do you cast it away, saying, "That cannot be for me"?

Do you know this? Can you prove it even against the Word of God and the Son of God Himself? Speak up, then. If there is such a sinner on this earth, speak out if you have such an accusation against God and if you can prove it to be true. Is there no hope? None at all? The difficulty is not that there is no salvation provided for and offered to you, but that there is no heart for it. *Wherefore is there a price put into the hands of a fool to get wisdom, seeing he hath no heart for it?* (Proverbs 17:16).

**16. Maybe you use the excuse, "I cannot change my own heart."** You cannot? Suppose Adam had made this excuse when God called him to repent after his first sin. "Make yourself a new heart and a right spirit," the Lord said to him. "I cannot change my own heart myself," replied Adam. "Indeed," responds his Maker, "how long has it been since you changed your heart yourself? You changed it a few hours ago from holiness to sin, and will you tell your Creator that you can't change it from sin to holiness?"

The sinner should consider that the change of heart is a voluntary thing. You must do it for yourself or it is never done. It is true that God changes the heart, but God influences the sinner to change, and then the sinner submits his heart to God. The change is the sinner's own voluntary act.

**17. You say that you cannot change your heart without more conviction.** Do you mean by this that you do not have enough knowledge of your duty and your sin? You cannot say this. You do know your sin and your duty. You know you should consecrate yourself to God.

What, then, do you mean? Can't you do that which you know you should do? There is the old lie – that shameless refuge of lies – that same foul doctrine of inability. What is implied in this new form of it? It is implied that God is not willing to convict you enough to make it possible for you to repent. There is a work and a responsibility for God, and He will not do His work. He will not bear His responsibility. Sadly, therefore, you have no alternative but to go down to hell, and this is all because God will not do His part toward your salvation! Do you really believe that, sinner?

**18. You might give the excuse that you must first have more of the Spirit.** Yet you resist the Spirit every day! God offers you His Spirit. Even more, God bestows His Spirit – but you resist it. What, then, do you mean when you pretend to want more of the Spirit's influence?

The truth is that you do not want it. You only want to make it appear that God does not do His part to help you to repent, and that since you cannot repent without His help, therefore the blame of your lack of repentance rests on God. This is only another refuge of lies – another form of the old slander upon God that He has made you unable and will not help you out of your inability.

**19. The sinner also makes an excuse by saying, "God must change my heart."** This is true in a sense, but in the sense in which God requires you to do it, He cannot do it Himself. God is said to change the heart only in the sense of persuading you to do it. In a person's change of politics, someone might say, "Such a man changed my heart. He brought me over to his side." This, however, by no means implies that you did not change your own mind. The plain meaning is that he persuaded you and you yielded.

This excuse made by the sinner, though, implies that there is something more for God to do before the sinner can become a follower of Christ. I have heard many professing Christians take this very ground. Yes, thousands of Christian ministers, too, have said to the sinner, "Wait for God. He will change your heart in His own good time. You can't do it yourself. All that you can do is to put yourself in the way for the Lord to change your heart. When the time comes, He will give you a new heart, maybe while you are asleep and in a state of unconsciousness. God acts in this matter as a sovereign, and He does His own work in His own way."

This is what they teach, filling the mouth of the sinner with excuses and making his heart like a stone against the real claims of God upon his conscience.

**20. Some sinners give the excuse, "I could not live a Christian life if I were to become a Christian. It is unreasonable for me to expect to succeed where I see so many fail."** I remember the case of a man who said, "It is of no use for me to repent and be a Christian, for it is completely irrational for me to expect to do better than others have done before me." Sinners who make this excuse come forward very timidly and tell God, "I am very humble. You see, Lord, that I have a very low opinion of myself. I am so zealous of Your honor and so afraid that I will bring disgrace upon Your cause that it does not seem at all best for me to think of becoming a Christian. I have such a fear of dishonoring Your name!"

Yes, and what then? "Therefore, I will continue to sin and trample the blessed gospel under my feet. I will persecute You, my God, and make war on Your cause, for it is better by far not to profess to follow Jesus than to profess and then disgrace my profession." What foolish logic!

This is a fair example of the absurdity of the sinner's excuses. This excuse assumes that there is not enough grace provided and offered to sustain the soul in a Christian life. The doctrine is that it is unreasonable to expect that we can, by any grace received in this life, perfectly obey the law of God – that God does not provide enough grace and help! This is actually taught by some people as biblical! Away with such teaching to the lowest pit from where it came!

What? Is God so weak that He cannot hold up the soul that casts itself on Him? Is He so uncharitable in bestowing His gracious aid that it must always be expected to fall short of meeting the needs of His dependent and depending child? This is what you seem to think. You seem to think that it is very difficult to persuade the Lord to give you a particle of grace, that you cannot get grace enough to live a Christian life with honor! This is accusing God of withholding sufficient grace.

But what do the Word of God and the oath of the Lord say? We read that *God, willing more abundantly to show unto the heirs of promise the immutability of his counsel, confirmed it by an oath: that by two immutable things, in which it is impossible for God to lie, we might have strong consolation, who have fled for refuge to lay hold upon the hope set before us* (Hebrews 6:17-18).

You say, however, "If I would flee and lay hold of this hope, I would fail for lack of grace. I could have no consolation in resting upon the word of Him who cannot lie. The oath of the immutable God can never be enough for me." You deny the Word of God and make up a miserably poor excuse for your lack of repentance.

**21. Another excuse is that this is a very obscure and mysterious subject.** You claim that you cannot understand this matter of faith and regeneration. Sinner, did you ever go to the Lord with this objection and say, "Lord, You have required me to do things that I cannot understand"?

You know that you can understand well enough that you are a sinner, that Christ died for you, and that you must believe on Him and turn away from and leave your sins by repentance. All this is so plain that *the wayfaring men, though fools, need not err therein* (Isaiah 35:8). Your excuse, therefore, is as false as it is corrupt. It is nothing better than a false accusation against God!

**22. Some people say, "I can't believe."** Do you mean that you cannot believe a God of infinite truth in the same way that you can believe a fellow man? Would you imply that God asks you to believe things that are really absurd – things so revolting to reason that you cannot accept them on any testimony that even God Himself can declare? Do you really expect to present this case against God? Do you even believe it yourself?

However, you insist that you cannot grasp these things. You know that these things are true, but you cannot comprehend that the Bible is true, that God does offer to forgive, and that salvation is actually provided and placed within your reach. What help can there be for a case like yours? What can make these truths more certain? As you admit, you do not need more evidence. Why not, then, act upon the known truth? What more can you ask?

Do you ever take your case before God and say, "O Lord, You say that Christ died for me, but I cannot believe that it is so, and therefore, Lord, I cannot possibly embrace Him as my Savior"? Would this be a rational excuse?

Yet you also give the excuse that you cannot repent. You cannot be sorry that you have offended God. You cannot make up your mind now to turn from your sin. If this is really so, then you cannot make up your mind to obey God, and you may as well make up your mind to go to hell! There is no alternative!

At any rate, you say that you cannot become a Christian now. You intend to be converted some time, but you cannot make up your mind to do so now. Well, God requires it now, and of course, you must yield or suffer the consequences.

Do you really say that you cannot now? Then God is very much to blame for asking you to do so now. If, however, the truth is that you can, then the lie is on your side, and it is a most offensive and unjust lie against your Maker.

## III. All excuses for sin add insult to injury

1. An excuse that reflects adversely upon the court or the lawgiver is an aggravation of the original crime. It is always so regarded in all courts. It must be preeminently so between the sinner and his infinite Lawgiver and Judge.

2. The same is true of any excuse made in self-justification. If it is false, it is considered an aggravation, or worsening, of the crime charged. This is a case that sometimes happens, and whenever it does, it is considered as adding fresh insult and wrong. For a criminal to come and spread out his lie upon the records of the court, to declare what he knows to be false – nothing can prejudice his case so fearfully.

On the other hand, when someone before the court appears to be honest and confesses his guilt, the judge, if he has any discretion in the case, puts down his sentence to the lowest point possible. However, if the criminal resorts to avoiding truth, if he evades and lies, then you will see the strong arm of the law come down upon him. The judge comes forth in all the thunders of judicial majesty and terror, and he feels that he may not spare his victim. Why? The man has lied before the very court of justice. The man has set himself against all law, and he must be put down, or the law itself is failing.

> It is truly detestable for the sinner to blame God and then excuse himself for it.

3. It is truly detestable for the sinner to blame God and then excuse himself for it. This is just the old way of the guilty. In the garden of Eden, Adam and Eve fled and hid themselves when they heard the voice of the Lord approaching. What had they done? The Lord called them out and began to examine them: "Adam what have you done? Have you eaten of the forbidden tree in the center of the garden?"

Adam trembled, but fled to an excuse: *The woman whom thou gavest to be with me, she gave me of the tree and I did eat* (Genesis 3:12). He said that God gave him his tempter. According to his excuse, God had been mainly to blame in the matter.

God next turned to the woman: *What is that thou hast done?* She, too, has an excuse: *The serpent beguiled me, and I did eat* (Genesis 3:13).

Oh, this perpetual shifting the blame back upon God! It has been kept up through the long line of Adam's imitators down to this day. For six thousand years, God has been hearing it, and still the world is spared. The vengeance of God has not yet burst forth to smite all His guilty slanderers to hell! Oh, what patience in God! Who has ever abused His patience and insulted Him by their excuses more than sinners here today?

## Remarks

1. No sinner under the light of the gospel lives a single hour in sin without some excuse, either implied or clearly stated, by which he justifies himself. It seems to be a law of man's intelligent nature that when he is accused of wrong, either by his conscience or by any other means, he must either confess or justify himself.

The latter is the course taken by all unrepentant sinners. This is the reason why they have so much cause for excuses, and why they find it convenient to have so great a variety. It is remarkable with what ease they move from one excuse to another, as if these refuges of lies might make up in number what they lack in strength. They are aware that not one of all the multitude of excuses is valid in point of truth and right, yet when confronted on one, they run to another, and when driven from all in succession, they are ready to come back and fight the same ground over again. It is very hard to abandon all excuses and admit the humbling truth that they themselves are all wrong and God is completely right.

Therefore, it becomes the great business of a gospel minister to search out and expose the sinner's excuses – to go all around and, if possible, demolish the sinner's refuges of lies and lay his heart open to the rays of truth.

2. Excuses make repentance impossible. Excuses are justifications, and justification is the very opposite of confession and repentance.

Therefore, to seek after and embrace excuses is to place oneself at the farthest possible point from repentance.

Of course, the self-excusing sinner makes it impossible for God to forgive him. He places the Deity in such a position toward himself and places himself in such an attitude toward the government of God that his forgiveness would be destructive to the very throne of God. What would heaven and earth say, and hell, too, if God were to forgive a sinner while he by his excuses is justifying himself and condemning his Maker?

3. Sinners should lay all their excuses at once before God. Surely this is most reasonable. Why not? If a man owed me money who thought he had a reasonable excuse for not paying the debt, he should come to me and let me understand the whole case. Maybe he will convince me that his views are right.

Sinner, have you ever done this in regard to God? Have you ever brought up one excuse before the Lord, saying, "You require me to be holy, but I can't be. Lord, I have a good excuse for not obeying You"? No, sinner, you are not in the habit of doing this. You probably have not done this even once in your life. In fact, you have no particular encouragement to present your excuses before God, for you do not yet have one that you believe is good for anything except to answer the purpose of a refuge of lies.

Your excuses will not stand the ordeal of your own reason and conscience. How, then, can you hope they will stand before the searching eye of God? The fact that you never come with your excuses to God shows that you have no confidence in them.

4. What infinite foolishness it is to rest on excuses that you dare not bring before God now! How can you stand before God in the judgment if your excuses are so weak that you cannot seriously think of bringing one of them before God in this world?

Sinner, that coming day will be far more searching and dreadful than anything you have yet seen. Observe that great crowd of sinners lined up before the great white throne as far as the eye can see. They come surging up – a countless multitude. Now they stand, and the dreadful trump of God summons them forward to bring forth their excuses for sin. Sinners, any one of you, what have you to say as to why sentence should not be passed on you? Where are all those excuses you were once so free and bold to make? Where are they all? Why don't you make them now?

Give heed! God waits. He listens. There is silence in heaven, all throughout the congregated crowd, for half an hour (Revelation 8:1). There is a dreadful silence that can be felt, but not a word is said, not a lip moves among the gathered multitude of sinners there. Now the great and dreadful Judge arises and lets loose His thunders. See the waves of dire damnation roll over the great crowd of self-condemned sinners!

Did you ever see the judge rise from his bench in court to pass the sentence of death on a criminal? Over there, look, the poor man staggers and falls prostrate. There is no longer any strength in him, for death is on him and his last hope has perished! Sinner, when that sentence from the dreadful throne falls on you, your excuses will be as millstones around your neck as you plunge down the sides of the pit to the lowest hell!

5. Sinners don't need their excuses. God does not ask for even one. He does not at all require you to justify yourself. If you needed them for your salvation, I could sympathize with you, and certainly would help you all I could. But you don't need them. Your salvation does not depend on your successful self-vindication. You do not need to rack your brain for excuses. It is better to say that you don't want them and don't deserve them than to have not even one that is worth a straw. It is better to say, "I am wicked. God knows that is the truth, and it would be useless for me to try to conceal it. I am wicked, and if I live, it must be on simple mercy!"

> It is better to say, "I am wicked. God knows that is the truth, and it would be useless for me to try to conceal it.

I can remember very well the year I lived on excuses, and how long it was before I gave them up. I had never heard a minister preach on the subject. I found, however, by my experience, that my excuses and lies were the obstacles in the way of my conversion. As soon as I let these completely go, I found the gate of mercy wide open – and so, sinner, would you.

6. Sinners should be ashamed of their excuses and repent of them. You might not have always seen this as plainly as you do now. With the light now before you, it would be good for you to beware. See to it that you never make another excuse unless you intend to slander God in the most horrible manner. Nothing can be a more grievous abomination in the sight of God than excuses made by a sinner who knows they are utterly false and blasphemous. You should repent of the insult you have already offered to God, and do so now so that you do not find yourself driven away from the gate of mercy.

7. You acknowledge your obligation, and of course are stopped from making excuses, for if you have any good excuse, you are not under obligation. If any one of you has a good excuse for disobeying God, you are no longer under obligation to obey. However, since you are obligated to admit your duty, you are also obligated to give up your excuses.

8. Inasmuch as you do and must admit your responsibility, then if you still give excuses, you insult God to His face. You insult Him by accusing Him of infinite tyranny.

Now, what good do you intend to make of this sermon? Are you ready to say, "I will from now on refrain from all my excuses, now and forever, and God will have my whole heart"? What do you say? Will you set out to come up with some new excuse? Do you at least say, "Let me go home first. Don't pressure me to yield to God here on the spot. Let me go home, and then I will"? Do you say this? Are you aware how tender this moment is – how critical this passing hour is?

Remember that it is not I who urge this claim upon you, but it is God. God Himself commands you to repent today – this hour. You know your duty. You know what true Christianity is. You know what it is to give God your heart.

Now I come to the final question: Will you do it? Will you abandon all your excuses? Will you fall, a self-condemned sinner, before a God of love, and yield to Him yourself – your heart and your whole being, from this moment on and forever? Will you come?

# Chapter 6

# The Sinner's Excuses Answered

Elihu also proceeded and said, Suffer me a little, and I
will shew thee that I have yet to speak on God's behalf.
I will fetch my knowledge from afar, and will ascribe
righteousness to my Maker.
—Job 36:1-3

E lihu was present and heard the controversy between Job and his
friends. His friends maintained that God's dealings with Job showed
that he was wicked. Job denied this and maintained that people could
not be judged to be good or bad based upon God's providential dealings with them because facts show that the present state is not a state
of rewards and punishments. However, they regarded this as taking
part with the wicked, and therefore did not back down from accusing
Job of doing this.

Elihu had previously said that his desire was for Job to be tried in regard
to what he had said regarding wicked men, but before the discussion
ended, he saw that Job had confounded his three friends, maintaining
unanswerably that it was not because of any hypocrisy or special guilt
that he was so specifically afflicted. Yet it was clear that not even Job
had the key to explain the reason for how God was dealing with him.
To him it was still a mystery. He did not see that God might have been

seeking to test and discipline his piety, or even to make an example of his integrity and submissiveness with which to confound the devil.

Elihu resolved to speak in God's behalf, and he ascribed righteousness to his Maker. It is my present intent to do the same in regard to sinners who refuse to repent and who complain of God's ways. But before I proceed, let me refer to a fact. Some years previously, in my labors as an evangelist, I became acquainted with a man who was prominent in his town for his general intelligence, and whose two successive wives were daughters of Old School Presbyterian clergymen. He had received many books through them to read on religious subjects, which they and their friends supposed would do him good, but that failed to do him any good at all. He denied the inspiration of the Bible, and on reasons that those books did not, in his view, counter at all. Indeed, they only served to increase his objections.

When I got to that town, his wife was very eager for me to see him and converse with him. I called on him, and she sent for him to come in and see the new minister. He replied that he was sure I could do him no good since he had conversed with so many others and had found no light on the points that so much hindered him. However, upon her urgent request, he agreed for her sake to come in.

I said to him at the beginning, "I have not come here to have a quarrel with you and provoke a dispute. I only want, at your wife's request, to talk with you if you are perfectly willing, upon the great subject of divine revelation."

He signified his pleasure to have such a conversation, and so I asked him to briefly state his position. He replied, "I acknowledge the truths of natural religion, and believe most fully in the immortality of the soul, but not in the inspiration of the Scriptures. I am a deist."

"But," I asked, "on what basis do you deny the inspiration of the Bible?"

He said, "I know it cannot be true."

"How do you know that?"

"It contradicts the affirmations of my reason. You agree and I hold that God created my nature, both physical and moral. Here is a Book, said to be from God, but it contradicts my nature. I therefore know that it cannot be from God."

This, of course, opened the door for me to draw from him the specific points of his objection to the Bible as teaching what his nature contradicted. These points and my reply to them will constitute the main part of this section.

"The Bible cannot be true because it represents God as unjust. I find myself possessed of convictions as to what is just and unjust. The Bible violates these convictions. It represents God as creating men and then condemning them for someone else's sin."

"Indeed," I said. "Where? Where does the Bible say this?"

"Does it not?" he said.

"No."

"Are you a Presbyterian?" he asked.

"Yes."

He then began to quote the catechism. "Stop, stop," I said. "That is not the Bible. That is only a human catechism."

"True," he said, "but does not the Bible connect the universal sin of the human race with the sin of Adam?"

"Yes," I said. "It does in a particular way, but it is quite essential to our purpose to understand in what way. The Bible makes this connection incidental and not direct. It always represents the sinner condemned as really sinning himself, and as condemned for his own sin."

"But," he continued, "children do suffer for their father's sins."

"Yes," I said, "in a certain sense it is so, and must be so. Do you not yourself see everywhere that children must suffer for the sins of their parents, and also be blessed by the piety of their parents? You see this, and you find no fault with it. You see that children must be intertwined in the good or bad conduct of their parents. Their relation as children makes this absolutely unavoidable. Is it not wise and good that the happiness or misery of children should depend on their parents, and thus this becomes one of the strongest possible motives to them to train them up in virtue? Yet it is also true that the child is never rewarded or punished punitively for his parents' sins. The evil that happens to him through his connection with his parents is always corrective, and never as punishment."

The man responded, "The Bible certainly represents God as creating people as sinners and as condemning them for their sinful nature."

"No," I replied, "for the Bible defines sin as voluntary transgression of law, and it is absurd to suppose that a nature can be a voluntary transgressor. Besides, it is in the nature of the case impossible that God would make a sinful nature. It is in fact doubly impossible, for the thing is a natural impossibility. Even if it were not, it would still be morally impossible that He would do it. He could not do it for the same reason that He cannot sin.

In harmony with this is the fact that the Bible never represents God as condemning people for their nature, either here or at the judgment. Nowhere in the Bible is there the slightest suggestion that God holds people responsible for their created nature, but only for the vile and persistent abuse of their nature. Other views of this matter that differ from this are not in the Bible, but are only false glosses put upon it – usually by those whose philosophy has led them into absurd interpretations. Everywhere in the Bible, people are condemned only for their voluntary sins, and they are required to repent of these sins, and of these only. Indeed, there cannot possibly be any other sins than these."

> The Bible never represents God as condemning people for their nature, either here or at the judgment.

Now I will continue with the general idea of the rest of my conversation with this man. He had several objections, and I discussed each one from reason and the Bible. I continued the conversation.

I told him that some people say that the Bible portrays God as being cruel since He commanded the Jews to wage a war of extermination against the ancient Canaanites. But why should this be called cruel? The Bible specifically informs us that God commanded this because of the awful wickedness of the Canaanites. They were too terribly wicked to live. God could not allow them to defile the earth and corrupt society. Therefore, He arose in His zeal for human welfare and commanded the Israelites to wash the land clean of such unutterable abominations. The good of the human race demanded it.

Was this cruel? No, not at all. This was simply kindness. It was one of the highest acts of benevolence to strike down such a society of people and sweep them from the face of the earth. To use the Jews as His executioners, allowing them to clearly understand why He commanded them to do it, was putting them in a position to acquire the highest moral benefit from the undertaking. In no other way could they have been so solemnly impressed with the holy justice of God. Will anyone find fault with God for this? None can reasonably do so.

Some will object because they say that the Bible allows slavery. What? The Bible allows slavery? In what sense is it allowed, and under what circumstances? What kind of slavery is it? These are all very important questions if we want to know the certainty and the meaning of the things we say.

The Bible did indeed allow the Jews, in the case of captives taken in war, to commute death for servitude. When the customs of existing nations put captives taken in war to death, God authorized the Jews in certain cases to spare their captives and use them as servants. By this means, they were taken out from among idolatrous nations and brought into contact with the worship and ordinances of the true God.

Moreover, God enacted laws for the protection of the Hebrew servant, which made his situation infinitely better than being cut off in his sins. Who would call this cruel? Jewish servitude was not American slavery, nor hardly any resemblance of it. It would require too much time to go into the detail of this subject here. All that I have stated can be abundantly substantiated.

Also, it is objected that God is unmerciful, vindictive, and unappeasable. The gentleman to whom I have alluded said, "I don't believe the Bible is from God when it represents Him as so vindictive and unmerciful that He would not forgive sin until He had first taken measures to kill His own Son."

Now it was by no means unnatural that, under such teaching as he had received, he should think so. I had once thought this way myself. This very objection had stumbled me. However, I later saw the answer so plainly that it left nothing more to be desired. The answer indeed is exceedingly plain. It was not an unmerciful disposition in God that led Him to require the death of Christ as the ground of forgiveness. It was simply His benevolent regard for the safety and blessedness of His kingdom. He knew very well that it was unsafe to forgive sin without such a restitution.

Indeed, this was the strongest possible demonstration of a forgiving nature – to consent to the sacrifice of His Son for this purpose. He loved

His Son, and certainly would not inflict any needless pain upon Him. He also loved a sinful race, and He saw the depth of that ruin toward which they were rushing. Therefore, He desired to forgive them and to prepare a way in which He could do so with safety. He only desired to avoid all misconception. To forgive without such an atonement that would adequately express His abhorrence of sin would leave the intelligent universe to think that He did not care how much we would sin. This would not do.

Let it be considered also that giving up Jesus Christ was only a voluntary offering on God's part to sustain law so that He could forgive without peril to His government. Jesus was not in any sense punished. He only volunteered to suffer for sinners so that they might be freed from the governmental necessity of suffering. Was not mercy manifested in this? Certainly. How could it be manifested more clearly?

"But," says the person objecting, "God is unjust since He requires impossibilities on pain of endless death." Does He really? Then where? Is it in the law or in the gospel? In these taken together, we have the totality of all God's requirements.

In what part, then, of either law or gospel, do you find the precept contained that requires impossibilities? Is it in the law? But the law only says, *Thou shalt love the* LORD *thy God with all thine heart* (Deuteronomy 6:5) – not with another person's heart, but simply with your own, and only with all your own heart, not with more than all. Read on still further: *and with all thy might.* You are not required to love God with the strength of an angel or with the strength of any other being than yourself, and only with such an amount of strength as you actually now have. The demands of the law you see exactly meet your ability – nothing more and nothing else.

> The demands of the law you see exactly meet your ability – nothing more and nothing else.

Some people might not have heard it explained like this before, but is this not just as it should be? Does not the law carry with it its own vindication in its very terms? How can anyone say that the law requires of us impossible service – things we have no power to do? The fact is that it requires us to do just what we can and nothing more. Where, then, is this objection to the Bible? Where is the impossibility of which you speak?

"But," the man continued, "is it not true that, as the catechism says, no mere man since the fall has been able wholly to keep the commandments of God, but daily breaks them in thought, word, and deed?"

"Yes, my friend, but that is the catechism, not the Bible. We must be careful not to attribute to the Bible all that human catechisms have said. The Bible only requires you to consecrate to God what strength and powers you actually have, and it is by no means responsible for the affirmation that God requires of man more than he can do. The Bible nowhere ascribes to God a demand so unreasonable and cruel. It is no wonder that the human mind would rebel against such a view of God's law. If any human law were to require impossibilities, there could be no end to the criticisms that must fall upon it. No human mind could possibly approve of such a law, nor can it be supposed that God can reasonably act on principles that would disgrace and ruin any human government."

"But," he resumed, "here is another objection. The Bible represents us as unable to believe the gospel unless we are drawn by God, for it says, *No man can come to me except the Father who hath sent me draw him* (John 6:44), yet sinners are required to believe on pain of damnation. How can this be?"

The first reply to this is that the connection shows that Christ referred to "drawing" by means of teaching or instruction, for to confirm what He had said, He appealed to the ancient Scriptures: *It is written in the prophets, They shall all be taught of God* (John 6:45). Without this teaching, then, no one can come. They must know Christ before they can come to Him in faith. They cannot believe until they know what to believe. In this sense of coming, untaught heathen are not required to come. God never requires any to come who have not been taught. Once taught, they are bound to come. They may be and are required to come, and they are without excuse if they refuse.

"But," he replied, "the Bible really does teach that people cannot serve the Lord, and still it holds them responsible for doing it. Joshua said to all the people, *Ye cannot serve the Lord: for he is an holy God* (Joshua 24:19)."

Let us see. Joshua had called all the people together and had laid before them their obligation to serve the Lord their God. When they all said so freely and with so little serious consideration that they would, Joshua replied, *Ye cannot serve the LORD: for he is an holy God; he is a jealous God; he will not forgive your transgressions nor your sins.*

What did he mean? He clearly meant this: You cannot serve God because you have not wholeheartedly abandoned your sins. You cannot get along with a God so holy and so jealous unless you give up sinning. You cannot serve God with a selfish heart. You cannot please Him until you really renounce your sins completely. You must begin by making to yourselves a new heart.

Joshua undoubtedly saw that they had not given up their sins and had not really begun to serve God at all, and did not even understand the first principles of true religion. This is the reason why he seemed to rebuke them so suddenly. It is as if he would say, "Stop. You must go back and begin with completely putting away all your sins. You cannot serve a holy and jealous God in any other way, for He will not go along with you as His people if you persist in sinning against Him."

It is a distasteful perversion of the Bible to try to make it mean that people have no power to do what God requires. It is true indeed, that in this connection it sometimes uses the words "can" and "cannot," but these and similar words should be explained according to the nature of the subject. All reasonable people interpret in this way intuitively in all common use of language. The Bible always uses the language of common life and in the way of common usage. This is how it should be interpreted here.

When it is said that Joseph's brethren hated him and could not speak peaceably to him, the meaning is not that their instruments of speech could not articulate kind words, but it points us to a difficulty in the heart. They hated him so much that they could not speak pleasantly. Nor does the sacred historian assume that they could not at once subdue this hatred and treat Joseph as brothers should treat a brother. The sacred writers are the last men in the world to apologize for sin on this account.

Then there is the case of the angels sent to hurry Lot out of guilty Sodom. One said, *Haste thee, escape thither, for I cannot do anything until thou be come thither* (Genesis 19:22). Does this mean that the Almighty God had no power to overwhelm Sodom as long as Lot was in it? Certainly not. It meant only that it was His purpose not to destroy the city until Lot was out.

All people use language like this in everyday life. You go into one of our village stores and say to the merchant, "Can you lift a ton of your goods at once?"

"No."

"Can you sell me that piece of cloth for a dollar a yard?"

"No."

Does the first "can" mean the same as the other? By no means. But how is it that you detect the difference? How is it that you come to know so quickly which is the physical "cannot" and which is the moral? The nature of the subject tells you.

But you say that the same word should always mean the same thing. Well, if it should, it does not in any language ever yet spoken by man, yet there is no difficulty in understanding even the most imperfect of human languages if people are honest in speaking and honest in hearing and will use their common sense. They intuitively understand language according to the nature of the subject spoken of.

The Bible always infers that sinners cannot do right and please God with a wicked heart. It always takes the ground that God abhors hypocrisy – that He cannot be satisfied with mere forms and professions of service when the heart is not in it, and therefore that all acceptable service must begin with making a new and sincere heart.

But here is another difficulty. Can I make myself a new heart? Yes, and you could not doubt so if you only understood what the language means and what the thing is.

Look at Adam and Eve in the garden. What was their heart? Did God create it? No. It is not possible that He did, for a heart in this sense is not the subject of physical creation. When God made Adam, giving him all the capabilities to act morally, he had no heart good or bad until he came to act morally. When did he first have a moral heart? It was when he was first awakened to moral consciousness and gave his heart to God, when he first saw God manifested and put confidence in Him as his Father, yielding up his heart to Him in love and obedience. Notice that Adam first had this holy heart because he yielded up his will to God in entire consecration. This was his first holy heart.

But at last the hour of temptation came, alluring him to withdraw his heart from God and turn to pleasing himself. The tempter said to Eve, *Hath God indeed said . . . Ye shall not surely die* (Genesis 3:1, 4). Ah, is that so? So he raised the question either as to the fact that God had really threatened death for sin, or as to the justice of doing so. In either case, it raised a question about obedience and opened the heart to temptation.

Then that fruit came before Eve's mind. It was attractive and seemed good for food. Her appetite awakened and demanded indulgence. Then, it was said to be able to *make one wise* (Genesis 3:6), and by eating it she might *be as gods, knowing good and evil* (Genesis 3:5). This appealed to her curiosity. Giving in to this temptation and making up her mind to please herself, she made herself a new heart of sin; she changed her heart from holiness to sin and fell from her first moral position. When Adam yielded to temptation, he made the same change in his heart; he gave himself up to selfishness and sin. This accounts for all future acts of selfishness later in life.

> While your leading motive is wrong, everything you do is selfish because it is all done for the single object of pleasing yourself.

Adam and Eve were again brought before God. God said to Adam, "Give Me Your heart. Change your heart."

"What!" said Adam. "I cannot change my own heart!"

God replied, "How long is it since you have done so? Only yesterday you changed your own heart from holiness to sin; why can't you change it back?"

It is this way in all cases. Changing the ruling preference, the governing purpose of the mind, is the thing needed, and who can say I cannot do that? Can you not do that? Can you not give yourself to God?

The reason you cannot please God in your governing acts is that your governing purpose is not right. While your leading motive is wrong, everything you do is selfish because it is all done for the single object of pleasing yourself. You do nothing for the sake of pleasing God, and you lack the governing design and purpose of doing all His holy will. Therefore, all you do, even your religious duties, only displease God. If the Bible had anywhere represented God as being pleased with your hypocritical services, it would be proven false, for this is perfectly impossible.

However, you say that the Bible requires you to begin with the inner man, the heart, and you say you cannot get at this – that you cannot reach your own heart and so cannot desire to change it.

Indeed, you are entirely mistaken. This is the very thing that is most entirely within your power. Of all things conceivable, this is the very thing that you can most certainly do. This is most absolutely within your power. If God had made your salvation depend upon your walking across the room, you might not be able to do it; or if it depended upon lifting your eyelids, rising from your seat, or even the least movement of your muscles, you might be completely unable to do it. You could will the motion required, and you could try, but the muscles might have no power to act.

You often think that if God had only conditioned your salvation upon some motions of your muscles, it would have been so easy. If He had only asked you to control the outside, you think you could have done so, but you wonder how you can control the inside. The inside is the very thing you can move and control. If it had been the outside, you might strive and groan until you die, and not be able to move a muscle, even on pain of an eternal hell.

But now because God only says, "Change your will," all is brought within your control. This is just the thing you always can do. You can always move your will. You can always give your heart, at your own option. Where, then, is your difficulty and objection? God requires you to act with your freedom, to exercise the powers of free voluntary action that He has given you. He asks you to put your hand on the fountainhead of all your own power, to act right where your central power lies – where you always have power as long as you have a rational mind and a moral nature.

Your liberty does not consist in a power to move your muscles at your own will, for the connection between your muscles and your will may be broken, and at all events is always necessary when your body is in its normal state; therefore, God does not require you to perform any particular movement of the muscles, but only to change your will.

This, compared with all other things, is that which you can always do, and can do more certainly than anything else.

Again, considering the will as distinct from ultimate purposes, and as our standing is considered before our governing acts, it is not the will that God requires, but He lays His demands directly upon the ultimate purposes. The ultimate purposes being given, these subordinate decisions of the will follow naturally and necessarily.

Your liberty, therefore, does not, strictly speaking, lie in these subordinate acts of the will, such as the will to sit, to walk, or to speak, but the ultimate purpose controlling all decisions of the will, and relating to the main object you will pursue – as for example, whether you will in all things strive to please God, or on the other hand, strive to please yourself – this, being the precise point wherein your liberty of free action lies, is the very point upon which God lays His moral demands. The whole question is: Will you please God or please yourself? Will you give your heart to Him, or will you give it to your own selfish enjoyment?

As long as you give your heart to selfish pleasure and withhold it from God, it will be perfectly natural for you to sin. This is precisely the reason why it is so natural for sinners to sin. It is because the will, the heart, is set upon it, and all they have to do is carry out this prevailing tendency and purpose.

However, if you simply change this governing purpose, you will find obedience equally natural and equally easy in all its governing acts. It will then become natural to please God in everything. Pleasing yourself is natural enough now. Why? Because you are consecrated to pleasing yourself. Change this purpose, though, and make a new and totally opposite consecration, reverse the committed heart, and let it be for God and not for self – and then all duty will be easy for the same reason that all sin is so easy now.

It is so far from being true that you are unable to make your heart new, that the truth is you would have done so long ago if you had not resisted God in His efforts to move you to repentance. Do you not know that you have often resisted God's Spirit? You know it well. So clear were your convictions that you should live for God that you had to resist every appeal of your own conscience and march right in the face of known duty, pressing your way along directly against God.

If you had only listened to the voice of your reason and to the demands of your conscience, you would have had a new heart long ago. However, you resisted God when He tried to persuade you to have a new heart. Sinner, how strong you have been to resist God! How strong to resist every consideration addressed to your intelligence and to your reason! How strangely you have listened to the considerations for sinning! Oh, the miserable petty things; tell me, what were they?

Suppose Christ should question you and ask you: "What is there in earth that you should love it so well? What is there in sin that you should prize it above My favor and My love? What are those little indulgences, those very small things that always perish with the using?"

*Vanity of vanities; all is vanity* (Ecclesiastes 1:2). This is most utterly contemptible! You have been holding on to sin with no reasonable motive for doing so, but consider what matters you have fought against and resisted! They are matters of almost infinite force! Think of the concerns resulting from God's law – so excellent in itself, but so dreadful in its penalties against transgressors; then think also of God's infinite love in the gospel – how He opened the life tides of His great heart and let blessings flow with His fullness!

Then consider how, despite this love, you have insulted your God exceedingly. You have gone on as if the motives to sin were all persuasive, as if sin's promises of good were more reliable than God's. When God spread out before you the glories of heaven, made all attractive and delightful in the beauties of holiness, you casually replied, "Earth is far better! Give me earth while I can have it, and heaven only when I can have earth no longer!" Sinner, you would have been converted a long time ago if you had not opposed God and trodden underfoot His invitations and His appeals.

Oh, what a thing this moral force is! How powerful it is, and how momentous, therefore, must its responsibilities be! When God is pouring forth influences in waves of light and power, with a kind of moral omnipotence, you resist and withstand it all as if you could do anything you pleased despite God – as if His influence were almost absolutely powerless to move your heart from its fixed purpose to sin!

Does it require great strength to lay down your weapons? Indeed, this is quite a new thing, for one would suppose it must instead require great strength to resist and to fight. So you put forth your great strength in fighting against God, and would willingly believe that you do not have enough strength to lay your weapons down! Oh, the absurdity of sin and of the sinner's excuse for sinning!

But you say that you must have the Holy Spirit. I answer yes – but only to overcome your voluntary opposition. That is all.

After I had gone over this ground with my friend, as I have already explained, he became very much agitated. The sweat started from every pore. His feelings overcame him. He dropped his head down upon his knees, buried in the most intense thought and full of emotion. I rose and went to the meeting. After it had progressed awhile, he came in – but oh, how changed he was! He said, "Dear wife, I don't know what has become of my unbelief. I should be sent to hell! What accusations I have been making against God, and yet with what amazing mercy did my God bear with me and let me live!" In fact, he realized that he had been all wrong, and he broke down and became as a little child before God.

You, too, sinner, know that you should live for God, yet you do not. You know that Jesus made Himself an offering to the injured dignity of that law that you violated, yet you have rejected Him. He gave Himself as a voluntary offering – not to suffer the penalty of the law, but as your legal substitute – and will He have done all this in vain? Do you say, "Oh, I am so prejudiced against God and the Bible!" What, so prejudiced that you will not repent? How horrible! Oh, let it be enough that you have played the fool so long and have erred so terribly. It has been all wrong! Return at once and devote yourself to God. Why should you live to yourself at all? You can get no good in that way!

Come to God! He is so easily pleased! It is so much easier to please Him than to please and satisfy yourself. The simplest little child can please Him. Children often have the most delightful piety because it is so simple-hearted. They know what to do to please God, and honestly intending to please Him, they cannot fail. No matter how simplehearted they are, if they desire to please God, they certainly will.

Cannot you at least do as much as to honestly choose and desire to please God?

# Chapter 7

# On Refuges of Lies

Judgment also will I lay to the line, and righteousness to
the plummet: and the hail shall sweep away the refuge
of lies, and the waters shall overflow the hiding place.
—Isaiah 28:17

All people know that they are sinners against God. They also know
that as sinners, they are in danger and are not safe. This is the
reason for their anxiety to find some refuge for safety. They know they
might find this in the way of forsaking sin and turning to the Lord,
but they do not choose to forsake their sins. Therefore, there seems to
be no convenient resource for them except to hide themselves under
some refuge.

Our text speaks of *the refuge of lies*, yet it is obvious that people who
resort to lies for a refuge do not regard those lies as lies, but as truth.
This fact leads us to raise the primary fundamental question: Do we
have any rule or standard that will show what is truth and what is falsehood? People have countless opinions about religion; these cannot all
be true. How can we determine which are true and which are not true?

We have an infallible test. Salvation, to be real and available, must
be salvation from sin. Everything else fails. A religion that does not
break the power of sin is a lie. If it does not drive out selfishness and
lust, and if it does not bring about love to God and man, joy, peace,

and the fruit of the Spirit, it is false and worthless. Any system that fails in this vital respect is a lie. It can be of no use. It is no better than a curse. That which does not bring about in us the spirit of heaven and make us godly, no matter where it comes from, or by what deception it is defended, is a lie, and if it is fled to as a refuge, it is a *refuge of lies*.

Also, if it does not bring about prayer, if it does not unify us with God, and if it does not bring us into fellowship and sympathy with Him, it is a lie.

If it does not produce a heavenly mind, expel a worldly mind, and detach us from the love of the world, it is a lie. If it does not produce in us the love required in the Scriptures, genuine love and worship of God and also love for His people – indeed, of all mankind – if it does not produce all those states of mind that fit the soul for heaven, then it completely fails of its purpose.

I must stop here a moment to notice an objection. It is said, "The gospel does not in fact do for people all that you claim. It does not make professed Christians heavenly minded, dead to the world, and full of love, joy, and peace."

I reply that here is medicine that, applied in the case of a given disease, will certainly cure. This healing power is just what it has and what we claim for it, but it must be properly applied. Someone may buy the medicine, and because it is bitter, may lay it up in his cupboard and never take it. He may provide himself with a counterfeit to take in its stead, or he may take the medicine and then also take something that will instantly counteract its influence in the system. In any such case, the effectiveness of the medicine is not disproved, but you have only proved that you have not used it properly and honestly.

It is the same with the gospel. You must take it and use it according to directions, or else its failure is not its fault, but yours. It is of no benefit, then, to say that the gospel does not save people from sin. It may indeed be counterfeited, and it may even be rejected; but he who receives it to his heart will surely find his heart blessed by it. The gospel does transform people from sin to holiness. It does make people peaceful, holy, and heavenly in life and in death. Millions of such cases can be found throughout the history of the world. The lives of such people demonstrate the reality and preciousness of the salvation that the gospel promises.

I will now proceed to name some things that lack this decisive characteristic and that do not save the soul from sin.

1. An unsanctifying hope of heaven. Speaking of what God's children will be, John says, *We know that when he shall appear, we shall be like him; for we shall see him as he is. And every man that hath this hope in him purifieth himself, even as he is pure* (1 John 3:2-3). A good hope, then, purifies the heart. However, there are certainly hopes that some people have that fail to purify the heart of those who hold them. Those hopes are lies. They cannot possibly be sound and true. On their very face, it stands revealed that they are worthless – a mere *refuge of lies*. The stronger and more unwavering they are, the more delusive they are. What hope in Christ is that which does not bring the heart to Christ?

2. An old religious experience, that is all old, is a lie. You might have heard of the man who had his old religious experience all written down and laid away with his deeds of land to keep until his time of need. This being all the evidence he had, he used to refer to it from time to time for his comfort. At last, when the time came for him to die, he felt the need of this record of his religion, and he sent his little daughter to bring it. She returned with only the sad story that the mice had found their way to his drawer and had eaten up the paper. All of the dying man's evidence of piety was gone! He must die in despair! He had no other hope but this! On the face of it, such a refuge is only lies.

3. There are two forms of self-righteousness, the legal and the gospel, both of which are refuges of lies. The legal form depends on doing duty – always trying to work out salvation by deeds of law. The gospel form sets itself to get grace by works. People try to get a new heart not by trying to turn from all sin, but by praying for it. Imagine that I meet such a man. He says, "I tried to become religious."

"Really? What did you do?"

"I prayed for a new heart."

You did, but you did not do what God says you must. You did not repent. You did not bow your heart to God. Therefore, all your efforts come short of what God requires. They fail to save the soul from sin.

There is a great deal of this gospel self-righteousness – this throwing off all the responsibility upon God.

4. Universalism is an old refuge of lies. I will tell you about one such situation. Being away from home in my carriage, I overtook a young man who was walking, and I invited him to ride. Almost immediately, he told me he was a Universalist, and he came out strongly in defense of his beliefs.

I said to him, "I am not well and may not live long, and I do not dare to be deceived in this matter." He said that he was sure enough of its truth. He had heard smart men say so, and they had proven it from Scripture.

I told him that I have one objection. There is a certain series of facts that I cannot account for if Universalism is true. I have known families who were once considered orthodox in their beliefs, who were then upright, moral, and justly respected. I have known these same families to become loose in morals, forsake the house of God, turn to strong drink, and become fearfully wicked. I have observed that along with this change, such families almost always become Universalists. This is one set of facts.

On the other hand, I have never known a holy, prayerful Universalist backslide into orthodoxy. I have never seen anyone forsake his Universalism and his morality and degenerate into vice and orthodoxy by one uniform and simultaneous descent. I have known people reformed from drunkenness and vice who then become orthodox, but I have never known people reform from wickedness into Universalism. It seems to me that thousands of facts reveal a natural sympathy between vice and Universalism on the one hand, and between virtue and orthodox Christianity on the other.

By this time, he began to feel troubled, and he said, "I am afraid I am all wrong. Would you believe it? I am running away from being converted. There is a revival in my place, and I am running away from it."

"You are," I said, "and do you think it will hurt you? Will it do you any harm?"

He looked deeply anxious and replied, "I had better go back. My good father and mother looked sad when I left my home. I don't believe Universalism can save me. Everybody knows it never did save anybody and never can."

The same must be said of proper Unitarianism. Some who bear the name of Unitarian are not actual Unitarians, but where you find people who deny depravity, regeneration, and atonement, you will certainly find that their system does not make them heavenly minded, holy, and humble. You do not need to reason with them to find this out. You only need to take the facts of their history.

It is the same with Davisism – the doctrines of Andrew Jackson Davis.[3] Do these doctrines make people holy? Never. I knew a man, once a friend and supporter of gospel reforms, who turned to Andrew Jackson Davis. Did this change make him more holy? No, indeed. He said that this way of belief made him more happy. This is undoubtedly true, for before he was always under conviction of sin and never enjoyed the peace of the gospel. What is the use of reasoning about his Universalism? Look at the facts! They alone are sufficient to show its complete falsehood. Universalism never saved anyone from sin. It throws no influence in that direction.

It is right for God to be displeased with these refuges of lies. He loves truth too well to have the least sympathy with lies.

This is also true of Mormonism and all similar delusions. We do not need to stop and write books against this and similar lies, for it stands out on the forefront of this system that it saves no one from sin. It is, therefore, a refuge of lies that deceives people into hopes that can never be realized, as is true of every creed and system that does not save people from sin and get them ready for heaven.

Now take notice of what God says. He declares, *The hail shall sweep away the refuge of lies, and the waters shall overflow the hiding place.* No

---

3    Andrew Jackson Davis (1826-1910) was a Spiritualist and believed that he had great powers of clairvoyance.

doubt this hail is the symbol of God's displeasure. It is right for God to be displeased with these refuges of lies. He loves truth too well to have the least sympathy with lies. He loves the souls of men too deeply to have any patience with forces so destructive. Therefore, He abhors all these refuges of lies, and He has solemnly declared that the hail will sweep them all away.

He declares that the waters will overflow the hiding places. Every refuge that leaves the soul in sin is a hiding place. All religious pretense is such, and is nothing better. To put on the mere appearance of devoutness and sanctimony, as if God could be made to believe that you are sincere and could not see through it all, is a flimsy hiding place indeed. This is true of all religious formality, such as going through the forms of worship, being in the church, and being baptized – these things do not help unless their piety is part of their life, and that life is the soul of real holiness.

A great many people hide in the church. Judas Iscariot crept in there to hide. A minister of the Dutch Reformed Church told me once of a case that is relevant here. A man who had been confirmed in that church was out at sea during a fearful storm. It was a time of intense distress, and many were exceedingly fearful of death, not to say also of that terrible state beyond. When they asked him, "How is it that you are so calm?" He replied, "What have I to fear? I belong to the South Dutch!"

Many people hide under orthodox creeds. They confidently boast that they are not Unitarians, they are not Mormons, and they are not Universalists; they are orthodox! They think that such religious opinions held so tenaciously must ensure their safety.

Others hide under the excuse of a sinful nature. They are naturally unable to do anything. Here they think they have found a sure retreat. They are very willing to do all their duty, but this sinful nature is all against them, and what can they do? This is a refuge of lies.

Some try to escape by hiding among those who profess to follow the Christian religion. I am afraid that there are many such people here now. Sadly, your hiding place will fail you in the day of trial! When the hail comes, the storm rolls up fearfully, and the dreadful thunder breaks with an appalling crash, you will try in vain to find the one who professes Christ in order to hide under his wing! Where is he now? If he were as bad as you claim, how much can he help you in that all-devouring storm? If he is not as good as he should be, you should be better than he and should not try to hide yourself under his shortcomings.

## Remarks

Sinners know these things to be refuges of lies because they do not save people from their sins. Certainly they must see this and know it to be the truth.

They resort to these refuges not because they are true, but to use them as an excuse for delay. This is miserable deceit! They are not honest, and therefore do not need to think it is strange if they are deceived.

They admit that if someone lives like Christ, all will be well, and they know that nothing less than this will avail for their safety. Of course, to seek a refuge of lies is to tempt God to destroy you. How can it be otherwise?

Remember the test – this one plain and simple principle: only that which saves from sin is true; all else is false and disastrous. You all have some hope of a happy future, but what is this hope? Is it good or bad? Is it truthful and sure, or is it a refuge of lies?

Does your hope sanctify you? Does it make you humble, holy, and prayerful? Does your faith purify your heart? Do you have the fruit of the Spirit, such as love, joy, peace, and long-suffering? Do you have daily communion with God? Are you so united to Him that you can say, "Truly we have fellowship with the Father" (1 John 1:3)? If so, this will be a hiding place indeed – not one that the hail will sweep away, but one that will save the soul.

Do you have the life of God in your soul? Does it permeate your heart and diffuse itself over all of your soul? Let nothing less than this avail to satisfy your mind.

Listen to Roman Catholics talk about the Virgin Mary and the sacraments and absolution; what are all these things (and a thousand more like them) good for if they do not save from sin? What is the use of running after these things that do not save?

Maybe you say that you love to believe that everyone will be saved, that it makes you so happy to believe that. But does it make you holy? Does it renew your heart? This is the only sure test.

Maybe you say, "I do not believe as you do." I answer that here are great facts. You are in sin. Are you saved from your sin by your system? If so, good; if not, then it is not good. Will your believing it to be one way or the other make it so? Does believing a lie make it the truth? If you were to believe that you could walk on the water, or that water could not drown you, and you would leap overboard, would your belief save you?

Dying sinner, all those refuges of lies will surely deceive and destroy you. It is time for you to arise and say, "I must have the religion of Jesus. If I do not have it, I cannot go where Jesus is. With a lie in my right hand, what have I to hope for?"

None of you, I hope, have reached that sad state described by the prophet: *A deceived heart hath turned him aside, that he cannot deliver his soul, nor say, Is there not a lie in my right hand?* (Isaiah 44:20).

O sinner, there is a refuge for you that is not one of lies. There is a hiding place for you that no waters can reach to overwhelm you. It lies far above their course. Take refuge in Christ! Away with these refuges of lies! Cry out, "Give me Christ and none besides! Christ and Him only, for what have I to do with lies and delusions? You need to come into such communion with Christ that His power and presence and fullness will flow through your heart fully and freely, and will be in you *a well of water springing up into everlasting life* (John 4:14).

# Chapter 8

# The Wicked Heart Set to Do Evil

Because sentence against an evil work is not executed speedily, therefore the heart of the sons of men is fully set in them to do evil.
—Ecclesiastes 8:11

This verse clearly infers that the present is not a state of rewards and punishments in which people are treated according to their character and conduct. This fact is not indeed affirmed, but it is assumed, as it is also everywhere throughout the Bible. Everybody knows that this life is not a state of present rewards and punishments. The experience and observation of everyone testifies to this fact with convincing power. Therefore, it is entirely proper that the Bible would assume it as a known truth.

Everyone who reads the Bible must see that many things in it are assumed to be true, and that these are precisely those things that everyone knows to be true and that no one could know more certainly even if God had affirmed them on every page of the Bible. In the case of this particular truth, every person knows that he is not punished as he has deserved to be in the present life. Everyone sees the same thing in the case of his neighbors. The psalmist was so astounded by the obvious injustice of things in this world, as between the various circumstances of the righteous and of the wicked, that he was greatly bothered *until*, he said, *I went into the sanctuary of God; then understood I their end* (Psalm 73:17).

It is also assumed in this passage that all people have a common heart by nature. One general fact is stated of them all, and in this way they are assumed to have a common character: *The heart of the sons of men is fully set in them to do evil.* This is also stated in Genesis 6:5: *God saw that the wickedness of man was great in the earth, and that every imagination of the thoughts of his heart was only evil continually.* This is the common method in which God speaks of sinners in His Word. He always assumes that by nature they have the same character.

The text also shows what the moral type of the sinner's heart is. It is *fully set . . . to do evil.* We must pause here a moment to inquire what is meant in our passage by the term "heart."

It is obvious that this term is used in the Bible in various shades of meaning. Sometimes it is used for the conscience, as in the passage that declares, *If our heart condemn us, God is greater than our heart* (1 John 3:20), and may be expected even more to condemn us. Sometimes the term is used for the intelligence, but here most evidently for the will, because this is the only capability of the mind that can be said to be set, fixed, bent, or determined upon a given course of voluntary action. The will is the capability that sets itself upon a chosen course. Therefore in our text, the will must be meant by the term "heart," for otherwise no understandable sense can be put upon the passage.

> The will of wicked people is fully set to do evil.

But in what direction and to what purpose is the will of wicked people fully set? The answer is that the will of wicked people is fully set to do evil. God's Word solemnly declares this.

Let it be said by way of explanation that this does not imply that people do evil for the sake of the evil itself. It does not imply that sinning, considered as disobedience to God, is their direct purpose. The drunkard does not drink because it is wicked to drink, but he drinks regardless of it being wicked. He drinks for the present good it promises, not for the sake of sinning. It is the same with the person who tells lies. His purpose is not to break God's law, but to get some good to himself by lying; yet he tells the lie despite God's prohibition. His heart may become fully set upon the practice of lying whenever it is convenient for him, and in pursuit of the good he hopes to gain by his lie. It is in vain that God labors by fearful prohibitions and penalties to discourage him from his course.

It is the same with stealing, adultery, and other sins. We are not to suppose that people set their hearts upon these sins out of love of pure wickedness, but they do wickedly for the sake of the good they hope to gain by the wickedness. The immoral person would probably be glad if it were not wicked to gratify his passion, but wicked though it is, he sets his heart to do it.

Why did Adam and Eve eat the forbidden fruit? Because they saw it was beautiful, and they were told it would make them wise. Therefore, for the good they hoped to gain, and despite God's prohibition, they took it and ate. I know it is sometimes said that sinners love sin for its own sake out of a pure love of sin as sin, with a natural delight (just as wolves love flesh), simply because it is disobedience to God, but this is not true – certainly not in many cases. The simple truth is that people do not set their hearts upon the sin for its own sake, but they set their hearts upon sinning for the sake of the good they hope to get from it.

Notice especially now the language: *the heart . . . is fully set in them to do evil.* One person is greedy. He sets his heart upon getting rich – honestly, if he can, but any way that he can. He wants to get money by honest means if possible, but he intends to be sure and get it. Another person is ambitious. The love of reputation fills and fires his soul, and therefore, he might become very polite and very gracious in his manners – and sometimes very religious, if religion is popular, but completely selfish, and nonetheless so for being so very religious.

Selfishness takes on a thousand forms and types, but each and all are sinful, for the whole mind should give itself up to serve God and to perform every duty as revealed to the reason. What did Eve do? She gave herself up to gratify her taste for knowledge, as well as for the good of self-indulgence. She consented to believe the lying spirit who told her it was *a tree to be desired to make one wise* (Genesis 3:6). She thought this must be very important. It was also, apparently, good for food, and her appetite became greatly excited. The more she looked, the more excited she became, and now what should she do? God had forbidden her to eat it. Would she obey God, or would she obey her own excited appetite? Despite God's command, she ate the fruit. Was that a sin? Many people would think it was only a very small sin, but it was real rebellion against God, and He could not do otherwise than visit it with great displeasure!

It is the same everywhere – to yield to the demands of appetite and passion against God's requirements and demands is grievous sin. All people are bound to fear and obey God, no matter how much self-denial and sacrifice it may cost.

Selfishness often acquires a religious side. At the beginning, the mind may be powerfully affected by some of the great and stirring truths of the gospel, but it soon takes an entirely selfish view, caring only to escape punishment and to make religion a matter of gain. It is astonishing to see how in such cases the mind completely misconstrues the intent of the gospel, completely losing sight of the great fact that it seeks to eradicate man's selfishness and draw out his heart into pure benevolence. Making this profound mistake, it perceives the whole gospel system as a scheme for gratification.

**Selfishness often acquires a religious side.**

You can see this demonstrated by the view that some people take of the imputation of Christ's righteousness, which they imagine is attributed to them while they are living in sin. That is, they suppose that they secure complete exemption from the penalty of violating the law, and even have the honors and rewards of full obedience while they still have all the self-indulgences of a life of sin. This is horrible! Were ever Roman Catholic indulgences worse than this?

Examine such a case thoroughly and you will see that selfishness is at the bottom of all the religion there is in it. The person was worldly before and is devout now, but he is devout for the same reason that he was worldly. The selfish heart forms the basis of both systems. The same goals are sought, and they are sought in the same spirit; the moral character remains unchanged. The person might pray, but if so, he asks God to do some great things for him in order to promote his own selfish purposes. He does not have the slightest intent of committing himself to God's interests so that he will from then on be in perfect affinity with God, desiring and seeking only God's interests, and serving no interests other than God's.

To illustrate this point, let us imagine that a parent would say to his children, "I will give you my property if you will work with me and truly identify your interests with mine. If you are not willing to do this, I will disinherit you." Some of the children may take a perfectly selfish view of this offer, and may say within themselves, "I will do just enough for my father to get his money. I will make him think that I am very zealous for his interests, and I will do just enough to secure the offered rewards, but why should I do more than that?"

Imagine the case of a human government that offers rewards to offenders on condition of their returning to obedience. The real spirit of the offer goes to the length of asking for the sincere devotion of their hearts to the best good of the government. However, they may take a completely selfish view of the case and determine to accept the proposal only just far enough to secure the rewards, and only for the sake of the rewards. The ruler wants and expects the actual affinity of their hearts – their real goodwill. If this is given, the ruler would love to reward them most abundantly, but how can he be satisfied with them if they are entirely selfish?

A person may be as selfish in praying as in stealing, and even far more wicked, for he may more grievously mock God and more impiously attempt to bribe the Almighty to promote his own selfish purposes. He may wrongly suppose that he can make the Searcher of hearts work for his own benefit. He may brazenly try to induce Him to play into his own hands, and so may most grievously tempt Him to His face.

The text affirms that the heart of men is *fully set in them to do evil*. Maybe some of you think otherwise. Maybe you don't believe in such depravity. That loving mother says, "I think my daughter is friendly to religion."

"Do you think she is converted?"

"No, not converted, but I think she is approving of religion and feels favorably toward it."

"Does she meet the demands of God like a friend to His government and to His reputation?"

"I cannot say that she does."

"Ask her to repent, and what does she say?"

"She will tell you she cannot."

How remarkable is the fact that you can go through the different classes of society and you will meet people almost everywhere with this position. The sinner says that he cannot repent and cannot believe. What is the matter? Where is the trouble? Go to that young woman who is thought to be so friendly to religion. She is so kind and gentle that she cannot bear to see any pain inflicted, but notice what happens. Present to her the claims of God, and what does she say? "I cannot. I cannot obey God in one of His demands. I cannot repent of my sin."

What is it about repentance that this kind lady, although so friendly to religion, would be incapable of repenting? What is the matter? Is God so unreasonable in His demands that He imposes upon you things that are quite impossible for you to do? Are you so indifferent to His feelings and so careless of the truth that for the sake of self-justification you will accuse Him of the most flagrant injustice and falsely imply that the wrong is all on His side and none on yours? Is this a very gracious trait of character in you? Is this one of your proofs that the human heart is not fully set to do evil?

> **Is God so unreasonable in His demands that He imposes upon you things that are quite impossible for you to do?**

You say that you cannot repent and love God! You find it quite impossible to make up your mind to serve and please God! What is the matter? Are there no sufficient reasons apparent to your mind why you should give up your heart to God? No reasons? Heaven, earth, and hell may all combine to pour upon you their reasons for fearing and loving God, and yet you cannot think of any? Why is this? It is because your heart is fully set within you to do evil rather than good.

You are completely committed to the pleasing of self. Jesus may plead with you. Your friends may plead with you. Heaven and hell may lift up their united voices to plead with you, and every motive that can press on the heart from reason, conscience, hope, and fear, and from angels and devils, God and man, may pass in long and flashing array before your mind – but sadly, your heart is so fully set to do evil that no motive to change can move you. What is this "cannot"? It is not a "cannot," but is nothing less or more than a mighty "will not"!

That kind woman insists that she is not much depraved. She will not steal! It is true that her selfishness takes on a most tender and delicate type. She has the most profuse sensitivities. She cannot bear to see a kitten in distress, but what does she care for God's rights? What does she care for the rights of Jesus Christ? What does she care for God's feelings? What does she care for the feelings and sympathies of the crucified Son of God? She cares nothing at all. What, then, are all her tender sensitivities worth? Doves and kittens have even more of this than she has. There is no doubt that she has many tender attachments, but they are all under the control of a perfectly selfish heart.

Eve, too, was most gracious. Indeed, she was a truly pious woman before she sinned, and Adam no doubt thought she could be trusted everywhere – but notice how terribly she fell! Just as Eve fell, so did her daughters. Giving up their hearts to a refined selfishness, they repel God's most righteous claims, and they are fallen!

You can go through all the levels of society and see the same thing. Go to the pirate ship with the captain armed to the teeth and the fire of hell in his eye; ask him to receive an offered Savior and repent of his sins, and he gives the very same answer as that gracious daughter does: he cannot repent. His heart, too, is so fully set within him to do evil that he cannot get his own consent to turn from his sins to God.

Oh, this horrible compulsion of the heart to do evil! It is the only reason why the Holy Spirit is needed to change the sinner's heart. Except for this, you would no more need the Holy Spirit than an angel of light does. Oh, how terribly strong is the sinner's heart against God! Right where the demands of God come in, he seems to have almost unlimited strength to oppose and resist! The motives of truth may roll as high as the mountains and beat upon his iron heart, yet see how he braces up his nerves to withstand God! What can he not resist rather than submit his will to God!

Another thing is seen in this text, incidentally brought out, assumed but not affirmed, and that is that sinners are already under sentence. The text, Ecclesiastes 8:11, says, *Because sentence . . . is not executed speedily,* implying that sentence is already passed and only waits its appointed time to be carried out. You who have attended courts of justice know that after the trial and conviction comes the sentence. The criminal takes his seat on the bench. The judge arises. Everything is as still as death. The judge reviews the case and quickly comes to the solemn conclusion: "You are convicted by this court of the crime alleged, and now you are to receive your sentence." Sentence is then delivered.

After this solemn transaction, execution of the sentence is commonly deferred for a period of time according to the circumstances. The purpose may be either to give the criminal an opportunity to obtain a pardon, or if there is no hope of this, at least to give him some days or weeks for serious reflection in which he may secure the peace of his soul with God. For such reasons, execution is usually delayed.

However, after the sentence is given, the case is fully decided. No further doubt of guilt can intervene to affect the case. The possibility of pardon is the only remaining hope. The dreadful sentence seals his doom, unless it is possible that a pardon can be obtained. That sentence – how it sinks into the heart of the guilty criminal! "You are now," says the judge, "remanded to the place from where you came. You are to be kept there in irons, under close confinement, until the day appointed. Then you are to be taken forth from your prison cell between the hours of ten and twelve as the case may be, and hung by the neck until you are dead. May God have mercy on your soul!" The sentence has passed now. The court has done its work. All that remains is for the executioner of justice to do his work, and the fearful scene closes.

This is how the Bible represents the case of the sinner. He is under sentence, but his sentence is not executed speedily. Some pause is given. The arrangements of the divine government require no court and no jury. The law itself says, *The soul that sinneth, it shall die* (Ezekiel 18:20), and *Cursed is every one that continueth not in all things which are written in the book of the law to do them* (Galatians 3:10), so that the mandate of the law involves the sentence of law on every sinner – a sentence from which there can be no escape and no deliverance except by a pardon. What a position this is for the sinner!

Next, consider another strange fact. Because sentence is not executed speedily, because there is some delay of execution, because mercy prevails to secure for the condemned criminal a few days' delay so that punishment will not tread close on the heels of crime, *therefore the heart of the sons of men is fully set in them to do evil*. How astounding! What a perversion and abuse of the gracious design of the King in granting a little delay from instant execution!

Let us see how it would look in the case of our friend or neighbor. He has committed a terrible crime. He is arrested, put on trial, convicted, sentenced, and handed over to the warden to await the day and hour of his execution. The judge says, "I delay the execution so that you may have opportunity to secure a pardon from the governor. I assure you that the governor is a most compassionate man. He loves to grant pardons. He has already pardoned thousands. If you will give up your spirit of rebellion, he will most freely forgive you. I beg you, therefore, that you will not try to attempt to justify yourself. Don't think of escaping death in any other way than by casting yourself upon his mercy. Don't deceive yourself by thinking that there can be any other refuge."

Now suppose this man says, "I have done nothing wrong – nothing at all. I am simply a martyr to truth and justice! Well, at least I have done nothing very bad – nothing that any government should notice. I don't believe I will be sentenced [the man is condemned already!]. I will live as long as the best of you." So he starts making excuses. He goes to work as if he were preparing for a trial and as if he expected to prove his innocence before the court. Maybe he even sets himself to oppose and curse the government, ranting against its laws and its officers, thinking nothing is too bad to say about them, indulging himself in the most outrageous opposition, and criticizing the very men whose mercy has spared his forfeited life!

People would be shocked to see such a case – to see someone who would so disrespect all that is right and just as to give himself up to insult the government whose righteous laws he had just broken and then whose leniency he had most flagrantly disregarded! Yet this text of Ecclesiastes 8:11 affirms this to be the case of the sinner, and all observation sustains it. You have seen it demonstrated over and over again ten thousand times. You can look back and see it in your own case. You know it is all true – fearfully and terribly true.

If it were revealed to you in some powerful and terrible manner tonight that your soul is damned, you would be stunned. You do not believe the simple declaration of God as it stands recorded on the pages of the Bible. You are continually saying to yourself, "I will not be condemned in the end. I will continue along. I will dare to continue to tempt His patience. I do not at all believe He will send me to hell. At least I will continue on a while longer before I eventually turn around if I find it advantageous, but for now, why should I fear to set my heart fully in the way God has forbidden?"

Where will you find a parallel to such wickedness? Only think of a state of moral boldness that can abuse God's richest mercies, that can calmly say, "God is so good that I will take advantage of Him all I can. God loves me so much that I will continue without fear to insult Him and abuse His mercy and patience to the utmost hardening of my soul in sin and rebellion!

> God does not wait because He is in doubt about the justice of the sentence but only that He may see if He can persuade you to embrace mercy.

Let each sinner observe that the day of execution is really set. God will not pass over it. When it arrives, there can be no more delay. God does not wait because He is in doubt about the justice of the sentence or because His heart is apprehensive in view of its terrible execution, but only that He may see if He can persuade you to embrace mercy. This is all. This is the only reason why judgment has lingered for such a long time and why the sword of justice has not long ago smitten you down.

Here is another extraordinary fact. Not only has God delayed execution, but at immense cost He has provided means for the safe application of mercy. You know that it is naturally a dangerous thing to bestow mercy. There is so much danger that it may weaken the force of law and encourage people to trample it down in hope of impunity. However, God has provided a glorious testimony in favor of law, showing that it is in His heart to sustain it at every sacrifice. He could not forgive sin until His broken and dishonored law was honored before the universe. Having done all this in the sacrifice of His own Son on Calvary, He can forgive without fear of consequences, provided that each candidate for pardon will first be truly repentant.

Now, therefore, God's heart of mercy is opened wide, and no fear of evil consequences from free pardons disturbs the exercise of mercy. Before atonement, justice stood with brandished sword, demanding vengeance on the guilty; but by and through the atoning blood, God rescued His law from danger. He lifted it up from beneath the defiled foot of the transgressor and set it on high in safety and glory, and now He opens wide the blessed door of mercy.

Now He comes in the person of His Spirit and invites you in. He comes to your very heart and room, sinner, to offer you the freest possible pardon for all your sin. Do you hear that gentle knock at your door? *Behold, I stand at the door and knock; if any man hear my voice and open the door, I will come in to him and sup with him, and he with me* (Revelation 3:20). Look at those hands. Have they not been pierced? Do you know those hands? Do you know where they have been to be nailed completely through? Notice the hair wet with the dew. How long has He been kept outside? How long has He been waiting for the door to open?

Who is it who comes? Is it the officer of justice? Has he come with his armed men to drag you away to execution? No, but One comes with the cup of mercy in His hands. He approaches your prison gate, His eye wet with the tear of compassion. Through the window of your door, He extends that cup of mercy to your parched lips. Do you see that face, disfigured more than any man's (Isaiah 52:14), and are you only the more fully set to do evil? Young man, young woman, is this how your heart is toward the God of mercy? Where can we find anything similar to such guilt? Can it be found anywhere else in the universe except in this demented world?

The scenes and activities on earth must inspire a wonderful interest in heaven. Angels desire to look into these things (1 Peter 1:12). The whole universe looks on with inquisitive wonder to see what Christ has done, and how the sinners for whom He has suffered and done all try to repay His amazing love! However, when they see you set your heart only the more fully to do evil, they stand back horrified at such unparalleled wickedness! What can be done for such sinners except leave them to the foolishness and doom of their choice?

God has no other alternative. If you wrong Him, He must execute His law and its fearful sentence of eternal death. Suppose it were a human government, and a similar situation occurs. Who does not see that government might as well abdicate at once as to refrain to punish?

It is the same with God. Although He has no pleasure in the sinner's death, and although He will never slay you because He delights in it, yet how can He do otherwise than execute His law if He would uphold it? How can He justify Himself for any failure in sustaining it? Will you oppose Him and then flatter yourself that He will fail to execute His terrible sentence upon you?

Oh, sinner, there is no possibility that you can pass the appointed time without execution. Human laws may possibly fail to be enforced, but God's laws can never fail! Who is it who says that their *judgment now of a long time lingereth not, and their damnation slumbereth not* (2 Peter 2:3)?

## Remarks

1. Let me ask those who profess to be true Christians: do you think you believe these truths? Let me suppose that there is a father and a mother reading this who have a child whom you know and acknowledge to be under sentence of death. You don't know this, but this is the very day and hour set for his execution. How do you feel? Does the knowledge and belief of such facts disturb your peace?

The case of your children could now be infinitely worse than this. You know that eternal death in hell must be far more terrible than any public execution on earth. If your own son were under sentence for execution on earth, how would you feel? How, then, would you feel if you believed that he were under the far more terrible sentence of hell?

Let us spread out this case a little. Place before you that aged father and mother. Their son went off to sea years ago. They have not seen him or even heard a word from him in a long time. How often have their troubled minds dwelt on his case! They do not know how he is, but they fear the worst. They had reason to know that his principles were not very well fixed when he left home, and they are afraid he has fallen into worse and worse company and may now be a bold transgressor.

As they are talking over these things and searching all the newspapers they can find from time to time to see if they can find some clue to their son's history, all at once the doorbell rings. A messenger hands a letter to the old father, who takes it, breaks the seal, reads a word, and suddenly falls back in his seat. The letter drops from his hand. He can't read it! The mother wonders what happened and she asks her husband about it. She rushes forward and grabs the fallen letter. She reads a word, and her heart breaks with agony. What is the matter? Their son is sentenced to die, and he wrote to see if his father and mother can come and see him before he dies.

In the early morning, they are off. The sympathetic neighbors gather around. They are all sorrowful, for it is a sad thing, and they feel it sharply. The parents hurry away to the prison and learn the details of the painful case. They see at once that there can be no hope of release except in a pardon. The governor lives nearby. They rush to his house, but sad for them, they find him stern and immovable. With palpitating and heavy hearts, they plead and plead, but all seems to be in vain.

He says, "Your son has been so wicked and has committed such crimes that he must be hung. The good of the nation demands it, and I cannot allow my sympathies to overrule my sense of justice and my convictions of the public good."

But the agonized parents must hold on. What a conflict is in their minds! How the case burns upon their hearts! At last the mother breaks out and says, "Sir, are you a father? Do you have a son?"

"Yes, one son."

"Where is he?"

"He has gone to California."

"How long has it been since you have heard from him? Suppose he, too, should fall! Suppose you were to feel such grief as ours and have to mourn over a fallen son!"

The governor finds himself to be a father. All the dormant affections of the father's heart are stirred within him. Calling to his private secretary, he says to make out a pardon for their son! Oh, what a flood of emotions they pour out!

All this is very natural. No one considers this strange at all. However, compare this to the case of the sinner condemned to an eternal hell. If your spiritual ears were opened, you would hear the chariot wheels rolling with the great Judge coming in His chariot of thunder. You would see the sword of death gleaming in the air, ready to smite down the hardened sinner.

However, hear the professedly Christian father pray for his ungodly son. He thinks he should pray for him once or twice a day, so he begins, but he has almost forgotten his subject. He hardly knows or thinks what he is praying about. God says, "Pray for your dying son! Lift up your cries for him while mercy still lingers and pardon can be found."

> Something is wrong when God says that your child is sentenced to die and yet the father or mother have no urgency in the case.

Where are the Christian parents who pray for their children as for a sentenced and soon-to-be-executed son! They say they believe the Bible, but do they? Do they act as if they believed even half of its terrible truths about sentenced sinners ready to go down to an eternal hell? Yet notice how they feel and how they act as soon as they are spiritually awake!

What is wrong with that professing Christian who has no spirit of prayer and no power with God? He is an unbeliever! Something is wrong when God says that your child is sentenced to die and his angel of death may come in one hour and cut him down in his guilt and sin and send his spirit quickly to hell, and yet the father or mother have no urgency in the case. They are unbelievers; they do not believe what God has said.

2. Here is another situation. Suppose that these distressed parents have gone to the governor. They have poured out their griefs before him and have at last wrestled a pardon from his stern hands. They rush from his house toward the prison, so delighted that they scarcely touch the ground. As they approach the prison, they hear songs of cheer, and they say, "Our son must be agonized with company and scenes so improper

and so disagreeable!" The parents meet the warden and ask him who can sing so happily in a prison.

The warden answers, "It is your own son. He has no idea that he is to be executed. He is promising to burn down the governor's house. Indeed, he has a most determined spirit, as if his heart were fully set on evil."

"That is distressing," they say, "but we can restrain his wicked and proud heart. We will show him the pardon and tell him how the governor feels. We are sure this will subdue him. He cannot withstand such kindness and compassion."

They go to the door of the prison cell. They enter and show their son the pardon. They tell him how much it has cost them and how tenderly the governor feels in the case. He seizes it, tears it to pieces, and tramples it under his feet! His parents think that he must be deranged! However, it is only depravity of the heart, and they come to realize it and know that this must be the case. They cry out, "This is worst of all! What! Not willing to be pardoned! Not willing to be saved! This is worse than all the rest. Well, we must go to our desolate home. We are done trying to save our son! We obtained a pardon for him with our tears, but he will not accept it. There is nothing more that we can do."

They turn sadly away, not caring even to bid him farewell. They go home doubly saddened not only because he deserved to die for his original crimes, but also for his yet greater crime of refusing the offered pardon.

The day of execution comes. The prison guard is on hand to do his duty. He escorts the prisoner from his cell to the place of execution. The witnesses crowd around and follow sadly along. Suddenly a messenger rushes up and says to the criminal, "You have torn in pieces one pardon, but here is another one. Will you accept this?"

With proud disdain, the condemned prisoner rejects even this last offer of pardon! Where are the sympathies of all the land now? Do they say, "How cruel to hang a young man, and for only such a crime"? No. They say no such thing at all. They see the need for law and justice. They know that a law so insulted must be allowed to vindicate itself in the criminal's execution. The warden now proclaims, "Just fifteen minutes to live." Even during these minutes, the criminal insults the governor and the dignity of law.

The fateful moment arrives. He trembles for a minute under the grasp of death, and all is still forever! He is gone, and the law has been sustained in the fearful execution of its sentence. All the people feel that this is righteous. They cannot possibly think otherwise. Even those aged parents do not have a word of complaint to utter. They approve the governor's course of action. They endorse the sentence. They say, "We thought that he would accept the pardon, but since he would not, let him be accursed! We love good government. We love the blessings of law and order in society more than we love iniquity and crime. He was indeed our son, but he was also the son of the devil!"

Now let us attend the execution of some of these sinners from our own congregation. You are sent for to face execution. We see the messenger and we hear the sentence read. We see that your fatal hour has come. Will we turn and curse God? No! We will do no such thing. When you are hung and you gasp and die, and your guilty, terror-stricken soul goes wailing down the sides of the pit, will we go away to complain of God and of His justice? No! Why not? Because you could have had mercy, but you would not (Isaiah 30:15; Jeremiah 6:16; Matthew 23:37). God waited on you patiently, but your heart only became more fully set to do evil. The universe looks on and sees the facts in the case, and with one voice that rings through the vast arch of heaven, they cry, "Just and righteous You are in all Your ways, most Holy Lord God!" (Revelation 15:3).

Who says this is cruel? Will the universe take up arms against God? No. When the universe gathers together around the great white throne, and the dreadful sentence goes forth, "Depart, accursed," and away they move in dense and vast masses as if the old ocean had begun to flow away – down, down, they sink to the depths of their dark home, then the saints with firm step and solemn heart will proclaim, "God's law is vindicated. The insulted majesty of both law and mercy is now upheld in honor, and all is right!"

Heaven is solemn, but joyful. Saints are solemn, yet they cannot help rejoicing in their own glorious Father. See the multitudes of people as they move up to heaven. They look back over the plains of Sodom and see the smoke of her burning ascend up like the smoke of a great furnace (Genesis 19:28), but they pronounce it just, and do not have one word of complaint to utter.

To the sinner who is still living, I say today that the hour of your execution has not yet arrived. Once more, the bleeding hand offers mercy's cup to your lips. Think for a moment. Your Savior now offers you mercy. Come now and accept it.

What will you say? "I will go on still in my sins." Then all we can say is that the heart of divine love is deeply moved for you, that God has done all to save you that He wisely can do. God's people have felt a deep and agonizing interest in you and are ready now to cry, "How can we give them up? But what more can we do? What more can even God do?"

Mercy has followed you with bleeding heart and quivering lip. Jesus Himself said, *O Jerusalem, Jerusalem, thou that killest the prophets, and stonest them which are sent unto thee, how often would I have gathered thy children together, even as a hen gathereth her chickens under her wings, and ye would not!* (Matthew 23:37). Will Jesus see you, weep over you, and say, *If thou hadst known, even thou, at least in this thy day, the things which belong unto thy peace! but now they are hid from thine eyes* (Luke 19:42)?

> When Christ comes so near to you, and would willingly draw you close to His warm heart, what will you do?

What will you say, dying sinner? Your response should be, "It is enough. I have dashed away salvation's cup long and wickedly enough. You do not need to say another word. Oh, that bleeding hand! Those weeping eyes! Is it possible that I have withstood a Savior's love so long? I am ready to beg for mercy now, and I rejoice to hear that our God has a father's heart."

He knows you have sinned greatly and grievously, but His compassions have been bleeding and flowing forth toward you these many days. Will you accept at once the terms of mercy and come to Jesus? What do you say?

Suppose an angel comes down in robes pure and white, unrolls his scroll, and produces a pardon in your name, sealed with Jesus' own blood. He opens the sacred Book and reads the very passage that reveals the love of God. Then he asks you if you will believe and embrace it. What will you do?

What will I say to my Lord and Master? When I come to report the matter, must I give my testimony that you would not hear? When Christ comes so near to you, and would willingly draw you close to His warm heart, what will you do? Will you still repeat the fatal choice to reject His love and defy His dishonored justice?

# Chapter 9

# Moral Insanity

The heart of the sons of men is full of evil, and madness is
in their heart while they live.
—Ecclesiastes 9:3

The Bible often ascribes to unconverted people one common heart
or character. It always makes two classes, and only two, of the
human race: saints and sinners. The one class is converted from their
sin and has become God's real friends. The other class remains His
unconverted enemies.

According to the Bible, therefore, the heart, in all unrenewed people,
is the same in its general character. In the days of Noah, God testified
*that the wickedness of man was great in the earth, and that every imagi-
nation of the thought of his heart was only evil continually* (Genesis 6:5).
Notice that he speaks of the thought of their heart, as if they had one
common heart, that they were all similar in moral character. Through
the apostle Paul, God testifies that *the carnal mind is enmity against
God* (Romans 8:7), testifying this not of only one person or of a few
people, but of all people of carnal mind.

So in our text, the wording is expressive: *the heart of the sons of men
is full of evil* – as if the sons of men had but one heart, all in common,
and this one heart were *full of evil*. You will notice that this affirmation

is not made of one or two people, nor only of some people, but *of the sons of men*, as if of them all.

**I. What is intended by affirming that *madness is in their heart while they live*?** This is not the madness of anger, but of insanity. It is true that sometimes people are mad with anger, but this is not the sense of our text. The Bible, as well as customary speech, uses this term "madness" to express insanity. We understand this to be its sense here.

Insanity is of two kinds: one is of the head, and the other is of the heart. In the former, the intellect is disordered. In the latter, the will and voluntary powers are disordered. Intellectual insanity destroys moral agency. The intellectually insane person is not, for the time, a moral agent. Moral responsibility is suspended because he cannot know his duty and cannot choose responsibly as to doing or not doing it.

It is true that when someone makes himself temporarily insane, as by drunkenness, the courts are obligated to hold him responsible for his acts committed in that state, but the guilt really attaches to the voluntary act that creates the insanity. A person who gets intoxicated by knowingly drinking what he knows is intoxicating must be held responsible for his acts during the ensuing intoxication. The reason of this is that he can foresee the danger and can easily avoid it.

The general law is that while the intellect retains its usual power, moral obligation remains unimpaired. Moral insanity, on the other hand, is madness of the will. The person retains his intellectual powers unimpaired, but he sets his heart fully to evil. He refuses to yield to the demands of his conscience. He practically discards the obligations of moral responsibility. He has the powers of free moral agency, but he persistently abuses them. He has a reason that affirms obligation, but he refuses obedience to its declarations. In this form of insanity, the reason remains unimpaired, but the heart deliberately disobeys.

The insanity spoken of in the text is moral – that of the heart. By the "heart" here is meant the will – the voluntary power. While the person is intellectually sane, he still acts as if he were intellectually insane.

**II. It is important to point out some of the indications of this state of mind.** Since the Bible affirms it to be a fact that sinners are mad in heart, we may naturally expect to see some manifestations of it. It is often astonishing to see how perfectly the Bible captures human character. Has it done so in reference to this point? Let us see.

Who are the morally insane? The morally insane are those who, not being intellectually insane, act as if they were. For example, those who are intellectually insane treat fiction as if it were reality, and reality as if it were fiction. They act as if truth were not truth, and as if falsehood were truth. Everyone knows that insane people actually follow the wild dreams of their own imagination, as if they were the most stern reality, and can hardly be made to feel the force of anything truly real.

In the same way, people, in their sins, treat the realities of the spiritual world as if they were not real, but follow the most empty delusions of this world as if they were stern realities. They also act as if self were of supreme importance and everything else were of relatively no importance. Suppose you were to see someone acting this out in everyday life. He goes around day after day assuming that he is the Supreme God, practically insisting that everybody should have a supreme regard to his rights and comparatively little or no regard for other people's rights. If you were to see someone saying this and acting it out, would you not consider him to be either a blasphemer or insane?

Now observe the astonishing fact that while wicked people talk so sensibly as to show that they know better, they act as if all this were true – as if they supposed that their own self-interest were more important than everything else in the universe, and that even God's interests and rights are nothing in comparison. Every sinner does this in practice. It is an essential element in all sin. Selfish people never regard the rights of anyone else unless they are in some way linked with their own.

If wicked people really believed that their own rights and interests were supreme in the universe, it would prove them to be intellectually insane, and we should hurry to place them in the nearest insane asylum. However, when they show that they know better, yet still act on this groundless assumption in the face of their better knowledge, we say with the Bible that *madness is in their heart while they live.*

Now consider this madness demonstrated in the person's relative estimate of time and of eternity. His whole life declares that, in his view, it is far more important to secure the good of time than the good of eternity. Yet if a person would reason this way, would argue to prove it, and would sincerely declare it, you would know him to be insane and you would help him to the insane asylum. However, suppose that he does not say this, that he dares not say it, and that he knows it is not true, yet he constantly acts it out and lives on the assumption of its truth – what then? Simply this: he is morally mad. Madness is in his heart.

This is precisely the practice of every one of you who is living in sin. You give the preference to time over eternity. You say in reality, "Oh, give me the joys of time. Why should I trouble myself yet about the trivial matters of eternity?"

In the same spirit, you assume that the body is more than the soul. If someone were to affirm this, though, and go around trying to prove it, you would consider him to be insane. If he were a friend of yours, your heart would break for his sad misfortune in that he has lost his reason. But if he knows better, yet lives in practice as if it were so, all you could say is that he is *morally* insane.

Suppose you see someone destroying his own property, not by accident or mistake, but deliberately. Suppose he were injuring his own health, also, as if he had no concern for his own well-being. You might bring his case before a judge and try to have him declared insane so that the person's goods would be taken out of his own control and he would no longer be able to waste them.

However, in spiritual things, wicked people will deliberately act against their own best interests. Having a price put into their hands to get wisdom, they will not use it. Having the treasures of heaven placed within their reach, they do not try to secure them. With an infinite wealth of blessedness offered for the mere acceptance, they will not take it as a gift. Indeed! How plain it is that if people were to act in worldly things as they do in spiritual, they would be declared insane by everyone. Anyone would take an oath in regard to this. They would say, "Just look. The man acts against his own interests in everything! Who can deny that he is insane? Certainly, sane people never do this!"

In moral questions, though, wicked people seem to take the utmost efforts to defeat their own interests and ruin themselves forever! Oh, how they impoverish their souls when they could have the riches of heaven!

They also try to realize clear impossibilities. For example, they try to make themselves happy in their sins and their selfishness, even though they know they cannot do it. If you ask them, they will admit that this is entirely impossible, yet despite this conviction, they perpetually keep up the effort to try, as if they expected to eventually accomplish a clear impossibility.

In moral things, this may not strike you as especially strange, for it is exceedingly common, but suppose that you were to see someone doing the same sort of thing in worldly matters. What would you think of him? For example, you might see him working hard to build a very long ladder, and you ask him why he is building the ladder. He answers, "I am going to climb to the moon." You see him expending his labor and his money with the efforts of his life in order to build an immense ladder with which to climb to the moon! Would you not say that he is certainly insane? Unless he were really insane, he would know that it were a complete impossibility.

In spiritual things, however, people are all the time trying to achieve a result that is at least equally impossible – that of being happy in sin, happy with a rebellion among their own inherent powers, with the heart at war against reason and conscience. The pursuit of happiness in sin is as if someone were seeking to bless himself by mutilating his own flesh, digging out his own eyes, and smashing in his teeth. Yet people just as truly know that they cannot obtain happiness in sin and selfishness as they know they cannot ensure health and comfort by mutilating their own flesh and severing their own nerves. Doing these foolish things, which they know will always result in defeat and will never ensure real happiness, they show themselves to be morally insane.

Another indication of intellectual insanity is loss of confidence in one's best friends. This is often one of the first and most painful evidences of insanity. The poor man will believe that his dearest friends are determined to ruin him. By no amount of evidence can he be persuaded to think they are his real friends.

This is the same way that sinners in their madness treat God. While they inwardly know that He is their real friend, they treat Him in practice as their worst enemy. Nothing can persuade them to confide in Him as their friend. In fact, they treat Him as if he were the greatest liar in the universe. Incredible to tell, they practically reverse the respect due to God and to Satan – treating Satan as if he were God, and God as if He were Satan. They believe and obey Satan, while they disown, dishonor, and disobey God. How strangely they want to reverse the order of things! They would gladly enthrone Satan over the universe, giving him the highest seat in heaven, yet they would send the almighty and holy God to hell. They do not hesitate to surrender to Satan the place of power over their own hearts that is due only to God.

I have already noted the fact that insane people treat their best friends as if they were their worst enemies, and I have mentioned that this is often the first proof of insanity. For example, a husband might think that his dear wife is trying to poison him. I remember a situation – the first case of real insanity I ever saw, and it might be for that reason that it made a strong impression on my mind. I was riding on horseback. Arriving near a house, I noticed a window of a room opened, and I heard a most unearthly cry. As soon as I got near enough to hear the words, I heard a most wild, imploring voice: "Stranger, stranger, come here; here is the great whore of Babylon. They are trying to kill me. They will kill me."

I dismounted and went up to the house, and there I found a man locked up in a cage and complaining most bitterly of his wife. As I turned toward her, I saw that she looked sad, as if a load of grief lay heavy on her heart. A tear trembled in her eye. Sadly, her dear husband was a maniac! It was then that I first learned how the insane are inclined to regard their best friends.

Sinners know better of God and of their other real friends, yet they very commonly treat them in precisely this way. It is as if they were to go into public places and yell to all bystanders, "Hello, there, everyone. Let it be known to you that the great God is an almighty tyrant! He should not be trusted or loved!"

Everybody knows they treat God in this way in practice. They regard the service of God, true religion, as if it were inconsistent with their real and highest happiness. I have often met with sinners who seemed to think that every attempt to make them Christians is a scheme to capture them and sell them into slavery. They by no means consider true religion as if it came forth from a God of love. Practically, they treat the Christian religion as if it would be their ruin if they embraced it. Yet in all this, they act entirely against their own convictions. They know better. If they did not, their sin would be exceedingly small compared with what it is.

Another remarkable characteristic of insanity is to be greatly excited about little things, and apathetic about the most important matters in the universe. Suppose you see someone excited about straws and pebbles. He takes much time and effort to gather them into piles and store them away as treasures, yet when a fire breaks out around his house and the village is in flames, he takes no notice of it and has no interest in it. Or people may die all around him with the plague, but he pays no attention to it. Would you not say that he must be insane?

> The conduct of unrepentant people is the perfection of irrationality.

However, this is precisely true of sinners. They are almost infinitely excited about worldly goods such as straws and pebbles as compared to God's offered treasures. How apathetic they are about the most momentous events in the universe! The vast concerns of their souls hardly stir up one sincere thought! If they did not know better, you would say that their reason is certainly dethroned; but since they do know better, you cannot say less than that they are morally insane. *Madness is in their heart while they live.*

The conduct of unrepentant people is the perfection of irrationality. When you see it as it is, you will get a more just and vivid idea of irrationality than you can get from any other source. You can see this in the goals to which they devote themselves and in the methods that they use to secure them. It is all utterly unreasonable. An end madly chosen, sought by means madly devised – this is the life history of the multitudes who reject God. If this were the result of wrong intellectual judgments, we would say at once that the human race has gone mad.

Insane asylums themselves provide no higher evidence of intellectual insanity than every sinner does of moral insanity. You can go to every room in the asylum, and you will not find one insane person who gives higher evidence of intellectual insanity than every sinner does of moral insanity. Every sinner provides evidence that he is mad morally.

Sinners act as if they were afraid that they would be saved. They often seem to be trying to make their salvation as difficult as possible. For example, they all know what Christ has said about the danger of riches and the difficulty of saving those who are rich. They have read His words: *How hardly shall they that have riches enter into the kingdom of God* (Mark 10:23) and *It is easier for a camel to go through the eye of a needle than for a rich man to enter into the kingdom of God* (Matthew 19:24). They know this, and yet how many of them are in a crazy rush to be rich! For this purpose, some are ready to sacrifice their conscience, and others their health. They all seem deliberately ready to sacrifice their souls! How could they more certainly ensure their own damnation!

They therefore regard damnation as if it were salvation, and salvation as if it were damnation. They rush upon damnation as if it were heaven, and flee salvation as if it were hell.

Is this exaggeration? No; this is only the simple truth. Sinners rush toward the way to hell as if it were the main good of their existence, and they avoid the way to heaven as if it were the culmination of evil. Sinner, this is your own moral state. The picture gives only the obvious facts of the case without exaggeration.

**III. This moral insanity is a state of complete wickedness.** The special feature of it that makes it a guilty state is that it is entirely voluntary. It does not result from the loss of reason, but from the abuse of reason. The will persists in acting against reason and conscience. Despite the affirmations of reason, and regardless of the admonitions of conscience, the sinner continues on in his career of rebellion against God and goodness. In such voluntary wickedness, must there not be deep-seated sin?

Besides, this action is oftentimes deliberate. The person sins in his calm, deliberate moments, as well as in his excited moments. If he sins quite openly and boldly in his excited moments, he does not repent and change his position toward God in his deliberate moments, but virtually endorses, then, the impulsive purposes of his more agitated hours. This heightens his sin.

His purposes of sin are obstinate and unyielding. In ten thousand ways, God is bringing influences to bear on his mind to change his purposes, but usually in vain. This career of sin is in violation of all his obligations. Who does not know this? The sinner never acts from right motives. He never yields to the influence of a sense of obligation. He never recognizes in practice his obligation to love his neighbor as himself or to honor the Lord his God.

It is a total rejection of both God's law and gospel. He will not obey the law, and he will not accept the gospel of pardon. He seems determined to brave the omnipotence of God and to dare His vengeance. Is he not *mad upon his idols* (Jeremiah 50:38)? Is it saying too much when the Bible affirms that *madness is in their heart while they live*?

## Remarks

1. Sinners strangely accuse saints of being mad and crazy. As soon as Christians begin to act as if the truth they believe is a reality, then wicked people cry out, "See, they are getting crazy." Yet those very sinners acknowledge that the Bible is true, and they admit that those things that Christians believe as true are indeed true. Further still, they admit that those Christians are doing only what they should do, and only what they themselves should be doing. Even so, they accuse them of insanity. It is curious that even those sinners themselves know that these Christians are the only rational people on the earth. I can well remember that I saw this plainly before my conversion. I knew then that Christians were the only people in all the world who had any valid claim to be deemed sane.

2. If intellectual insanity is a shocking fact, much more so is moral insanity. I have referred to my first impressions at the sight of one who was intellectually insane, but a case of moral insanity should be considered far more distressing and astounding. Imagine the case of a great man such as Daniel Webster. If his brain becomes weak and he would

become insane, there is not a person in all the land who would not feel somber. What? Daniel Webster, that great man, insane! How have the mighty fallen! What a horrible sight!

How much more horrible it would be to see him become morally insane – to see a selfish heart run wild with the clear decisions of his gigantic intellect, to see his moral principles fading away before the demands of selfish ambition, to see such a man become a drunkard, immoral, and lazy – if this were to occur in someone such as Daniel Webster, how inexpressively shocking it would be! Intellectual insanity is not to be named in the comparison!

3. Although some sinners may be outwardly decent, and may seem to be agreeable in temper and character, yet every real sinner is actually insane. In view of all these serious matters of eternity, he insists on being controlled only by the things of time. With the powers of an angel, he does not try to rise above the low pursuits of a selfish heart. How must angels look upon such a case! Eternity is so vast, and its issues are so dreadful, yet this sinner drives furiously to hell as if he were on the high road to heaven! And all this only because he is obsessed with the pleasures of sin for a season.

At first glance, he seems to have really made the mistake of hell for heaven, but upon a closer examination, you see it is no real mistake of the intellect. He knows very well the difference between hell and heaven, but he is basically deceiving himself under the impulses of his mad heart! The mournful fact is that he loves sin, and that is what he will pursue! So very tragically, so insane, he rushes greedily on toward his own damnation just as if he were in pursuit of heaven!

We shudder at the thought that any of our friends might become insane, but this is not half as bad as to have one of them become wicked. It is better to have a whole family become insane than to have one of them become a hardened sinner. Indeed, the former compared with the latter is as nothing. The insane person will not always be so. When this mortal body is laid away in the grave, the soul may look out again in the free air of liberty as if it had never been confined in a dark prison, and the body, raised again, may blossom in eternal vigor and beauty; but sadly, moral insanity only grows worse and worse forever! The root of this is not in a diseased brain, but in a diseased heart and soul. Death cannot cure it. The resurrection will only raise him *to shame and everlasting contempt* (Daniel 12:2). The eternal world will only give free reign to his madness to rage on with increased vigor and wider reach forever.

Some people are more afraid of being called insane than of being called wicked. Surely they show the fatal delusion that is on their hearts. Intellectual insanity is only deserving of pity, but it is not disgraceful. Moral insanity, though, is unspeakably disgraceful. No one needs to be amazed that God would say that some will arise *to shame and everlasting contempt.*

Conversion to God is becoming morally sane. It consists in restoring the will and the affections to the just control of the intelligence, the reason, and the conscience so as to put the person once more in harmony with himself. All his abilities are adjusted to their true positions and proper functions.

> Intellectual insanity is only deserving of pity, but it is not disgraceful. Moral insanity, though, is unspeakably disgraceful.

Sometimes people who have become converted, but not well established in the truth, backslide into moral insanity – just as people sometimes relapse into intellectual insanity after being apparently quite restored. This is a sad situation, and it brings sorrow upon the hearts of friends. Yet in no case can it be so sad as a case of backsliding into moral insanity.

An intellectual asylum is a sorrowful place. How can a heart of any human feeling contemplate such a scene without intense grief? As you pass through the halls of this asylum, notice the traces of intellectual ruin. There is a noble-looking woman – completely insane. Over there is a man of splendid appearance and presence – all in ruins! How awful! If this is so, then what a dreadful place hell must be! These intellectual asylums are awful; how much more the moral asylum!

Suppose we go to a large city and visit its insane asylum. We go around to all its wards and study the case of each inmate. Then we will go to another asylum and another, visiting the asylums of several states. Would not this be a sorrowful scene? You would cry out long before we had finished, "Enough! Enough! How can I bear these sights of insane people? How can I endure to behold such desolation?"

Suppose, then, we go next to the great moral asylum of the universe

– the hell of lost souls. For if people will make themselves crazy, God must close them up in one vast asylum. Why should He not? The well-being of His empire demands that all the moral insanity of His kingdom should be withdrawn from the society of the holy, and should be closed up alone and apart. There are those whose intellects are right but whose hearts are all wrong. What a place must that be in which to spend one's eternity! The great asylum of the universe!

Sometimes sinners here, aware of their own insanity, get glimpses of this fearful state. I recall that I once had this idea that Christians are the only people who can claim to be rational, and then I asked myself, "Why should I act the way I do? Would it hurt me to obey God? Would it ruin my peace or damage my prospects for either this life or the next? Why do I go on in this way?"

I said to myself, "I can give no reason for it except that I am mad. All that I can say is that my heart is set on iniquity, and it will not turn."

Alas, poor maniac! Not unfortunate, but wicked! How many of you know that this is your actual situation? Oh, young man, did your father think you were sane when he sent you to a university? You might have been intellectually sane, but not morally. Your moral nature and functions were all completely deranged. My dear young friend, does your own moral course commend itself to your conscience and your reason? If not, what are you but a moral maniac? Young man, young woman, must you in truth write yourselves down as morally insane?

Finally, the subject shows the importance of not quenching the Spirit. This is God's instrument for the cure of moral maniacs. If you put out His light from your souls, there remains to you only the blackness of darkness forever (Jude 1:13)! A young man in Lane Seminary who was then dying in his sins said, "Why did you not tell me there is such a thing as eternal damnation? Why did not you tell me?"

"I did."

"Oh, I am going there! How can I die in this way? It is growing dark. Bring in a light!"

And so he passed away from this world of light and hope!

Oh, sinner, take care that you do not put out the light that God has cast into your dark heart. If you do, when you pass away it will grow dark to your soul at midday – the opening into the blackness of darkness forever.

# Chapter 10

# Conditions of Being Saved

What must I do to be saved?

—Acts 16:30

I bring forward this subject today not because it is new to many who are reading this, but because it is greatly needed. I am happy to know that the great question of our text is beginning to be deeply and extensively asked in this community, and under these circumstances it is the first duty of a Christian pastor to answer it fully and plainly.

The circumstances that gave occasion to the words of the text were these. Paul and Silas had gone to Philippi to preach the gospel. Their preaching stirred up much opposition and outcry. They were arrested and thrown into prison, and the jailer was commanded to keep them safely. At midnight, Paul and Silas were praying and singing praises. God came down. The earth quaked and the prison was shaken. Its doors burst open, and the prisoners' chains fell off. The jailer jumped up afraid. Supposing that his prisoners had fled, he was about to take his own life when Paul cried out, *Do thyself no harm: for we are all here* (Acts 16:28). The jailer then called for a light. He rushed in trembling, and he fell down before Paul and Silas. He then brought them out and said, *Sirs, what must I do to be saved?*

This is briefly the context of our text. I will develop it now by showing what sinners must not do to be saved and what they must do to be saved.

# I. What sinners must not do to be saved

It has now come to be necessary and very important to tell people what they must *not* do in order to be saved. When the gospel was first preached, it seems Satan had not introduced as many delusions to mislead people as he has now. It was then enough to give, as Paul did, the simple and direct answer, telling people only what they must at once do. This does not seem to be enough now, though. So many delusions and corruptions have confused and darkened the minds of men that they often need a great deal of instruction to lead them back to those simple views of the subject that prevailed at first. This is why it is important to show sinners what they must not do if they intend to be saved.

**1. You must not imagine that you have nothing to do.** In Paul's time, nobody seems to have thought of this. The doctrine of Universalism was not much developed then. People had not begun to dream that they could be saved without doing anything. They had not learned that sinners have nothing to do to be saved. If this idea, so current of late, had been popular at Philippi, the question of our text would not have been asked. No trembling sinner would have cried out, *What must I do to be saved?*

If people imagine that they have nothing to do, they are never likely to be saved. It is not in the nature of falsehood and lies to save people's souls, and certainly nothing is more false than this idea. People know they have something to do to be saved. Why, then, do they pretend that all people will be saved whether they do their duty or whether they constantly refuse to do it? The very idea is absurd, and it is supported only by the most evident insult upon common sense and an enlightened conscience.

**2. You should not mistake what you have to do.** The duty required of sinners is very simple, and it would be easily understood if it were not for the false ideas that prevail as to what true religion is and as to the exact things that God requires as conditions of salvation. False opinions prevail on these points to a most alarming extent. Because of this, there is much danger of mistake. Beware that you are not deceived in a matter of such importance.

**3. Do not say or imagine that you cannot do what God requires.** On the contrary, always assume that you can. If you assume that you cannot, this very assumption will be fatal to your salvation.

**4. Do not procrastinate.** If you ever intend or hope to be saved, you must set your face like a flint against this most damaging delusion. Probably no other method of evading one's present duty has ever prevailed as extensively as this, or has destroyed so many souls. Almost all people in gospel lands intend to prepare for death. They intend to repent and become religious before they die. Even Universalists expect to become religious at some time – maybe after death, or maybe after being purified from their sins by purgatorial fires – but somehow they expect to become holy, for they know that they must do so before they can see God and enjoy His presence.

You will notice, though, that they put off this matter of becoming holy to the most distant time possible. Having a strong dislike to it now, they flatter themselves that God will take care of this properly in the next world, no matter how much they oppose His efforts to do so in this world. As long as it remains in their power to choose whether to become holy or not, they use the time to enjoy sin, leaving it up to God to make them holy in the next world – if they can't prevent it there! Consistency is a jewel!

All those who put off being religious now in the fond hope of becoming so in some future time, whether in this world or the next, are acting out this same inconsistency. You fondly hope that what you are striving now to prevent will occur.

In this way, sinners by multitudes press their way down to hell under this delusion. They often, when confronted with the claims of God, will even name the time when they will repent. It may be very near – maybe as soon as they get home from the meeting or as soon as the sermon is over – or it may be much later, as for example, when they have finished their education, or have become settled in life, or have made a little more money, or after they abandon some business of questionable morality; but no matter whether the set time is near or far away, the delusion is fatal. The thought of procrastination is murder to the soul.

Such sinners are not very aware that Satan himself has poured out his spirit upon them and is leading them wherever he desires. He does not care whether they put God off for a longer time or a shorter time. If he can persuade them to a long delay, he likes it well; if only to a short one, he feels quite sure he can renew the delay and get another extension – so it serves his purpose fully in the end.

Now observe, sinner, that if you ever want to be saved, you must resist and grieve away this spirit of Satan. You must cease to procrastinate. You can never be converted as long as you operate only in the way of delaying and promising yourself that you will seek God at some future time. Did you ever accomplish anything in your worldly business by procrastination? Did procrastination ever begin, perform, and accomplish any important business?

Suppose you have some business of much consequence that involves your character, your possessions, or your life, to be transacted in a certain city, but you do not know exactly how soon it must be done. It may be done with safety now, and with greater ease and success now than it ever can be later, but it might possibly still be done even though you would delay a little time. However, every moment's delay involves an absolute uncertainty of your being able to do it at all. You do not know if even a single hour's delay will make you too late.

In these circumstances, what would a person of sense and discretion do? Would he not be awake and get ready in an instant? Would he continue to sleep when a matter of such importance is at stake, involved in such risks and uncertainties? No. You know that the risk of a thousand dollars, depending on such conditions, would stir the warm blood of any man of business, and you could not tempt him to delay an hour. "Oh," he would say, "this is the important business to which I must attend, and everything else must be pushed aside."

Suppose he would act as a sinner does about repentance, and promise himself that tomorrow will be as this day and will be much more abundant, and so would do nothing today, or tomorrow, or the next month, or the next year; would you not think that he is out of his mind? Would you expect his business to be done, his money to be secured, and his interests to be furthered by his delay?

In the same way, the sinner accomplishes nothing but his own ruin as long as he procrastinates. Until he says, "The time is now. I will do all my duty today," he is only playing the fool and laying up his wages accordingly. It is infinite madness to defer a matter of such great importance and of such perilous uncertainty!

**5. If you want to be saved, you must not wait for God to do what He commands you to do.** God will certainly do all that He can for your salvation. All that the nature of the case allows for Him to do, He either has done or stands ready to do as soon as your position and course will allow Him to do it. Long before you were born, He anticipated your needs as a sinner, and He began on the most generous scale to make provision for them. He gave His Son to die for you, doing all that needed to be done by way of an atonement. Long ago, He began shaping His providence so as to give you the needed knowledge of duty – He has sent you His Word and Spirit.

Indeed, He has given you the highest possible evidence that He will be active and prompt on His part, as one who is in earnest for your salvation. You know this. What sinner fears that God would be negligent on His part in the matter of His salvation? Not one. Many of you are even annoyed that God would urge you so earnestly and would be so energetic in the work of securing your salvation. Can you now quiet your conscience with the excuse of waiting for God to do your duty?

> There are things for you to do that God cannot do for you.

The fact is that there are things for you to do that God cannot do for you. Those things that He has ordered and revealed as the conditions of your salvation, He cannot and will not do Himself. If He could have done them Himself, He would not have asked you to do them. Every sinner should consider this. God requires repentance and faith of you because it is naturally impossible that anyone else except you should do them. They are your own personal matters – the voluntary exercises of your own mind – and no other being in heaven, earth, or hell can do these things for you in your place. As far as substitution was naturally possible, God has introduced it, as in the case of the atonement. He has never hesitated to march up to meet and to bear all the self-denials that the work of salvation has involved.

**6. If you intend to be saved, you must not wait for God to do anything whatsoever.** There is nothing to be waited for. God has either done all on His part already, or if anything more remains, He is ready and waiting this moment for you to do your duty so that He may impart all necessary grace.

**7. Do not flee to any refuge of lies.** Lies cannot save you. It is truth, not lies, that alone can save. I have often wondered how people could think that Universalism, or any other lie, could save anyone.

People must be sanctified by the truth. There is no plainer teaching in the Bible than this, and no Bible doctrine is better sustained by reason and the nature of the case. Does Universalism sanctify anybody? Universalists say you must be punished for your sins, and that they will be put away because of this – as if the fires of purgatory would thoroughly consume all sin and bring out the sinner pure. Is this being sanctified by the truth? You might as well hope to be saved by eating liquid fire! You might as well expect fire to purify your soul from sin in this world as in the next! Why not?

It is amazing that people would hope to be sanctified and saved by this great error, or indeed by any error whatsoever. God says you must be sanctified by the truth (John 17:17). Even if you could believe this delusion, would it make you holy? Do you believe that it would make you humble, heavenly minded, sin-hating, and benevolent? Can you believe any such thing? Be assured that Satan is only the father of lies (John 8:44), and he cannot save you. In fact, he would not save you even if he could. His lies are not intended to save you, but to destroy your very soul, and nothing could be more adapted to its purpose. Lies are only the natural poison of the soul. You take them at your peril!

**8. Don't seek for any self-indulgent method of salvation.** The great effort among sinners has always been to be saved in some way of self-indulgence. They are slow to admit that self-denial is indispensable and that total, unqualified self-denial is the condition of being saved. I warn you against supposing that you can be saved in some easy, self-pleasing way. People should know, and always assume, that it is naturally imperative for selfishness to be completely put away and its demands resisted and put down.

I often ask, "Does the system of salvation that I preach so well harmonize with the intuitions of my reason that I know from within myself that this gospel is the thing I need? Does it in all its parts and relations meet the demands of my intelligence? Are its demands obviously just and right? Do its specified conditions of salvation obviously satisfy man's moral position before God and his moral relations to the government of God?"

To these and similar questions, I am constrained to answer in the affirmative. The longer I live, the more fully I see that the gospel system is the only one that can both meet the demands of the human intelligence and supply the needs of man's sinning, depraved heart. The duties required of the sinner are just those things that I know must in the nature of the case be the conditions of salvation. Why, then, should any sinner think of being saved on any other conditions? Why desire it even if it were possible?

**9. Don't imagine that you will ever have a more favorable time.**
Unrepentant sinners are inclined to think that right now is by no means as convenient a time as may be expected later, so they put it off in hope of a better time. They think that they might later have more conviction, fewer obstacles, and fewer hindrances.

That is what Felix thought. He did not intend to neglect salvation any more than you do, but he was very busy just then. He had certain matters to be handled that seemed especially urgent, and so he asked to be excused on the promise of very faithful attention to the subject at the expected convenient season. But did the convenient season ever come? Never. Nor does it ever come to those who in a similar manner resist God's solemn call and grieve away His Spirit. Thousands are now waiting in the agonies of hell who said just as Felix did: *Go thy way for this time; when I have a convenient season, I will call for thee* (Acts 24:25).

Oh, sinner, when will your convenient season come? Are you aware that no time will ever be "convenient" for you unless God calls your attention earnestly and solemnly to the subject? Can you expect Him to do this at the time of your choice, when you disregard His call at the time of His choice? Have you not heard Him say what is written in His Word about this?

> Because I have called, and ye refused; I have stretched out
> my hand, and no man regarded; but ye have set at nought
> all my counsel, and would none of my reproof; I also will
> laugh at your calamity; I will mock when your fear cometh.
> When your fear cometh as desolation, and your destruc-
> tion cometh as a whirlwind, when distress and anguish
> cometh upon you; then shall they call upon me, but I will
> not answer; they shall seek me early, but they shall not find
> me. (Proverbs 1:24-28)

Oh, sinner, that will be a fearful and a final fate, and the innumerable voices of God's universe will say, "Amen!"

**10. Do not suppose that you will find another time as good, and one in which you can just as well repent, as now.** Many people are ready to suppose that although there may not be a better time for themselves, there will at least be one just as good. That is a vain delusion! Sinner, you already owe ten thousand talents (Matthew 18:24), and will you find it just as easy to be forgiven of this debt while you are showing that you don't care how much and how long you add to it? In a case like this, where everything depends upon your securing the goodwill of your creditor, do you hope to gain His goodwill by positively insult-ing Him to His face?

Take another view of the case. You know that your heart must one day give up sin, or you are forever damned. You know also that each successive sin increases the hardness of your heart and makes it a more difficult matter to repent. How, then, can you reasonably hope that a future time will be equally favorable for your repentance? When you have hardened your neck like an iron muscle, and made your heart like an immovable stone, can you hope that repentance will still be as easy to you as ever?

You know, sinner, that God requires you to leave your sins now, but you look up into His face and say to Him, "Lord, it is just as good if I stop wronging You at some future convenient time. Lord, if I can only be saved later, I will think it is all to my benefit to go on insulting and wronging You as long as I possibly can. Since You are so very compassionate and patient, I think I may still continue on in sin and rebellion against You for many more months and years. Lord, don't hurry me. Let me have my way. Let me offend You, if You please, and spit in Your face. All will be just as well if I only repent in time so as to be saved in the end. I know indeed that You are pleading with me to repent now, but I much prefer to wait longer, and it will be just as good to repent at some later time."

> You know, sinner, that God requires you to leave your sins now.

Do you suppose that God will approve of this – that He will say, "You are right, sinner. I set my seal of approval upon your plan. It is good that you take such proper views of your duty to your Maker and your Father. Proceed as planned. Your course of action will ensure your salvation"? Do you expect such a response from God as this?

**11. If you ever expect to be saved, do not wait to see what others will do or say.** I was recently astounded to find that a young lady here under conviction of sin was greatly bothered about what a beloved brother would think of her if she would give her heart to God. She knew what she needed to do, but he was unrepentant, and she did not know what he would think if she would repent now.

It amounts to this. She would come before God and say, "O great God, I know I should repent, but I can't because I don't know if my brother will like it. I know that he, too, is a sinner and must repent or lose his soul, but I am much more afraid of his displeasure than I am of Yours, and I care more for his approval than I do for Yours. Because of this, I dare not repent until he does!" How shocking this is! It is strange that on such a subject, people will always ask, "What will others say about me?" Are you answerable to God? What, then, do others have to say about your duty to Him? God requires you and them also to repent, so why don't you do it at once?

Not long ago, as I was preaching abroad, one of the leading men of the city came to the meeting for those seeking God, apparently much convicted and in great distress for his soul. But being a man of high political standing, and supposing himself to be very dependent upon his friends, he insisted that he must consult them and have a regard for their feelings in this matter. I could not possibly convince him otherwise, although I spent three hours in the effort. He seemed almost ready to repent. I thought he certainly would, but he slipped away, relapsed by a perpetual backsliding. I expect he will be found at last among the lost in the lake of fire. Would you not expect such a result if he tore himself away under such an excuse as that?

Oh, sinner, you must not care what others say of you. Let them say what they please. Remember, the question is between your own soul and God. *If thou be wise, thou shalt be wise for thyself: but if thou scornest, thou alone shalt bear it* (Proverbs 9:12). You must die for yourself, and you must appear before God in judgment for yourself!

Go, young woman, and ask your brother, "Can you answer for me when I come to the judgment? Can you pledge yourself that you can stand in my place and answer for me there?" Until you have reason to believe that he can, it is wise for you to disregard his opinions if they stand at all in your way. If anyone steps in and offers any objection to your immediate repentance, do not fail to ask him, "Can you shield my soul in the judgment? If I can be assured that you can and will, I will make you my savior; but if not, then I must attend to my own salvation and leave you to attend to yours."

I will never forget the scene that occurred while my own mind was pondering this important point. Seeking a secluded place for prayer, I went into a deep grove, found a perfectly secluded spot behind some large logs, and knelt down. All of a sudden, a leaf rustled and I jumped up. I thought that somebody must be coming and I would be seen praying there. I had not been aware that I cared about what others said about me, but looking back upon my exercises of mind there, I could see that I did care infinitely too much what others thought of me.

Closing my eyes again for prayer, I heard a rustling leaf again, and then the thought came over me like a wave of the sea: "I am ashamed of confessing my sin!" I thought, "What! Ashamed of being found speaking with God!" Oh, how ashamed I felt of this shame! I can never describe the strong and overpowering impression that this thought made on my mind. I cried aloud at the very top of my voice, for I felt that even if all the people on earth and all the devils in hell were present to hear and see me, I would not retreat and would not cease to cry unto God, for what does it matter to me if others see me seeking the face of my God and Savior? I am hastening to the judgment. I will not be ashamed to have the Judge as my friend there. I will not be ashamed there to have sought His face and His pardon here. There will be no turning away from the gaze of the universe.

If sinners at the judgment could get away, how gladly they would, but they cannot! Nor can they stand there in each other's places to answer for each other's sins. That young woman, can she then say, "Oh, my brother, you must answer for me, for I rejected Christ and lost my soul to please you"? That brother is himself a guilty rebel, cursed, anguished, and trembling before the fearsome Judge, and how can he assist you in such a dreadful hour? Do not fear his displeasure now, but rather warn him while you can to escape for his life before the wrath of the Lord grows fierce against him, and there is no remedy (2 Chronicles 36:16).

**12. If you would be saved, you must not entertain animosity against God, His ministers, Christians, or against anything Christian.** There are some people of a particular temperament who are much in danger of losing their souls because they are tempted to strong prejudices. Once committed either in favor of or against any persons or things, they are exceedingly inclined to become so rigid as never more to be really honest. When these people or things in regard to which they become committed are so connected with Christianity that their prejudices stand aligned against their fulfilling the great conditions of salvation, the effect can be nothing else than disastrous. It is naturally imperative to salvation that you should be entirely honest. Your soul must act before God in the open sincerity of truth, or you cannot be converted.

I have known people in revivals to remain under great conviction for a long time without submitting themselves to God. By careful inquiry, I have found them completely hedged in by their prejudices, and yet so blind to this fact that they would not admit that they had any prejudice at all. In my observation of convicted sinners, I have found this to be among the most common obstacles in the way of the salvation of souls. People become committed against Christianity, and remaining in this state, it is naturally impossible that they would repent. God will not indulge your prejudices or lower His prescribed conditions of salvation to accommodate your feelings.

You must give up all hostile feelings in cases where you have really been hurt. Sometimes I have seen people evidently shut out from the kingdom of heaven because, having been really hurt, they would not forgive and forget, but maintained such a spirit of resistance and revenge that they could not in the nature of the case repent of the sin toward God, nor could God forgive them. Of course, they lost heaven. I have heard people say, "I cannot forgive. I will not forgive. I have been hurt, and I will never forgive that wrong." Notice that you must not hold on to such feelings; if you do, you cannot be saved.

Also, you must not allow yourself to fall because of the prejudices of others. I have often been struck with the state of things in families in which the parents or older members of the family had prejudices against the minister, and I have wondered why those parents were not more wise than to lay stumbling blocks before their children to ruin their souls. This is often the true reason why children are not converted. Their minds are turned against the gospel by being turned against those from whom they hear it preached. I would rather have people come into my family and curse and swear before my children than to have them speak against those who preach the true gospel to them. Therefore, I say to all parents, be careful what you say if you do not want to shut the gate of heaven against your children!

For another thing, do not allow yourself to take some inflexible position, and then allow the stand you have taken to prevent you from doing any obvious duty. People sometimes allow themselves to be committed against taking what is called "the anxious seat."[4] Consequently,

---

4   The anxious seat was a seat near the front of the building during preaching where people who were troubled in conscious or seeking peace with God would go in order to find spiritual counsel.

they refuse to go forward under circumstances when it is obviously proper that they should, and where their refusal to do so places them in an unfavorable mindset that could be fatal to their conversion. Let every sinner beware of this!

Do not hold on to anything about which you have any doubt of its lawfulness or uprightness. Cases often occur in which people are not fully satisfied that a certain thing is wrong, yet are not satisfied that it is right. In cases like this, it should not be enough to say, "Those Christians do so." You should have better reasons than this for your course of conduct. If you ever expect to be saved, you must abandon all practices that you even suspect to be wrong. This principle seems to be involved in the passage, *He that doubteth is damned if he eat, because he eateth not of faith; for whatsoever is not of faith is sin* (Romans 14:23). To do that which you are not certain is right is to allow yourself to tamper with the divine authority, and it cannot fail to break down in your mind that solemn fear of sinning that you must carefully cherish if you would ever be saved.

> It often happens that convicted sinners try to justify themselves for delaying their duty because some professing Christians are delaying theirs.

If you want to be saved, do not look at those who profess to be Christians and wait for them to become engaged as they should be in the great work of God. If they are not what they should be, let them alone. Let them bear their own dreadful responsibility. It often happens that convicted sinners compare themselves with professing Christians, and they try to justify themselves for delaying their duty because some professing Christians are delaying theirs. Sinners must not do this if they ever want to be saved. It is very probable that you will always find enough sinful people who claim to be Christians to stumble over into hell if you will allow yourself to do so.

On the other hand, many people who are professing Christians may not be nearly as bad as you suppose, and you must not be so critical as to put the worst constructions upon their conduct. You have other work to do than this. Let them stand or fall to their own master (Romans 14:4). Unless you abandon the practice of looking for flaws in the conduct of professing Christians, it is utterly impossible that you would be saved.

Do not depend upon professing Christians – on their prayers or influence in any way. I have known children to depend a long time upon the prayers of their parents, putting those prayers in the place of Jesus Christ, or at least in the place of their own present efforts to do their duty. This approach pleases Satan entirely. He would ask nothing more to make sure of you. Therefore, do not depend on any prayers – not even those of the holiest Christians on earth. The matter of your conversion lies between you and God alone, as truly as if you were the only sinner in all the world, or as if there were no other beings in the universe except you and your God.

Do not seek for any apology or excuse whatsoever. I dwell upon this and emphasize it because I so often find people resting on some excuse without being aware of it. In conversation with them about their spiritual condition, I see this and point out that they are resting on a certain excuse. "Am I?" they say. "I did not know it."

Do not look for stumbling blocks. Sinners, sometimes a little uneasy in their ignorance, begin to look around for stumbling blocks for self-vindication. All at once they become wide awake to the faults of professing Christians, as if they had to bear the care of all the churches. The real fact is that they are all busy trying to find something to which they can take offense to so that they can thereby blunt the sharp edge of truth upon their own consciences. This never helps along their own salvation.

> **Do not presume that you may continue any longer in your sins and still find the gate of mercy.**

Do not tempt the patience and kindness of God. If you do, you are in the utmost danger of being abandoned forever. Do not presume that you may continue any longer in your sins and still find the gate of mercy. This presumption has paved the way for the destruction of many souls.

Do not despair of salvation and settle down in unbelief, saying, "There is no mercy for me." You must not despair in any such sense as to shut yourself out from the kingdom of God. You may well despair of being saved without Christ and without repentance, but you are obligated to believe the gospel. To do this is to believe the glad tidings that Jesus Christ has come to save sinners, even the worst, and that *him that cometh to Him He will in no wise cast out* (John 6:37). You have no right to doubt this and act as if there were no truth in it.

You must not wait for more conviction. Why do you need any more?

You know your sin and you know your present duty. Nothing can be more ridiculous, therefore, than to wait for more conviction. If you did not know that you are a sinner, or that you are guilty of sin, there might be some appropriateness in seeking for conviction of the truth on these points.

Do not wait for more or for different feelings. Sinners are often saying, "I must feel differently before I can come to Christ," or "I must have more feeling," as if this were the great thing that God requires of them. They are completely mistaken in this.

Do not wait to be better prepared. While you wait, you are growing worse and worse, and you are quickly rendering your salvation impossible.

Don't wait for God to change your heart. Why would you wait for Him to do what He has commanded you to do and waits for you to do in obedience to His command?

Don't try to recommend yourself to God by prayers or tears or by anything else whatsoever. Do you think that your prayers place God under any obligation to forgive you? Suppose you owed someone a million dollars, and you would go a hundred times a week and beg him to cancel this debt. Then you would enter your prayers in your ledger as payment to him. Suppose you should pursue this course until you had canceled the debt according to the records in your ledger. Could you hope to prove anything by this course except that you were insane? Yet sinners seem to think that their many prayers and tears place the Lord under real obligation to them to forgive them.

Never rely on anything else whatsoever other than Jesus Christ and Him crucified (1 Corinthians 2:2). It is ridiculous for you to hope, as many do, to make some payment by your own sufferings. In my early experience, I did not think that I could be converted at once, but must be burdened for a long time. I said to myself, "God will not have compassion on me until I feel worse than I do now. I cannot expect Him to forgive me until I feel a greater agony of soul than this." Even if I could have gone on increasing my sufferings until they equaled the miseries of hell, it could not have changed God. The fact is that God does not ask you to suffer. Your sufferings cannot in the nature of the case avail for atonement. Why, therefore, would you attempt to throw aside the system of God's providing, and bring in one of your own?

There is another view of the case. God demands for you to bow your stubborn will to Him. This is just like the case of a child in the attitude of disobedience who is required to submit who starts crying and groaning and showing expressions of agony, and might even afflict himself in hope of moving the compassion of his father, but all the time refuses to submit to parental authority. He would be very glad to put his own sufferings in the place of the submission demanded. This is what the sinner is doing. He would gladly put his own sufferings in the place of submission to God and move the compassion of the Lord so much that He would back away from the hard condition of repentance and submission.

If you want to be saved, you must not listen at all to those who pity you and who indirectly take your side against God and try to make you think you are not as bad as you are. I once knew a woman who after a long season of distressing conviction fell into great despair. Her health sank, and she seemed about to die. All this time she found no relief, but only seemed to grow worse and worse, sinking down in grim and terrible despair. Instead of dealing plainly and faithfully with her and searching her guilty heart to the bottom, her friends had taken the course of pitying her, and they almost complained that the Lord would not have compassion on the poor, agonized, dying woman.

Eventually, as she seemed in the last stages of life, being so weak as to hardly be able to speak in a low voice, a minister who better understood how to deal with convicted sinners happened to stop by. The woman's friends cautioned him to deal very carefully with her since she was in a dreadful condition and was greatly to be pitied, but he judged it best to deal with her very faithfully. As he approached her bedside, she raised her faint voice and begged for a little water. He said, "Unless you repent, you will soon be where there is not a drop of water to cool your tongue."

"Oh," she cried, "must I go down to hell?"

"Yes, you must, and you will do so soon unless you repent and submit to God. Why don't you repent and submit immediately?"

"Oh," she replied, "it is a dreadful thing to go to hell!"

"Yes, and for that very reason, God has provided an atonement through Jesus Christ – but you won't accept it. He brings the cup of salvation to your lips, and you push it away. Why will you do this? Why will you persist in being an enemy of God and reject His offered salvation when you could become His friend and have salvation if you wanted to?"

This was the manner of their conversation, and its result was that the woman saw her sin and her duty, and turning to the Lord, she found pardon and peace.

Therefore, I say that if your conscience convicts you of sin, do not let anybody take your side against God. Your wound does not need a bandage, but a surgical probe. Do not fear the probe; it is the only thing that can save you. Do not seek to hide your sin or veil your eyes from seeing it. Do not be afraid to know the worst, for you must know the very worst, and the sooner you know it, the better. I warn you not to look for some physician to give you a drug to make you feel at ease, for you don't need it. Shun, as you would shun death itself, all those who would speak smooth things to you and would prophesy that which is not true. They would surely ruin your soul.

> Christianity never interferes with any real duty.

Do not suppose that becoming a Christian will interfere with any of the necessary or appropriate duties of life, or with anything whatsoever to which you should attend. Christianity never interferes with any real duty. So far is this from being the case, that a proper attention to your various duties is in fact indispensable to following Jesus. You cannot serve God without this.

Additionally, if you want to be saved, you must not attend to anything that would hinder you. It is infinitely important that your soul should be saved. No consideration thrown in your way should be allowed to have the weight of even a straw or a feather. Jesus Christ has illustrated and applied this by several parables, especially in the one that compares the kingdom of heaven to *a merchant man seeking goodly pearls, who, when he had found one pearl of great price, went and sold all that he had and bought it* (Matthew 13:45-46). In another parable, the kingdom of heaven is said to be like *treasure hid in a field, which, when a man hath found, he hideth, and for joy thereof goeth and selleth all that he hath, and buyeth that field* (Matthew 13:44). We see that God's Word strongly teaches us that we must be ready to make any sacrifice whatsoever that may be required of us in order to gain the kingdom of heaven.

You must not seek Christianity selfishly. You must not make your own salvation or happiness the primary goal. Beware, for if you make this your primary goal, you will get a false hope, and you will probably slide along down the pathway of the hypocrite into the deepest hell.

## II. What sinners must do to be saved

**1. You must understand what you have to do.** It is of the utmost importance that you clearly see this. You need to know that you must return to God, and you must understand what this means. The difficulty between yourself and God is that you have stolen yourself and have run away from His service. You rightfully belong to God. He created you for Himself, and therefore He has a perfectly righteous claim to the loyalty of your heart and the service of your life. But you, instead of living to meet His claims, have run away. You have deserted from God's service and have lived to please yourself. Now your duty is to return and give yourself to God.

> You have deserted from God's service and have lived to please yourself. Now your duty is to return and give yourself to God.

**2. You must return and confess your sins to God.** You must confess that you have been completely wrong and that God has been completely right. Go before the Lord and lay open the depth of your sin. Tell Him that you deserve just as much damnation as He has threatened.

These confessions are naturally indispensable to your being forgiven. In accordance with this, the Lord says, *If then their uncircumcised hearts be humbled, and they then accept of the punishment of their iniquity, then will I remember my covenant* (Leviticus 26:41-42). Then God can forgive. However, as long as you dispute this point and will not concede that God is right, or admit that you are wrong, He can never forgive you.

Moreover, you must confess to anyone if you have hurt them. Is it not a fact that you have hurt some, and likely many, of your fellow men? Have you not slandered your neighbor and said things that you have no right to say? Have you not in some instances, that you could call to mind if you tried, lied to them, or about them, or covered up or twisted the truth? Have you not been willing for others to have a false impression of you or of your conduct? If so, you must renounce all such iniquity, for *he that covereth his sins shall not prosper: but whoso confesseth and forsaketh them shall have mercy* (Proverbs 28:13).

Furthermore, not only must you confess your sins to God and to the people you have hurt, but you must also make restitution. You have not taken the position of a repentant sinner before God and man until you have done this. God cannot treat you as a repentant sinner until you have done so. I do not mean by this that God cannot forgive you until you have completed your purpose of restitution by finishing the outward act, for sometimes it may demand time, and in some cases it might not be possible to do. But the purpose must be sincere and thorough before you can be forgiven by God.

**3. You must renounce yourself.** In this is implied the following:

- You must renounce your own righteousness, forever abandoning the very idea of having any righteousness in yourself.

- You must forever let go of the idea of having done any good that could commend you to God, or ever be thought of as a reason for your justification.

- You must renounce your own will and be always ready to say not in word only, but in heart, *Thy will be done in earth, as it is in heaven* (Matthew 6:10). You must consent most wholeheartedly that God's will shall be your supreme law.

- You must renounce your own way and let God have His own way in everything. Never allow yourself to worry and be aggravated by anything whatsoever, for since God's arm extends to all events, you should recognize His hand in all things. Of course, to be troubled about anything at all is to be troubled against God, who has at least permitted that thing to occur as it does. As long, therefore, as you allow yourself to worry, you are not right with God. You must become before God as a little child, subdued and trustful at His feet. Whether the weather is fair or foul, agree that God should have His way. Whether all things go well with you, or poorly (as people see it), yet let God do His will, and let it be your part to submit in perfect submission. Until you take this position, you cannot be saved.

**4. You must come to Christ.** You must accept of Christ truly and completely as your Savior. Renouncing all thought of depending on anything you have done or can do, you must accept of Christ as your atoning sacrifice and as your ever-living Mediator before God. Without the least restriction or reserve, you must place yourself under His wing as your Savior.

**5. You must seek primarily to please Christ, and not yourself.** It is naturally impossible that you would be saved until you enter this attitude of mind – until you are so well pleased with Christ in all respects as to find your pleasure in doing His will. It is in the nature of things impossible that you could be happy in any other state of mind, or unhappy in this, for His will is infinitely good and right. When, therefore, His will becomes your delight, and your will harmonizes entirely with His, then you will be happy for the same reason that He is happy, and you cannot fail to be happy any more than Jesus Christ can. Becoming supremely happy in God's will is essentially the idea of salvation. In this state of mind, you are saved. Out of it, you cannot be.

It has often struck my mind with great force that many who profess to be Christian are severely and completely mistaken on this point. Their real feeling is that Christ's service is an iron collar, an unbearably hard yoke. Therefore, they labor exceedingly to throw off some of this burden. They try to make it seem that Christ does not require much, if any, self-denial, or much, if any, deviation from the course of worldliness and sin. Oh, if they could only get the standard of Christian duty quite down to a level with the ways and customs of this world! How much easier, then, they think, it would be to live a Christian life and wear Christ's yoke!

In their view, taking Christ's yoke as it really is becomes an iron collar. Doing the will of Christ instead of their own is a hard business. If doing Christ's will is true religion (and who can doubt it?), then in their mind, even a little of it will cause them to be very miserable.

Let me ask those who groan under the idea that they must be religious – who consider it extremely difficult, but they must do so – how much religion of this kind would it take to make hell? Surely not much! When it gives you no joy to do God's will, yet you are confined to doing His will as the only way to be saved, and are thereby perpetually forced into doing what you hate as the only means of escaping hell, would not this be itself a hell? Can you not see that in this state of mind you are not, and cannot be, saved?

To be saved, you must come into a state of mind in which you will ask no greater joy than to do God's will. This alone will be forever enough to fill your cup to overflowing.

**6. You must have complete trust in Christ, or you cannot be saved.** You must absolutely believe in Him. You must believe all His words of promise. They were given to you to be believed, and unless you believe them, they can do you no good at all. Not only will the promises not help you if you do not exercise faith in them, but they will only increase your sin of unbelief.

> You must have complete trust in Christ, or you cannot be saved.

God wants to be believed when He speaks in love to lost sinners. He gave them these *exceeding great and precious promises*, that they by faith in them might *escape the corruption that is in the world through lust* (2 Peter 1:4). But thousands of people who profess the Christian religion do not know how to use these promises, and as to them or any profitable use they make, the promises might as well have been written on the sands of the sea.

Sinners, too, will go down to hell in endless multitudes unless they believe and take hold of God by faith in His promise. His awful wrath is out against them! He says, "I will go through them and will burn them up together; or let them take hold of My strength, that they may make peace with Me, and they will make peace with Me. Let him stir himself up and take hold of My arm, which is strong to save, and then he may make peace with Me." Do you ask how to take hold? By faith. Yes, by faith. Believe His words and take hold. Take hold of His strong arm and swing right out over hell, and don't be afraid any more than if there were no hell.

But you say, "I do believe, and yet I am not saved." No, you don't believe.

A woman said to me, "I believe – I know I do, and yet here I am in my sins."

"No," I said, "you don't. Do you have as much confidence in God as you would have in me if I had promised you a dollar? Do you ever pray to God? If so, do you come with the same confidence that you would have if you came to me to ask for a promised dollar? Until you have as much faith in God as this, and more – until you have more confidence in God than you would have in ten thousand people, your faith does not honor God, and you cannot hope to please Him. You must say, *Let God be true, though every man be a liar* (Romans 3:4).

**You must no longer think to own yourself.**

But you say, "I am a sinner, and how can I believe?" I know you are a sinner, and so are all people to whom God has given these promises.

You say, "But I am a great sinner!" Well, *It is a faithful saying and worthy of all acceptation, that Jesus Christ came into the world to save sinners, of whom I am chief,* Paul said (1 Timothy 1:15). So you do not need to despair.

**7. You must forsake all that you have, or you cannot be Christ's disciple.** There must be absolute and total self-denial. I do not mean by this that you are never to eat again, or never again to clothe yourself, or never again to enjoy the society of your friends, but that you should cease entirely from using any of these enjoyments selfishly. You must no longer think to own yourself, including your time, your possessions, or anything you have ever called your own. You must consider all these things as God's, and not yours. You are to forsake all that you have in the sense of laying all upon God's altar to be devoted supremely and only to His service.

When you come back to God for pardon and salvation, lay all that you have at His feet. Come with your body, to offer it as a living sacrifice upon His altar. Come with your soul and all its powers, and yield them in willing consecration to your God and Savior. Come, bring them all along. Bring everything – body, soul, intellect, thought, possessions – all, without reserve. Do you ask if you must bring them all? Yes, all – absolutely all. Do not keep back anything. Don't sin against your own soul like Ananias and Sapphira by keeping back a part (Acts 5:1-11), but renounce your own claim to everything and recognize God's right to all.

Say, "Lord, these things are not mine. I had stolen them, but they were never mine. They were always Yours. I will have them no longer. Lord, these things are all Yours, now and forever. Now, Lord, what is Your will for me? I have no business of my own to do. I am entirely Yours to do Your will. What work do You have for me to do?"

In this spirit, you must renounce the world, the flesh, and Satan. Your fellowship is from now on to be with Christ, and not with those objects. You are to live for Christ and not for the world, the flesh, or the devil.

**8. You must believe the record that God has given of His Son.** He who does not believe does not receive the record. He does not affirm that God is true. *This is the record, that God has given to us eternal life, and this life is in his Son* (1 John 5:11). The condition of your having it is that you believe the record, and of course that you act accordingly.

Suppose there is a poor man living next door to you, and he gets a letter in the mail stating that a rich man has died and has left him $1,000,000, and the cashier of a neighboring bank tells him that he has received the amount on deposit for him, and they are holding it for him at the bank until he lets them know what he wants them to do with it. The poor man says, "I can't believe the record. I can't believe there ever was any such rich man. I can't believe there is $1,000,000 for me." Therefore, he must live and die as poor as Lazarus because he won't believe the record.

Notice that this is just how it is with the unbelieving sinner. God has given you eternal life, and it waits for you, but you don't get it because you will not believe, and therefore you will not accept into your possession what is there for you.

Maybe you say that you must have some feeling before you can believe, that you cannot believe until you have the feeling. The poor man might say the same thing. "How can I believe that the $1,000,000 is mine? I do not have even a penny of it now. I am as poor as ever."

Yes, you are poor because you will not believe. If you would believe, you could go and buy out every store in this county. Still you cry, "I am as poor as ever. I can't believe it. See my poor worn clothes. I was never more ragged in my life. I do not have even a fragment of the feeling and comforts of a rich man." In the same way, the sinner says that he cannot believe until he gets the inward experience! He must wait to have some of the feeling of a saved sinner before he can believe the record and take hold of the salvation! That is ridiculous enough! This is similar to the poor man who must wait to get his new clothes and fine house before he can believe the account and withdraw his money. Of course, he dooms himself to everlasting poverty, even though mountains of gold were all his own.

Sinner, you must understand this. Why should you be lost when eternal life is bought and offered to you by the last will and testament of the Lord Jesus Christ? Will you not believe the record and withdraw what is waiting for you at once? For mercy's sake, understand this and do not lose heaven by your own foolishness!

I must conclude by saying that if you want to be saved, you must accept a prepared salvation – one that is already prepared, complete, and present. You must be willing to give up all your sins and to be saved from them all – now and from now on! Until you consent to this, you cannot be saved at all. Many people would be willing to be saved in heaven if they could hold on to some sins while on earth – or rather, they think that they would like heaven on such terms. The fact is, though, that they would dislike a pure heart and a holy life in heaven just as much as they do on earth. They entirely deceive themselves in thinking that they are ready or even willing to go to such a heaven as the one that God has prepared for His people. There can be no heaven except for those who accept a salvation from all sin in this world. They must take the gospel as a system that allows no compromise with sin, that aspires to full deliverance from sin even now, and makes provision accordingly. Any other gospel is not the true one, and to accept of

Christ's gospel in any other sense is not to accept it at all. Its first and last condition is an affirmed and eternal renunciation of all sin.

## Remarks

1. Paul did not give the same answer to this question that a consistent Universalist would give. The latter would say, "You are to be saved by being first punished according to your sin. All people must expect to be punished all that their sins deserve." But Paul did not answer in this way. He would have been a miserable comforter if he had said, "You must all be punished according to the letter of the law you have broken." This could hardly have been called good news.

Nor did Paul give the Universalist's answer and say, "Do not concern yourself about this matter of being saved. All people are sure enough of being saved without any particular anxiety about it." No, for Paul understood and did not refrain from expressing the necessity of believing on the Lord Jesus Christ as the condition of being saved.

> The most terrible damnation will fall on the head of those who knew their duty, but who did not do it.

2. Take care that you do not sin willfully after having understood the truth concerning the way of salvation. Your danger of this is great and is precisely in proportion as you see your duty clearly. The most terrible damnation will fall on the head of those who knew their duty, but who did not do it. When, therefore, you are told plainly and truly what your duty is, be on your guard so that you do not let salvation slip out of your hands. It may never come as near your reach again.

3. Do not wait, even to go home, before you obey God. Make up your mind now, at once, to deal with the offers of salvation. Why not? Are they not most reasonable?

4. Let your mind act upon this great proposal. Embrace it just as you would any other important proposition. God lays the proposition before you. You hear it explained, and you understand it. The next and only remaining step is to embrace it with all your heart. Just as any other

great question (we may suppose it is a question of life or death) might come before a community, the case is fully stated, the conditions are explained, and then the argument is made. Will you consent? Will you agree to meet these conditions? Do you wholeheartedly embrace the proposition? Now all this would be understandable.

This is how it is in the case of the sinner. You understand the proposition. You know the conditions of salvation. You understand the contract into which you are to enter with your God and Savior. You agree to give your all to God, to lay yourself upon His altar to be used up there however He desires to use you. The only remaining question is: Will you consent to this at once? Will you consent to full and everlasting consecration with all your heart?

5. The jailer made no excuse. When he knew his duty, he yielded in a moment. Paul told him what to do, and he did it. He might possibly have heard something about Paul's preaching before this night, but probably not much – but now he hears for his life. How often have I been struck with this case! He was a sinful-minded heathen. He had heard, we must suppose, a great deal of negative talk about these apostles, but despite that, he went to them for truth. Hearing the truth, he is convinced, and being convinced, he surrenders at once. Paul uttered a single sentence, and the jailer received it and embraced it, and it was done.

Now, sinner, you know and admit all this truth, and yet as infinitely strange as it is, you will not in a moment believe and embrace it with all your heart. Will not Sodom and Gomorrah rise up against you in the judgment and condemn you? How could you bear to see that heathen jailer on that dreadful day and stand rebuked by his example there?

6. It is remarkable that Paul said nothing about the jailer needing any help in order to believe and repent. He did not even mention the work of the Spirit or allude to the jailer's need of it. It should be noticed, though, that Paul gave the jailer precisely those instructions that would most effectively secure the Spirit's aid and promote His action.

7. The jailer seems to have made no delay at all, waiting for no future or better time, but he surrendered and embraced the conditions as soon

as they were presented to him. No sooner was the proposition made than he seized upon it.

I was once preaching in a village in New York, and a lawyer sat before me who had been greatly offended by the gospel. That day, though, I noticed that he sat with fixed eye and open mouth, leaning forward as if he would seize each word as it came. I was explaining and simplifying the gospel, and when I stated just how the gospel was offered to people, he said to me afterward, "I snatched at it. I put out my hand, adapting the action to the thought, and I seized it – and it became mine."

This was how it was in my own situation while I was in the woods praying. After I had burst away from the fear of man and began to give room to the achings of my heart, this passage fell upon me: *Ye shall seek me, and find me, when ye shall search for me with all your heart* (Jeremiah 29:13). For the first time, I found that I believed a passage in the Bible. I had supposed that I had believed before, but surely never before as I did now. I said to myself, "This is the word of the everlasting God. My God, I take You at Your word. You say that I will find You when I search for You with all my heart, and now, Lord, I know that I do search for You with all my heart." True enough, I did find the Lord. Never in all my life was I more certain of anything than I was now that I had found the Lord.

This is the very idea of His promises. They were made to be believed, to be laid hold of as God's own words, and to be acted upon as if they actually meant just what they say. When God says, *Look unto me, and be ye saved* (Isaiah 45:22), He wants us to look unto Him as if He really had salvation in His hands to give, and also a heart to give it, for He does. The true spirit of faith is well expressed by the psalmist: *When thou saidst, Seek ye my face; my heart said unto thee, Thy face, LORD, will I seek* (Psalm 27:8). This is the way. Let your heart at once respond to the blessed words of invitation and of promise.

But you say that you are not a Christian. You never will be until you believe on the Lord Jesus Christ as your Savior. If you never become a Christian, the reason will be because you do not and will not believe the gospel and embrace it with all your heart.

The promises were made to be believed, and they belong to anyone who will believe them. They reach forth their precious words to all, and whoever will may take them as his own. Now will you believe that the Father has given you eternal life? This is the fact declared; will you believe it?

You have now been told what you must not do and what you must do to be saved. Are you prepared to act? Do you say, "I am ready to renounce my own desires, and from now on seek no other pleasure than to please God"? Can you forsake everything else for the sake of this?

Sinner, do you want to please God, or will you choose to please yourself? Are you willing now to please God and to begin by believing on the Lord Jesus Christ unto salvation? Will you be as simplehearted as the jailer was, and will you act as promptly?

Make your decision now. I do not want you to delay, or you might start talking about something else and let these words of life and this precious opportunity to grasp an offered salvation slip by you. Whom do you suppose I am now addressing? I am speaking to every unrepentant sinner. I call heaven and earth to record that I have set the gospel before you today (Deuteronomy 30:19). Will you take it? Is it not reasonable for you to decide at once? Are you ready now to say before high heaven and before those around you, "I will renounce myself and yield to God. I am the Lord's, and let all people and angels bear me witness that I am forevermore the Lord's"?

Sinner, the infinite God waits for your assent!

# Chapter 11

# The Sinner's Natural Power and Moral Weakness

Of whom a man is overcome, of the same is he brought in bondage.
—2 Peter 2:19

Now, I intend to discuss the moral condition of the sinner.

**I. The first important fact to be noted is that all people naturally have free will, and not any less so for being sinners.** By natural freedom, I do not mean that they have a right to do as they please, for this can by no means be true. Nor do I mean that they are free agents merely in the sense of being able to do as they will to do. In fact, people sometimes can and sometimes cannot accomplish their purposes of will. Be this as it may, however, moral liberty does not consist in the power to accomplish one's purposes.

You are aware that some old philosophers defined liberty of will as the power to do what you will to do. For many reasons, this cannot be the true idea of freedom of the will. Look at the department of doing that is embraced in muscular action. The simple fact is that some of our muscles are not under the control of the will at all, while others are under its control by a law of the sternest necessity. In regard to this latter class, all the freedom there is pertains to the will; none of it pertains to the action of the muscles controlled by the will.

It is, then, an absolute mistake to deny the location of freedom where it is, and to place it where it is not. If there is any such thing as necessity in the universe, it is found in the absolute control held by the will over those physical muscles that are placed under its control. The obedience of the muscles is absolute; it is not free or voluntary in any sense whatsoever. Therefore, it is absurd to place human freedom there.

This freedom is in the will itself, and it consists in its power of free choice. To do or not to do – this is its option. It has by its own nature the function of determining its own choices. The soul wills to do or not to do, and thus is a moral sovereign over its own activities. In this fact lies the foundation for moral activity. A being so constituted that he can will to do or not to do, and also has knowledge and appreciation of his moral obligations, is a moral agent. None other can be.

It deserves special notice here that every person knows that he has a conscience that tells him how he should act, as well as a moral power in the exercise of which he can either follow or resist its admonitions.

That a person is free in the sense of determining his own activities is proved by each person's own consciousness. This proof does not require any series of reasoning. It is as strong as it needs to be without any reasoning at all. A person is just as much aware and as well aware of originating his own acts as he is of acting at all. Does he really act himself? Yes. Does he know that he acts himself? Yes. How does he know these things? By consciousness. But he has the same evidence of being free, for this is equally proved by his own consciousness.

Even further, a person can distinguish between those acts in which he is free and those in which he is acted upon by influences independent of his own choice. He knows that in some things he is a recipient of influences and of actions exerted upon himself, while in other things he is not a recipient in the same sense, but is a voluntary actor. The fact of this distinction proves the possession of free agency.

The difference to which I now refer is one of everyday consciousness. Sometimes a person cannot tell where his thoughts come from. He cannot trace the origins of the impressions made upon his mind. They may be from above or they may be from beneath. He knows only a little of their source, and little about them, except that they are not his own free choices. Of his own acts of will, there can be no such uncertainty. He knows their origin. He knows that they are the product of an original power in himself for which he is compelled to hold himself primarily responsible for the actions thereof.

Not only does he have this direct consciousness, but he has, as already suggested, the testimony of his own conscience. This ability, by its very nature, takes notice of his moral acts, requiring certain acts of will and forbidding others. This ability is an essential condition of free moral agency. Possessing this and man's other mental powers, he must be free and under moral obligation.

It is inconceivable that man should be under moral law and government without the power of free moral action. The logical condition of the existence of a conscience in man is that he should be free.

It is evident that man is free from the fact that he is conscious of praise or blame. He could not reasonably blame himself unless it were a "first truth" that he is free. By a first truth, I mean one that is known to all by a necessity of their own nature. There are such truths – those that no one can help knowing, no matter how much they may desire to ignore them. Unless it were a first truth, necessarily known to all, that man is free, he could not praise or blame himself.

> It is inconceivable that man should be under moral law and government without the power of free moral action.

As conscience implies moral force, so, where there is a conscience, it is impossible for people really to deny moral responsibility. They cannot blame anyone except themselves for wrongdoing. Aware of the forewarning of conscience against the wrong act, how can they escape the conviction that the act was wrong?

The Bible always treats people as free agents, commanding them to do or not to do things as if, of course, they had all the power necessary to obey such commands. A young minister once said to me, "I preach that people should repent, but never that they can."

I asked, "Why not also preach that they can?"

He replied, "The Bible does not say that they can."

I replied that it would be most utter foolishness for a human legislature, having required certain action, to proceed to state publicly that people have the power to obey. The requirement is the strongest possible affirmation that, in the belief of the enacting power, the subjects are able to do the things required. If the lawmakers did not believe this, how could they reasonably require it? The very first assumption to be made concerning good rulers is that they have common sense and common honesty. To basically deny that God has these qualities is blasphemous.

Freedom of will lies among the earliest and most resistless convictions. Probably no one living can remember his first idea of what he should do – his first convictions of right and wrong. It is also among our most irresistible convictions. We assume the freedom of our own will from the very beginning. The little child affirms it in his first juvenile efforts to accomplish his purposes. See him reach forth to get his food or his playthings. The little machinery of a freely acting agent begins to play long before he can understand it. He begins to act on his own responsibility, long before he can estimate what or how great this responsibility is. The fact of personal responsibility is attached to us so that we might as well escape from ourselves as from this conviction.

**II. While it is true and cannot be rationally denied that people have this attribute of moral liberty, it is equally true that they are morally enslaved.** They are in moral bondage. They have liberty by created nature; the bondage comes by voluntary corruption and misuse of their powers.

The Bible represents people as being in bondage – as having the power to resist temptation to sin, but as voluntarily yielding to those temptations. This reminds me of our doughfaced politicians who could, but do not and will not, resist the demands of the slave power.[5] This is how it is with the bondage of sinners under temptation. The Bible represents Satan as ruling the hearts of men at his will, just as the men who exert the slave power of the South rule the doughfaces of the North at their will, dictating the choice of our presidents and the entire legislation of the federal government. As Satan ruled Eve in the garden, so he now *works in the children of disobedience* (Ephesians 2:2).

What the Bible here represents, experience proves to be true. Wicked

---

5    A "doughface" refers to Northern congressmen before or during the American Civil War
     who were not opposed to slavery, but were controlled, or molded, by others.

people know that they are in bondage to Satan. Who do you think puts it into the hearts of young men to plan iniquity and drink it in like water? Is it not the devil? How many young men do we meet with who, when tempted, seem to have no moral stamina to resist, but are swept away by the first gust of temptation?

People are in bondage to their desires and appetites. Desire that is excited leads them away just as it led Eve and Adam. What can be the reason that some young men find it so hard to give up the use of tobacco? They know that the habit is filthy and disgusting. They know it is not good for their health. However, appetite craves, and the devil helps on its demands. The poor victim makes a feeble effort to deliver himself, but the devil turns the screw again and holds him even tighter, and then drags him back to a harder bondage.

It is the same when someone is in bondage to alcohol, and so with every form of worldly indulgence. Satan helps promote the influence of worldly desires, and he does not care much what the particular form of it may be as long as its power is strong enough to ruin the soul. It all plays into his hand and promotes his main purpose.

Some people are in bondage to the love of money, to the fashions of the world, or to the opinions of mankind. They are enslaved by these and are led on in the face of the demands of duty. Every person is really enslaved who is in reality led counter to his convictions of duty. He is free only when he acts in accordance with those convictions. This is the true idea of liberty. A person is only free when reason and conscience control the will, for God made man, intelligent and moral beings, to act normally under the influence of their own enlightened conscience and reason. This is the type of freedom that God exercises and enjoys; none can be higher or nobler. However, when a moral force is in bondage to his ignoble appetites and passions, and is led by them to disregard the dictates of his conscience and of his reason, he is simply a galley slave to a very hard and cruel master.

God made people to be free, giving them just such mental powers that they need in order to control their own activities as a rational being should want to do. Their bondage, then, is completely voluntary. They choose to resist the control of reason and submit to the control of appetite and passion.

Every unrepentant person is aware of actually being in bondage to temptation. What person who is not saved from sin through grace does not know that he is an enigma to himself? I would have little respect for anyone who would say that he was never ashamed of himself and who never found himself doing things he could not properly justify. I would be especially ashamed and afraid, too, if I were to hear a student say he had never been affected with a sense of his moral weakness. Such ignorance would only show his complete lack of reflection and his consequent failure to notice the most obvious moral incidents of his inner life. Does he not know that his weakest desires still carry his will – the strongest convictions of his reason and conscience – to the contrary?

> Every unrepentant person is aware of actually being in bondage to temptation.

This is a most guilty condition because it is so completely voluntary. It is very needless. It is quite contrary to the convictions of his reason and of his understanding, and it is opposed to his convictions of God's righteous demands. To go counter to such convictions, he must be exceedingly guilty.

Of course, such conduct must be most detrimental. The sinner acts in most certain opposition to his own best interests so that if he has the power to ruin himself, this path will certainly do it. The course he pursues is of all others best suited to destroy both body and soul. How, then, can it be anything except detrimental to himself? He practically denies all moral obligation, yet he knows the fact of his moral obligation, and he denies it in the face of his clearest convictions. How can this be otherwise than harmful?

I have often asked sinners how they could explain their own conduct. The honest ones answer, "I cannot at all. I do not understand it myself." The real explanation is that while by created nature they are free moral agents, yet by their obsession with sin they have sold themselves into moral bondage, and they are really slaves to Satan and their own lusts.

This is a state of deep moral degradation. It is most disgraceful. Everybody feels this in regard to certain forms of sin and certain classes of sinners. We all feel that drunkenness is beastly. We regard a drunkard as being well on the way to acting like a beast. See him staggering about, mentally intoxicated, and reeking in his own filth! Is he not almost a beast? No, for we must ask pardon of beasts for this comparison, for not one beast is so vulgar and vile. Not one beast stirs up in our hearts such a sense of voluntary degradation. Compared with the self-intoxicated drunkard, any one of them is a noble creature.

We all say this as we look only from our human standpoint, but there is another and a better standpoint. How do angels look upon this self-made drunkard? They see in him someone who was made only a little lower than themselves, and one who might have aspired to be their companion, yet he chose rather to lower himself to a level with swine! Oh, how their souls must shudder at the sight of such self-made degradation! It is too much for angels to bear to see the noble quality of intellect discarded, and still nobler moral qualities rejected and trodden under foot as if they were only a hindrance. How they must feel!

The drunkard is not alone in the contempt that his carnal degradation results in. Observe the tobacco smoker. The correct judgment of community demands that by conventional laws the smoker should be excluded from waiting rooms, hotel rooms, public transportation, churches, and indeed all really decent places. Yet for the sake of this offensive indulgence, the smoker is willing to descend into places that are not decent. See him sneak out of his place among respectable people and gather with rough and rebellious people for the sake of his filthy indulgence. If he were only required to assemble all day in the society to which he sinks himself by this indulgence, it might warn him of the cost of his filthy habit! It might help to open his eyes!

I have taken these examples of fleshly indulgence as illustrations of the real degradation of sin. In these cases, the good sense of mankind has been displayed by the level of corruption to which they entrust these adherents of low self-indulgence. If we only saw things in their right light, we would take the same view of the moralist. I remember talking with one leading moralist who said, "How can I act from regard to God or to what is right? How can I go to a religious meeting from the high motive of pleasing God? I can go from a desire to promote my own selfish ends, but how can I go for the sake of pleasing God?"

Yes, that is precisely his difficulty and his sin. He does not care how little he pleases God! That is the least of his concerns. The very lowest class of causes influences his will and his life. He stands a great distance away from the reach of the highest and noblest. His self-made degradation and his exceeding great sin consists in this.

It is the same with the miser when he gets beyond all causes except the love of hoarding – when his practical question is not how he will honor the human race, or bless his generation, or glorify his Maker, but how he can make a few dollars. Even when urged to pray, he would ask, "What profit will I have if I do pray to Him?" When you find a man so incapable of being moved by noble motives, what a wretch he is! How unspeakably miserable!

I could also bring before you the ambitious scholar who is too low in his aims to be influenced by the exalted motive of doing good, and who feels only that which touches his reputation. Is not this exceedingly low and ignoble? What would you think of the preacher who would lose all regard for the welfare of souls and care only about building up his reputation? What would you say of him? You would declare that he was too shameful and too wicked to live, and was fit only for hell!

What would you think of one who could shine like Lucifer among the morning stars of intellect and genius, but who would reduce himself to the low and miserable business of seeking applause and desiring to be complimented for his talents? Would you not say that such self-seeking is unutterably contemptible? With all heaven from above calling them on to lofty purposes and efforts, there they are, working their manure rakes and searching after some little recognition for their small selves!

See that ambitious man who so wants to please everybody that he conforms his own opinion to everyone else's opinions, and never has one that is really his own. Must not he be low enough to satisfy any of those whose ambition seems strangely reversed, who only strive to dive and sink, but never to soar, whose inclinations all tend downward and never up? One would suppose they would have degradation enough to satisfy any common ambition.

All this comes because of bondage to low-minded selfishness. It is sad that there should be so much of this in our world that public sentiment rarely measures it in any way near its real nature!

## Remarks

Our subject reveals the case of those who are convicted of what is right, but cannot be persuaded to do it. For example, on the subject of temperance, or abstaining from alcohol, he is convicted as to his duty. He knows that he should completely reform, yet he will not change. Every temperance lecture carries conviction, but the next temptation sweeps it away, and he returns like the dog to his vomit. Observe, though, that every successive course of temperance, conviction, and temptation's triumph leaves him weaker than before, and very soon will find him completely defeated. Miserable man! How certainly he will die in his sins!

No matter what the form of the temptation may be, he who is convinced of his duty, yet takes no corresponding action, is on the high road to perdition. Inevitably, this bondage grows stronger and stronger with every fresh trial of its strength. Every time you are convinced of duty and yet resist that conviction and refuse to act in accordance with it, you become more and more helpless. You commit yourself more and more to the control of your iron-hearted master. Every new case renders you only the more fully a helpless slave.

There may be some young men and women reading this who have already made themselves a moral wreck. There may be boys not yet sixteen who have already trampled upon their consciences. You might have already learned to go against all your convictions of duty. How horrible! Your chains are growing stronger every day. With each day's resistance, your soul is more deeply and hopelessly lost. Poor, miserable, dying sinner! *He, that being often reproved hardeneth his neck, shall suddenly be destroyed, and that without remedy* (Proverbs 29:1).

Suddenly, the waves dash you upon the rocks and you are gone! Your friends move solemnly along the shore and look out upon those rocks of damnation on which your soul is wrecked. Weeping as they go, they mournfully

say, "There is the wreck of one who knew his duty, but did not do it. Thousands of times the appeals of conviction came home to his heart, but he learned to resist them. He made it his business to resist, and tragically, he was only too successful!"

How insane is the delusion that the sinner's situation, while still in his sins, is growing better! The drunkard might as well imagine that he is growing better because every temperance lecture convicts him of his sin and shame, even though every next day's temptation leaves him as drunk as ever! Growing better! There can be no delusion as false and so fatal as this!

You see the force of this delusion in clearer light when you notice how insignificant the issues are that influence the soul against all the tremendous purposes of God's character and kingdom. Must not that be a strong and fearful delusion that can make considerations so insignificant outweigh motives so vast and momentous?

The sin of this condition is to be estimated by the insignificance of the motives that control the mind. What would you think of a youth who could murder his father for a dollar? You would exclaim, "What! He was bribed to murder his father for such a small amount!" You would consider his sin to be even greater by how much less the temptation was.

Our subject shows the need of the Holy Spirit to impress the truth on the hearts of sinners. You can also see how certainly sinners will be lost if they grieve the Spirit of God away. Your earthly friends might be discouraged, yet you still might be saved; but if the Spirit of God becomes discouraged and leaves you, then your doom is sealed forever. *Woe also to them when I depart from them!* (Hosea 9:12). This departure of God from the sinner signals the knell of his lost soul. Then the mighty angel begins to ring the great bell of eternity – one more soul going to its eternal doom!

# Chapter 12

# On the Atonement

How that Christ died for our sins according to the scriptures.
—1 Corinthians 15:3

For he hath made him to be sin for us, who knew no sin; that we might be made the righteousness of God in him.
—2 Corinthians 5:21

But God commendeth his love toward us, in that, while we were yet sinners, Christ died for us.
—Romans 5:8

The LORD is well pleased for his righteousness' sake; he will magnify the law, and make it honorable.
—Isaiah 42:21

Whom God hath set forth to be a propitiation through faith in his blood, to declare his righteousness for the remission of sins that are past, through the forbearance of God; to declare, I say, at this time his righteousness; that he might be just, and the justifier of him which believeth in Jesus.
—Romans 3:25-26

In this last passage, the apostle Paul states, with unusual fulness, the theological design, and I might even say the philosophical design, of Christ's mission to our world: to set forth before created beings God's righteousness in forgiving sins. It is here said that Christ is set forth as a propitiation so that God may be just in forgiving sin, assuming that God could not have been just to the universe unless Christ had been first set forth as a sacrifice.

When we seriously consider the irresistible convictions of our own minds in regard to our relationship with God and His government, we cannot help but see that we are sinners and are lost beyond hope when based upon law and justice. The fact that we are grievous sinners against God is an ultimate fact of human knowledge, testified to by our irresistible convictions, and is no more to be denied than the fact that there is such a thing as wrong.

Now if God is holy and good, it must be that He disapproves of wrongdoing, and will punish it. The penalty of His law is pronounced against it. Under this penalty, we stand condemned and have no relief except through some adequate atonement that is satisfactory to God because it is safe to the interests of His kingdom.

We may advance this far safely and on solid ground by the simple light of nature. If there were no Bible, we might know this much with absolute certainty. Even atheists are compelled to go this far.

Here, then, we are under absolute and most righteous condemnation. Is there any way of escape? If so, it must be revealed to us in the Bible, for it cannot come from any other source. The Bible does profess to reveal a method of escape. This is the great burden of its message.

It opens with a very brief allusion to the circumstances under which sin came into the world. Without being very detailed as to the manner in which sin entered, it is exceedingly full, clear, and precise in showing the fact of sin in the human race. It is as plain as can be that God regards the human race as being in sin and rebellion. It is worthy of notice that this fact and the connected fact of possible forgiveness are affirmed on the same authority and with the same sort of simplicity and clearness. These facts stand or fall together.

God clearly intended to impress on all minds these two great truths: first, that man is ruined by his own sin, and second, that he may be saved through Jesus Christ. To deny the former is to deny both our own irresistible convictions and God's most explicit revealed testimony. To deny the latter is to shut the door of our own free act and accord against all hope of our own salvation.

The philosophical explanation of the reasons and governmental meaning of the atonement must not be confused with the fact of an atonement. People may be saved by the fact if they simply believe it while they may know nothing about the philosophical explanation. The apostles did not make much account of the explanation, but they asserted the fact most earnestly, gave miracles as testimony to prove their authority from God, and so urged people to believe the fact and be saved. The fact, then, may be savingly believed while the explanation is unknown. This has been the case, no doubt, with many thousands of people.

> God clearly intended to impress on all minds that man is ruined by his own sin *and* that he may be saved through Jesus Christ.

It is very useful, though, to understand the reasons and governmental basis of the atonement. It often serves to remove skepticism. It is very common for lawyers to reject the fact until they come to see the reasons and governmental basis of the atonement. Once this is seen, they usually admit the fact. There is a large class of people who need to see the governmental aspect, or they will reject the fact. The reason why the fact is so often doubted is that the explanations given have been unsatisfactory. They have misrepresented God. It is no wonder that people would reject them, and along with them, the fact of any atonement at all.

The atonement is a governmental expedient to sustain law without the execution of its penalty on the sinner. Of course, it is always a difficult thing in any government to sustain the authority of law, and the respect due to it, without the execution of penalty, yet God has accomplished it most perfectly.

A distinction must be made here between public and retributive justice. The latter punishes the individual sinner according to the nature of his offense. The former, public justice, looks only toward the general good, and must do that which will secure the authority and influence of law, as well as the carrying out of the penalty. It may accept a substitute, though, if it is equally effective to the support of law and the assurance of obedience.

Public justice, then, may be satisfied in one of two ways: either by the full execution of the penalty, or by some substitute that will serve the purposes of government at least equally well. What is necessary for the purposes of public justice?

1. Not the literal execution of the penalty, for if so, it must necessarily fall on the sinner and on no one else. Besides, it could be no gain to the universe for Christ to suffer the full and exact penalty due to every lost sinner who would be saved by Him. Since the amount of suffering is the same in the one case as in the other, where is the gain? Further, if the administration of justice is to be disciplinary and corrective, then it cannot fall on Christ, but must fall on the sinner himself. If not disciplinary and corrective, it certainly may be, as compared with that due the sinner, far different in kind and less in degree.

It has sometimes been said that Christ suffered everything in the same degree and the same in kind as all the saved together would have suffered, but human reason revolts at this assumption, and certainly the Scriptures do not affirm it.

2. Some people say that God needs to be appeased and to have His feelings pacified. This is an absolute mistake. It completely misrepresents God and misunderstands the atonement.

3. It is not part of public justice for an innocent being to suffer penalty or punishment, in the proper sense of these terms. Punishment implies crime, of which Christ had none. Christ, then, was not punished.

Let it be clearly understood that the divine law originates in God's kindness, and it only has compassionate ends in view. It was revealed only and solely to promote the greatest possible good by means of obedience. Such a law can allow for forgiveness, provided an expression can be given that will equally secure obedience and make an equal revelation of the lawgiver's firmness, integrity, and love. Since the law is perfect and is most essential to the good of His creatures, God must not set aside its penalty without some equivalent influence that will lead to obedience.

The penalty was designed as a testimony to God's regard for the dictates of His law and to His purpose to sustain it. An atonement, therefore, that would answer as a substitute for the administering of this penalty must be able to show God's regard for both the precept and the penalty of His law. It must be adapted to enforce obedience. Its moral power must be in this respect equal to that of the administration of the penalty on the sinner. Consequently, we find that in this atonement God has expressed His high regard for His law and for obedience to it.

The method of administering the penalty of the law was to make a strong impression of the majesty, excellence, and utility of the law. Anything may answer as a substitute that will as thoroughly demonstrate the evil and wickedness of sin, God's hatred of it, and His determination to carry out His law in all its demands. The proposed substitute may especially avail if it will also make a significant demonstration of God's love to sinners. The atonement, by the death of Christ, has most emphatically done this.

Every act of rebellion denounces the law. Therefore, before God can pardon rebellion, He must make such a demonstration of His attitude toward sin that will excite the heart of the created universe and make every ear tingle. For the purpose of the highest obedience, it was especially necessary to make such a demonstration that will appropriately secure the confidence and love of subjects toward their Lawgiver that will show that He is no tyrant and that He seeks only the highest obedience and resultant happiness of His creatures. Once this is done, God will be satisfied.

What can be done to teach these lessons and to impress them on the universe with great and everlasting emphasis? God's testimony must be so given as to be well understood. Obviously, the testimony to be given must come from God, for it is His view of law, penalty, and substitution that needs to be revealed. Everyone must see that if He were to enact law on the sinner, this would show at once His view of the value of the law. But plainly, His view of the same thing must be shown with equal force by any proposed substitute before He could accept it as such.

In this transaction, the decree of the law must be accepted and honored both by God and by Jesus as Mediator. The latter, as the representative of the human race, must honor the law by obeying it and by publicly endorsing it; otherwise, the necessary honor cannot be shown to the divine law in the proposed atonement. This has been done.

To make adequate provision for the application of mercy to the human race, it is plainly essential that, in the person of their Mediator, both the divine and the human should be united. God and man are both to be represented in the atonement. The divine Word represented the Godhead, and the man Jesus represented the race to be redeemed. What the Bible thus asserts is verified in the history of Jesus, for He said and did things that could not have been said and done unless He had been man, and equally could not have been unless He were also God. On the one hand, He was too weak to carry His cross through exhaustion of the human; on the other hand, He was mighty to calm the storm and to raise the dead through the abundance of divine power. We see, then, that God and man are both represented in Jesus Christ.

The thing to be done, therefore, required that Jesus Christ would honor the law and fully obey it. He did just that. Standing for the sinner, He must, in an important sense, bear the

**The sacrifice made on Calvary is to be understood as God's offering to public justice.**

curse of the law – not the literal penalty, but a vast amount of suffering that is sufficient in view of His relationship to God and the universe to make the necessary demonstration of God's displeasure against sin, yet also of His love for both the sinner and all His moral subjects. On the one hand, Jesus represented the human race, and on the other hand, He represented God. This is a most divine philosophy.

The sacrifice made on Calvary is to be understood as God's offering to public justice. God Himself gave up His Son to death, and this Son poured forth His life's blood in atonement for sin, thus throwing open the folding gates of mercy to a sinning, lost race. This must be regarded as demonstrating His love to sinners. This is God's ransom provided for them. Look at the state of the case. The supreme Lawgiver, and indeed the government of the universe, had been scorned by rebellion; of course, there can be no pardon until this dishonor done to God and His law is thoroughly washed away. This is done by God's freewill offering of His own Son for these great sins.

Sinners, what do you think of all this being done for you? What do you think of that appeal that Paul writes and that God makes through him: *I beseech you, therefore, brethren, by the mercies of God, that ye present your bodies a living sacrifice, holy, acceptable to God, which is your reasonable service* (Romans 12:1)? Think of those mercies. Think how Christ poured out His life for you.

Suppose He were to appear to you today, and holding up His hands dripping with blood, would say, "I implore you by the mercies shown to you by God, that you present your bodies a living sacrifice, holy, acceptable to God!" Would you not feel the force of His appeal that this is a *reasonable service*? Would not this love of Christ constrain you (2 Corinthians 5:14)? What do you think of it? Did He die for all so that *they which live should not henceforth live unto themselves*, but unto Him that loved them and gave Himself for them (2 Corinthians 5:15; Ephesians 5:25)?

What do you say? Just as the uplifted ax would otherwise have fallen on your neck, He caught the blow on His own. You could have had no life if He had not died to save it. What, then, will you do? Will you have this offered mercy, or will you reject it? Will you yield to Him the life He has spared in such mercy, or will you refuse to yield it?

## Remarks

1. The governmental significance of this design is perfectly apparent. The whole transaction tends powerfully to sustain God's law and to reveal His love and even mercy to sinners. It shows that He is personally ready to forgive, and needs only to have such an arrangement made so that He can do it safely in regard to His government. What could show His readiness to forgive so remarkably as this? See how carefully He guards against the abuse of pardon! He is always ready to pardon, yet ever watchful over the great interests of obedience and happiness so that they are not jeopardized by its freeness and fullness!

2. Why would it ever be thought inconceivable that God would devise such a plan of atonement? Is there anything in it that is unlike God or

that is inconsistent with His revealed character? I doubt whether any moral agent can understand this system and still think it is unbelievable. Those who reject it as unbelievable must have failed to understand it.

3. The question might be asked, Why did Christ die at all, if not for us? He had never sinned. He did not die on His own account as a sinner. He did not die as the infants of our race do, with a moral nature yet undeveloped, yet who belong to a sinful race. The only account to be given of His death is that He did not die for Himself, but for us.

It could also be asked why He died in the way that He did. See Him dying between two thieves, crushed down beneath a mountainous weight of sorrow. Why was this? Other martyrs have died shouting. He died in anguish and grief, cast down and afflicted and hidden from His Father's face.

All nature seemed to sympathize with His agony. The sun was clothed in darkness. The rocks were split. The earth quaked. All nature was shaken. Even a heathen philosopher exclaimed, "Surely the universe is coming to an end, or the Maker of the Universe is dying!" Listen to that piercing cry: *My God, My God; why hast thou forsaken me?* (Matthew 27:46).

On the belief that He was dying as a Savior for sinners, it is all plain. He died for the kingdom of God, and He had to suffer these things to make a just expression of God's abhorrence of sin. While He stood in the place of guilty sinners, God had to frown on Him and hide His face from Him. This reveals both the spirit of God's government and His own infinite wisdom.

4. Some have criticized the atonement as likely to encourage sin, but such people neglect the very important distinction between the proper use of a thing and its abuse. No doubt the best things in the universe may be abused, and by abuse can be corrupted to evil, and all the more by how much the better they are in their correct use.

It would seem that no one can rationally doubt of the natural tendency of the atonement to good. The tendency of displaying such love, meekness, and self-sacrifice for us is to make the sinner trust and love, and to make him bow before the cross with a broken and contrite heart.

Many people do abuse it, though, and the best things, abused, become the worst. The abuse of the atonement is the very reason why God sends sinners to hell. He says, *He that despised Moses' law died without mercy under two or three witnesses; of how much sorer punishment, suppose ye, shall he be thought worthy, who hath trodden under foot the Son of God, and hath counted the blood of the covenant, wherewith he was sanctified, an unholy thing, and hath done despite to the Spirit of grace?* (Hebrews 10:28-29).

Therefore, if any sinner will abuse the atoning blood and trample down the holy law and the very idea of returning to God in repentance and love, God will say of him, *Of how much sorer punishment . . . shall he be thought worthy"* than he who despised Moses' law and fell beneath its vengeance?

5. It is a matter of fact that this manifestation of God in Christ does break the heart of sinners. It has subdued many hearts, and will subdue thousands more. If they believe it and hold it as a reality, must it not subdue their heart to love and grief? Do you not think so? Certainly if you saw it as it is and felt the force of it in your heart, you would break down in tears and cry out, "Did Jesus love me so much, and will I love sin any longer?"

Your heart would melt just as thousands of hearts have been broken and melted in every age when they have seen the love of Jesus as revealed on the cross. That beautiful hymn puts the case truthfully:[6]

> I saw one hanging on a tree,
>> In agony and blood;
> Who fixed His languid eyes on me,
>> As near the cross I stood.
> But it was not the first look that fully broke his heart.
>> A second look He gave, which said,
> "I freely all forgive;
>> This blood is for thy ransom paid;
> I died that thou mayest live."

---

6    This hymn was written by John Newton, author of the hymn "Amazing Grace."

It was only after the second look that his whole heart broke, tears fell like rain, and he gave his all in the full consecration of his soul to the Savior.

This is the genuine result of the sinner's understanding of the gospel and giving Jesus Christ credit for His lovingkindness in dying for the lost. Faith thus breaks the stony heart. If this demonstration of God's love in Christ does not break your heart, nothing else will. If this death and love of Christ do not cause you to surrender to Him, nothing else can.

However, if you do not look at it and will not set your mind upon it, it will only work your destruction. To know this gospel only enough to reject and renounce it can serve no other purpose except to make your sin even greater and your fate even more fearful.

6. Jesus was made a sin offering for us. This was beautifully illustrated under the Mosaic system! The victim was brought out to be slain. The blood was carried in and sprinkled on the mercy seat. This mercy seat was no other than the sacred cover or lid of the ark that contained the tables of the law and other sacred memorials of God's ancient mercies. There they were, in that deep recess within which none might enter on pain of death except the high priest, and he only once a year, on the great Day of Atonement.

> If this demonstration of God's love in Christ does not break your heart, nothing else will.

On this eventful day, the sacred rites culminated to their highest solemnity. Two goats were brought forward, upon which the high priest laid his hands and publicly confessed his own sins and the sins of all the people. Then one goat was driven far away into the wilderness to signify how God removes our sins as far as the east is from the west. The other goat was slain, and its blood was carried by the high priest into the Most Holy Place, where it was sprinkled upon the mercy seat beneath the cherubim. Meanwhile, the vast congregation stood outside, confessing their sins and expecting remission only through the shedding of blood. It was as if the whole world had been standing around the base of Calvary confessing their sins while Jesus carried His cross to the summit to hang upon it and to bleed and die for the sins of mankind. How fitting that while Christ is dying, we would be confessing our sins!

Some of you may think it is a great thing to go on a foreign mission, but Jesus has led the way. He left heaven on a foreign mission. He came down to this more-than-heathen world, and no one ever faced such self-denial. Yet He fearlessly marched up without the least hesitation to face the consequences. Never did He back away from disgrace, humiliation, or torture. Can you, then, hesitate from following the footsteps of such a leader? Is anything too much for you to suffer while you follow in the lead of such a Captain of your salvation?

# Chapter 13

# Where Sin Occurs, God Cannot Wisely Prevent It

It must needs be that offences come; but woe to that
man by whom the offence cometh!
—Matthew 18:7

It is impossible but that offences will come; but woe
unto him through whom they come!
—Luke 17:1

An offense, as used in this passage, is an occasion of falling into
sin. It is anything that causes another to sin and fall. It is plain
that the author of the offense is understood of in this passage as being
voluntary and as sinful in his act, or else the curse of God would not
be denounced upon him.

Consequently, the passage assumes that this sin is in some sense
necessary and unavoidable. What is true of this sin in this respect is
true of all other sin. Indeed, any sin may become an offense in the
sense of a temptation to others to sin, and therefore its necessity and
unavoidableness would then be affirmed by these texts.

The doctrine of these texts, therefore, is that sin, under the government of God, cannot be prevented. I intend to examine this doctrine

and to show that, nevertheless, sin is completely inexcusable as to the sinner. Then I intend to answer some objections and conclude with a few remarks.

1. When we say it is impossible to prevent sin under the government of God, the statement still calls for another inquiry, and that is, Where does this impossibility lie? Is it on the part of the sinner or on the part of God? Which is true: that the sinner cannot possibly refrain from sinning, or that God cannot prevent him from sinning?

The first supposition answers itself, for it could not be sin if it were completely unavoidable. It might be his unfortunate situation, but nothing could be more unjust than to attribute it to him as his sin.

We will better understand where this impossibility does and must lie if we will first review some of the elementary principles of God's government. Let us then consider that God's government, or rule, over people is moral, and is known to be such by every intelligent being. By the term "moral," I mean that it governs by motives and does not move by physical force. It adapts itself to mind and not to matter. It contemplates mind as having intellect to understand truth, sensibility to appreciate its relevance to happiness, conscience to judge of what is right, and a will to determine a course of voluntary action in view of God's claims.

We see that God governs mind, but does not do the same in regard to matter. The planetary worlds are controlled by quite a different sort of agency. God does not move them in their orbits by motives, but by a physical agency.

All people know that this government is moral by their own consciousness. When its precepts and its penalties come before their minds, they are conscious that an appeal is made to their voluntary powers. They are never conscious of any physical agency trying to force their obedience.

God's government implies in us the power to will, or not to will – to will what is right or to will what is wrong, to choose to accept or to refuse the great good that God promises. It also implies intelligence. The beings to whom law is addressed are capable of understanding it.

They also have a conscience by which they can appreciate and must affirm its obligations.

You need to generally distinguish between the influence of motive on mind and of mechanical force upon matter. The former implies it being voluntary; the latter does not. The former is adapted to mind and has no adaptation to matter; the latter equally is adapted to matter but has no possible application to mind.

In God's government over the human mind, all is voluntary; nothing is coerced as by physical force. Indeed, it is impossible that physical force would directly influence mind. Compulsion is precluded by the very nature of moral agency. Where compulsion begins, moral agency ends. If it were possible for God to force the will as He forces the moon along in its orbit, to do so would subvert the very idea of a moral government. Neither praise nor blame could be attached to any actions of beings who were moved by force.

> Neither praise nor blame could be attached to any actions of beings who were moved by force.

Persuasion, brought to bear upon the mind, is always such in its nature that it can be resisted. By the very nature of the case, God's creatures must have power to resist any amount of even His persuasion. There can be no power in heaven or earth to coerce the will as matter is coerced. The nature of mind forbids its possibility. If it were possible, it would still be true that in just so far as God should coerce the human will, He would cease to govern morally.

God is infinitely wise. People can no more doubt this than they can doubt their own existence. He has infinite knowledge. He knows every- thing – all objects of knowledge – and He knows them all perfectly. He is also infinitely good. His will is always conformed to His perfect knowledge and is always controlled by infinite benevolence.

His infinite goodness implies that He does the best He can, always and everywhere. In no instance does He ever fail to do the very best He can do, so that He can appeal to every person and say, "What more can I do to prevent sin than I am doing?" Indeed, He appeals in this way to every intelligent mind. He made this appeal through Isaiah to the ancient Jews: *And now, O inhabitants of Jerusalem, and men of Judah, judge, I pray you, betwixt me and my vineyard. What could have been done more to my vineyard, that I have not done in it?* (Isaiah 5:3-4).

Every moral agent in the universe knows that God has done the best He could do in regard to sin. Do not each one of you know this? Certainly you do. He Himself, in all His infinite wisdom, could not suggest a better course than that which He has taken. People know this truth so well that they can never know it better. At some future time, you might realize it more fully when you will come to see its millions of illustrations drawn out before your eyes, but no demonstration can make its proof more perfect than it is to your own minds today.

Sin does in fact exist under God's government. God is either to blame or not to blame for this sin. Everyone knows that God is not to blame for this sin, for man's own nature affirms that He would prevent it if He wisely could. Certainly if He was able wisely to prevent sin in any case where it actually occurs, then not to do so nullifies all our conceptions of His goodness and wisdom. He would be the greatest sinner in the universe if, with power and wisdom adequate to prevent sin, He had failed to prevent it.

> Everyone knows that God is not to blame for sin.

Let me here mention also that what God cannot do wisely, he cannot (speaking morally) do at all. For He cannot act unwisely. He cannot do things that wisdom forbids. To do so would be to un-deify Himself. The supposition would make Him cease to be perfect, and this would be equivalent of Him ceasing to be God.

We could also look at it this way: if He were to intercede unwisely to prevent a sinner from sinning, He Himself would sin. I speak now of each instance in which God does not in fact intercede to prevent sin. In any of these cases, if He were to intercede unwisely to prevent sin, He would prevent someone from sinning at the expense of sinning Himself. Here, then, is the case. A sinner is about to fall due to temptation – or in more correct language, is about to rush into some new sin. God cannot wisely prevent his doing so. Now what will be done? Will He let that sinner rush on to his chosen sin and self-made ruin, or will He step forward unwisely, sin Himself, and incur all the unpleasant consequences of such a step? God lets the sinner bear his own responsibility. Why should He not? Who would want to have God sin?

This is a full explanation of every case in which man does in fact sin and God does not prevent it. This is not conjecture, but is logical certainty. No truth can be more overwhelmingly and necessarily certain than this. I once heard a minister say in a sermon, "It is not irrational to suppose that in each case of sin, it occurs as it does because God cannot prevent it." After he stepped down from the pulpit, I said to him, "Why did you leave the matter like that? You left your hearers to infer that perhaps it might be in some other way, that this was only a possible theory, while some other theory might have been even more probable. Why did you not say that this theory is certain and must necessarily be true?"

The impossibility of preventing sin does not lie in the sinner, but entirely with God. It should be remembered that sin is nothing else than an act of free will that is always committed against one's conviction of right. Indeed, if someone did not know that selfishness is sin, it would not be sin in his case.

Once more, sin is always committed against and despite motives that are of infinitely greater weight than those that lead one to sin. The very fact that his conscience condemns the sin is his own judgment on the question, proving that in his own view the motives to sin are infinitely contemptible when put in the scale to measure those against the sin in question.

Every sinner knows that sin is a willful abuse of his own powers as a moral agent. It is an abuse of those noblest powers of his being – in view of which he is especially said to be made in the image of God. Made like God with these exalted attributes, capable of determining his own voluntary activities intelligently if he wants to do so, and in accordance with his reason and his conscience if he desires, he still in every act of sin abuses and degrades these powers, tramples down in the very dust the image of God stamped on his being, and with the capacities of becoming an angel, makes himself a fool.

Clothed with a dignity of nature similar to that of his Maker, he chooses to debase himself to the level of beasts and of devils. With a face naturally looking upward, with an intelligence that grasps the great truths of God, with a reason that accepts and affirms the great necessary principles involved in his moral duties and relations, and with abilities that qualify him to sit on a nation's throne, he still says, "Let me take this glorious image of God and dishonor it in the dust! Let me cast myself down until there will be no lower depth of degradation to which I can sink!"

In every instance, sin is a dishonoring of God. Every sinner must know this. It rejects His authority, disregards His advice, and mistreats His love. Truly does God Himself say, *A son honoreth his father, and a servant his master; if then I be a father, where is mine honor? And if I be a master, where is my fear?* (Malachi 1:6).

What sinner ever imagined that God neglects to do anything He wisely can do to prevent sin? If this is not true, what is conscience except a lie and a delusion? Conscience always affirms that God is clear of all guilt in reference to sin. In every instance in which conscience condemns the sinner, it necessarily must and actually does fully acquit God.

These comments are enough to show that sin in every instance of its commission is entirely inexcusable.

Next we will note some objections.

1. If God is infinitely wise and good, why do we need to pray at all? If He will certainly do the best possible thing always and all the good He can do, why do we need to pray?

I answer that it is because His infinite goodness and wisdom require us to do so. Who could ask for a better reason than this? If you believe in His infinite wisdom and goodness, and make this belief the basis of your objection, you will certainly, if honest, be satisfied with this answer.

I also answer that it might be wise and good for God to do many things if He is asked in prayer that He could not wisely do if not asked. You cannot therefore conclude that prayer never changes the course that God voluntarily pursues.

2. You offer another objection and ask why we should pray to God to prevent sin if He cannot prevent it. If, under the circumstances in which sin exists, God cannot, as you believe, prevent sin, why go to Him and ask Him to prevent it?

I answer that we pray for the very purpose of changing the circumstances. This is our reason. Prayer does change the circumstances. If we step forward and offer fervent, effectual prayer, this very much changes the state of the case. Look at Moses pleading with God to spare the nation after their great sin in the matter of the golden calf. God said to him, *Let me alone, that I may destroy them, and . . . I will make of thee a great nation* (Exodus 32:10; Deuteronomy 9:14). "No," said Moses, "for what will the Egyptians say? What will all the nations say? They have said for a long time that the God of that people will not be able to get them through that vast wilderness. Now, therefore, what will You do for Your great name?" Then he said, *Yet now, if thou wilt, forgive their sin – ; and if not, blot me, I pray thee, out of thy book which thou hast written* (Exodus 32:32).

This prayer that came up before God greatly changed the circumstances of the case. Because of this prayer, God could honorably spare the nation; it was honorable for Him to answer this prayer.

3. For yet another objection, you ask, "Why did God create moral agents at all if He foresaw that He could not prevent their sinning?"

I answer that it is because He saw that in general it was better to do so. He could prevent some sin in this race of moral agents. He could overrule what He could not wisely prevent so as to bring out from it a great deal of good. He saw that it was better in the long run, with all the results before Him, to create than to cease. Therefore, wisdom and love made it necessary that He should create. Having the power to create a race of moral beings, having power to convert and save a vast multitude of them, and also having power to overrule the sin He would not prevent so that it should result in immense good, how could He cease to create as He did?

4. But if God cannot prevent sin, will He not be unhappy?

No. He is entirely satisfied to have offered us redemption and accept the results.

5. Some will say, "Is this not limiting the Holy One of Israel?"

No. It is not a proper limitation of God's power to say that He cannot do anything that is unwise. Nor do we limit His power when we say that He does not move the mind just as He moves a planet. That is not a proper subject of power that is absurd and impossible in its own nature. Yet these are the only areas in which we have spoken of any limitations to His power.

But you ask if God could not prevent sin by annihilating each moral agent the instant before he would sin. Undoubtedly He could, but we say that if this were wise, He would have done it. He has not done it, certainly not in all cases, and therefore it is not always wise.

But you say that God, then, should give him more of His Holy Spirit. I answer that He does give all He can give wisely under existing circumstances. To suppose that He should give more than He does, with circumstances being the same, is to criticize His wisdom or His goodness.

Some people seem greatly horrified at the idea of setting limits to God's power, yet they make assumptions that inevitably criticize His wisdom and His goodness. Such people need to consider that if we must choose between limiting His power on the one hand, or His wisdom and His love on the other hand, it is infinitely more honorable to Him to adopt the former alternative than the latter. To strike a blow at His moral attributes is to annihilate His throne. Further, let it be also considered, as we have already suggested, that you do not in any offensive sense limit His power when you assume that He cannot do things that are naturally impossible, and that He cannot act unwisely. Let these remarks be sufficient to answer the objections.

You know that it is entirely impossible for God to act unwisely.

I know that you who are Bible students will say that this must be true. You are used to noticing the action of your own moral powers. You have a moral sense, and it has been in some good degree developed. You know that it is entirely impossible for God to act unwisely. You know He must act benevolently, always doing the best thing He can do. He has given you a nature that affirms, asserts, and recognizes these truths, or else there could be no conscience. The presence and action of a conscience implies that these great truths respecting the moral nature of God are indisputably affirmed in your soul by your own moral nature.

I address you, therefore, as those who have a conscience. Suppose it were otherwise. Suppose all that we call conscience – the entire moral side of your nature – would suddenly drop out, and I would find myself speaking to a mob of moral imbeciles – beings completely void of a conscience! How desolate the scene would be! However, I am not speaking to such an audience. Therefore, I am sure that you will understand and appreciate what I say.

## Remarks

1. We may see the only sense in which God could have allowed the existence of sin. It is simply negative. He did not intend to prevent it in any case where it does actually occur. He does not intend to make moral agents sin – not, for example, Adam and Eve in the garden, or Judas in the matter of betraying Christ. All He planned to do Himself was to leave them with only a certain amount of restraint – as much as He could wisely impose – and then if they would sin, let them bear the responsibility. He left them to act freely, and He did not positively prevent their sinning. He never uses means to make people sin. He only abstains from using unwise means to prevent their sinning. Therefore, His agency in the existence of sin is only negative.

2. The existence of sin does not prove that it is the necessary means of the greatest good. Some of you are aware that this point has been often brought up in theological discussions. I do not now intend to go into it at length, but will only say that in all cases wherein people sin, they could obey God instead of sinning. The question here is, If they were to obey rather than sin, would not a greater good result? We have these two reasons for the affirmative: (1) that by natural tendency, obedience promotes good and disobedience promotes evil, and (2) that in all those cases, God earnestly and positively demands obedience. It is fair to presume that He would demand that which would secure the greatest good.

3. The human conscience always justifies God. This is an undeniable fact – a fact of universal knowledge. The proof of it can never be made stronger, for it stands recorded in each person's heart.

A very remarkable book by Edward Beecher has recently appeared, though, titled *The Conflict of Ages*, which is obviously built upon the opposite assumption – that the human conscience does not categorically condemn people, but except under the light of this specific theory, it does in fact condemn God. This theory, adopted presumedly to place God against the human conscience, holds that there was a preexistent state in which we all lived and sinned, and we there forfeited our title to a moral nature, unbiased toward sinning. There we had a fair probation. Here, if we suppose this to be the commencement of our moral agency, we do not have a fair trial period, and conscience therefore does not, and in truth cannot, justify God except on the assumption of a preexistent state.

The entire book, therefore, is built upon the assumption of a conflict between the human conscience and God. That is a shocking assumption! A brother remarked to me about this that it seemed to him to be the most outrageous and blasphemous indictment against God that could be drawn. Yet the author intended no such thing. He is undoubtedly a good man, but in this particular area, he is egregiously mistaken.

The fact is that conscience always condemns the sinner and justifies God. It could not affirm obligation without justifying God. The real controversy, therefore, is not between God and the conscience, but between God and the heart. In every instance in which sin exists, conscience condemns the sinner and justifies God. This of itself is a perfect and sufficient answer to the whole doctrine of that book. It knocks out the only and whole foundation on which it is built. If that book is true, then people never would have had a conscience until that book was published, read, understood, and believed. No one would have ever been convicted of sin until he came to see that he had existed in a previous state and began his sinning there.

Yet the facts are contrary to this. Everywhere in all ages, with no regard to this book, and with no inclination to wait for its refined knowledge, everywhere and through all time, the human conscience has stood up to condemn each sinner, to compel him to sign his own death warrant, and to acquit his Maker of all blame. These are the facts of human nature and life.

4. Conversion consists precisely in the heart's consent to these decisions of the conscience. It is for the heart to come over to the ground occupied by the conscience and to thoroughly assent to it as right and

true. Conscience has been speaking for a long time. It has always held one doctrine, and has long been resisted by the heart. Now, in conversion, the heart comes over and gives its full assent to the decisions of conscience – that God is right, and that sin and himself, a sinner, are entirely wrong.

Do any of you want to know how you may become a Christian? This is how: let your heart justify God and condemn sin, even as your conscience does. Let your voluntary powers yield to the necessary affirmations of your reason and conscience. Then all will be peaceful within because all will be right.

But you say, "I am trying to do this!" Yes, I know this is the case with some of you who you are trying to resist to your utmost. You settle down as it were with your whole weight while God would gladly draw you by His truth and Spirit, yet you imagine that you are really trying to surrender your heart to God. This is a most unexplainable delusion!

5. In the light of this subject, we can see the reason for a general judgment. God intends to clear Himself from all allegation of wrong in the matter of sin before the entire moral universe. Strange facts have transpired in His universe, and strange insinuations have been made against His course. These matters must all be set right. He will take time enough for this. He will wait until all things are ready. Obviously, He could not bring out His great day of trial until the deeds of earth have all been performed – until all the events of this wondrous drama have had their full development. Until then, He will not be ready to make a full exposé of all His doings. Then He can and will do it most triumphantly and gloriously.

> God intends to clear Himself from all allegation of wrong in the matter of sin before the entire moral universe.

The revelations of that day will undoubtedly show why God did not intervene to prevent every sin in the universe. Then He will satisfy us as to the reasons He had for allowing Adam and Eve to sin and for letting Judas betray his Master. We know now that God is wise and good, although we do not know all the specific reasons for His conduct in the permission of sin. He will then reveal those specific reasons as far as it may be best and possible. No doubt He will then show that His reasons were so wise and good that He could not have done better.

6. Sin will then appear infinitely inexcusable and abhorrent. It will then be seen inexpressibly blameworthy and guilty in its true relationship toward God and His intelligent creatures.

Let me give you an example. Suppose a son has gone far away from the paths of obedience and virtue. He has had one of the best of fathers, but he would not hear his counsel. He had a wise and affectionate mother, but he sternly resisted all the appeals of her tenderness and tears. Despite the most watchful care of parents and friends, he went astray. As someone foolishly determined to ruin himself, he pushed on, unconcerned of the sorrow and grief he brought upon those he should have honored and loved.

At last, the consequences of such a course stand revealed. The guilty youth finds himself ruined in health, in fortune, and in good name. He has sunk far too low to retain even self-respect. Nothing remains for him but agonizing reflections on past foolishness and sin. Hear him lament his own desires: "I have almost killed my honorable father, and I had completely broken my mother's heart long ago. All that foolishness and sin in a son could do, I have done to bring down their gray hairs with sorrow to the grave. It is no wonder that having done so much to ruin my best friends, I have pulled down a double ruin on my own head. No sinner ever deserved to be doubly damned more than me."

And so truth flashes upon his soul. His heart trembles and his conscience thunders condemnation. So it must be with every sinner when all his sins against God will stand revealed before his eyes and there will be nothing left for him except intense and unqualified self-condemnation.

7. God's omnipotence is no guarantee to anyone that either himself or any other sinner will be saved. I know the Universalist affirms it to be. He will ask, "Does not the fact of God's omnipotence, taken in connection with His infinite love, prove that all people will be saved?"

I answer, "No!" It does not prove that God will save one soul. Even with so much proof of God's perfect wisdom, love, and power, we could not conclude that He would save even one sinner. We might just as reasonably suppose that He would send the whole human race to hell. How could we know what His wisdom would determine? How could we know what the necessities of His government might demand? In fact, the only basis we have for the belief that He will save any sinner is not at all our assumption from His wisdom, love, and power, but is entirely and only His own declarations as to this matter. Our knowledge is entirely from revelation. God has said so, and this is all we know about it.

8. How bitter the reflections that sinners must have on their deathbeds, and how fearfully agonizing it must be when they pass behind the veil and see things in their true light! When you have seen a sinner dying in his sins, have you ever thought about what a dreadful thing it is for a sinner to die? You notice the lines of anguish on his face. You see the look of despair. You observe that he cannot bear to hear about the dreadful future.

There he lies, and death advances in its stern assault. The poor victim struggles in vain against his dreaded foe. He sinks and sinks. His pulse runs lower, and still lower. Look into his glazed eye. Observe that withered brow. It seems that he has stopped breathing, but all at once he stares as one frightened. He throws up his hands wildly, screams frightfully, sinks down, and is gone to return no more!

Where is he now? He is not beyond the realm of thought and reflection. He can see back into the world he has left. He can still think. Sadly, his misery is that he can do nothing except think! As the prisoner in his solitary cell said, "I could bear torture or endure toil, but oh, to have nothing to do except to think! To hear the voice of friends no more, to say not a word, to do nothing from day to day and from year to year except to think – that is awful."

It is the same with the lost sinner. Who can measure the misery of unceasing self-agonizing thought? While you are yet alive, when at any time your thoughts weigh uncomfortably upon you and you feel that you will almost go insane, you can find some drop of comfort for your fevered lips. You can for a few moments, at least, fall asleep, and so forget your sorrows and find a brief rest; but oh, when you will reach the world where the wicked find no rest, where there can be no sleep, where not one drop of water can reach you to cool your tongue – how can your heart endure or your hands be strong in that dreadful hour? God tried in vain to cleanse and save you. You fought against Him and pulled down on your guilty head a fearful damnation!

9. What infinite consolation will remain to God after He will have closed up the entire scenes of earth! He has banished the wicked and has taken home the righteous to His arms of love and peace. He says, "I have done all I wisely could to save the human race. I made sacrifices cheerfully. I sent My well-beloved Son gladly. I waited as long as it seemed wise to wait, and now it only remains to overrule all this pain and woe for the utmost good, and to rejoice in the joy of the redeemed forevermore."

These are the guilty lost. Their groans roll out and echo up the walls of their pit of woe. It is only so much evidence to those who are holy that God is good and wise and will surely sustain His throne in justice and righteousness forever. It teaches most impressive lessons upon the dreadful destruction of sin. Let it stand there and bear its testimony in order to warn others against a path so shameful and a fate so dreadful!

Some of our students, maybe even some of our own children, could be there in that world of woe. However, God is just, and His throne is undefiled of their blood. It will not spoil the eternal joy of His kingdom that they would pull down such damnation on their heads. They insisted that they would take the responsibility, and now they have it.

Sinner, do you not care about this today? Will you seek God about your salvation? I can tell you when you will not think this is inconsequential. When the great bell of time will toll the death knell of earth and call her millions of sons and daughters to the final judgment, you will not be in a mood to fool around! You will certainly be there one day soon! It will be a time for serious thought – a terrible time of dread.

Are you ready to face its revelations and decisions, or do you say, "Enough, enough! I have long enough opposed His grace and rejected His love. I will now give my heart to God. I will forevermore be His alone"?

# Chapter 14

# The Inner and the Outer Revelation

There are many people who believe that a careless, general faithlessness has rarely, if ever, been more prevalent in our country than at this time, especially among young men. I am not prepared to say it is an honest faithlessness, yet it may very probably be real. Young men may really doubt the inspiration of the Christian Scriptures, not because they have honestly studied those Scriptures and their numerous evidences, but because they have read them little and reasoned legitimately even less. Particularly, they have almost universally failed to study the intuitive affirmations of their own minds. They have not examined the original revelation that God has made in each human soul to see how far this would carry them and how wonderfully it opens the way for understanding and, indeed, for embracing the revelation given in God's Word.

To bring these and similar points before your minds, I have taken as my text the words of Paul from 2 Corinthians 4:2: *By manifestation of the truth commending ourselves to every man's conscience in the sight of God.*

Paul is speaking of the gospel ministry that he received, and he is stating how he fulfilled it. He shows plainly that he should preach to the human conscience. He found in each person's heart a conscience to which he could appeal and to which the manifestation of the truth commended itself.

Probably no thoughtful person has ever read the Bible without noticing that there has been a previous revelation given in some way to man. It assumes many things as being already known. Some of you might know that I was studying in my law office when I bought my first Bible, and that I bought it as one of my law books. No sooner had I opened it than I was struck to see how many things it assumed as being known, and therefore states much with no attempt at proof. For instance, the first verse in the Bible says, *In the beginning God created the heavens and the earth* (Genesis 1:1). This assumes the existence of God. It does not try to prove this truth, but it goes on the presumption that this revelation – the existence of a God – has been made already to all who are mature enough to understand it.

The apostle Paul also, in his epistle to the Romans, asserts that the real Godhead and eternal power of the one God, though in some sense *invisible things*, are still *clearly seen* in the creation of the world, *being understood by the things that are made*, so that all wicked people are *without excuse* (Romans 1:20). Paul's doctrine is that the created universe reveals God. If this is true of the universe without us, it is no less true of the universe within us. Our own minds – their convictions and their necessary affirmations – truly reveal God and many of the great truths that note our relations to Him and to His government.

When we read the Bible attentively and notice how many things of the utmost importance it assumes, and bases its precepts on them without attempting to prove them, we cannot resist asking if these assumptions are properly made.

The answer to this question is found when we turn our eye within and inquire for the intuitive affirmations of our own minds. When we do so, we will see that we possess an intellectual and moral nature that just as truly reveals great truths concerning God and our relations to Him and to law as the material world reveals His eternal power and Godhead.

For instance, we will see that man has a moral nature related to spiritual and moral truth just as certainly as he has a physical nature related to the physical world. As his senses – sight, touch, hearing – perceive certain truths respecting the external world, so does his spiritual nature perceive certain truths respecting the spiritual world. No one can well consider the first class of truths without being forced to consider and believe the second.

Let us see if this is true. Not long ago, I met with a young lady of considerable intelligence who was a skeptic. She professed to believe in God and in those great truths pertaining to His attributes that are embraced in deism, but she quite rejected the Bible and all that pertains to a revealed way of salvation.

I began by presenting to her mind some of the great truths taught by the mind's own affirmations concerning God, His attributes, and His government, and then I proceeded to show her how the Bible came in to make out a system of truth needful to man as a lost sinner. Of course, she admitted the first, and then she saw that the second must be true if the first was true, or else there could be nothing for man but hopeless ruin. Recoiling in horror from the gulf of despair, she saw that only her unbelief was ruining her soul. She then renounced this, yielded her heart to God, and found gospel peace and joy in believing.

> If anyone is ever afraid of God at all, it is because He is good – He is just and holy.

I plan now to present much the same course of thought to you as I did to her. The first great question is, What ideas does our own nature – God's first revelation – give us?

1. Undoubtedly, man's own nature gives him the idea of God. Our own minds affirm that there is and must be a God, and that He must have all power and all knowledge. Our minds also give us God's moral attributes. No one can doubt that God is good and just. People are never afraid that God will do anything wrong. If anyone is ever afraid of God at all, it is because He is good – He is just and holy.

2. Man's nature gives him the idea of law – moral law. He can no more doubt the existence of a moral law, imposed also on himself, than he can doubt the existence of his own soul and body. He knows he should not be selfish, but should be compassionate. He knows he is obligated to love his neighbor as himself.

How is it that people get these ideas? I answer that they must have them by nature. They must be in the mind before they receive any direct instruction from human lips, or else you could never teach a child these ideas any more than you could teach them to a horse. The child knows these things before he is taught, and he cannot remember when he first knew them.

Suppose you were to close your Bible and ask, "Apart from all that this Book teaches, how much do I know?" You would find that your moral nature gives you the idea of a God and affirms His existence. It gives you His attributes, natural and moral, and also your own moral relations to Him and to your fellow beings.

In proof of this, I can appeal to you that not one of you can say that you are under no obligation to love God and your fellow humans. Your moral nature teaches you these things. It affirms to you these truths, even more directly and undeniably than your senses give you the facts of the external world. Moreover, your moral nature not only gives you the law of supreme love to God and of love equal and impartial toward your fellow men, but it affirms that you are sinners – that you have displeased God and have utterly failed to please Him – and of course that you are under condemnation from His righteous law. You know that God's good law must condemn you because you have not been good in the sense required by that law. Therefore, you must know that you are in the position of a criminal, condemned by the law and without hope from the administration of justice.

Another thing it teaches you is that you are still unrepentant (I speak of those who know this to be their case). Your own conscience affirms this to you beyond all contradiction. It affirms that you are still living in sin and have not reformed in such a way that God can accept your reformation. You know that you do harm to your own conscience, and that while you are doing this, you can neither respect yourself nor be respected by God. You know that as long as this is the case with you, God cannot forgive you. Even more, if He would, it would not do any good. You could not be happy. You could not respect yourself, even if you were told that you were forgiven.

Even if your nature spoke out honestly, it would not let you believe that you are really forgiven as long as you are doing harm to your conscience. I can remember when these thoughts were in my mind like fire.

I saw that no one could doubt them any more than he could doubt his own existence. Certainly you may see these truths and feel their force.

You know, then, that you have forfeited the favor of God by your sins, and you have no claim on Him at all based upon the score of justice. You have cast off His authority and have refused subjection to His law and government. Indeed, you have cast all His precepts beneath your feet. You can no longer come before God and say, "You should not have cast me off. I have not deserved it at Your hand." You can no more say this honestly than you can deny your own existence.

Did you ever think of this? Have you ever tried to see what you can honestly do and say before God? Have you ever tried to go into God's presence and seriously tell Him that He has no right to punish you? Not one of you can tell Him so without being conscious in yourself of blasphemy.

It is a good method because it may serve to show you how the case really stands. Suppose you try it. See what you can honestly and with an approving conscience say before God when your soul is deeply impressed with the sense of His presence. Consider that I am not asking you whether you can harden your heart and violate your conscience enough to blaspheme God to His face, but I am asking you to put the honest convictions of your own conscience to the test and see what they are and what they will allow you to do and to say before God. Can you kneel down before Him and say, "I deny that I have cast off God. I have never refused to treat Him as a friend. I have never treated Him as an enemy"? You know you can make no issue of this kind with God without meeting the rebukes of your own mind.

Maybe you can see no reason to hope for forgiveness under the law. With all the light of your deism, you can discern no ground of pardon. Outside the Bible, all is as dark as death. There is no hope. If you cling to any hope, it must be directly in the teeth of your own solemn convictions. Why do you think it is so difficult to persuade a wise governor to grant a pardon?

When Jerome Bonaparte was monarch of Spain, why did his brother Napoleon send him that earnest rebuke for pardoning certain criminals? What were the principles that underlaid that remarkably able state paper? Have you ever studied those principles as they were grasped and presented so powerfully by the mighty mind of Napoleon?

You can never infer from the goodness of God that He can forgive – much less, that He must. One of the first Universalist preachers I ever heard announced at the beginning that he would infer from the goodness of God that He would save all people. I can well remember how perfectly shallow his arguments appeared to me and how absurd his assumptions seemed. I was not a Christian then, but I quickly saw that he could much better infer from the goodness of God that He would forgive none than that He would forgive all. It seemed to me most clear that if God were good and had made a good law, He would sustain it. Why not? I must suppose that His law is a good one. How could a Being of infinite wisdom and love impose any other law than a good law? And if it were a good law, it had a good end to answer, and a good God could not allow it to fail to answer those ends by letting it come to nothing through inefficiency in its administration.

I knew enough about law and government then to see that a firm hand in administration is essential to any good results from ever so good a law. Of course, I knew that if law were left to be trampled underfoot by hardened, blasphemous transgressors, and then to add to that, an broad pardon were given, and nothing done to sustain the law, there would be an end of all authority and a positive annihilation of all the good hoped for under its administration. Will rational people attempt to presume from God's goodness that He will pardon all sinners?

Suppose the spirit of riot and lawlessness now so rampant at Erie, Pennsylvania, goes from bad to worse – that the rioters commit every form of mischief in their power. Suppose that they tear up the rails, burn down the bridges, shoot into the cars, and run entire trains off the track, crushing the quivering flesh of hundreds all at once into heaps of blood and bones. Then, when the guilty are arrested and convicted by due course of law, the question comes up, Will the governor pardon them? He might be very much inclined to do so, if he wisely could, but could a good governor do so? What would a purely good and truly wise governor do?

Will you say, "Oh, he is too good to punish. He is so good, he will certainly pardon"? Will you say that pardon broadly given, and given to all, will secure the highest respect for law and the best obedience? Everybody knows that this is absolute nonsense. No one who ever had anything to do under the responsibilities of government, or who has ever learned the basics of human nature in this relation, can for one moment suppose that pardon in such ways can replace punishment with any other result than complete ruin. No. If the ruler is good, he will certainly punish, and all the more certainly by how much more predominant the element of goodness in his character is.

You, sinners, are under the law. If you sin, you must see much reason why God should punish and not forgive.

Here is another fact. When you look upon yourself and your moral position, you find yourself twice dead. You are civilly dead in the sense of being condemned by law, an outcast from governmental favor. You are also morally dead, for you do not love God, do not serve Him, and have no tendencies that will lead you to care about the things of God. On the other hand, you are dead to all considerations that could lead this way. You are indeed alive to your own low, selfish interests, but dead to God's interests. You care nothing for God except to avoid Him and escape His judgment. You know all this beyond all question. In this condition, without a further revelation, where is your hope? You have none, and have no reason for any.

> You, sinners, are under the law. If you sin, you must see much reason why God should punish and not forgive.

Furthermore, if a future revelation is to be made, revealing some reason for pardon, you can see with the light now before you on what basis it must rest. You can see what more you need from God. The first revelation closes you up to God. It shows you that if help ever comes, it cannot come from yourself, but must come from God. It cannot come from His justice, but must come from His mercy. It cannot come from the law, but must come from some extra provision whereby the law may have its demands satisfied other than through the execution of its penalty on the offender. You can see that somebody must intercede for you who can take your part and stand in your place before the offended law.

Did you ever think of this? In the position where you stand, and where your own nature and your own convictions place you, you are compelled to say, "My case is hopeless! I need a double salvation – from condemnation and from sinning. I need to be saved first from the curse, and then from the heart to sin – from the tendency and inclination to commit sin. Where can I find a revelation to meet these needs of my lost soul?"

Is the answer to be found in all the book of nature? No. Look into the irresistible convictions of your own moral being. They tell you of your needs, but they do not supply those needs. They show what you need, but they entirely fail to give it. Your own moral nature shows that you need an atoning Savior and a renewing Spirit. Nothing less can meet the case of a sinner condemned, unlawful, and doubly dead by the moral corruption of all his voluntary powers.

The worst trouble with unbelief is that it ignores all this. It takes no notice of one entire side of our nature, and that side is the most important side. It talks much about philosophy, yet restricts itself to the philosophy of the outer world and has no interest in the inner and higher nature. It ignores the fact that our moral nature affirms one entire class of great truths, and does so with even more force and certainty than the senses affirm the facts of the external world. Truly, this is a tremendous and a fatal omission!

## Remarks

1. Without the first revelation, the second could not be satisfactorily proved. When the Bible reveals God, it assumes that our minds affirm His existence and that we need no higher proof. When it reveals His law, it presupposes that we are capable of understanding it and of appreciating its moral claims. When it prescribes duty, it assumes that we would feel the force of obligation to obey it.

The fact that the Bible makes many arguments of this sort establishes an intimate and dependent connection between the Bible on the one hand, and the laws of the human mind on the other. If these assumptions are well and truly made, then the divine authority of the Bible is abundantly sustained by its correspondence and harmony with the intellectual and moral nature of man. It suits the beings to whom it is given. On the other hand, if these assumptions had on examination proved false, it would be impossible to sustain the credit of the Scriptures as coming from a wise and honest Being.

2. Having the first revelation, it is most absurd to reject the second. The second is to a great extent a reaffirmation of the first, with various important additions of a supplementary sort, such as the atonement (and therefore the possibility of pardon) and the gift and work of the Spirit (and therefore the related possibility of being saved from sinning).

Now those things that the first revelation affirms and the second reaffirms are so fundamental in any revelation of moral duty to moral beings that having them taught so naturally and so undeniably, we are left self-convicted of extreme absurdity if we then reject the second. Logically, there seems no ground left on which to base a denial of the written revelation. Its supplementary doctrines are not, to be sure, intuitive truths, but they are so related to man's needs as a lost sinner, and they so richly supply those needs. Moreover, they are so beautifully related to the requirements of God's government, and they so sufficiently meet those requirements, that no intelligent mind, once understanding all these things in their actual relationships, can fail to recognize their truthfulness.

> A person can no more deny the Bible after knowing all his own moral relations than he can deny his own existence.

3. The study of the first secures an intellectual reception of the second. I do not believe it is possible for anyone to read and understand the first thoroughly and then come to the second and properly understand its relation to his own moral nature and moral convictions, and also his moral needs, without being compelled to say that it is all true – that the Bible is entirely true! They coincide so wondrously, and the former sustains the latter so admirably and so triumphantly, that a person can no more deny the Bible after knowing all his own moral relations than he can deny his own existence.

4. You see why so many people reject the Bible. They have not read it well themselves. They have not looked within to read carefully the volume God has put on record there. They have labored to quiet and

extinguish the ever-rising convictions of their own moral nature. They have refused to listen to the cry of need that swells up from their troubled heart of sin. Therefore, there is still one entire volume of revelation of which they are strangely ignorant. This ignorance accounts for their rejection of the Bible.

A little attention to the subject will show you that the reason here indicated is beyond question that basis on which the multitudes in every Christian land really rest their faith in the Bible. Hardly one in ten thousand of them has studied the historical argument for divine revelation extensively and carefully so as to intelligently make this a cornerstone for his faith in the Bible. It is not reasonable to demand that they should.

There is an argument that is shorter and infinitely more convincing. It is a simple problem: a soul is guilty, condemned, and lost, and some adequate relief is required. The gospel solves the problem. Who will not accept the solution? It answers every condition perfectly. Therefore, it must come from God. It is at least our highest wisdom to accept it.

Someone might reply to this that such a problem fits the situation only of those who give their hearts to God. However, this may be adapted to yet another group of people. Some know that their moral nature affirms God, law, obligation, sin, and ruin, and they have a need to know whether a written revelation is reliable that is built upon the broad basis of man's intuitive affirmations, that gives them the approval of man's Creator, that adds a system of duty and of salvation of such a kind that it interlocks itself inseparably with truth intuitive to man, and that clearly fills out an accompaniment of moral instructions and agencies in perfect adaptation to both man and his Maker.

In the Bible, we have the very thing required. A key that threads the countless obstacles of such a lock must have been made to fit. Each came from the same Author. You cannot grant to man an origin from God without granting the same origin to the Bible. When I came to examine these things in the light of my own convictions, I wondered how I had not seen them truly before.

Suppose I would now announce to you the two great precepts of the moral law; would not their obvious nature and meaning enforce on your mind the conviction that these precepts must be true and must be from God? As I would discuss these things more specifically, you would still affirm that these must be true and that these must certainly have come down from heaven.

Even if I were to go back to the Mosaic law (a law that many object to because they do not understand the circumstances that called for such a law) and would explain their special circumstances and the reasons for such statutes, everyone must affirm the righteousness of even those statutes. I am aware that the Old Testament reveals truth under a veil since the world was not then ready for its clearer revelation. The veil was taken away when, in the fullness of time, people were prepared for God in the flesh being clearly revealed (Galatians 4:4).

The reason, therefore, why so many people receive the Bible is not that they are gullible and therefore accept absurdities with ease, but the reason is that because it commends itself so irresistibly to each person's own nature and to his deep and resistless convictions, he is compelled to receive it. He would do harm to his inner convictions if he rejects it. Man's whole nature cries out, "This is just what I need!"

That young lady of whom I spoke could not help but abandon her unbelief and surrender her heart to God when she had reached this point. I asked her, "Do you admit that there is a God?"

She answered, "Yes."

"Do you admit that there is law?"

"Yes."

"Do you admit your personal sin?"

"Yes."

"And your need of salvation?"

"Oh, yes."

"Can you help yourself?"

"Oh, no," she said. "I do not believe I can ever be saved."

"But God can save you. Certainly nothing is too hard for Him."

"Oh," she replied, "my own nature has closed me in. I am in despair. There is no way of escape for me. The Bible, you know, I don't receive, and here I am in darkness and despair!"

At this point, I began to speak of the gospel. I said to her, "Listen

– God has done such and such things as revealed in the gospel. He came down and dwelt in human flesh to meet the case of such sinners as you are. He made a sufficient atonement for sin. What do you think of that?"

"That is exactly what I need," she said. "If it were only true!"

"If it is not true," I said, "you are lost beyond hope. Why, then, not believe?"

"I cannot believe it," she answered, "because it is inconceivable. It is much too good to be true!"

"And is not God good," I said, "infinitely good? Then why do you object that anything He does is too good to be true?"

"That is what I need," she repeated again, "but how can it be so?"

"Then you cannot give God credit for being so good!" I said.

"I see that it is my unbelief, but I cannot believe. I can clearly see that it is what I need, but how can I believe it?"

At this point I rose up and said to her seriously, "The crisis has come! There is now only one question for you: Will you believe the gospel?"

She raised her eyes, which had been sad and covered for half an hour or more. Every feature declared the most intense discomfort. I asked again, "Will you believe God? Will you give Him credit for sincerity?"

> The Bible presumes that you have enough light to see and to do your duty.

She threw herself upon her knees and began to loudly weep. What a scene – to see a skeptic beginning to give God credit for love and truth – to see the door of light and hope opened, and heaven's blessed light breaking in upon a desolate soul! Have you ever witnessed such a scene? When she next opened her lips, it was to proclaim the Savior's praise!

The Bible presumes that you have enough light to see and to do your duty, and to find the way to heaven. A great many of you are perhaps confused as to your religious beliefs, holding undefined and cynical ideas. You have not seen that it is the most reasonable thing in the world to acknowledge and embrace this glorious truth. Will you allow yourself to go on confused, without considering that you are yourself a living, walking revelation of truth? Will you refuse to come into such a relationship to God and Christ that will save your soul?

In my early life, when I was tempted with doubt, I can well remember that I said to myself that it is much more probable that ministers and the multitudes of good people who believe the Bible are right, than that I am. I knew that they had examined the subject, while I had not. It was therefore entirely unreasonable for me to doubt.

Certainly you can say, "I know that the gospel is suited to my needs. I know I am afloat on the vast ocean of life, and if there is no gospel, there is nothing that can save me. It is therefore not right for me to stand here and criticize. I must examine it. I must look into this matter. I can at least see that if God offers me mercy, I must not reject it."

Does not this gospel show you how you can be saved from hell and from sin? Then believe it! Let the blessed truth find your heart open for its acceptance. When you will dare to give God credit for all His love and truth, and when you will bring your heart under the power of this truth and surrender yourself to its blessed influence – that will be the dawn of morning to your soul! *Whosoever will, let him come and take of the waters of life freely* (Revelation 22:17).

# Chapter 15

# Quenching the Spirit

Quench not the Spirit.
—1 Thessalonians 5:19

In discussing the subject presented in this text, I will try to do the following:

I.   Show how the Holy Spirit influences the mind

II.  Draw some conclusions from the known method of the Spirit's operations

III. Show what it is to quench the Spirit

IV. Show how this may be done

V.  Explain the consequences of quenching the Spirit

## I. How does the Holy Spirit influence the human mind?

The Holy Spirit does not influence the human mind by physical means. He does not do so by using direct physical power. The action of the will is not influenced in this way and cannot be. The very idea is absurd. It is both absurd and at war with the very idea of free agency to think that physical means would produce voluntary mental phenomena just as it does physical. It is absurd to think that the same physical means that move a planet would move the human will.

Also, the Bible informs us that the Spirit influences the human mind by means of truth. The Spirit persuades people to act in view of truth, just as we ourselves influence our fellow men by presenting truth to their minds. I do not mean that God presents truth to the mind in the same way that we do. Of course, His way of doing it must differ from ours. We use writing, speech, and gestures. We use the language of words and the language of nature. God does not use these means now, yet He still reaches the mind with truth. Sometimes His providence suggests it, and then His Spirit gives it power, setting it home upon the heart of the recipient.

> Whatever the method, the purpose is always the same: to produce voluntary action in conformity to His law.

Sometimes the Lord makes use of preaching. Indeed, His ways are various. But whatever the method, the purpose is always the same: to produce voluntary action in conformity to His law.

If the Bible were entirely silent on this subject, we would still know from the nature of the mind and from the nature of those influences that only can move the human mind that the Spirit must exert not physical, but moral influences on the mind. However, we are not now left to a merely theoretical opinion, for we have the plain testimony of the Bible to the fact that the Spirit uses truth in converting and sanctifying people.

## II. We next inquire what is implied in this fact, and what conclusions can be drawn from it.

God is physically omnipotent, yet His moral influences exerted by the Spirit may be resisted. You will easily see that if the Spirit moved people by physical omnipotence, no mortal could possibly resist His influence. The Spirit's power would of course be irresistible, for who could withstand omnipotence?

We know it is a fact that people can resist the Holy Spirit, for the nature of moral agency implies this, and the Bible declares it. The nature of moral agency implies the voluntary action of one who can yield to motive and follow light or not as he pleases. Where this power does not exist, moral agency cannot exist; and at whatever point this power ceases, moral agency ceases there also.

Therefore, if our action is that of moral agents, our moral freedom to do or not do must remain. It cannot be set aside or in any way overruled. If God would in any way set aside our voluntary ability, He would of necessity terminate at once our moral and responsible action. Suppose God would grab hold of someone's arm with physical omnipotence and forcibly use it in acts of murder or of arson. Who does not see that the moral, responsible power of that person would be entirely set aside? Yet this is not more than if, in an equally irresistible manner, God would seize the person's will and compel it to act as He desired.

The very idea that moral influence can ever by itself be irresistible originates in an entire mistake as to the nature of the will and of moral action. The will of man can never act in any way other than freely in view of truth and of the motives it presents for action. Increasing the amount of such influence has no sort of tendency to impair the freedom of the will. Under any possible vividness of truth perceived, or under any amount of motive present to the mind, the will still has the same changeless power to yield or not yield – to act or refuse to act in accordance with this perceived truth.

This fact shows that any work of God carried on by moral and not by physical power not only can be resisted by man, but also that man may be in very special danger of resisting it. If the Lord carries the work forward by means of revealed truth, there may be most imminent danger that people will neglect to study and understand this truth, or that knowing this truth, they will refuse to obey it. Surely it is very much within the power of each person to shut out this truth from his consideration and close his heart against its influence.

## III. We next inquire what it means to quench the Spirit.

We will easily understand this when we come to see clearly what the work of the Spirit is. We have already seen that the Spirit's work is to enlighten the mind into truth concerning God, ourselves, and our duty. For example, the Spirit enlightens the mind into the meaning and self-application of the Bible. It takes the things of Christ and shows them to us.

There is such a thing as refusing to receive this light. You can shut your eyes against it. You have the power to turn your eye entirely away and barely see it at all. You can absolutely refuse to follow it when seen, and in this case, God ceases to hold up the truth before your mind.

Almost everyone knows by personal experience that the Spirit has the power to shine a marvelous light upon revealed truth so that this truth will stand before the mind in a new and most impressive form and will operate upon it with astonishing strength. But this light of the Spirit may be quenched.

There is, so to speak, a sort of heat – a warmth and vitality attending the truth when it is enforced by the Spirit. That is why we say that if one has the Spirit of God, his soul is warm, and if he does not have the Spirit, his heart is cold. This vital heat produced by the divine Spirit may be quenched. If someone resists the Spirit, he will certainly quench this vital power that it exerts upon the heart.

## IV. We will now point out some of the ways in which the Spirit may be quenched.

1. People often quench the Spirit by directly resisting the truth He presents to their minds. Sometimes people set themselves deliberately to resist the truth, determined that they will not yield to its power, at least for now. In such cases, it is amazing to see how great the influence of the will is in resisting the truth. Indeed, the will can always resist any moral considerations, for as we have seen, there is no such thing as forcing the will to yield to truth.

In those cases in which the truth presses strongly on the mind, there is credible evidence that the Spirit is present by His power. It is in precisely these cases that people are especially prone to set themselves against the truth, and therefore are in the utmost danger of quenching the Spirit. They hate the truth presented. It frustrates their chosen path of indulgence. They feel irritated and harassed by its claims. They resist and quench the Spirit of the Lord.

You have undoubtedly often seen such cases, and if so, you have undoubtedly noticed this other remarkable fact that often occurs: after a short struggle in resisting truth, the conflict is over, and that particular truth almost completely stops affecting the mind. The individual becomes hardened to its power. He seems quite able to disregard it and drive it from his thoughts, or if this fails and the truth is thrown before his mind, he still finds it relatively easy to resist its claims. He felt greatly annoyed by that truth until he had quenched the Spirit, and now he is no longer bothered by it.

If you have seen cases like this, you have undoubtedly seen how, as the truth pressed upon their minds, they became agitated, offended, and then even angry, but they remained stubborn in resisting until at last the conflict eases. The truth makes no more impression upon them, and is from then on quite dead to them. They grasp it only with the greatest dimness, and care nothing about it.

Let me ask here: Have not some of you had this very experience? Have you not resisted some truth until it has ceased to affect your minds? If so, then you may conclude that you have quenched the Spirit of God in that case.

2. The Spirit is often quenched when people try to support error. People are sometimes foolish enough to attempt to support a position by an argument that they have good reason to know is a false position. They argue it until they get committed to it. They indulge in a dishonest state of mind, and so quench the Spirit. They are usually left to believe the very lie that they so unwisely attempted to support. I have seen many such cases when people began to defend and maintain a position that they know is wrong, and they continued in it until they quenched the Spirit of God. They believed their own lie, and it is to be feared that they will die under its delusions.

> Perhaps nothing more certainly quenches the Spirit than to question the motives of others and judge them harshly.

3. The Spirit of God is quenched by unkind judgments. Perhaps nothing more certainly quenches the Spirit than to question the motives of others and judge them harshly. It is so unlike God, and so hostile to the law of love, that it is no wonder that the Spirit of God is completely opposed to it and turns away from those who take part in it.

4. The Spirit is grieved by harsh and indecent language. People often grieve the Spirit of God by using such language toward those who disagree with them. It is always safe to presume that people who give in to such behavior have already grieved the Spirit of God completely away,

5. The Spirit of God is quenched by a bad temper. When a bad temper and spirit are stirred up in individuals or in a community, a revival of religion suddenly ceases. The Spirit of God is repressed and quenched. There is no more prevailing prayer, and no more sinners are converted.

6. Often the Spirit is quenched by diverting the attention from the truth. Since the Spirit operates through the truth, it is most obvious that we must pay attention to this truth that the Spirit wants to keep before our minds. If we refuse to listen, as we always can if we choose to do so, we will almost certainly quench the Holy Spirit.

7. We often quench the Spirit by giving in to excessive excitement on

any subject. If the subject is outside of practical, divine truth, strong excitement diverts attention from such truth and makes it almost impossible to feel its power. While the mind sees and feels strongly about the subject in which it is excited, it sees dimly and feels distant regarding the vital things of salvation. Therefore, the Spirit is quenched.

The extreme enthusiasm may even be on some really religious topic. Sometimes I have seen a burst – a real tornado of feeling in a revival – but in such cases, truth loses its hold on the minds of the people. They are too much excited to take serious views of the truth and of the moral duties it instills. However, by no means is all religious excitement to be condemned. There must be enough emotion to stir up the mind to serious thought – enough to give the truth an edge and power. It is always good, though, to avoid that measure of excitement that throws the mind from its balance and renders its understanding of truth uncertain or irregular.

8. The Spirit is quenched by entertaining preconceived ideas. Whenever the mind is made up on any subject before it is thoroughly examined, that mind is closed against the truth and the Spirit is quenched. When there are strong preconceived ideas, it seems impossible for the Spirit to act, and of course, His influence is quenched. The mind is so committed that it resists the first efforts of the Spirit.

Thousands have done so. Thousands of people have ruined their souls for eternity in this way. Therefore, let everyone keep his mind open to conviction and be sure to carefully examine all important questions, especially great questions about duty to God and man.

I am not speaking now against being firm in maintaining your position after you thoroughly understand it and are sure it is the truth, but while pursuing your investigations, be sure you are really honest and yield your mind to all the reasonable evidence you can find.

9. The Spirit is often quenched by violating one's conscience. There are circumstances under which violating one's conscience seems to quench the light of God in the soul forever. Maybe you have seen cases like this where people have had a very tender conscience on some subject, but all at once they come to have no conscience at all on that subject.

I am aware that change of conduct sometimes results from change of views without any violation of conscience, but the situation I speak of is where the conscience seems to be killed. All that remains of it seems as hard as a stone.

I have sometimes thought that the Spirit of God had much more to do with conscience than we usually think. The fact is undeniable that people sometimes experience very great and sudden changes in the amount of sensibility of conscience that they feel on some subjects. This is only to be accounted for by the premise that the Spirit has power to awaken the conscience and make it pierce like an arrow. Then when people sin, despite the reproof of conscience, the Spirit is quenched. The conscience loses all its sensitivity. A complete change takes place, and the person continues in sin as if he never had any conscience to forbid it.

It sometimes happens that the mind is awakened just prior to committing some particular sin. Something seems to say to the person, "If you do this, you will be forsaken of God." A strange apprehension warns him to stop. If he continues, the whole mind receives a dreadful shock. The very eyes of the mind seem to be almost put out. The moral perceptions are strangely irrational and confused. A deadly harm is done to the conscience on that specific subject at least, and indeed the injury to the conscience seems to affect all departments of moral action. In such circumstances, the Spirit of God seems to turn away and say, "I can do no more for you. I have warned you faithfully and can warn you no more."

If people continue to commit the sin despite the Spirit's warnings, the soul is left in dreadful darkness.

All these results sometimes accumulate from neglect of plainly revealed duty. People avoid known duty through fear of the opinions of others, or through dislike of some self-denial. In this crisis of trial, the Spirit does not leave them in a state of doubt or inattention as to duty, but keeps the truth and the claims of God vividly before the mind. Then, if people continue to commit the sin despite the Spirit's warnings, the soul is left in dreadful darkness. The light of the Spirit of God may be quenched forever.

I do not know in how many cases I have seen people in great agony, and even despair, who have evidently quenched the Spirit in the manner just described. There is the case of a young man whom I know. He had a long trial on the question of preparing himself for the ministry. He contemplated the question for a long time. The claims of God were clearly set before him, but at last he resisted the convictions of duty, went away and got married, and turned away from the work to which God had seemed to call him. Then the Spirit left him.

For a few years after, he remained entirely hardened as to what he had done and as to any claims of God upon him, but finally his wife became sick and died. Then his eyes were opened. He saw what he had done. He sought the Lord, but sought in vain. No light returned to his darkened, desolate soul. It no longer seemed his duty to prepare for the ministry. That call of God had ceased. His cup of wretchedness seemed to be filled to the brim. He often spent whole nights in most intense agony – groaning, crying for mercy, or reflecting in anguish upon the dire despair that spread its universe of desolation all around him. He was so absolutely miserable under these reproaches of a guilty conscience and these thoughts of deep despair that I have often feared he would take his own life.

I could mention many other similar cases. People refuse to do known duty, and this refusal does deadly harm to their own moral sense and to the Spirit of the Lord. Consequently, there remains for them only *a certain fearful looking for of judgment and fiery indignation* (Hebrews 10:27).

10. People often quench the Spirit by indulging their appetites and passions. You would be astonished if you knew how often the Spirit is grieved by this means until a crisis is formed of such a nature that they seem to quench the light of God at once from their souls. Some people indulge their appetite for food to the injury of their health. Although they know they are hurting themselves, and the Spirit of God objects and implores them to desist from ruinous self-indulgence, they persist in their course and are given up by God. From that point on, their appetites control them to the ruin of their spirituality and of their souls. The same may be true of any form of physical indulgence.

11. The Spirit is often quenched by indulging in dishonesty. People engaged in business will take little advantages in buying and selling.

Sometimes they are powerfully convinced of the great selfishness of this, and they see that this is not at all loving their neighbor as themselves. It may happen that someone who is about to drive a good bargain will ask himself the question, "Is this right?" He will consider it in his mind for a while and will say to himself, "Now this neighbor of mine needs this article very much, and he will suffer if he does not get it. This will give me a great chance to add to the price – but then would this be doing to him what I would want him to do to me?" He looks and thinks. He sees his duty, but he ends up deciding in favor of his selfishness.

Eternity alone will disclose the consequences of such a decision. When the Spirit of God has followed such people for a long time, has made them see their danger, has kept the truth before them, and finally, seizing the favorable moment, makes a last effort to save them, and this proves futile – then the die is cast. From then on, all restraints are gone and the selfish person is abandoned by God. He continues to go from bad to worse. He possibly ends up in the state prison, and certainly in hell!

12. People often quench the Spirit by casting concern aside and suppressing prayer. It is true that suppressing prayer will always quench the Spirit. It is wonderful to see how naturally and earnestly the Spirit leads us to pray. If we were really led by the Spirit, we would be drawn many times a day to secret prayer, and would be continually lifting up our hearts in silent prayers whenever the mind unwinds itself from other urgent obligations. The Spirit in the hearts of saints is preeminently a spirit of prayer, and of course, to suppress prayer will always quench the Spirit.

Some of you might have been in this very situation. You once had the spirit of prayer, but now you have lost it. You once had access to God, but you have it no longer. You have no more enjoyment in prayer. You no longer groan and agonize over the state of the church and of sinners.

If this spirit of prayer is gone, where are you now? Sadly, you have quenched the Spirit of God. You have put out His light and have driven His influences from your soul.

13. The Spirit is quenched by empty and useless conversation. Few people seem to be aware how wicked this is and how certainly it quenches the

Holy Spirit. Christ said that for *every idle word that men shall speak, they shall give account thereof in the day of judgment* (Matthew 12:36).

14. People quench the Holy Spirit by a spirit of levity and foolishness. People also quench the Holy Spirit by indulging a quick-tempered and irritable spirit. A spirit of laziness can also quench the Spirit. Many people indulge in this to such an extent as to completely drive away the Holy Spirit. Another sure way to quench the Spirit of God in the soul is by a spirit of procrastination and by indulging themselves in making excuses for neglect of duty.

15. It is to be feared that many people have quenched the Spirit by resisting the doctrine and duty of sanctification. This subject has been widely discussed for a few years past, and the doctrine has also been greatly opposed. Several church bodies have taken a stand against it, and it is sometimes to be feared that clergy members have said and done at these denominational meetings what they would not by any means have said or done in their own homes or pulpits.

Is it not also probable that many ministers and some laymen have been influenced by this very action of these groups to oppose the doctrine – the fear of man having become a snare to their souls? May it not also be the case that some have really opposed the doctrine because it raises a higher standard of personal holiness than they like – too high, perhaps, to be able to consider themselves to be Christians, too high for their own experience, and too high for their own tastes and conduct for future life?

Who does not see that opposition to the doctrine and duty of sanctification on any such grounds must certainly and fatally quench the Holy Spirit? No work can lie nearer to the heart of Jesus than the sanctification of His people. Therefore, nothing can so greatly grieve Him as to see this work hindered – much more to see it opposed and discouraged.

An earnest and dire emphasis is given to these considerations when you consider the facts respecting the current state of piety in very many churches throughout the land. You do not need to ask if revivals are experienced, if Christians are prayerful, self-denying, alive in faith, and in love to God and to others. You do not need to ask if the work of sanctifying the church is moving on rapidly and is displaying itself by abundant fruits of righteousness. The answer is seen before you can even ask the question.

How sad that the Spirit would be quenched under the spreading of the very truth that should sanctify the church! What can save if the gospel promise in all its fullness is so twisted or resisted as to quench the Spirit, serving only to harden the heart?

## V. I will now speak of the consequences of quenching the Holy Spirit.

1. One consequence is great darkness of mind. Abandoned by God, the mind sees truth so dimly that it makes no useful impression. Such people read the Bible without interest or benefit. It becomes to them a dead letter, and they generally lay it aside unless some disagreement leads them to search it. They take no such spiritual interest in it that would make its study delightful.

Have not some of you been in this very state of mind? This is that darkness of nature that is common to people when the Spirit of God is withdrawn.

2. Another result is usually much coldness and dullness of mind in regard to Christianity generally. It leaves to the mind no such interest in spiritual things as people take in worldly things.

People often get into such a state that they are greatly interested in some worldly matters, but not in true religion. Their souls are all awake while worldly things are being discussed, but if some spiritual matter is brought up, their interest is gone at once. You can hardly get them to attend a prayer meeting. You know that they are in a worldly state of mind, for if the Spirit of the Lord was with them, they would be more deeply interested in Christ and what draws them nearer to Him than in anything else.

But observe them. See them at a political meeting or a theatrical show, and their souls are all on fire – but go and appoint a prayer meeting or a meeting to promote a revival, and they do not attend, or if they do, they feel no interest in the matter.

Such people often seem not to know themselves. They might think they attend to these worldly things only for the glory of God. I will believe this when I see them interested in spiritual things as much as in worldly things.

When someone has quenched the Spirit of God, his religion is all outside. His vital, heart-affecting interest in spiritual things is gone. It is indeed true that a true Christian will take some interest in worldly things because he regards them as a part of his duty to God, and to him they are spiritual things.

3. The mind falls very naturally into various errors in religion. The heart wanders from God, loses its hold on the truth, and the person might insist that he now takes a much more broad-minded and enlightened view of the subject than before.

I recently had a conversation with a man who had given up the idea that the Old Testament was inspired. He had given up the doctrine of the atonement, and indeed every distinctive doctrine of the Bible. He remarked to me, "I used to think as you do, but I have now come to take a more progressive and enlightened view of the subject."

Indeed! This is not a more progressive and enlightened view! He is so blinded that he cannot see that Christ confirmed the Old Testament as the oracles of God, and yet he flatters himself that he now takes a more broad-minded and enlightened view! There can be nothing stronger than Christ's affirmations respecting the inspiration of the Old Testament, and yet while this man admits that these affirmations are true, he denies the very thing they affirm! Most liberal and enlightened view indeed!

> When someone has quenched the Spirit of God, his religion is all outside. His vital, heart-affecting interest in spiritual things is gone.

How can you possibly account for such views except on the basis that for some reason the man has fallen into a strange, unnatural state of mind – a sort of mental absurdity in which moral truths are hidden or distorted? Everyone knows that there cannot be a greater absurdity than to acknowledge the divine authority of the teachings of Christ, and yet reject the Old Testament. The language of Christ affirms and implies the authority of the Old Testament in all those ways in which, on the belief that the Old Testament is inspired, He might be expected to affirm and imply this fact.

The Old Testament does not indeed exhaust divine revelation. It left more things to be revealed. Christ taught much, but He taught nothing more clearly than the divine authority of the Old Testament.

4. Quenching the Spirit often results in unfaithfulness to God. What can account for such a case as that I have just mentioned unless God has allowed the mind to fall into very great darkness?

5. Another result of quenching the Holy Spirit is great hardness of heart. The mind becomes callous to all that class of truths that make it pliable and tender. The mobility of the heart under truth depends entirely upon its moral hardness. If it is very hard, truth makes no impression. If it is soft, then it is as pliant as air, and moves quickly to the touch of truth in any direction.

6. Another result is deep delusion in regard to their spiritual state. It is remarkable that people will claim to be Christians when they have rejected every distinctive doctrine of Christianity. Indeed, such people sometimes claim that by rejecting in this way almost all of the Bible and all its great design of salvation by an atonement, they have become real Christians. They think that they now have got the true light! Indeed!

How can such a delusion be accounted for except on the basis that the Spirit of God has abandoned the person to his own ways and left him to complete and absolute delusion?

7. People in this condition often justify themselves in the most obvious wrong because they *put darkness for light, and light for darkness* (Isaiah 5:20). They entrench themselves in entirely false principles as if those principles were true and could adequately justify their sin.

## Remarks

1. People are often not aware what is going on in their minds when they are quenching the Spirit of God. Duty is presented and pressed upon

them, but they do not realize that this is really the work of the Spirit of God. They are not aware of the present voice of the Lord to their hearts, nor do they see that this solemn impression of the truth is nothing other than the effect of the Holy Spirit on their minds.

2. So when they accept different views and abandon their former opinions, they do not seem aware of the fact that God has departed from them. They flatter themselves that they have become very tolerant and very much enlightened, and have only given up their former errors. Sadly, they do not see that the light they now walk in is darkness – complete darkness! *Woe unto them that call evil good, and good evil; that put darkness for light, and light for darkness; that put bitter for sweet, and sweet for bitter!* (Isaiah 5:20).

3. You see how to account for the spiritual state of some people. Without the clue that this subject provides, you might be much misled. In the case just described, suppose that I had taken it for granted that this man was in truth taking a more enlightened and reasonable view. I would have been misguided entirely.

I have good reason to know how people become Unitarians and Universalists, having seen hundreds of instances. It is not by becoming more and more people of prayer and real spirituality. It is not by getting nearer and nearer to God. They do not go on progressing in holiness, prayer, and communion with God until in their great achievements they reach a point where they deny the inspiration of the Bible, give up public prayer, leave the ordinances of the gospel, and probably stop private prayer too.

Those who give up these things are not led away while wrestling in prayer and while walking humbly and closely with God. No one ever moved away from biblical views while in this state of mind. Rather, people first get away from God and quench His Spirit. Then they embrace one error after another. Truth, and we could almost say truthfulness itself, leaves the mind, or those qualities or moral attributes that enable the mind to discern and understand the truth. Then darkness becomes so universal and so deceptive that people imagine themselves to be entirely in the light.

4. Such a state of mind is most tragic and often hopeless. What can be done when someone has grieved away the Spirit of God?

5. When an individual or a group of people have quenched the Spirit, they are in the utmost danger of being given up to some delusion that will soon bring them to destruction.

6. They take entirely false ground who maintain that a religious movement that is the work of God cannot be resisted. For example, I have often seen cases where people would stop a revival, and then say, "It was not a real revival, for if it had been, it would not have stopped."

Nothing can be more dangerous than for someone to think that he cannot stop the work of God in his own soul. Let a group of people adopt the belief that revivals come and go without our activity and intercession, and by the instrumentality of God only, and it will bring absolute ruin on them. There never was a revival that could exist three days under such a delusion. The solemn truth is that the Spirit is most easily quenched. There is no moral work of His that cannot be resisted.

> When the Spirit is dealing with an individual, there is the greatest danger that something might be said that could be ruinous to the soul.

7. An immense responsibility pertains to revivals. There is always fearful danger that the Spirit would be resisted. When the Spirit is dealing with an individual, there is the greatest danger that something might be said that could be ruinous to the soul. Many people who have attended these meetings are in the greatest danger. The Spirit often labors with sinners here, and many have grieved Him away.

8. Many people do not seem to realize the nature of the Spirit's operations, the possibility always of resisting, and the great danger of quenching that light of God in the soul. I could name many young people who were once considering the matters pertaining to their soul whose hearts are now dull. Where are those young people who were so serious, and who attended the inquiry meeting so long in our last revival? Sadly, they have quenched the Holy Spirit.

Is not this the case with you, young man? Is it not this way with you, young woman? Have you not quenched the Spirit until your mind is now darkened and your heart is severely hardened? How long before the church bells ring to announce your death and your soul goes down to hell? How long before you lose your hold on all truth and the Spirit will have left you completely?

Let me bring this appeal home to the hearts of those who have not yet entirely quenched the light of God in the soul. Do you find that truth still takes hold of your conscience, that God's Word flashes on your mind, that heaven's light is not yet completely extinguished, and that there is still a quivering of conscience? You hear of a sudden death, like that of the young man the other day, and trembling seizes your soul, for you know that another blow may single you out.

Then by all the mercies of God, I beseech you to be careful what you do. Quench not the Holy Spirit so that your sun does not go down in everlasting darkness. Just as you may have seen the sun dim when it hid behind a dark, intense, ominous thunder cloud, so an ignorant sinner dies! Have you ever seen such a death? Dying, he seemed to sink into a dreadful cloud of fire and storm and darkness. The scene was fearful, like a sunsetting of storms, gathering clouds, rolling thunders, and forked lightnings. The clouds gather low in the west. The spirit of storm rides on the blast. Erupting thunders seem as if they would divide the solid earth. Behind such a fearful cloud, the sun hides, and all is darkness! In a similar way, I have seen sinners give up the ghost and drop into a world of storms, howling tempests, and flashing fire.

How unlike the setting sun of a mild summer evening! All nature seems to put on her sweetest smile as she bids the king of day adieu. This is how the saint of God dies. There may be paleness on his lip and cold sweat on his brow, but there is beauty in that eye and glory in the soul.

I think of a woman recently converted who became very sick. She was brought down to the gates of death, yet her soul was full of heaven. Her voice was the music of angels. Her countenance shone, and her eyes sparkled as if the forms of heavenly glory were embodied in her dying features. Nature at last sinks. The moment of death has come. She stretches out her dying hands and hails the waiting spiritual assembly.

She cries out, "Glory to God! I am coming! I am coming!" Notice that she did not say that she was going, but that she was coming!

Now compare this to the dying sinner. A frightful glare is on his countenance as if he saw ten thousand demons – as if the sun were descending into an ocean of storms to be lost in a world filled with tornadoes, storms, and death!

Young man and young woman, you will die just so if you quench the Spirit of God. Jesus Himself has said, *If ye believe not that I am he, ye shall die in your sins* (John 8:24). Beyond such a death, there is a dreadful hell.

# Chapter 16

# The Spirit Not Striving Always

And the LORD said, My Spirit shall not always strive with man.

—Genesis 6:3

In discussing this text, I will pursue the following outline of thought, and will attempt to explain the following points:

I.   What is implied in the assertion, *My Spirit shall not always strive with man*

II.  What is not intended by the Spirit's striving

III. What is intended by it

IV.  How it can be known when the Spirit strives with an individual

V.   What is intended by His not striving always

VI.  Why He will not always strive

VII. Some consequences of His ceasing to strive with people

## I. What is implied in the assertion, *My Spirit shall not always strive with man*?

1. It is implied in this assertion that the Spirit does sometimes strive with people. It is nonsense to affirm that He will not always strive if the fact that He does sometimes strive is not implied. Beyond all question, the text assumes the doctrine that God, by His Spirit, does strive sometimes with sinners.

2. It is also implied that people resist the Spirit, for there can be no strife unless there is resistance. If sinners always yielded at once to the teachings and guidance of the Spirit, there could be no striving on the part of the Spirit in the sense implied here, and it would be totally improper to use the language that is used here. In fact, the language of our text implies long-continued resistance. It continues for so long that God declares that the struggle will not be kept up on His part forever.

I am well aware that sinners are inclined to think that they do not resist God. They often think that they really want the Spirit of God to be with them and to strive with them. What? Indeed! Think of this! If a sinner really wanted the Spirit of God to convert or to lead him, how could he resist the Spirit? But in fact, he does resist the Spirit. What Stephen affirmed of the Jews of his time is true in general of all sinners: *Ye do always resist the Holy Spirit* (Acts 7:51).

If there were no resistance on the sinner's part, there could be no striving on the part of the Spirit. Therefore, it is absolutely absurd to think that a sinner in a state of mind to resist the Spirit would still sincerely desire to be led into truth and duty by the Spirit. However, sinners are sometimes so deceived about themselves and are so blinded to their true character as to imagine that they want God to strive with them while really they are resisting all He is doing and are ready to resist all He will do.

## II. We must notice secondly what is not intended by the Spirit's striving.

The main thing to be observed here is that it is not any form of physical struggling, or any effort whatsoever. It is not any force applied to our bodies. The Spirit's striving does not attempt to urge us literally along toward God or heaven. This is not to be thought of at all.

## III. What, then, is the striving of the Spirit?

The striving of the Spirit is a power of God, applied to the mind of man, that sets truth before his mind – debating, reasoning, convincing, and persuading. The sinner resists God's claims, criticizes them, and argues against them, and then God, by His Spirit, meets the sinner and debates with him, similar to how two people might debate and argue with each other. You are not, however, to think that the Holy Spirit does this with an audible voice to the human ear, but rather He speaks to the mind and to the heart. The inner ear of the soul can hear the Spirit's whispers.

Our Savior taught that when the Comforter would come, He would *reprove the world of sin, and of righteousness, and of judgment* (John 16:8). "Reprove" as used here refers in its proper sense to judicial proceedings. When the judge has heard all the testimony and the arguments of counsel, he sums up the whole case and lays it before the jury, bringing out all the strong points and conveying them, with all their condensed and accumulated power, upon the condemnation of the criminal. This is reproving him in the original and legitimate sense of the word used here by our Savior. It is in this way that the Holy Spirit reproves the world of sin, of righteousness, and of judgment. Therefore, the Spirit convinces or convicts the sinner by testimony, by argument, and by gathering all the strong points of the case against him under circumstances of impactful solemness and power.

## IV. How can it be known when the Spirit of God strives with an individual?

When the Spirit of God strives with an individual, it is not known by direct recognition of His action through any of your physical senses, for His presence is not revealed to these senses. It is not known directly by our consciousness, for the only proper subjects of consciousness are the acts and states of our own minds. However, we know the presence and operation of the Spirit by His works. The results He produces are the legitimate proofs of His presence.

Therefore, a person under the Spirit's influence finds his attention focused on the great concerns of his soul. The solemn questions of duty and responsibility to God are continually pushing themselves upon his mind. If he is a student studying his lesson, his mind is drawn away continually, before he realizes, to think of God and of the judgment to come. He turns his attention back to his books, but soon it is off again. How can he neglect these matters of infinite importance to his future well-being?

It is the same with people of every calling. The Spirit of God turns the mind and draws it to God and the concerns of the soul. When such results take place, you may know that the Spirit of God is the cause, for who does not know that this drawing and leaning of the mind toward God is by no means natural to the human heart? When it does occur, therefore, we may know that the special influence of God is in it.

Again, when a person finds himself convicted of sin, he may know that this is the Spirit's work. It is one thing to know that you are a sinner, and quite another to feel a realizing sense of it and to have the truth take mighty hold of the deepest sensibilities of the soul. The latter sometimes takes place. You may see the person's countenance fallen and his eyes downcast, and his whole demeanor is as if he had disgraced himself by some terrible crime, or as if he had suddenly lost all the friends he ever had. I have often met with unrepentant sinners who looked condemned, as if conscious guilt had taken hold of their inmost soul. They would not be aware that they were revealing in their countenances the deep workings of their hearts, but the observing eye could not help seeing it. I have also seen the same among backslidden professors of Christianity, resulting from the same cause – the Spirit of God reproving them of sin.

> When a person finds himself convicted of sin, he may know that this is the Spirit's work.

Sometimes this conviction is of a general nature, and sometimes it is more specific. It may enforce only the general impression: "I am all wrong. I am completely abhorrent and hateful to God. My whole heart is a cesspool of abomination in His sight." In other cases, it may seize upon some specific form of sin, hold it up before the sinner's mind, and make him see his infinite horridness before God for this sin. It may be a sin he has never thought of before, or he may have considered it a very light matter; but now, through the Spirit, it will rise up before his mind in such features of ugliness and loathsomeness that he will abhor himself. He sees sin in a perfectly new light. Many things are sins now that he never considered to be sins before.

Again, the Spirit not only convinces people of the fact that such things are sins, but He also convicts the mind of the great offense and deserved punishment of sin. The sinner is made to feel that his sin deserves the most dreadful damnation.

The case of an unbeliever whom I know may serve to illustrate this. He had lived in succession with two pious wives. He had read almost every book he could find on the inspiration of the Scriptures. He had disputed with, criticized, and often thought himself to have triumphed over believers in the Bible. In fact, he was the most skillful unbeliever I ever saw. It was remarkable that in connection with his unbelief, he had no proper views of sin. He had indeed heard much about some dreadful depravity that had come down in the flow of human blood from Adam, and was itself a physical thing, but as usual, he had no oppressive consciousness of sin, even though he had his share of this original stain. His mind consequently was quite at ease in respect to the guilt of his own sin.

In time, however, a change came over him, and his eyes were opened to see the horrible enormity of his sin. I saw him one day so weighed down with sin and shame that he could not look up. He bowed his head upon his knees, covered his face, and groaned in agony. I left him in this condition and went to the prayer meeting. Before long, he entered the meeting as he never entered before. As he left the meeting, he said to his wife, "You have long known me as a strong-hearted unbeliever, but my unbelief is all gone. I cannot tell you what has become of it. It all seems to me now as complete nonsense. I do not understand how I could ever have believed and defended it. I seem to myself like a man called to view some glorious and beautiful structure in order to pass his judgment upon it, but who dares to judge and condemn it after having caught only a dim glimpse of one obscure corner. This is just what I have done in condemning the glorious Bible and the glorious government of God."

The secret of all this change in his mind toward the Bible lay in the change of his views as to his own sin. Before, he had not been convicted of sin at all. Now he sees it in some of its true light, and he really feels that he deserves the deepest hell. Of course, he now sees the relevance, beauty, and glory of the gospel system. He is now in a position in which he can clearly see one of the strongest confirmations of the truth of the Bible – its perfect adaptation to meet the needs of the sinful human race.

It is remarkable to see what power there is in conviction of sin to break up and annihilate the delusions of error. For instance, no one can fully see his own sin and remain a Universalist, considering it unjust for God to send him to hell. When I hear someone talking in defense of Universalism, I know he does not understand anything about sin. He has not begun to see his own sin in its true light. It is the blindest of all mental obsessions to think that the little inconveniences of this life are all that sin deserves. Once someone sees his own sin as God sees it, he will be amazed to think that he ever held such an idea. The Spirit of God, pouring light upon the sinner's mind, will soon overthrow Universalism.

I once labored in a village in the state of New York where Universalism prevailed extensively. The leading man among them had a sick wife who agreed with him in this belief. She was near death, and I called to see her to try to expose the utter fallacy of her delusion. After I had left, her husband returned, and his wife, her eyes being now opened, cried out to him as he entered, "O my dear husband, you are on the way to hell. Your Universalism will ruin your soul forever!"

He was greatly enraged, and learning that I had been talking with her, his rage was kindled against me. "Where is he now?" he asked.

"He has gone to the meeting," was the reply.

"I'll go there and shoot him," he said. He grabbed his loaded pistol, as I was informed, and he headed out. When he entered the meeting, I was preaching, I think, from Matthew 23:33: *Ye serpents, ye generation of vipers, how can ye escape the damnation of hell?*

At the time, I knew nothing about his purpose and nothing about his pistol. He listened awhile, and then all at once, in the midst of the meeting, he leaned back on his seat and cried out, "Oh, I am sinking to hell. O God, have mercy on me." His Universalism went away in a moment. He saw his sin and realized that he was sinking to hell. This change in him was not my work, for I could produce no such effects as these. I was indeed trying to show from my text what sinners deserve, but the Spirit of God, and nothing less, could bring conviction of sin like this.

Another result of the Spirit is developed in the case of those people who are aware of much hardness and coldness of heart. It frequently happens that people think they are Christians because they have so much emotion on religious subjects. To undeceive them, the Spirit directs their attention to some truth that dries up all their feeling and leaves their hopes stranded on the beach. Now they are in great agony. "The more I hear," they say, "the less I feel. I was never in the world so far from being convicted of sin. I will certainly go to hell. I do not have an ounce of feeling. I cannot feel if I die."

The explanation of this remarkable condition is usually that the

Spirit of God sees their danger – He sees them deceiving themselves by relying on their feelings, and therefore He brings some truths before their minds that arrange the opposition of their hearts against God and dry up the fountains of their feelings. Then they see how perfectly hard their hearts are toward God. This is the work of the Spirit.

The Spirit also convicts the soul of the sin of unbelief. Sinners are very inclined to think that they do believe the gospel. They confuse faith with a mere intellectual assent, and so blind themselves into thinking that they believe God in the sense of gospel faith.

However, once the Spirit reveals their own hearts to them, they will see that they do not believe in God in the same way that they believe in their fellow men, and that instead of having confidence in God and resting on His words of promise as they do on promises of people, they do not rest on God at all, but are full of anxiety lest God should fail to fulfill His own words. They see that instead of being childlike and trustful, they are full of trouble, apprehension, and unbelief. They also see that this is a horribly sinful state of heart. They see the sin of not resting in His promises. The see the horrible sin of not believing with the heart every word God ever uttered.

**This is the work of the Spirit this making a sinner see that everything else is only straw compared with the eternal rock of God's truth.**

This change is the work of the Spirit. Our Savior mentions it as one of the effects brought about by the Spirit, that He will *reprove the world of sin, and of righteousness, and of judgment: of sin, because they believe not on me* (John 16:8-9). In fact, we find that this is one of the characteristic works of the Spirit. In conversing recently with a man who has been for many years a professor of religion, but having little victory over sin, he remarked, "I have been thinking of this truth, that God cares for me and loves me, and through Jesus Christ has offered me eternal life, and that now I deserve to be damned if I do not believe." Stretching out his pale hand, he said with great energy, "I will go to hell if I will not believe." All this is the work of the Spirit – this making a person see the sin and deserving of hell because of unbelief – this making a sinner see that everything else is only straw compared with the eternal rock of God's truth.

The Spirit also makes people see the danger of dying in their sins. A young man said, "I am afraid to go to sleep at night, for I am afraid that I might awake in hell." Sinners often know what this feeling is. I remember having this thought once impressed upon my mind, and I was so much agonized, that I almost thought I was dying right then and there! I can never express the terror and the agony of my soul in that hour! Sinner, if you have these feelings, it is a solemn time with you.

Moreover, the Spirit makes sinners feel the danger of being given up by God. It often happens that sinners, convicted by the Spirit, are made to feel that if they have not been given up already, they are in the most imminent danger of it, and must rush for the gate of life now or never. They see that they have so terribly sinned and have done so much to provoke God to give them over, that their last hope of being accepted is fast dying away. Sinners, have any of you ever felt this way? Have you ever trembled in your very soul lest you should be given over to a reprobate mind before another Lord's Day, or maybe even before another morning? If so, you may attribute this to the Spirit of God.

Even more, the Spirit often convicts sinners of the great blindness of their minds. It seems to them that their minds are full of complete darkness – a darkness that can be felt.

This is really the natural state of the sinner, but he is not aware of it until enlightened by the Spirit of God. When thus enlightened, he begins to appreciate his own exceeding great blindness. He now becomes aware that the Bible is a sealed book to him, for he finds that although he reads it, its meaning is immersed in impenetrable darkness.

Have not some of you been aware of such an experience as this? Have you not read the Bible with the distressing awareness that your mind was by no means appropriately affected by its truth? Did you not have the conviction that you did not get hold of its truth to any good purpose at all? This is how people are enlightened by the Spirit to see the real state of their case.

The Spirit shows sinners their total alienation from God. I have seen sinners so strongly convicted of this that they would come right out and say, "I know that I do not have the least inclination to return to God. I am aware that I don't care whether I have any Christianity or not."

I have often seen professed Christians in this state, aware that their hearts are entirely alienated from God and from all harmony with His character or government. Their deep backslidings, or their complete lack of all Christianity has been so revealed to their minds by the Spirit as to become a matter of most distinct and impressive consciousness.

Sinners made to see themselves this way by the Spirit often find that when they pour out their words before God for prayer, their heart won't go. I once said to a sinner, "Come, now, and give up your heart to God."

"I will," he said, but in a moment he cried out, "My heart won't go." Have not some of you been compelled to say the same? "My heart won't go." If so, then you know by experience one of the results of the Spirit's convicting power.

When the Spirit of God is not with people, they can speak out their long prayers before God and never think or seem to care how prayerless their hearts are all the time and how utterly far from God they are. But when the Spirit sheds His light on the soul, the sinner sees how miserable a hypocrite he is; then he cannot pray so smoothly, so loosely, and so self-complacently.

The Spirit of God often convinces people that they are ashamed of Christ, and that in truth they do not want Christianity. It sometimes happens that sinners do not feel ashamed of being thought seriously inclined until they come to be convicted of sin. This is how it was with me. I bought my first Bible as a law book, and I laid it beside my Blackstone's law commentary. I studied it as I would any other law book, my only purpose being to find in it the great principles of law. I never once thought of being ashamed of reading it then. I read it as freely and as openly as I read any other book. However, as soon as I became awakened to the concerns of my soul, I put my Bible out of sight. If it were lying on my table when people came into my office, I was careful to throw a newspaper over it. Before long, however, the conviction that I was ashamed of God and of His Word came over me with overwhelming force and served to show me the horrible state of my mind toward God. I suppose that the general course of my experience is by no means uncommon among unrepentant sinners.

The Spirit also convicts people of worldly mindedness. Sinners are always in this state of mind, but are often not fully aware of the fact until the Spirit of God makes them see it. I have often seen people pushing their worldly projects most intensely, but when addressed on the subject, they would say, "I don't care much about the world. I am pursuing this business right now mainly because I want to be doing something." However, when the Holy Spirit shows them their own hearts, they are in agony that they might never be able to break away from the dreadful power of the world upon their souls. They then see that they have been the most absolute slaves on earth – slaves to the passion for worldly good.

The Holy Spirit also often makes such a personal application of the truth as to give the impression that the preacher is speaking to a person personally and intends to describe the case and character of him who is the subject of his influence. The individual thus convinced of sin may think that the preacher has in some way come to a knowledge of his character and intends to describe it. He thinks that the preacher is referring specifically to him and is preaching to him. He wonders who has told the preacher so much about him. All this often takes place when the preacher likely does not even know that such a person is in the assembly, and knows absolutely nothing of his history. In this way, the Holy Spirit, who knows his heart and his entire history, becomes very personal in the application of truth.

Do any of you have this experience? Has it now or at any other time seemed to you as if the preacher meant you and that he was describing your case? Then the Spirit of the living God is upon you. I have often seen individuals drop their heads under preaching almost as if they had been shot. They might have been unable to look up again during the whole service. Afterward, I have often heard that they thought I was referring specifically to them, and they thought others were thinking of them too. Maybe they imagined that many people were looking at them, and therefore they did not look up, when in fact neither I nor anyone in the congregation, in all probability, so much as thought of them. In this way, a bow drawn at random often lodges an arrow between the joints of the sinner's coat of armor (1 Kings 22:34). Sinner, is it so with you?

The Holy Spirit often convinces sinners of the enmity of their hearts against God. Most unrepentant sinners, and perhaps all deceived professors of religion, unless convinced to the contrary by the Holy Spirit, think that they are in general friendly to God. They are far from believing that this *carnal mind is enmity against God* (Romans 8:7). They think that they do not hate God, but on the contrary, they think that they love Him. This delusion must be torn away or they will be lost.

To do this, the Spirit so arranges it that some truths are presented that clearly show their real enmity against God. The moralist who has been the almost Christian, or the deceived professor of Christianity, begins to criticize, to find fault, and finally to condemn – to oppose the preaching and the meetings, the methods, and the men. It is possible that the man who has a pious wife and who has thought of himself, and has been thought by her, to be almost a Christian, begins by criticizing the truth and finding fault with the measures and the methods. Then he refuses to go to church meetings, and finally forbids his wife and family going.

Very frequently, his enmity of heart will boil over in a horrible manner. He may have no thought that this boiling up of hell within him is occasioned by the Holy Spirit revealing to him the true condition of his heart. His Christian friends also may mistake his situation and be ready to conclude that something is wrong in the matter or manners or measures of the preacher that is causing difficulty for this man. But beware what you say or do. In many such cases that have come under my own observation, it has turned out that the Holy Spirit was at work in those hearts, revealing to them their real enmity against God. He does this by presenting those truths in that manner and under those circumstances that produce these results. He pushes this process until He compels the person to see that his heart is filled with enmity to God and to what is right; that it is not man, but God to whom he is opposed; that it is not error, but truth; that it is not the manner, but the matter; and that it is not the measures, but the God of truth that he hates.

**The Spirit often convicts sinners powerfully of the deceitfulness of their own hearts.**

Additionally, the Spirit often convicts sinners powerfully of the deceitfulness of their own hearts. Sometimes this conviction becomes really appalling. They see that they have been deceiving themselves in matters too plain to justify any mistake, and too consequential to give any excuse for willful blindness. They are perplexed with what they see in themselves.

The Spirit also frequently strips the sinner of his excuses and shows him clearly their great foolishness and absurdity. I recall that this was one of the first things in my experience in the process of conviction. I lost all confidence in any of my excuses, for I found them to be so foolish and futile that I could not stand by them. This was my state of mind before I had ever heard of the work of the Spirit or knew at all how to judge whether my own mind was under His influence or not. I found that whereas before I had been very strong in my excuses and objections, I was now completely weak, and it seemed to me that any child could defeat my arguments. In fact, I did not need to be defeated by anyone, for my excuses and criticisms had sunk to nothing of themselves, and I was deeply ashamed of them. I had essentially worked myself out of all their mazes, so they could bewilder me no longer. I have since seen many people in the same condition – weak as to their excuses, their old defensive armor all torn off, and their hearts laid naked to the arrows of God's truth.

Sinners, have any of you known what it is to have all your excuses and explanations fail you – to feel that you have no courage and no defensible reasons for pushing forward in a course of sin? If so, then you know what it is to be under the convicting power of the Spirit.

The Spirit convicts people of the foolishness of seeking salvation in any other way than through Christ alone. Often, without being aware of it, a sinner will be really seeking salvation in some other way than through Christ, and he will be looking to his good deeds, to his own prayers, or to the prayers of some Christian friends; but if the Spirit ever saves him, He will tear away these delusive schemes and show him the utter uselessness of every other way than through Christ alone. The Spirit will show him that there is only this one way in which it is naturally possible for a sinner to be saved, and that all attempts toward any other way are forever vain and worse than worthless. All self-righteousness must be rejected entirely, and Christ alone must be sought. Have you ever been made to see this? You who are professed Christians, is this your experience?

The Spirit convinces people of the great foolishness and insanity of clinging to a hope that will not sanctify. The Bible teaches that everyone who has the genuine gospel hope purifies himself, even as Christ is pure (1 John 3:3). In this passage, the apostle John plainly intends to affirm a universal proposition. He states a universal characteristic of the Christian hope. Whoever has a Christian hope should ask, "Do I purify myself even as Christ is pure?" If not, then mine is not the true gospel hope.

Yet thousands of professed Christians have a most inefficient hope. What is it? Does it really lead them to purify themselves as Christ is pure? Nothing like it. It is not a hope that they will see Christ as He is, will be forever with Him, and will be like Him, too, but it is mainly a hope that they will escape hell and go as an alternative to some unknown heaven.

Such professed Christians cannot but know that their experience lacks the witness of their own consciences that they are living for God and bearing His image. If such people are ever saved, they must first be convinced of the foolishness of a hope that leaves them unsanctified.

You professors of religion who have lived a worldly life so long, are you not ashamed of your hope? Do you not have good reason to be ashamed of a hope that has no more power than yours has had? Are there not many here who in the honesty of their hearts must say, "Either there is no power in the gospel, or I don't know anything about it"? The gospel affirms as a universal fact of all those who are not under the law but under grace, that *sin shall not have dominion over you* (Romans 6:14). Will you then go before God and say, "Lord, You have said, *Sin shall not have dominion over you* – but Lord, that is all false, for I believe the gospel and am under grace, but sin still has dominion over me"? No doubt in this case there is a mistake somewhere, and you should sincerely ask, "Will I blame this mistake and falsehood upon God, or will I admit that it must be in me alone?"

The apostle Paul has said that the gospel *is the power of God unto salvation to every one that believeth* (Romans 1:16). Is it so to you?

Paul has also said, *Being justified by faith, we have peace with God through our Lord Jesus Christ* (Romans 5:1). Do you know this by your own experience? Paul adds that we *rejoice in hope of the glory of God. And not only so, but we glory in tribulations also; knowing that tribulation worketh patience; and patience, experience; and experience, hope; and hope maketh not ashamed; because the love of God is shed abroad in our hearts by the Holy Spirit which is given unto us* (Romans 1:2-5).

Is all this in accord with your experience, professed Christian? Is it true that your hope makes not ashamed? Does it produce such glorious fruits unto holiness as are here described? If you were to test your experience by the Word of the living God and open your heart to be searched by the Spirit, would you not be convinced that you do not embrace the gospel in reality?

The Holy Spirit also convinces people that all their goodness is selfish and that self is the end of all their efforts – of all their prayers and religious exercises. I once spent a little time with the family of a man who was a leading member in a Presbyterian church. He asked me, "What would you think of a man who is praying for the Spirit every day, but does not get the blessing?"

I answered, "I would suppose that he is praying selfishly."

"But suppose," he replied, "that he is praying for the sake of promoting his own happiness?"

"He can be purely selfish in that," I replied. "The devil might do as much, and would perhaps do just the same if he supposed he could make himself happier by it." I then cited the prayer of David: *Take not thy Holy Spirit from me. Restore unto me the joy of thy salvation; . . . Then will I teach transgressors thy ways; and sinners shall be converted unto thee* (Psalm 51:11-13).

This seemed to be a new doctrine to him, and he turned away, as I later learned, in great anger and trouble. In the first rush of feeling, he prayed that God would cut him down and send him to hell so that he would not have to confess his sin and shame before all the people. He saw that in fact his past religion had been all selfish, but the dread of confessing this was at first horrifying to him. However, he saw the possibility of mistake, that his hopes had been all misleading, and that he had been working his self-deceived course while quickly headed toward the depths of hell.

Finally, it is the Spirit's work to make self-deceived people feel that they are now having their last call from the Spirit. When this impression is made, let it by all means be heeded. It is God's own voice to the soul. Out of a great multitude of cases under my observation, in which God has distinctly made sinners feel that the present call by God was their last call, I do not remember one in which it did not prove to be so.

This is a truth of solemn importance to the sinner, and should make the warning voice of God ring in his ear like the forewarning knell of the second death.

## V. What is meant by the Spirit's not always striving?

I understand the meaning to be not that He will at some period withdraw from among mankind, but that He will withdraw from the individual in question, or maybe, as in the text, from a whole generation of sinners. In its general application now, the principle seems to be that the Spirit will not follow the sinner onward down to his grave. There will be a limit to His efforts in the case of each sinner, and this limit is perhaps ordinarily reached a longer or a shorter time before death. At some uncertain, terrible point, he will reach it and pass it. Therefore, every sinner needs to understand his danger of grieving the Spirit away forever.

## VI. Next, we are to inquire why God's Spirit will not always strive.

God's Spirit will not always strive, but it is not because God is not compassionate, patient, slow to anger, and great in mercy. It is not because He runs out of patience and acts unreasonably – by no means. It is nothing like this at all. Why, then, will the Spirit not always strive?

1. Longer striving will do the sinner no good. By the very laws of mind, conversion must be brought about through the influence of truth. But it is a known law of mind that when truth is resisted, it loses its power upon the mind that resists it. Every successive instance of resistance weakens its power. If the truth does not take hold with power when fresh, it is not likely to do so ever after. Therefore, when the Spirit reveals truth to the sinner, and he hardens himself against it and resists the Spirit, there remains little hope for him. We may expect God to give him up for lost. This is what the Bible teaches.

> When the Spirit reveals truth to the sinner, and he hardens himself against it and resists the Spirit, there remains little hope for him.

2. Why does God's Spirit cease to strive with sinners? A second reason may be because to strive longer not only does the sinner no good, but it results in positive evil. Sin is measured by light. The more light, the greater the sin. Therefore, more light revealed by the Spirit, along with longer striving, might serve only to increase the sinner's guilt, and of course, his final woe. It is better, then, for the sinner himself, after all hope of his repentance is gone, that the Spirit would leave him than that his efforts would be prolonged in vain, to no other result than to increase the sinner's light and guilt, and consequently his endless curse. It is in this case a real mercy to the sinner that God would withdraw His Spirit and let him alone.

3. God's Spirit may cease to strive with sinners because sinners sin willfully when they resist the Holy Spirit. It is the very work of the Spirit to shine light before their minds. Of course, in resisting the Spirit, they must sin against light. Therefore, their sin is dreadful.

We are often greatly shocked with the bold and daring sins of people who may not, after all, have much illumination of the Spirit, and of course have comparatively little guilt. But when God's ministers come to the souls of men with His messages of truth, and people despise or neglect them, and when God's providence also enforces His truth, yet people still resist, then they are greatly guilty. How much more so when God comes by His Spirit, and they resist God under the blazing light of His Spirit's illuminations! How infinitely increased is their guilt now!

4. Another reason why the Spirit of God will not always strive is because their resistance tempts the forbearance of God. Sinners never so grievously tempt the forbearance of God as when they resist His Spirit. You may see this advanced in the Jews of Stephen's time. Stephen said, *Ye stiff-necked and uncircumcised in heart and ears, ye do always resist the Holy Spirit; as your fathers did, so do ye* (Acts 7:51). He had been summarizing their national history and running fearlessly across their Jewish prejudices, laboring in the deep sincerity and faithfulness of his soul, to set before them their sin in persecuting and murdering the Son of God. And what do they do? Enraged at these rebukes, they gnashed at him with their teeth. They attacked him with the spirit of demons

and stoned him to death, even though they saw the very glory of God beaming in his eye and on his countenance as if it had been an angel's.

Did not this fearful deed of theirs seal up their damnation? Read the history of their nation and see. They had tempted God to the last limit of His forbearance, and now what remained for them but swift and terrible judgments? The wrath of God arose against them, and there was no remedy (2 Chronicles 36:16). Their resistance of the Holy Spirit pressed the forbearance of God until it could bear no more.

It is a solemn truth that sinners tempt God's forbearance most dangerously when they resist His Spirit. Think how long some of you have resisted the Holy Spirit. The claims of God have been presented and urged upon you again and again, but you have just as often put them away. You have said unto God, *Depart from us; for we desire not the knowledge of thy ways* (Job 21:14). Now do you not have the utmost reason to expect that God will take you at your word?

> God intends to have people converted young and one reason for this is that He intends to convert the world, and therefore must have laborers.

5. There is a point beyond which forbearance is not a virtue. This is and must be true in all governments. No government could possibly be maintained that would push the indulgence of a spirit of forbearance toward the guilty beyond all limits. There must be a point beyond which God cannot go without peril to His government, and we can be assured that He will never go past this point.

Suppose we would just as often see old, gray-headed sinners converted as youthful sinners, and this would be the general course of things. Would not this bring harm to God's government – and even to sinners themselves? Would not sinners take encouragement from this and remain in their sins until their lusts were worn out, and until they themselves would rot in their corruptions? They would say, "We will be just as likely to be converted in our old age, corrupt with long-indulged lusts and filthy with the unchecked growth of every abomination of the heart of man, as if we were to turn to God in the freshness of our youth. Let us, then, have the pleasures of sin first, and the unwelcomeness of Christianity when the world can give us no more to enjoy."

However, God intends to have people converted young, if at all, and one reason for this is that He intends to convert the world, and therefore must have laborers trained up for the work in the morning of life. If He were to make no discrimination between the young and the aged, converting from each class alike, or mainly from the aged, the means for converting the world would utterly fail, and in fact, on such a plan, the result would be that no sinners at all would be converted. Therefore, there is a necessity for the general fact that sinners must submit to God in early life.

## VII. Consequences of the Spirit's ceasing to strive with men.

One consequence will be a confirmed hardness of heart. It is inevitable that the heart will become much more hardened, and the will more fully set to do evil.

Another consequence will be a confirmed opposition to Christianity. This will be likely to manifest itself in dislike to everything on the subject, often with great impatience and anger when urged to attend to the subject seriously. People are often so settled in their opposition to God and His Word that they might refuse to have anything said to them personally.

You may also expect to see them opposed to revivals and to gospel ministers, and especially to those ministers who are most faithful to their souls. All those means of promoting revivals that are used to awaken the conscience will be especially abhorrent to their hearts. Usually such people become bitter in their dispositions, cynical, haters of all Christians, delighting if they dare to distribute slander and abuse against those whose piety annoys and disturbs their senseless ease in sin.

Another consequence of being forsaken by the Spirit is that people will commit themselves to some refuge of lies and will settle down in some form of fatal error. I have often thought that it was almost impossible for people to embrace fatal error completely unless they are first forsaken by the Spirit of God. From observation of numerous cases, I believe this to be the case with the great majority of Universalists. They are described by Paul: *They received not the love of the truth, that they may be saved, and for this cause God shall send them strong delusion, that they should believe a lie* (2 Thessalonians 2:10-11). They hate the truth, they are more than willing to be deceived, and they are uneasy when pressed with gospel claims; therefore, they are ready to grasp at any form of delusion that sets aside these claims and boldly asserts, *Ye shall not surely die* (Genesis 3:4).

It has long been an impression on my mind that this is the usual course of feeling and thought that leads to Universalism. There may be exceptions, but the great majority go into this delusion from the starting point of being abandoned by the Spirit. Thus abandoned, they become disagreeable and unfriendly. They hate all Christians, as well as all those truths that God and His people love. This could not be the case if they had the love of God in their hearts. It could not well be the case if they were enlightened and restrained by the present influence of the divine Spirit.

Generally, those who have been left by God end up with a seared conscience. They are distinguished by great numbness of mind. They are by choice blind and hardened in respect to the nature and guilt of sin. Although their intelligence affirms that sin is wrong, yet they do not feel it or care about it. They can know the truth and still be thoughtless of its application to their own hearts and lives. God has left them, and of course, the natural tendencies of a depraved heart are developed without restraint.

This type of sinner will inevitably grow worse and worse. They become loose in habits. They become careless in their observance of the Lord's Day. They slide backward in regard to alcohol and all similar moral subjects. They slip into some of the many forms of sin, and perhaps immorality and crime. If they have been conscientious against the use of tobacco, they relinquish their conscientiousness and throw a loose rein on their lusts. Basically, they are inclined to grow worse and worse in every branch of morals, and often become so changed that you would hardly recognize them. It is common for them to become profane swearers and to steal a little at first and then to later steal much. If God does not restrain them, they go down by a short and steep descent to the depths of hell.

Another consequence of being abandoned by the Spirit will be certain damnation. There can be no mistake about this. It is just as certain as if they were already there.

This state is not always attended with indifference of feeling. There may be at times a most intense excitement of the emotion. The Bible describes the case of some who *sin willfully* after they have *received a knowledge of the truth*, and there remains for them only *a certain fearful looking for of judgment and fiery indignation* (Hebrews 10:26-27). I have seen some people like this, and I pray that I will never see such agony and wretchedness again. They are the very pictures of despair and horror. Their eyes are fully open to see their ruined state, and they exclaim, "I know I am abandoned by God forever. I have sinned away my day of hope and mercy, and I know I will never repent. I have no heart to repent, although I know that I must, or I will be damned." They will speak such language as this with a settled, positive tone, and with an air of agony and despair that is enough to break a heart of stone.

Another common consequence is that Christians find themselves unable to pray in faith for such sinners. There are some in almost every community for whom Christians cannot pray. I believe it is common for many Christians, without being aware of each other's state, to have a similar experience. For example, several Christians are praying in secret for some specific individual, and they have considerable freedom in prayer up to a certain moment – and then they find that they cannot pray for him any longer. They happen to meet together, and one of them says, "I have been praying a long time with great interest for that certain unrepentant sinner, but at a particular time I found myself all closed up in prayer. I could not get hold of the Lord again for him, and have never been able to since."

Another person, and then another, says, "I have felt just so myself. I did not know that anyone else felt as I have, but you have described my case precisely."

If you will go to that sinner, he will tell you a story that will explain the whole situation. He will show that he came at that eventful moment to some fatal decision, grieved the Spirit, and was abandoned by God. The Spirit ceased to strive with him, and consequently ceased to draw out prayer in his behalf in the hearts of God's people.

Finally, when God has ceased to strive with sinners, no means whatsoever used for the purpose can be successful for their salvation. If you, sinner, have passed that dreadful point, you will no longer be profited by my preaching, even if I were to preach to you five thousand sermons. No, you could not be profited even though an angel, or even Christ Himself, would come and preach to you. All would be only in vain. You are left by God to fill up the measure of your iniquities (Genesis 15:16).

## Remarks

1. Christians may understand how to account for the fact already noticed – that there are some for whom they cannot pray. Even while they are walking with God and are trying to pray for particular individuals, they may find themselves utterly unable to do so, and this may be the explanation. I would not, however, in such a case take it for granted that all is right with myself, for perhaps it is not. However, if I have the best evidence that all is right between myself and God, then I must conclude that God has forsaken that sinner and does not want me to pray for him any longer.

2. Sinners should be aware that light and guilt keep pace with each other. They are increased and lessened together, which explains the solemn responsibility of being under the light and the strivings of the Spirit.

While enlightened and urged to duty by the Spirit, sinners are under the most solemn circumstances that can ever occur in their entire lives. Indeed, no period of the sinner's existence through its eternal duration can be so momentous as this. Yes, sinner, while the Spirit of God is pleading and striving with you, angels appreciate the solemnity of the hour. They know that the destiny of your soul is being decided for eternity. What an object of infinite interest! An immortal mind is on the turning point of its eternal destiny. God is debating and persuading. The sinner is resisting, and the struggle is about to be broken off as hopeless forever.

Suppose, sinner, that you could set yourself aside and could look on and be a spectator of such a scene. Were you ever in a court of justice when the question of life and death was about to be decided? The witnesses have all been heard. The lawyers have been heard. It is announced that the jury is ready to deliver its verdict. Now pause and observe the scene. Note the anxiety depicted in every countenance and how eagerly, yet with what awful solemnity, they wait for the decision about to be made – and with good reason, for a question of momentous interest is to be decided.

If this question involving only the earthly life is so momentous, how much more so is the sinner's situation when the life of the soul for eternity is pending! How solemn while the question still is unanswered – while the Spirit still strives, and the sinner still resists, and no one can tell how soon the last moment of the Spirit's striving may come!

This should be the most solemn world in the universe. In other worlds, the destinies of the souls are already established. It is so in hell. All there is determined and changeless forever. It is a solemn thing indeed for a sinner to go to hell, but the most solemn point in the whole duration of his existence is that one in which the decision is made.

Oh, what a world this is! Throughout all its years and centuries, we cannot see one moment on whose tender point there does not hang a balancing of the question of eternal life or eternal death! Is this a place to mess around? Is this a place to be irrational and foolish and vain? No! It would be more reasonable to trifle in any other world than in this one. The awful destinies of the soul are being determined here. Heaven sees it and hell, too, and all are filled with anxiety, swelling almost to agony. But you who are the subjects of all this anxiety – you can somehow mess around and play the fool and dance on the brink of everlasting woe. Isaac Watts, in his hymn based upon Psalm 73, wrote:

> I heard the wretch profanely boast,
>> Till at thy frown he fell;
> His honors in a dream were lost,
>> And he awoke in hell.

God represents the sinner as on a slippery steep, his feet just sliding

– on the very edge of a dreadful chasm.[7] God holds him up for a short moment, and he wastes away even this short moment in insane foolishness. All hearts in heaven and in hell are beating and throbbing with intense emotion – but he is unconcerned! Oh, what madness!

If sinners rightly estimated this danger of resisting the Spirit, they would be more afraid of it than of anything else whatsoever. They would consider no other dangers worthy of a moment's thought or care compared with this.

It is a very common thing for sinners to grieve away the Spirit long before death. I believe this, although I am aware that some people are greatly opposed to this doctrine. Do you doubt it? Think of almost the whole Jewish nation in the time of the Savior. They were given up to unbelief and corruption. They were abandoned by the Spirit of God, yet they sinned against far less light and, of course, with much less guilt than sinners now do. If God could give them up then, why may He not do so with sinners now?

If He could give up the whole population of the world in Noah's time when Noah alone stood forth as a preacher of righteousness (2 Peter 2:5), why may He not give up individual sinners now who are incomparably more guilty than they were because they have sinned against greater light than had ever shone then? It is infinitely cruel to sinners themselves to conceal this truth from them. Let them know that long before they die, they are in danger of grieving away the Spirit beyond recall. This truth should be proclaimed over all the earth. Let its echo ring out through every valley and over every mountaintop throughout the world. Let every living sinner hear it and heed the timely warning!

We see why so few aged sinners are converted. The fact is unmistakable and unquestionable. Take the age of sixty, and count the number converted past that age. You will find it small indeed. Few and scattered are they, like beacons on mountaintops, just barely enough to prevent the aged from utter despair of ever being converted. I am aware that unbelievers seize upon this fact to try to criticize Christianity, saying, "How does it happen that the aged and wise, whose minds are developed by thought and experience, and who have passed by the period of

---

7    This is reminiscent of "Sinners in the Hands of an Angry God," a sermon by Jonathan Edwards based upon Deuteronomy 32:35: *Their foot shall slide in due time.*

warm youthful passion, never embrace the gospel?" They would eagerly try to say that none but children and women become Christians, and that this is to be accounted for on the ground that the Christian religion rests on its appeal to the emotions and not to the intelligence. But unbelievers make a most grievous mistake in this line of reasoning. The fact under consideration should be assigned to an entirely different class of causes. The aged are only rarely converted because they have grieved away the Spirit. They have become entangled in the mazes of some loved and soul-ruinous delusion, and

> Let me ask the people of God if you should not be awake in such an hour as this.

hardened in sin past the moral possibility of being converted. Indeed, it would be unwise on the part of God to convert many sinners in old age. It would be too great a temptation for human nature to bear, for at all the earlier periods of life, sinners would be looking forward to old age as the time for conversion.

I have already said what I want to repeat here – that it is an immensely remarkable time when God's Spirit strives with sinners. I have reason to believe that the Spirit is striving with some of you. Even within the past week, your attention has been solemnly captured, and God has been calling upon you to repent. Are you now aware that while God is calling, you must listen – that when He speaks, you should stop and give Him your attention? Does God call you away from your lesson, and are you replying, "Oh, I must study my lesson"?

Ah, your lesson! What is your first and main lesson? *Prepare to meet thy God* (Amos 4:12). But you say, "The bell will ring in a few minutes, and I have not finished my lesson!"

Yes, sinner, soon the great bell will ring. Unseen spirits will seize hold of the bell's rope and will sound the dread death knell of eternity, echoing the summons for you to come to judgment. The bell will be rung, and where will you be then, sinner? Are you prepared? Have you grasped that one great lesson: *Prepare to meet thy God*?

In the long passing ages, you will be asked of your lost doom how and why you came into this place of torment, and you will have to answer, "Oh, I was studying my lesson when God came by His Spirit, and I could not stop to hear His call! So I exchanged my soul for my lesson! Oh, what a fool I was!"

Let me ask the people of God if you should not be awake in such an hour as this. How many sinners during the past week have pleaded with you to pray for their perishing souls? Have you no heart to pray? How full of critical concern and peril are these passing moments? Have you ever seen the magnetic needle of the compass go back and forth, quiver, and finally settle down fixed to its position? So it is with the sinner's destiny today.

Sinners, think of your destiny as being now about to assume its fixed position. Soon you will decide it forever and forever!

Do you say, "Let me first go home, and there I will give myself up to God"? No, sinner, no! Do not go away from here in your sin. Now is your accepted time (2 Corinthians 6:2). Now – today, after so long a time – now is the only hour of promise. Now might be the last hour of the Spirit's presence and grace to your soul!

# Chapter 17

# Christ Our Advocate

If any man sin, we have an advocate with the Father,
Jesus Christ the righteous; and he is the propitiation
for our sins; and not for ours only, but also for the sins
of the whole world.
—1 John 2:1-2

The Bible abounds with governmental analogies. These are designed for our instruction, but if we receive instruction from them, it is because there is a real analogy in many points between the government of God and human governments.

## I. What is the idea of an advocate when the term is used to express a governmental office or relation?

An advocate (often one such as an attorney) is one who pleads the cause of another, who represents another, and who acts in his name; one who uses his influence in behalf of another by his request.

## II. Purposes for which an advocate may be employed.

1. To secure justice, in case any question involving justice is to be tried.

2. To defend the accused. If one has been accused of committing a crime, an advocate may be employed to conduct his trial on his behalf, to defend him against the charge, and to prevent his conviction if possible.

3. An advocate may be employed to secure a pardon when a criminal has been justly condemned and is under sentence. That is, an advocate may be employed either to secure justice for his client or to obtain mercy for him in case he is condemned. An advocate may be employed either to prevent his conviction, or if convicted, may be employed in setting aside the execution of the law upon the criminal.

## III. The sense in which Christ is the advocate of sinners.

He is working to plead the cause of sinners, not at the bar of justice, and not to defend them against the charge of sin, because the question of their guilt is already settled. The Bible represents them as condemned already; and such is the fact, as every sinner knows. Every sinner in the world knows that he has sinned, and that consequently he must be condemned by the law of God. This office, then, is exercised by Christ in respect to sinners – not at the bar of justice, but at the throne of grace and at the footstool of sovereign mercy. He is working, not to prevent the conviction of the sinner, but to prevent his execution; not to prevent his being condemned, but being already condemned, to prevent his being damned.

## IV. What is implied in His being the advocate of sinners.

1. His working is at a throne of grace and not at the bar of justice, to plead for sinners as sinners, and not for those who are merely charged with sin without the charge being established. This implies that the guilt of the sinner is already ascertained, the verdict of guilty has been given, the sentence of the law has been pronounced, and the sinner awaits his execution.

2. His being appointed by God as the advocate of sinners implies a merciful disposition in God. If God had not been mercifully disposed toward sinners, no advocate would have been appointed and no question of forgiveness would have been raised.

3. It implies also that the exercise of mercy on certain conditions is possible. Not only is God mercifully disposed, but to manifest this disposition in the actual pardon of sin is possible. If this had not been the case, no advocate would have been appointed.

4. It implies that there is hope, then, for the condemned. Sinners are prisoners, but in this world, they are not yet prisoners of despair, but are prisoners of hope.

5. It implies that there is a governmental necessity for the intervention of an advocate – that the sinner's relations are such, and his character such, that he cannot be admitted to plead his own cause in his own name. He is condemned. He is no longer on trial. In this respect, he is under sentence for a capital crime. Consequently, he is an outlaw, and the government cannot recognize him as being capable of performing any legal act. His relations to the government forbid that in his own name, or in his own person, he should appear before God. So far as his own personal influence with the government is concerned, he is as a dead man – he is civilly dead. Therefore, he must appear by his friend, or by his advocate, if he is heard at all. He may not appear in his own name and in his own person, but must appear by an advocate who is acceptable to the government.

## V. I next call attention to the essential qualifications of an advocate under such circumstances.

1. He must be the uncompromising friend of the government. Notice that he appears to pray for mercy to be extended to the guilty party whom he represents. Of course, he must not himself be the enemy of the government of whom he asks so great a favor, but he should be known

to be the devoted friend of the government whose mercy he desires to be extended to the guilty.

2. He must be the uncompromising friend of the dishonored law. The sinner has greatly dishonored, and by his conduct denounced, both the law and the lawgiver. By his consistent disobedience, the sinner has proclaimed, in the most emphatic manner, that the law is not worthy of obedience and that the lawgiver is a tyrant. The advocate must be a friend to this law. He must not sell himself, to the dishonor of the law, nor consent to its dishonor. He must not reflect upon the law, for in this case he places the lawgiver in a condition in which, if he should set aside the penalty and exercise mercy, he would consent to the dishonor of the law, and by a public act would himself condemn the law.

The advocate seeks to dispense with the execution of the law, but he must not offer as a reason that the law is unreasonable and unjust. For in this case, he renders it impossible for the lawgiver to set aside the execution of the law without consenting to the assertion that the law is not good. In that case, the lawgiver would condemn himself instead of the sinner. It is plain, then, that he must be the uncompromising friend of the law, or he can never secure the exercise of mercy without involving the lawgiver himself in the crime of dishonoring the law.

3. The advocate must be righteous. That is, he must be clear of any complicity in the crime of the sinner. He must have no fellowship with his crime; there must be no charge or suspicion of guilt resting upon the advocate. Unless he himself is clear of the crime of which the criminal is accused, he is not the proper person to represent him before a throne of mercy.

4. He must be the compassionate friend of the sinner – not of his sins, but of the sinner himself. This distinction is very plain. Everyone knows that a parent can be greatly opposed to the wickedness of his children while having great compassion for the children themselves. He is not a true friend to the sinner who really sympathizes with his sins. I have several times heard sinners give as an excuse for not being Christians that their friends were opposed to it. They have a great many close

friends who are opposed to their becoming Christians and obeying God. They want them to continue in their sins. They do not want them to change and become holy, but desire them to remain in their worldly mindedness and sinfulness.

I tell such people that those "friends" are their friends in the same sense that the devil is their friend. Would they call the devil their good friend, their kind friend, because he sympathizes with their sins and does not want them to become Christians? Would you call someone your friend who wanted you to commit murder, or robbery, or tell a lie, or commit any crime? Suppose he would come and appeal to you, and because you are his friend would ask you to commit some great crime; would you regard that person as your friend?

> No one is a true friend of a sinner unless he desires the sinner to abandon his sins.

No! No one is a true friend of a sinner unless he desires the sinner to abandon his sins. If any person wants you to continue in your sins, he is the adversary of your soul. Instead of being in any proper sense your friend, he is playing the devil's part to ruin you.

Notice that Christ is the compassionate friend of sinners. He is a friend in the best and truest sense. He does not sympathize with your sins, but His heart is set upon saving you from your sins. I said that the advocate must be the compassionate friend of sinners, and his compassion must be stronger than death, or he will never meet the necessities of the case.

5. Another qualification must be that he is sufficiently able to honor the law, which sinners by their transgression have dishonored. He seeks to avoid the execution of the dishonored law of God. The law, having been dishonored by sin in the highest degree, must either be honored by its execution on the criminal, or the lawgiver must in some other way bear testimony in favor of the law before he can justly dispense with the execution of its penalty. The law is not to be repealed. The law must not be dishonored. It is the law of God's nature, the unalterable law of His government, the eternal law of heaven, and the law for the government of moral agents in all worlds, and in all time, and to all eternity. Sinners have borne their most emphatic testimony against it

by pouring contempt upon it in utterly refusing to obey it. Sin must not be treated lightly; this law must be honored.

God may pour a flash of glory over it by executing its penalty upon the whole human race that has despised it. This would be the solemn testimony of God to sustain its authority and vindicate its claims. If our advocate appears before God to ask for the remission of sin and for the penalty of this law to be set aside and not executed, the question immediately arises, But how will the dishonor of this law be avoided? What will compensate for the careless and blasphemous contempt with which this law has been treated? How will sin be forgiven without apparently making light of it?

It is plain that sin has placed the whole question in such a light that God's testimony must in some way be produced in a most emphatic manner against sin and to sustain the authority of this dishonored law. It is necessary for the advocate of sinners to provide himself with a plea that will meet this difficulty. He must meet this necessity if he wants to secure the setting aside of the penalty. He must be able to provide an adequate substitute for its execution. He must be able to do that which will as effectively bear testimony in favor of the law and against sin as the execution of the law upon the criminal would do. In other words, he must be able to meet the demands of public justice.

6. He must be willing to volunteer a willing and free service. He cannot be called upon in justice to volunteer a service or to suffer for the sake of sinners. He may volunteer his service, and it may be accepted, but if he does volunteer his service, he must be able and willing to endure whatever pain or sacrifice is necessary to meet the case.

If the law must be honored by obedience; if, *without the shedding of blood, there is no remission* (Hebrews 9:22); if an emphatic governmental testimony must be borne against sin and in honor of the law; and if he must become the representative of sinners, offering himself before the whole universe as a propitiation for sin, then he must be willing to meet the case and make the sacrifice.

7. He must have a good plea. In other words, when he appears before the mercy seat, he must be able to present such considerations as will

actually meet the necessities of the case and render it safe, proper, honorable, and glorious in God to forgive.

## VI. I now come to inquire what His plea in behalf of sinners is.

It should be remembered that the appeal is not to justice. Since the fall of man, God has plainly suspended the execution of strict justice upon the human race. To us, as a matter of fact, He has sat upon a throne of mercy. Mercy, and not justice, has been the rule of His administration since people have been involved in sin.

This is a simple fact. People do sin, and they are not cut off immediately and sent to hell. The execution of justice is suspended, and God is represented as seated upon a throne of grace, or upon a mercy seat. It is here at a mercy seat that Christ executes the office of advocate for sinners.

2. Christ's plea for sinners cannot be that they are not guilty. They are guilty and condemned. No question can be raised in respect to their guilt and their deserving of punishment; such questions are settled. It has often appeared strange to me that people overlook the fact that they are condemned already and that no question respecting their guilt or their deserving punishment can ever be raised.

3. Christ, as our Advocate, cannot and need not plead a justification. A plea of justification admits the fact charged, but asserts that under the circumstances, the accused had a right to do as he did. Christ can never make this plea. This is entirely out of place, the case having been already tried and the sentence given.

4. He may not plead what will reflect, in any way, upon the law. He cannot plead that the law was too strict in its precept or too severe in its penalty, for in that case, He would not really plead for mercy, but for justice. He would plead in that case that no injustice could be done to the criminal. For if He implies that the law is not just, then the sinner does not deserve the punishment. Therefore, it would be unjust to punish him, and His plea would amount to this – that the sinner should not be punished because he does not deserve it. If this plea would be allowed to prevail, it would be a public acknowledgment on the part of God that His law was unjust – and this can never be.

5. Christ, as our Advocate, may not plead anything that will reflect upon the administration of the Lawgiver. If He would plead that people had been harshly treated by the Lawgiver, either in their creation, by His providential arrangements, or by allowing them to be so tempted – or if, in any way, He brings forward a plea that reflects upon the Lawgiver in creation or in the administration of His government, the Lawgiver cannot listen to His plea and forgive the sinner without condemning Himself. In that case, instead of insisting that the sinner should repent, the Lawgiver would be essentially called upon Himself to repent.

6. He may not plead any excuse whatsoever for the sinner in reduction of his crime or in justification of his conduct, for if He does, and the Lawgiver would forgive in answer to such a plea, He would confess that He had been wrong and that the sinner did not deserve the sentence that had been pronounced against him.

He must not plead that the sinner does not deserve the damnation of hell, for if He would urge this plea, it would virtually accuse the justice of God and would be equivalent to begging that the sinner might not be sent unjustly to hell. This would not be a proper plea for mercy, but rather would be an issue with justice. It would be asking that the sinner might not be sent to hell, not because of the mercy of God, but because the justice of God forbids it. This will never be.

7. He cannot plead as our Advocate that He has paid our debt in such a sense that He can demand our release on the ground of justice. He has not paid our debt in such a sense that we do not still owe it. He has not atoned for our sins in such a sense that we would not still be justly punished for them. Indeed, such a thing is impossible and absurd. One being cannot suffer for another in such a sense as to remove the sin of that other. He may suffer for another's sin in such a sense that it will be safe to forgive the sinner for whom the suffering has been endured, but the suffering of the substitute can never, in the slightest degree, diminish the fundamental sin of the criminal.

Our Advocate may urge that He has borne such suffering for us to honor the law that we had dishonored, and that now it is safe to extend mercy to us, but He can never demand our release on the ground that we do not deserve to be punished. The fact of our fundamental guilt remains, and must forever remain. Our forgiveness is just as much an act of sovereign mercy as if Christ had never died for us.

8. Christ may plead His sin offering to confirm the law, as fulfilling a condition upon which we may be forgiven. However, this offering is not to be regarded as the ground upon which justice demands our forgiveness. Our Advocate does not appeal to this offering as payment in such a sense that now in justice He can demand that we should be set free. No. As I said before, it is simply the fulfilling of a condition upon which it is safe for the mercy of God to stop and set aside the execution of the law in the case of the repentant sinner.

Some theologians appear to me to have been unable to see this distinction. They insist that the atonement of Christ is the ground of our forgiveness. They seem to assume that He literally bore the penalty for us in such a sense that Christ now no longer appeals to mercy, but demands justice for us. To be consistent, they must maintain that Christ does not plead at a mercy seat for us, but having paid our debt, He appears before a throne of justice and demands our release.

I cannot accept this view. I insist that His offering could not touch the question of our basic deserving of damnation. His appeal is to the infinite mercy of God and to His loving disposition to pardon. He points to His atonement, not as demanding our release, but as fulfilling a condition upon which our release is honorable to God. He may plead His obedience to the law and the shedding of His blood as a substitute for the execution of the law upon us. Basically, He may plead the entirety of His work as God-man and Mediator. Therefore, He may give us the full benefit of what He has done – to sustain the authority of law and to vindicate the character of the Lawgiver as fulfilling conditions that have made it possible for God to be just and still justify the repentant sinner.

9. The plea is directed to the merciful disposition of God. He may point to the promise made to Him in Isaiah 52:13-53:2:

> Behold, my servant shall deal prudently, he shall be exalted and extolled, and be very high. As many were astonished at thee; his visage was so marred more than any man, and his form more than the sons of men: so shall he sprinkle many nations; the kings shall shut their mouths at him: for that which had not been told them shall they see; and that which they had not heard shall they consider. Who hath believed our report? and to whom is the arm of the LORD revealed? For he shall grow up before him as a tender plant, and as a root out of a dry ground: he hath no form nor comeliness; and when we shall see him, there is no beauty that we should desire him.

10. He may plead also that He becomes our surety, that He advocates for us, and that He is our *wisdom, and righteousness, and sanctification, and redemption* (1 Corinthians 1:30). He can point to His official capacity – His infinite fullness, willingness, and ability to restore us to obedience and to prepare us for the service, the activities, and enjoyments of heaven. It is said that He is made the *surety of a better covenant* than the legal one (Hebrews 7:22), and a covenant founded *upon better promises* (Hebrews 8:6).

11. He may urge as a reason for our pardon the great pleasure it will give to God to set aside the execution of the law. *Mercy rejoiceth against judgment* (James 2:13). Judgment is His strange work, but He *delighteth in mercy* (Micah 7:18).

It is said of Queen Victoria that when her prime minister presented a pardon and asked her if she would sign a pardon in the case of some individual who was sentenced to death, she seized the pen and said, "Yes – with all my heart!" Do you think that such an appeal could be made to a woman's heart without its leaping for joy to be placed in a position in which it could save the life of a fellow being?

It is said that *there is joy in the presence of the angels of God over one sinner that repenteth* (Luke 15:10), and do you not think that it gives God the sincerest joy to be able to forgive the miserable sinner and save him from the doom of hell? He has no pleasure in our death (Ezekiel 33:11).

It is a grief to Him to be bound to execute His law on sinners, and no doubt it gives Him infinitely higher pleasure to forgive us than it does us to be forgiven. He knows very well what the unutterable horrors of hell and damnation are. He knows the sinner cannot bear it. He says, "Can your heart endure, and can your hands be strong in the day that I will deal with you? And what will you do when I will punish you?" (Ezekiel 22:14). Our Advocate knows that to punish the sinner is that in which God has no delight – that He will forgive and sign the pardon with all His heart.

Do you think that such an appeal to the heart of God, to His merciful disposition, will be of no use? It is said of Christ, our Advocate, that *for the joy that was set before him, he endured the cross, despising the shame* (Hebrews 12:2). So great was the love of our Advocate for us that He regarded it a pleasure and a joy so great to save us from hell that He counted the shame and agony of the cross as a mere trifle; He despised them.

This, then, is a disclosure of the heart of our Advocate. How certainly He may assume that it will give God the sincerest joy, eternal joy, to be able to honorably seal to us a pardon.

12. He may urge the glory that will be given to the Son of God for the part that He has taken in this work. Will it not be eternally honorable

in the Son to have advocated the cause of sinners, to have undertaken at such great expense to Himself a cause so desperate, and to have carried it through at the expense of such agony and blood?

Will not the universe of creatures forever wonder and adore as they see this Advocate surrounded with the innumerable multitude of souls for whom His advocacy has prevailed?

13. Our Advocate may plead the gratitude of the redeemed and the profound thanks and praise of all good beings. Do you not think that the whole family of virtuous beings will forever feel indebted for the intervention of Christ as our Advocate, and for the mercy, forbearance, and love that has saved us?

## Remarks

1. You see what it is to become a Christian. It is to engage Christ as your Advocate by committing your cause entirely to Him. You cannot be saved by your works, by your sufferings, or by your prayers. You cannot be saved in any way except by the intervention of this Advocate. *He ever lives to make intercession for them* (Hebrews 7:25). He offers to take up your cause. To be a Christian is to at once surrender your whole cause, your whole life and being, to Him as your Advocate.

2. He is an Advocate that loses no causes. Every cause committed to Him, and continued in His hands, is infallibly gained. His advocacy is all-prevalent. God has appointed Him as an Advocate, and wherever He appears in behalf of any sinner who has committed his cause to Him, one word of His is sure to prevail.

3. Therefore, you see the safety of believers. Christ is always at His post, always ready to attend to all the concerns of those who have made Him their Advocate. *He is able also to save unto the uttermost all that come unto God by him* (Hebrews 7:25), and abiding in Him, you are forever safe.

4. You see the position of unbelievers. You have no advocate. God has appointed an Advocate, but you reject Him. You hope to get along without Him. Maybe some of you think you will be punished for your sins,

and do not ask forgiveness. Others of you may think you will approach in your own name, and that you will plead your own cause without any atonement or without any advocate. But God will not allow it. He has appointed an Advocate to act in your behalf, and unless you approach through Him, God will not hear you.

If you are out of Christ, He is to you a consuming fire (Hebrews 12:29). When the judgment will begin, and you appear in your own name, you will certainly appear unsanctified and unsaved. You will not be able to lift up your head. You will be ashamed to look in the face of the Advocate, who will then sit both as Judge and Advocate.

5. I ask, Have you engaged Him? Have you by your own consent made Him your Advocate? It is not enough that God would have appointed Him to act in this way. He cannot act for you in this way, unless you individually commit yourself and your case to his advocacy. This is done, as I have said, by entrusting, or committing, the whole question of your salvation to Him.

6. Do any of you say that you are unable to engage Him? Remember that the fee that He requires of you is your heart. You have a heart. It is not money that He seeks, but your heart. The poor, then, may employ Him as well as the rich. The children who do not have a penny of their own can engage Him as their Advocate just as well as their rich parents. All may employ Him, for all have hearts.

7. He offers His services freely to all, requiring nothing of them but confidence, gratitude, love, and obedience. The poor and the rich alike must give this to Him, and this they are all able to give.

8. Can any of you do without Him? Have you ever considered how it will be with you? The question now comes down to this: Will you consent to give up your sins and trust your souls to the advocacy of Christ? Will you give Him the fee that He asks – your heart, your trust, your grateful love, and your obedience? Will He be your Advocate, or will He not?

Suppose He stood before you, and in His hand He held the Book of Life. Then, with a pen dipped in the very light of heaven, He would ask,

"Who of you will now consent to make Me your Advocate?" Suppose He would ask of you, sinner, "Can I be of any service to you? Can I do anything for you, dying sinner? Can I support and help you in any way? Can I speak a good word for you? Can I interpose My blood, My death, My life, and My advocacy to save you from the depths of hell? Will you consent? May I write down your name in the Book of Life? Will it today be told in heaven that you are saved? May I report that you have committed your cause to Me, and thus give joy in heaven? Or will you reject Me, stand upon your own defense, and attempt to carry your cause through at the solemn judgment?"

Sinner, I warn you in the name of Christ, do not tell Him no. Consent here and now, and let it be written in heaven.

9. Have any of you made His advocacy certain by committing all to Him? If you have, He has attended to your cause because He has secured your pardon. You have the evidence in your peace of mind. Has He attended to your cause? Do you have the inward sense of reconciliation, the inward witness that you believe that you are forgiven, that you are accepted, that Christ has taken up your cause, that He has already prevailed and secured pardon for you? Has He given in your own soul the peace of God that passes understanding to rule in your heart (Philippians 4:7)?

It is a remarkable fact in Christian experience that whenever we really commit our cause to Jesus, He secures our pardon without delay, and in the inward peace that follows, He gives us the assurance of our acceptance that He has interposed His blood, that His blood is accepted for us, that His advocacy has prevailed, and that we are saved.

Do not stop short of this, for if your peace with God is truly made, if you are in fact forgiven, then the sting of remorse is gone. There is no longer any grating or any irritation between your spirit and the Spirit of God. The sense of condemnation and remorse has given place to the spirit of gospel liberty, peace, and love.

The stony heart is gone; the heart of flesh has taken its place (Ezekiel 11:19). The dry sensation is melted, and peace flows like a river. Do you have this? Is this a matter of realization with you?

If so, then leave your cause, by a continual commitment of it, to the advocacy of Christ. Abide in Him, and let Him abide in you, and you will be as safe as the surroundings of Almighty arms can make you.

# Chapter 18

# God's Love Commended to Us

But God commendeth his love toward us, in that, while
we were yet sinners, Christ died for us.
—Romans 5:8

W hat is meant here by "commend"? It means to recommend – to
set forth in a clear and strong light. Toward whom is this love
exercised? It is exercised toward us – toward all beings of our lost human
race. God manifests this love to each one of us. Is it not written, *God
so loved the world, that he gave his only begotten Son, that whosoever
believeth in him should not perish, but have everlasting life* (John 3:16)?

How does He commend this love? He does so by giving His Son to
die for us – His well-beloved Son. It is written that Jesus *gave himself a
ransom for all* (1 Timothy 2:6) and that He tasted *death for every man*
(Hebrews 2:9). We are not to suppose that He died for the sum total of
mankind in such a sense that His death is not truly for each one in particular. It is a great mistake into which some fall to suppose that Christ
died for the human race in general, and not for each one in particular.
By this mistake, the gospel is likely to lose much of its practical power
on our hearts. We need to understand it as Paul did, who said of Jesus
Christ, He *loved me and gave himself for me* (Galatians 2:20).

We need to make this personal application of Christ's death.
Undoubtedly, this was the great secret of Paul's holy life and of his great

power in preaching the gospel. We, too, are to regard Jesus as having loved us personally and individually. Let us consider how much effort God has taken to make us feel that He cares for us personally. It is this way in His providence, and also in His gospel. He would gladly make us single ourselves out from the crowd and feel that His loving eye and heart are upon us individually.

For what purpose does He commend His love to us? Is it a desire to make a public display? No, for certainly there can be no affection in this. God is infinitely above all pretense. He must from His very nature act honestly. Of course, He must have some good reason for this manifestation of His love. No doubt He seeks to prove to us the reality of His love. Feeling the most perfect love toward our lost race, He thought it best to reveal this love and make it obvious, both to us and to all His creatures. And what could display His love if this gift of His Son does not? Oh, how gloriously is love revealed in this great sacrifice! How this makes divine love stand out prominently before the universe! What else could He have done that would prove His love so powerfully?

God demonstrated that His love is unselfish, for Jesus did not die for us as friends, but as enemies. It was while we were still enemies that He died for us. On this point, Paul suggests that *scarcely for a righteous man will one die; yet peradventure for a good man some would even dare to die* (Romans 5:7). But the human race was as far as possible from being good. Indeed, they were not even righteous, but were utterly wicked. One might be willing to die for a very dear friend. There have been soldiers who, to save the life of a beloved officer, have taken into their own chest the spear of death, but for one who is merely just and not so much as good, this sacrifice  could scarcely be made. How much less for an enemy! Herein we may see how greatly *God commendeth his love to us, in that, while we were yet sinners, Christ died for us* (Romans 5:8).

Notice still further, that this love of God to us cannot be the love of esteem or complacency because there is in us no basis for such a love.

It can be no other than the love of unselfish kindness. This love had been called in question. Satan had questioned it in Eden. He boldly insinuated it when he asked, *Hath God said, Ye shall not eat of every tree in the garden?* (Genesis 3:1). Why would He want to keep you from such a pleasure? The old Serpent tried to cast suspicion on the goodness of God. Therefore, there was even more reason why God would vindicate His love.

He would also commend the great strength of this love. We would think that we gave evidence of strong love if we were to give our friend a great amount of money. But what is any amount of money compared with giving up a dear son to die? Oh, certainly it is surpassing love, beyond measure wonderful, that Jesus would not only labor and suffer, but that He would really die! Was ever love like this?

**God must maintain the honor of His throne. He must show that He could never brush aside sin.**

God also wanted to reveal the moral character of His love for mankind, and especially its justice. He could not show favors to the guilty until His government was made secure and His law was properly honored. Without this sacrifice, He knew it could not be safe to pardon. God must maintain the honor of His throne. He must show that He could never brush aside sin. He felt the solemn necessity of giving a public rebuke of sin before the universe. This rebuke was even more expressive because Jesus Himself was sinless. Of course, it must be seen that in His death, God was not disapproving of His sin, but of the sin of those whose sins He bore and in whose place He stood.

This shows God's abhorrence of sin since Jesus stood as our representative. While He stood in this position, God could not spare Him, but laid on Him the chastisement of our iniquities (Isaiah 53:5). Oh, what a rebuke of sin that was! How revealingly did it show that God abhorred sin, yet loved the sinner! These were among the great objects in view – to create in our souls the twofold conviction of His love for us and of our sin against Him. He wanted those convictions to be strong and abiding, so He set forth Jesus crucified before our eyes – a far more expressive thing than any mere words. No saying that He loved us could compare with the strength and impressiveness of this manifestation.

In no other way could He make it seem so much a reality – so touching and so overpowering.

By this He commends it to our regard. He invites us to look at it. He tells us that angels desire to look into it (1 Peter 1:12). He wants us to consider this great fact and examine all its significance until it comes powerfully upon our souls with its power to save. He delivers it to us to be reciprocated, as if He would inspire us to love Him who has so loved us. Of course He wants us to understand this love and appreciate it so that we may repay it with responsive love in return. It is an example for us that we can love our enemies and, much more, our brethren. Oh, when this love has taken its effect on our hearts, how deeply we feel that we cannot hate anyone for whom Christ died! Then, instead of selfishly pushing our neighbor aside and grabbing the good to which his claim is just as great as ours, we love him with a love so deep and so pure that it cannot be in our heart to do him wrong.

It was therefore a part of the divine purpose to show us what true love is. Someone said in prayer, "We thank You, Father, that You have given us Your Son to teach us how to love." Yes, God wants us to know that He Himself is love, and therefore, if we want to be His children, we must love Him and love one another. He desires to reveal His love so as to draw us into union with Himself and make us like Him.

Do you not believe that a thorough consideration of God's love, as manifested in Christ, actually teaches us what love is and serves to draw our souls into such love? The question is often asked, How should I love? The answer is given in this example. *Herein is love* (1 John 4:10)! Look at it and savor its spirit. Man is inclined to love himself first and foremost, but there is a completely different kind of love from that. This love commends itself in that *while we were yet sinners, Christ died for us.* How powerfully this rebukes our selfishness! How much we need this lesson to overcome our small-minded selfishness and shame our unbelief!

How strange it is that people do not realize the love of God! The wife of a minister who had herself labored in many revivals said to me, "Until a few days ago, I never knew that God is love."

"What do you mean?" I asked.

"I mean that I never understood it in all its significance before."

Oh, I assure you that it is a great and blessed truth, and it is a great thing to see it as it is! When it becomes a reality to the soul and you come under its powerful tenderness, then you will find the gospel to indeed be the power of God unto salvation. Paul prayed for his Ephesian converts that they might *be able to comprehend with all saints what is the breadth and length and depth and height; and to know the love of God that passeth knowledge, that you might be filled with all the fulness of God* (Ephesians 3:18-19).

By commending His love to us in this way, God wanted to subdue our oppressive fear. Someone said, "When I was young, I was sensible of fearing God, but I knew I did not love Him. The instruction I received led me to fear, but not to love." As long as we think of God only as one to be feared and not to be loved, there will be a prejudice against Him as more an enemy than a friend.

> Every sinner knows that he deserves to be hated by God. He plainly sees that God must have good reason to be displeased with him.

Every sinner knows that he deserves to be hated by God. He plainly sees that God must have good reason to be displeased with him. The selfish sinner judges God from himself. Knowing how he should feel toward someone who had wronged him, he unconsciously infers that God must feel the same way toward every sinner. When he tries to pray, his heart won't; it is nothing but terror. He feels no attraction toward God, no real love.

The childlike spirit comes before God, weeping indeed, but loving and trusting. God would gladly put away the state of feeling that only fears Him, and He desires to make us know that He loves us still. We must not regard Him as being entirely such as ourselves. He would want to take away what deceives us and make us realize that although He has spoken against us, yet He does *earnestly remember* us still (Jeremiah 31:20). He wants us to understand His dealings fairly and without preconceptions. He sees how, when He frustrates men's plans, they are intent on misunderstanding Him. They will think that He is unconcerned about their well-being, and they are blind to the precious truth that He shapes all His ways toward them in love and kindness. He would lead us to judge that if God spared not His own Son, but gave Him up freely for us all, then He will much more give us all other things most freely (Romans 8:32).

God wants to lead us to serve Him in love, not in bondage. He wants to draw us forth into the liberty of the sons of God. He loves to see the obedience of the heart. He desires to inspire love in us that is enough to make all our service to Him willing and cheerful and full of joy. If you want to make others love you, you must give them your love. Show your servants the love of your heart, and you will break their bondage and make their service one of love. In this way, God commends His love toward us in order to win our hearts to Himself, thus getting us ready and preparing us to dwell forever in His eternal home. His ultimate aim is to save us from our sins so that He may fill us forever with His own joy and peace.

## Remarks

1. We see that saving faith must be the heart's belief of this great fact that God so loved us. Saving faith receives the death of Christ as an expression of God's love to us. No other kind of faith, no faith in anything else, wins our hearts to love God. Saving faith saves us from our bondage and our prejudice against Him. It is this that makes it saving. Any faith that leaves out this great truth will fail to save us. If any element of faith is vital, it is this. Let anyone doubt this fact of God's love in Christ, and I would not give much for all his religion. It is worthless.

2. The Old Testament system is full of this idea. All those bloody sacrifices are filled with it. When the priest, in behalf of all the people, came forward and laid his hand on the head of the innocent victim and then confessed his sins and the sins of all, and then when this animal was slain and its blood was poured out before the Lord, and He gave indications that He accepted the offering, it was a solemn manifestation that God substituted the death of an innocent lamb for the sufferings due to the sinner. Throughout that ancient system, we find the same idea, showing how God wants people to see His love in the gift of His own dear Son.

3. One great reason why people find it so difficult to repent and submit

to God is that they do not receive this great fact. They do not accept it in simple faith. If they were to accept it and let it come home to their hearts, it would carry with it a power to subdue the heart to submission and to love.

4. One reason why young men are so afraid that they will be called into the ministry is their lack of confidence in this love. Oh, if they saw and believed this great love, certainly they would not let eight hundred million people go down to hell in ignorance of this gospel! Oh, how it would agonize their hearts that so many would go to their graves and to an eternal hell without ever knowing the love of Jesus to their perishing souls!

Yet here is a young man for whom Christ has died who cannot bear to go and tell them that they have a Savior! What do you think of his compassion? How much is his heart like Christ's heart? Do you wonder that Paul could not hold his peace, but felt that he must go to the ends of the earth and preach the name of Jesus where it had never been known before? How deeply he felt that he must let the world know these glad tidings of great joy! How amazing that young men now can let the gospel die unknown and not go forth to bless the lost! Have they never tasted its blessedness? Have they never known its power? Do you seriously intend to conceal it so that it may never bless your dying brethren?

5. This manner of commending God's love is the strongest and most expressive that He could use. In no other way possible could He so powerfully demonstrate His great love to our human race. Therefore, if this fails to overcome men's enmity, prejudice, and unbelief, what can avail? What methods can He use if this proves unsuccessful? The Bible demands, *How shall we escape, if we neglect so great salvation?* (Hebrews 2:3). It may well make this appeal, for if this fails to win us, what can succeed?

6. If we had been His friends, there would have been no need for Him to die for us. It was only because we were still sinners that He died for us. How great, then, are the claims of this love on our hearts!

7. Sinners often think that if they were pious and good, the Lord might love them – so they try to win His love by doing some good things. They try in every way to make God love them, especially by mending their manners rather than their hearts. Sadly, they seem not to know that the very fact of their being sunk so low in sin is moving God's heart to its very foundations! A sinless angel enjoys God's complacency, but not His compassion. He is not an object of mercy, and there is no call for it. The same is true of a good child. He receives the complacency of his parents, but not their compassion.

But suppose this child becomes wicked. Then his parents mourn over his fall, and their compassion is moved. They look on him with compassion and concern as they see him going down to the depths of iniquity, crime, and degradation. As he sinks lower and lower in the filth and abominations of sin, they mourn over him more and more. As they see how changed he is, they stand in tears, saying, "This is our son, our own once-honored son – but he is fallen now! Our hearts are moved for him, and there is nothing we would not do or suffer if we could save him!"

> Christ died for us so that He could save us – not in our sins, but from our sins.

In the same way, the sinner's great degeneration moves the compassion of his divine Father to their very depths. When the Lord passes by and sees him lying in his blood in the open field (Ezekiel 16:6), He says, "That is My son! He bears the image of his Maker." *Since I have spoken against him, I do earnestly remember him still; therefore my bowels are troubled for him; I will surely have mercy upon him, saith the LORD* (Jeremiah 31:20). Sinners should remember that the very fact that they are sinners is the thing that moves God's compassion and kindness. Do you say, "I do not see how God can make it consistent with His holiness to pardon and love such a sinner as I am"? I can tell you how: by giving His own Son to die in your place!

8. Christ died for us so that He could save us – not in our sins, but from our sins. Then must it not exceedingly grieve Him that we would continue in sin? What do you think? Suppose you were to see Jesus face to face, and He were to show you those wounds in His hands and in His side, and were to say, "I died for you because I saw that you were lost

and beyond hope, and because I wanted to save you from your sins; and now will you repeat those sins again? Can you go on still longer in sinning against Me?"

9. You may suppose from our subject that Jesus must be willing to save you from wrath if you truly repent and accept Him as your Savior. How can you doubt it? Since Jesus suffered unto death for this very purpose, it certainly only remains for you to meet the conditions, and you are saved from wrath through Him.

10. You may also suppose that God, having spared not His Son, will also with Him freely give you all other things else – enough grace to meet all your needs, the kind care of His providence, the love of His heart – everything you can need. To continue in sin despite such grace and love must be heinous! It must grieve His heart exceedingly.

A friend of mine who is in charge of 150 boys in a reform school is accustomed, when they misbehave, to put them for a time on bread and water. What do you think he does himself in some of these cases? He puts himself with them on bread and water! The boys in the school see this, and they learn the love of the superintendent and father. Then when tempted to do wrong, they must say to themselves, "If I do wrong, I will have to live on bread and water; but the worst of all is that my father will come and eat bread and water with me and for my sake, and how can I bear that? How can I bear to have my father who loves me so well confine himself to bread and water for my sake?"

In the same way, Jesus puts Himself on pain and shame and death so that you might have joy and life – that you might be forgiven and saved from sinning. Will you then continue to sin more? Have you not the heart to appreciate His dying love? Can you go on and sin even more despite all the love shown to you on Calvary?

You understand that Christ died to redeem you from sin. Suppose your own eyes were to see Him face to face, and He would tell you all He has done for you. "Sister," He says, "I died to save you from that sin; will you do it again? Can you go on and sin just the same as if I had never died for you?"

In that reform school of which I spoke, the effects produced on even the worst boys by the love shown them is really remarkable. The superintendent had long insisted that he did not want locks and bars to confine his boys. The directors had said, "You must lock them in; if you don't, they will run away." On one occasion, the superintendent was to be gone for two weeks. A director came to him and urged him to lock up the boys before he left, for he thought that while the superintendent was gone, the boys would certainly run away.

The superintendent replied, "I do not think they will. I have confidence in those boys."

"But," responded the director, "give us some guarantee. Are you willing to pledge your city lot – that if they do run away, the lot goes to the reform school fund?"

After a little reflection, he consented. "I will give you my lot – all the little property I have in the world – if any of my boys run away while I am gone."

Before he left, he called all the boys together and explained to them his pledge. He asked them to look at his dependent family, and then he appealed to their honor and their love for him. "Would you be willing to see me stripped of all my property? I think I can trust you."

He left, and then returned a little unexpectedly – late one Saturday night. He had hardly entered the yard when the word rang through the sleeping halls: "Our father has come!" Almost in an instant, they were there greeting him and shouting, "We are all here! We are all here!"

Cannot Christ's love have as much power as that? Will the love the reform school boys bear to their official father hold them to their place during the long days and nights of his absence, and will not Christ's love to us restrain us from sinning? What do you say? Will you say, "If Christ loves me so much, then it is clear that He won't send me to hell, and therefore I will continue to sin all I want"? Do you say that? If so, then there is no hope for you. The gospel that should save you can do nothing for you but sink you deeper in moral and eternal ruin. You are fully resolved to twist it to your utter damnation!

If those reform school boys had said, "Our father loves us so much that he will eat bread and water with us, and therefore we know he will not punish us to hurt us," would they not certainly bring a curse on themselves? Would not their reformation be completely hopeless? It is the same with the sinner who can trivialize the Savior's dying love. Is it possible that when Jesus has died for you to save your soul from sin and from hell, you can continue to willingly sin again and again? Will you continue in sin even more because He has loved you so much?

Think of this and make up your mind. "If Christ has died to redeem me from sin, then I will put away all sinning from this moment on and forever! I forsake all my sins from this hour! I am able to live or to die with my Redeemer; why not? With God's help, I will have no more to do with sinning forever!"

# Chapter 19

# Prayer and Labor for the Gathering of the Great Harvest

But when he saw the multitudes, he was moved with compassion on them, because they fainted, and were scattered abroad, as sheep having no shepherd. Then saith he unto his disciples, The harvest truly is plenteous, but the laborers are few. Pray ye therefore the Lord of the harvest, that he will send forth laborers into his harvest.
—Matthew 9:36-38

In discussing this subject, I intend to discuss the following:

I.  To whom this precept is addressed

II.  What is intended by this precept

III. What is implied in the prayer required

IV. To show that the state of mind that constitutes obedience to this precept is an indispensable condition of salvation

## I. The precept is addressed to all who are under obligation to be benevolent.

Therefore, it is addressed to all classes and all beings upon whom the law of love is imposed. Consequently, it is addressed to all human beings – for all who are human bear moral responsibility, should care for the souls of their fellows, and of course fall under the broad sweep of this request.

Notice the occasion of Christ's remark. He was visiting the cities and villages of His country, *teaching in their synagogues, and preaching the gospel of the kingdom, and healing every sickness and every disease among the people* (Matthew 9:35). He saw multitudes before Him, mostly in great ignorance of God and salvation, and His deeply compassionate heart was moved because He saw them fainting and scattered abroad as sheep without a shepherd. They were perishing for lack of the bread of heaven, and who should go and provide it for their needy souls!

> Let no one think that merely using the words of prayer is real obedience.

His feelings were even more affected because He saw that they felt hungry. They not only were famishing for the bread of life, but they seemed to have some awareness of the fact. They were just then in the condition of a harvest field, the white grain of which is ready for the sickle and awaits the coming of the reapers. In the same way, the multitudes were ready to be gathered into the granary of the great Lord of the harvest. No wonder this sight would touch the deepest compassions of His compassionate heart.

## II. What is really intended in this precept: *Pray ye the Lord of the harvest, that he would send forth laborers into his harvest?*

Every precept relating to external conduct has its spirit and also its letter (the letter referring to the external, but the spirit to the internal), yet both are involved in real obedience. In the present situation, the letter of the precept requires prayer. However, let no one think that merely using the words of prayer is real obedience. In addition to the words, there must be a praying state of mind. The precept does not require us to lie and play the hypocrite before God. No one can for a moment suppose this to be the case. Therefore, it must be admitted that the precept requires the spirit of prayer as well as the letter. It requires first a praying state of mind, and then also its proper expression in the forms of prayer.

What, then, is the true spirit of this precept? I answer that it is love for souls. Certainly it does not require us to pray for people without any heart in our prayer, but that we should pray with a sincere heart, full of real love for human well-being – a love for immortal souls and a deep concern for their salvation. It undoubtedly requires the same compassion that Jesus Himself had for souls. His heart was filled with real compassion for dying souls, and He was conscious that His own state of mind was a right one. Therefore, He could not do less than require the same state of mind of all His people, and so He requires us to have real and deep compassion for souls – such compassion that really moves the heart, for such most obviously was His.

This involves a full commitment of the soul to this purpose. Christ had committed His soul to the great labor of saving people. He labored and toiled for this. His heart agonized for this. His life was ready to be offered for this. Therefore, He could do no less than require the same of His people.

Again, an honest offering of this prayer implies a willingness on our part for God to use us in His harvest field in any capacity He pleases. When the farmer gathers his harvest, many things are to be done, and he often needs many hands to do them. Some he sends in to cut the grain, and others to bind it. Some gather into the barn, and others glean the field so that nothing is lost. In the same way, Christ will have a variety of labors for His servants in the great harvest field, and no one can be of real use to Him unless they are willing to work in any department of their Master's service, thankful for the privilege of doing the humblest service for such a Master and in such a cause.

Therefore, it is implied in honest prayer

for this purpose that we are really committed to the work and that we have given ourselves up most sincerely and entirely to do all we can for Christ and His cause on earth. We are always on hand, ready for any work – or for any suffering. For, clearly, if we do not have this mind, we do not need to think that we are praying to any good purpose. It would simply be a pitiful and insulting prayer to say, "Lord, send somebody else to do all the hard work, and let me do little or nothing." Everybody knows that such a prayer would only insult God and curse the one praying. Therefore, sincere prayer for Christ's cause implies that you are willing to do anything you can do to promote its interests by the actual and absolute devotion of all your powers and resources for this purpose. You may not withhold even your own children. Nothing will be too dear for you to offer on God's altar.

Suppose a person would give nothing. Suppose he would withhold all his substance and withhold all efforts, except he says that he will pray. He professes to really pray, but do you suppose that his prayer has any heart in it? Does he mean what he says? Does he love the purpose more than anything else? Truly, no. You could never say that a young person does all he can for Christ's harvest if he refuses to go into the field to work, nor that an aged but wealthy person is doing all he can if he refuses to give anything to help sustain the field laborers.

## III. What, then, is implied in really obeying this precept?

A sense of personal responsibility in respect to the salvation of the world is implied in obeying this precept. No one ever begins to obey this command who does not feel a personal responsibility in this thing that brings it home to his soul as his own work. He must really believe that "This is my work for life; for this I am to live and spend my strength." It does not matter on this point whether you are young enough to go abroad into the foreign field, or whether you are qualified for the gospel ministry. You must feel such a sense of responsibility that you will gladly and most wholeheartedly do all you can. You can do the hewing of the wood or the drawing of the water (Joshua 9:21), even if you cannot fill the more responsible trusts. An honest and consecrated heart is willing to do any sort of work and bear any sort of burden. Unless you are willing to do anything you can successfully and wisely do, you will not be conforming to the conditions of a prayerful state of mind.

Another aspect is a sense of the value of souls. You must see solemnly that souls are precious – that their guilt while in unpardoned sin is fearful and their danger is most alarming. Without such a sense of the value of the interests at stake, you will not pray with fervent, strong desire. Without a proper understanding of their sin, danger, and remedy, you will not pray in faith for God's interposing grace. Indeed, you must have so much of the love of God – a love like God's love for sinners in your soul – that you are ready for any sacrifice or any labor.

You need to feel as God feels. *God so loved the world, that he gave his only begotten Son, that whosoever believeth in him should not perish* (John 3:16). You need to love the world in such a way that your love will draw you to make similar sacrifices and put forth similar labors. Each servant of God must have a love for souls – the same kind that God had in giving up His Son to die, and that Christ had in coming cheerfully down to make Himself the offering – or his prayers for this object will have little heart and no power with God. This love for souls is always implied in acceptable prayer that God would send forth laborers into His harvest. I have often thought that the reason why so many people pray only in form and not in heart for the salvation of souls is that they lack this love, like God's love, for the souls of the perishing.

**No one can pray for what he thinks might be opposed to God's will.**

Acceptable prayer for this purpose implies confidence in the ability, wisdom, and willingness of God to push forward this work. No one can pray for what he thinks might be opposed to God's will, or that is beyond His ability or is too complicated for His wisdom. If you ask God to send forth laborers, the very prayer assumes that you trust in His ability to do the work well, and in His willingness, in answer to prayer, to carry it forward.

The very idea of prayer implies that you understand this to be a part of the divine plan – that Christians should pray for God's intervening power and wisdom to carry forward this great work. You do not pray until you see that God gives you the privilege, commands the duty, and encourages it by assuring you that it is an essential method, an indispensable condition of His inserting His power to give success. You remember that it is said, *I will yet for this be inquired of by the house of Israel to do it for them* (Ezekiel 36:37).

No one complies with the spirit of this condition who does not pray with his might, fervently and with great perseverance and urgency, for the blessing. He must feel the pressure of a great cause and must also feel that it cannot prosper without God's intervening power. Weighed down by these considerations, he will pour out his soul with intensely fervent supplications.

Unless the body of Christ is filled with the spirit of prayer, God will not send forth the laborers into His harvest. The command to pray for such laborers plainly implies that God expects prayer and that He will wait until it is made. This prayer comes into His plan as one of the appointed methods, and it can by no means be done away with. It was undoubtedly in answer to prayer that God sent out such a multitude of strong men after the ascension. How obviously did prayer and the special hand of God bring in a Saul of Tarsus and send him forth to call in whole tribes and nations of the gentile world! Along with him were a host of others. *The Lord gave the word: great was the company that published it* (Psalm 68:11).

That this prayer should be in faith, resting in assurance on God's everlasting promise, is too obvious to need proof or illustration. Honest, sincere prayer implies that we lay ourselves and all we have upon His altar. We must feel that this is our business, and that our disposable strength and resources are to be committed to its pursuit. It is only then, when we are given up to the work, that we can honestly ask God to raise up laborers and carry the work forward. When a person's lips say, "Lord, send forth laborers," but his life suggests, "I don't care whether anyone goes or not; I will not help with the work," you will of course know that he is only playing the hypocrite before God.

I do not imply by this that every honest servant of Christ must feel himself called to the ministry and must enter it; by no means. God does not call every pious man into this field, but has many other fields and labors that are essential parts of the great whole. The thing I have to say is that we must be ready for any part whatsoever that God's providence assigns us.

When we can go, and are in a situation to obtain the necessary education, then the true spirit of the prayer in our text implies that we pray that God would send us. If we are in a condition to go, then plainly this prayer implies that we have the heart to ask for the privilege for ourselves that God would put us into His missionary work. Then we will say with the ancient prophet, Lord, *here am I; send me* (Isaiah 6:8).

Do you not think that Christ expected His disciples to go, and to desire to go? Did He not assume that they would pray for the privilege of being put into this precious group of laborers? How can we be in real sympathy with Christ unless we love the work of laboring in this gospel harvest and desire to be commissioned to go forth and put in our sickle with our own hand? Most certainly, if we were have the heart of Christ, we would say, *I have a baptism to be baptized with, and how am I straitened till it be accomplished!* (Luke 12:50). We would cry out, "Lord, let me go! Let me go, for dying millions are right now perishing in their sins." How can I ask God to send out others if I am unwilling in heart to go myself? I have heard many say that they would go themselves if they were young. This seems like a state of mind that can honestly pray for God to send forth laborers.

The spirit of this prayer implies that we are willing to make any personal sacrifices in order to go. Are not people always willing to make personal sacrifices in order to gain the great object of their heart's desire? Did ever a merchant, seeking fine pearls, find one of great value without being quite willing to go and sell all that he had and buy it (Matthew 13:45-46)?

Additionally, an honest heart before God in this prayer implies that you are willing to do all you can to prepare yourselves to accomplish this work. Each young man or young woman should say, "God requires something of me in this work." God might want you as a helper in some missionary family; if so, you are ready to go. No matter what the work may be, no labor done for God or for others is demeaning. In the spirit of this prayer, you will say, "If I may only wash the feet of my Lord's servants, I will richly enjoy it."

All young people especially, feeling that life is before them, should say, "I must devote myself, in the most effective way possible, to the promotion of my Savior's cause." Suppose someone bows his soul in earnest prayer before God, saying, "O Lord, send out hosts of people into this harvest field." Does not this imply that he is getting himself ready for this work with his might? Does it not imply that he is ready to do the best he can in any way whatsoever?

This prayer, made honestly, also implies that we do all we can to prepare others to go out. Our prayer will be, "Lord, give us hearts to prepare others, and get as many people ready as possible, and as well prepared as possible, for the gathering in of this great harvest."

Of course, it is also implied that we abstain from whatever would hinder us, and that we would not make any arrangements that would tie our hands. Many young Christians do this, sometimes carelessly, often in a way that shows that they are by no means fully set to do God's work anyway.

When we honestly ask God to send out laborers, and our own circumstances allow us to go, we are to expect that He will send us. What! Does God need laborers of every description, and will He not send us? Depend on it that He will send out the person who prays properly and whose heart is deeply and fully with God. We do not need to be concerned that God would lack the needful wisdom to manage His matters well.

> He will put all His workers where they should be, into the fields they are best qualified to fill.

He will put all His workers where they should be, into the fields they are best qualified to fill. The good reaper will be put into his post, sickle in hand. If there are feeble ones who can only glean, He puts them there.

When youth have health and the means for obtaining an education, they must assume that God calls them to this work. They should assume that God expects them to enter the field. They will fix their eye upon this work as their own. Thinking of the multitudes of God's true children who are lifting up this prayer, "Lord, send forth laborers to gather in the nations to Your Son," they will certainly presume that the Lord will answer these prayers and send out all His faithful, ready, and true workers into this field. Most certainly, if God has given you the mind, the training, the tact, the heart, and the opportunity to get all needful preparation, you may know that He will send you forth. Is it possible that I am prepared, ready, and waiting, with the hosts of the church praying that God would send forth laborers, yet He will not send me? Impossible!

One indispensable part of this preparation is to have a heart for it – most plainly so, for God wants no one in His harvest field whose heart is not there. You would not want laborers in your field who have no heart for their work. Neither does God. However, He expects us to have this preparation of a ready and willing heart, and He will accept no one's excuse from service that he has no heart to engage in it. The lack of a heart for this work is not your misfortune, but your fault – your great and damning sin!

## IV. This state of mind is an indispensable condition of salvation.

Many people in the church are dreadfully in the dark about the conditions of salvation. I was once preaching on this subject, urging that holiness is one condition of salvation, *without which no man can see the Lord* (Hebrews 12:14), when I was confronted and strenuously opposed by a Doctor of Divinity. He said that the Bible makes faith the sole and only condition of salvation. He said that Paul preached that faith is the condition, and plainly meant to exclude every other condition.

I answered that Paul emphasized so earnestly and held up so prominently the doctrine of salvation by faith because he had to oppose the great Jewish error of salvation by works. Such preaching was greatly and specifically needed then, and Paul charged onto the field to meet the emergency. But when Antinomianism developed itself, James was called out to uphold with equal determination the doctrine that faith without works is dead, and that good works are the legitimate fruit of living faith and are essential to demonstrate its life and genuineness. This at once raised a new question about the nature of gospel faith. James held that all true gospel faith must work by love. It must be an affectionate filial trust that draws the soul into agreement with Christ and leads it forward powerfully to do all His will.

Many professed Christians believe that nothing is necessary except simply faith and repentance, and that faith can exist without real benevolence, and consequently, without good works. This is a great mistake. The great demand that God makes upon man is for him to become truly benevolent. This is the essence of all true religion – a state of mind that has compassion like God's compassion for human souls, that cries out in earnest prayer for their salvation, and that does not shy away from any labor to achieve this purpose. If, therefore, true religion is a condition of salvation, then the state of mind developed in our text is also a condition.

## Remarks

1. This state of mind is as much required upon sinners as upon saints. All people should feel this compassion for souls. Why not? Can any reason be given why a sinner should not feel as much compassion for souls as a Christian, or why he should not love God and man as fervently?

2. Professors of Christianity who do not obey the true spirit of these precepts are hypocrites, without one exception. They profess to be truly religious, but are they? Certainly not, unless they are on the altar, devoted to God's work and in heart sincerely sympathizing in it. Without this, every one of them is a hypocrite. You profess to have the spirit of Christ, but when you see the multitudes as Jesus saw them, perishing for lack of gospel light, do you cry out in mighty prayer with compassion for their souls? If you do not have this spirit, you can consider yourself a hypocrite.

3. Many people do not pray that God would send forth laborers because they are afraid He will send them. I can remember when Christianity was repulsive to me because I was afraid that if I would be converted, God would send me to preach the gospel. But I thought further on this subject. I said that God has a right to deal with me as He pleases, and I have no right to resist. If I do resist, He will put me in hell. If God wants me to be a minister of His gospel and I resist and rebel, He should certainly put me in hell, and undoubtedly He will.

There are many young men and women in Christian colleges who never give themselves to prayer for the conversion of the world for fear that God would send them into this work. You would be ashamed to pray, "Lord, send forth laborers, but don't send me." If the reason you don't want to go is that you have no heart for it, then without mistake, you can consider yourself a hypocrite.

If you say, "I have a heart for the work, but I am not qualified to go," then you may consider that God will not call you unless you are or can be qualified. He does not want unfit workers in the service.

4. For the last quarter of a century, the ministry has fallen into disgrace for this reason: many young men have entered it who never should have entered. Their hearts are not established, and they shy away from making sacrifices for Christ and His cause. Therefore, they do not go straight forward, true to what is right, firm for the oppressed, and strong for every good word and work. By entire groups, they back out from the position that they have sworn to maintain. The hearts of multitudes of lay brethren and sisters are in great distress, crying out over this fearful defection.

To a minister who was complaining of the public reproach cast on his profession, a layman of Boston replied, "I am sorry there is so much need for it. God intends to rebuke the ministry, and He should rebuke them since they so richly deserve it." Do not understand me to say that this wavering in the ministry is universal. No, indeed. I am glad to know there are exceptions. However, the painful fact still remains that many have relapsed, and consequently as a class they have lost character – and this has discouraged many young men from entering the ministry.

Let this be so no longer. Let the young men now preparing for the ministry come up to the spirit of their Master and rush to the front of the battle. Let them labor for the good of souls and love this work as their great Lord has done before them. Let them by their faithfulness redeem the character of this class of men from the reproach under which it now lies. Let them rally in their strength and lay themselves with one heart on the altar of God. So doing, not one generation should pass away before it will be said, "Behold the faithful men. Notice the men whose heart is in and on their work. The ministry is redeemed!"

5. With sorrow, I am compelled to say that many people don't care whether the work is done or not. They are all consumed with ambitious, selfish

desires. Who does not know that they do not identify with Jesus Christ?

Beloved, let me ask you if you are honestly aware of identifying with your great Leader. I can never read the passage before us without being affected by the demonstration it makes of Christ's tenderness and love. The thronging multitudes were there before Him. To the merely external eye, all might have seemed fine, but to those who thought of their spiritual state, there was enough to move the deep fountains of compassion. Christ saw them scattered abroad as sheep who have no shepherd. They had no teachers or guides in whom they could commit their trust. They were in darkness and moral death. Christ wept over them and called on His disciples to sympathize in their case and to unite with Him in mighty prayer to the Lord of the harvest that He would send forth laborers. Such was His spirit. And now, dear young men and women, do you care whether or not this work is done?

6. Many people seem determined to avoid this labor and leave it all for others to do. Indeed, they will hardly consider the question of what part God wants them to take and do. Now let me ask you if such people will be welcomed and applauded in the end by the herald of judgment, crying out, "Well done, good and faithful servants; enter into the joy of your Lord" (Matthew 25:21). No, never!

7. Many people say that they are not called, but really they are not devoted to this work so as to care whether they are called or not. They do not want to be called!

The very fact that you have the necessary qualifications, means, and skills for preparation indicates God's call. These constitute the voice of His providence, saying, "Go forth, and prepare for labor in My vineyard!" There is your instruction; use it. There are the classes for you to enter. Go in and work and learn until you are ready to enter the great white fields of the Savior's harvest. If God is preparing you, you must work and apply yourself to keep up with His call. Pray for the baptism of the Holy Spirit, seek the divine anointing, and give yourself no rest until you are in all things equipped for the work God assigns to you.

> If God is preparing you, you must work and apply yourself to keep up with His call.

It is painful to see that many people are committing themselves in some way or other against the work. They are putting themselves in a position which of itself prevents their taking part in it. Let me ask you, young people, can you expect ever to be saved if, when you have the power and the means to engage in this work, you have no heart for it? No, indeed! You knock in vain at the gate of the blessed! You may go there and knock, but what will be the answer? "Are you My faithful servants? Were you among the few, faithful among the faithless, willing servants always ready at your Master's call? Oh, no! You studied how you could avoid the labor and the self-denial! I do not know you! Your portion lies outside the city walls!"

Let no one excuse himself as not called, for God calls everyone to some sort of labor in the great harvest field. Therefore, you never need to excuse yourself as not called to some service for your Lord and Master. Let no young man excuse himself from the ministry unless his heart is on the altar and he himself is praying and longing to go, but is only held back by an obvious call of God, through His providence, to some other part of the great labor.

Many people will be sent to hell in the end for treating this subject as they have – with so much selfishness at heart! I know a young man who for a long time struggled between a strong conviction that God called him to the ministry and a great resistance against engaging in this work. I know what this feeling is, for I felt it a long time myself. For a long time, I had a secret conviction that I should be a minister, although my heart resisted it. In fact, my conversion depended very much upon my giving up this contest with God and subduing this resistant feeling against God's call.

8. You can see what it is to be a Christian and what God demands of people at conversion. The turning point is, Will you really and honestly serve God? With students especially, the question is likely to be, Will you abandon all your ambitious plans and devote yourself to the humble, unambitious work of proclaiming Christ's gospel to the poor? Most young men and women in Christian colleges are ambitious and aspiring. They have plans of self-elevation, which can be difficult to completely renounce. For this reason, your being a Christian and being

saved at last will depend much, and perhaps completely, on your giving yourself up to this work in the true self-denial of the gospel spirit.

9. Many people have been called to this work who afterward backslide and abandon it. They begin well, but backslide. They get into a state of great perplexity about their duty. Possibly, like Balaam, they are so unwilling to see their duty and so eager to get away from it that God will not struggle with them any longer, but gives them up to their covetousness, or their ambition.

Young man, are you earnestly crying out, "Lord, what will You have me do"? Be assured that God wants you in His field somewhere. He has not abandoned His harvest to perish. He wants you in it, but He first wants you to repent and prepare your heart for the gospel ministry. You do not need to enter it until you have done this.

Many people are waiting for a miraculous call. This is a great mistake. God does not often call people in any miraculous way. The finger of His providence points out the path, and the competence He gives you indicates the work for you to do. You do not need to fear that God will call you wrong. He will point out the work He wants you to do. Therefore, ask Him to guide you to the right place in the great field. He will certainly do it.

Young men, will you deal kindly and truly with my Master in this matter? Do you pray, "God, I am available, ready for any part of the work You have for me to do"? What will you say? Are you prepared to take this ground? Will you consecrate your education to this work? Are you ready and yearning to consecrate your all to the work of your Lord? Do you say, "Yes. God will have my all, entirely and forever"?

*I beseech you therefore, brethren, by the mercies of God, that ye present your bodies a living sacrifice, holy, acceptable unto God, which is your reasonable service* (Romans 12:1). The altar of God is before you. A complete sacrifice is the thing required. Are you ready to forsake all your selfish plans? You who have gifts that are preparing you for the ministry, will you devote them with all your soul to this work? Will you deal honestly and truly with my Master? Do you love His cause and regard it as your highest glory to be a laborer together with God in gathering in the nations of lost people to the fold of your Redeemer?

# Chapter 20

# Converting Sinners Is a Christian Duty

Brethren, if any of you do err from the truth, and one
convert him, let him know, that he which converteth
the sinner from the error of his way shall save a soul
from death, and shall hide a multitude of sins.
—James 5:19-20

A matter of present duty and of great practical importance is brought
before us in this text. In order for us to clearly understand it, let
us look into the true idea of a sinner.

What constitutes a sinner?

1. A sinner is basically a moral agent. He must be this, no matter what
else he may or may not be. He must have free will in the sense of being
able to originate his own activities. He must be the responsible author
of his own acts in such a sense that he is not forced irresistibly to act one
way or another in any way other than according to his own free choice.

He must also have intellect so that he can understand his own
actions and his moral responsibilities. An insane person who lacks this
aspect of his fundamental character is not a moral agent and cannot
be a willing sinner.

He must also have emotion so that he can be moved to action – so that there can be persuasion to voluntary activity, as well as the capability to act upon the impulses for right or wrong action.

These are the essential elements of mind, necessary to constitute a moral agent, yet these are not all the facts that develop themselves in a sinner.

2. He is a selfish moral agent, devoted to his own interests, making himself his own supreme end of action. He looks on his own things, not on the things of others (Philippians 2:4). His own interests are his main concern rather than the interests of others. We see, then, that every sinner is a moral agent who is acting under this law of selfishness, having free will and all the powers of a moral agent, but making self the great end of all his action. This is a sinner.

3. We have here the true idea of sin. In an important sense, it is error. A sinner is one who "errs" – *He which converteth the sinner from the error of his way.* It is not a mere mistake, for mistakes are made through ignorance or incompetence. Nor is it a mere defect of character that is blamed on its author. Rather, it is an "error in his ways." It is missing the mark in his voluntary course of conduct. It is a willing separation from the line of duty. It is not an innocent mistake, but it is a reckless yielding to desire. It involves a wrong purpose, a bad intention, or being influenced by desire or passion in opposition to reason and conscience. It is an attempt to secure some present gratification at the expense of resisting convictions of duty. This is most emphatically missing the mark.

> To convert him from the error of his ways is to turn him from this course to a tenderhearted consecration of himself to God and to the well-being of others.

## What is conversion?

What does it mean to *convert the sinner from the error of his way*? This error lies in his having a wrong ambition of life – his own present worldly interests. Therefore, to convert him from the error of his ways is to turn him from this course to a tenderhearted consecration of himself to

God and to the well-being of others. This is precisely what is meant by conversion. It is changing the great moral reason of action. It removes selfishness and substitutes compassion in its place.

## In what sense does a person convert a sinner?

Our text says, *If any of you do err from the truth, and one convert him* – implying that a person may convert a sinner. But in what sense can this be said and done?

I answer that the change must of necessity be a voluntary one. It is not a change in the essence of the soul or in the essence of the body. It is not any change in the created inherent abilities, but it is a change that the mind itself, acting under various influences, makes as to its own voluntary purpose of action. It is an intelligent change. The mind, acting intelligently and freely, changes its moral course, and does so for understood reasons.

The Bible attributes conversion to various means:

I.   To God. God is spoken of as converting sinners, and Christians rightly pray to God to do so.

II.  Christians are spoken of as converting sinners. We see this in our text.

III. The truth is also said to convert sinners.

Again, let it be considered that no one can convert another without the cooperation and consent of that other person. His conversion consists in his surrendering his will and changing his voluntary course. He can never do this against his own free will. He may be persuaded and induced to change his voluntary outward actions, but to be persuaded is simply to be led to change one's chosen course and choose another.

Even God cannot convert a sinner without his own consent. He cannot, for the simple reason that the thing involves a contradiction. Being converted implies one's own consent, or else it is not conversion at all. Therefore, God converts people only as He persuades them to turn from the error of their selfish ways to the rightness of compassionate ways.

So also, a person can convert a sinner only in the sense of presenting the reasons that bring about the voluntary change, thus persuading him to repent. If he can do this, then he converts a sinner from the error of his ways. However, the Bible informs us that man alone never does or can convert a sinner. It stands to reason, however, that when man acts, humbly depending on God, God works with him and by him.

People are *laborers together with God* (1 Corinthians 3:9). They present reasons, and God enforces those reasons on the mind and heart.

> When man acts, humbly depending on God, God works with him and by him.

When the minister preaches, or when you speak with sinners, man presents truth, and God causes the mind to see it with great clearness and to feel its personal application with great power. Man persuades and God persuades; man speaks to his ear, and God speaks to his heart. Man presents truth through the means of his senses to reach his free mind; God presses it upon his mind so as to secure his voluntary yielding to its claims.

It is for this reason that the Bible speaks of sinners as being persuaded: *Almost thou persuadest me to be a Christian* (Acts 26:28). The language of the Bible is entirely natural in this. It is just as if you would say that you had turned someone from his purpose, or that your arguments had turned him, or that his own convictions of truth had turned him. In the same way, the language of the Bible on this subject is altogether simple and plain, speaking right out in perfect harmony with the laws of the mind.

## We must next inquire into the kind of death of which the text speaks: *Shall save a soul from death.*

Notice that it is a soul, not a body, that is to be saved from death. Therefore, we may dismiss all thought of the death of the body in this connection. However truly converted, his body must nevertheless die. The passage speaks of the death of the soul. By the death of the soul is sometimes meant spiritual death – a state in which the mind is not influenced by truth as it should be. The person is under the dominion of sin and repels the influence of truth.

The death of the soul may also be eternal death – the complete loss of the soul and its final destruction. The sinner is, of course, spiritually dead, and if this condition were to continue through eternity, this would become eternal death. Yet the Bible represents the sinner, dying unpardoned, as going away *into everlasting punishment* (Matthew 25:46) and as being *punished with everlasting destruction from the presence of the Lord, and from the glory of his power* (2 Thessalonians 1:9). To be always a sinner is terrible enough. It is a death of fearful horror, but how terribly increased is even this when you conceive of it as intensified by everlasting punishment, far away *from the presence of the Lord, and from the glory of his power*!

## We now consider the importance of saving a soul from death.

Our text says that he who converts a sinner saves a soul from death. Consequently, he saves him from all the misery he otherwise would have had to endure. So much misery is saved. This amount is greater in the case of each sinner saved than all that has been experienced in our entire world up to this hour. This may startle you at first and may seem incredible, yet you have only to consider the matter attentively and you will see that it must be true. That which has no end – that which increases entirely beyond all our ability to compute, must surpass any finite amount, no matter how great.

Yet the amount of actual misery experienced in this world has been very great. As you go about the great cities in any country, you cannot fail to see it. Suppose you could ascend to some great height and stretch your vision over a whole continent just to take in at one glance all its miseries. Suppose you had an eye to see all forms of human woe and measure their magnitude – all the woes of slavery, oppression, intemperance, war, lust, disease, anguished hearts, etc. Suppose you could stand above some battlefield and hear as in one ascending volume all its groans and curses and take the gauge and dimensions of its unutterable woes. Suppose you could hear the echo of its agonies as they roll up to the very heavens.

If you were able to do so, you must say that there is indeed an ocean of agony here – yet all this is only a drop in the bucket compared with that vast amount, defying all calculation, that each lost sinner must endure, and from which each converted sinner is saved. If you were to see a train rumble over a dozen people at once, grinding their flesh and bones, you could not bear the sight. Perhaps you would even faint. Oh, but if you could see all the agonies of the earth accumulated, and could hear the terrible groans ascending in one deafening roar that would shake the very earth, how must your nerves quiver! Yet all this would be merely nothing compared with the eternal sufferings of one lost soul! And this is true, no matter how low may be the degree of this lost soul's suffering, each moment of his existence.

Even more, the amount of suffering thus saved is greater not only than all that ever has been, but it is greater than all that ever will be endured in this world. This is true, even though the number of inhabitants would increase a million-fold, and their miseries be increased in a similar proportion. No matter how low the degree of suffering the sinner would endure, yet our supposition is that if the earth's population increased a million-fold and its increase of miseries increased in a similar proportion, it could not begin to measure the agonies of the lost spirit.

We can also extend our comparison and take in all that has already been endured in the universe – all the agonies of earth and all the agonies of hell combined, up to this hour; yet even so, our total is utterly too meager to measure the amount of suffering saved when one sinner is converted. Even more, the amount thus saved is greater than the created universe ever can endure in any finite duration. It is even greater, countless times greater, than all finite minds can ever conceive. You may embrace the entire understanding of all finite minds, of every person and every angel, of all minds except that of God, and still the person who saves one soul from death saves in that single act more misery from being endured than all this immeasurable amount. He saves more misery, by countless times, than the entire universe of created minds can conceive.

I am afraid that many of you have never troubled yourselves to consider this subject. You are not to escape from this fearful conclusion by saying that suffering is only a natural consequence of sin and that there is no governmental infliction of pain. It does not matter at all whether the suffering is governmental or natural. The amount is all I speak of now. If a person continues in his sins, he will be miserable forever by natural law, and therefore the person who converts a sinner from his sins saves all this immeasurable amount of suffering.

You may remember the illustration used by an old preacher who attempted to give an approximate understanding of this idea, a greater appreciation by means of the understanding. There are two methods of studying and of trying to comprehend the infinite. One is by the reason, which simply affirms the infinite, and the other is by the understanding, which only approximates toward it by ideas and estimates of the finite. Both these modes of understanding may be developed by culture.

If someone stands on the deck of a ship and casts his eye abroad upon the shoreless expanse of waters, he may get some idea of the vast. Even better, if he goes out and looks at the stars in the dimmed light of evening, he can get some idea of their number and of the vastness of that space in which they are scattered abroad. On the other hand, his reason tells him at once that this space is unlimited. His understanding only helps him to approximate toward this great idea. Let him suppose, as he gazes upon the countless stars, that he has the power of rising into space at his will, and that he ascends at the speed of light for thousands of years. Approaching those glorious orbs one after another, he takes in more and more clear and grand conceptions of their magnitude as he soars on past the moon, the sun, and other suns of surpassing splendor and glory. It is the same with the conceptions of the understanding in reference to the great idea of eternity.

The old writer to whom I alluded thinks of it as a bird that is removing a globe of earth by taking away a single grain of sand once in a thousand years. What an eternity, almost, it would take – and yet this would not measure eternity!

Suppose, sinner, that you are the one suffering during all this period and that you are destined to suffer until this supposed bird has removed the last grain of sand away. Suppose you are to suffer nothing more than you have sometimes felt, yet suppose that bird must remove, in this slow process, not this world only – for this is but a little speck, comparatively – but also the whole material universe, just a single grain at a time!

Or suppose the universe were a million times more extensive than it is, and that you must suffer through all this time while the bird removes slowly a single tiny grain once every thousand years! Would it not seem to you like an eternity? If you knew that you must be deprived of all happiness for all time, would not the knowledge sink into your soul with a force that is perfectly crushing?

However, this concept only gives a basic understanding. Let this time measured in this way roll on until all is removed that God ever created or ever can create, and even so, it hardly provides a comparison, for eternity has no end. You cannot even begin to come near its end. After the lapse of the longest period you can conceive, you have approached no nearer than you were when you first began. Sinner, can your heart endure, or your hands be strong, in the day when God will deal in this way with you? (Ezekiel 22:14).

Let us look at still another view of the situation. He who converts a sinner not only saves more misery, but bestows more happiness than all the world, or even all the created universe, has yet enjoyed. You have converted a sinner, have you? Indeed! Then think what has been gained! What happens then? Let the facts of the case give the answer. The time will come when he will say, "In my experience of God and divine things, I have enjoyed more than all the created universe had done up to the general judgment – more than the total happiness of all creatures during the whole duration of our world – and yet my happiness is only just begun! Onward, still onward! Onward forever rolls the deep tide of my blessedness, and it is evermore increasing!"

> He who converts a sinner not only saves more misery, but bestows more happiness than all the world has yet enjoyed.

Also look at the work in which this converted person is occupied. Just look at it. In some sunny hour, you have caught glimpses of God and of His love and have said, "Oh, if this could only last forever! Oh, if this stormy world were not around me! Oh, if my soul had wings like a dove, then I would fly away and be at rest." Those were only longings for the rest of heaven; that which the converted person enjoys above is heaven. You must add to this the rich and glorious idea of eternal and perpetual increase. His blessedness not only endures forever, but it increases forever! This is the joy of every converted sinner.

## If these things are true, then the following things are also true:

I. Converting sinners is the work of the Christian life. It is the great work to which we, as Christians, are especially appointed. Who can doubt this?

II. It is the great work of life because its importance demands that it should be. It is so much beyond any other work in importance that it cannot be rationally regarded as anything other or less than the great work of life.

III. It can be made the great work of life because Jesus Christ has made provision for it. His atonement covers the human race and lays the foundation so broad that whosoever will may come (Revelation 22:17). The promise of His Spirit to aid each Christian in this work is equally broad, and it was designed to open the way for each one to become a laborer together with God in this work of saving souls.

IV. Compassion can never stop short of it. Where so much good can be done and so much misery can be prevented, how is it possible that compassion can fail to do its utmost?

V. Living to save others is the condition of saving ourselves. No one is truly converted who does not live to save others. Every truly converted person turns from selfishness to compassion, and compassion certainly leads him to do all he can to save the souls of his fellow men. This is the changeless law of benevolent action.

VI. The self-deceived are always to be differentiated by this characteristic: they live to save themselves. This is the main purpose of all their religion. All their religious efforts and activities lean toward this sole purpose. If they can secure their own conversion so as to be pretty sure of it, they are satisfied. Sometimes the ties of natural compassion embrace those who are especially near to them, but selfishness commonly goes no further – except that a desire for a good reputation may urge them on.

VII. Some people make no effort to convert sinners, but act as if this were a matter of no importance whatsoever. They do not labor to persuade people to be reconciled to God.

Some seem to be waiting for miraculous intervention. They take no efforts even with their children or friends. Very much as if they felt no interest in the great issue, they wait and wait for God, or a miracle, to move. Sadly, they do nothing in this great work of human life!

Many professed Christians have no faith in God's blessing, and no expectation by that of success. Consequently, they make no effort in faith. Their own experience is good for nothing to help them, because never having had faith, they have never had success. Many ministers preach so as to do no good. Having failed so long, they have lost all faith. They have not gone to work expecting success, and therefore they have not had success.

> Every Christian, male or female, of every age, and in any position in life whatsoever, should make it a business to save souls.

Many professors of Christianity who are not ministers also seem to have lost all faith. Ask them if they are doing anything, and they answer that they are truly doing nothing. However, if their hearts were full of the love of souls, or of the love of Christ, they would certainly make much effort. They would at least try to convert sinners from the error of their ways. They would live Christianity. They would hold up its light as a natural, instinctive thing.

Every Christian, male or female, of every age, and in any position in life whatsoever, should make it a business to save souls. There are indeed many other things to be done, and they should have their place – but don't neglect the greatest thing of all.

Many professed Christians never seem to convert sinners. Let me ask you how it is with you. Some of you might reply, "Under God, I have been the means of saving some souls." But some of you cannot even say this. You know you have never labored honestly and with all your heart for this purpose, and you do not know that you have ever been the means of converting one sinner.

What will I say of those young converts here? Have you given yourselves up to this work? Are you laboring for God? Have you gone to your unrepentant friends, even to their homes, and by personal, warmhearted appeal pleaded with them to be reconciled to God? By writing and speaking and by every form of influence you can command, have you tried to save souls and do what you can in this work? Have you succeeded?

Suppose all who professed Christianity were to do this, each in their sphere and each doing all they individually could do – how many would be left unconverted? Suppose each one would say, "I lay myself on the altar of my God for this work. I confess all my past neglect. From now on, God helping me, this will be the labor of my life." Imagine if each person would begin by removing all the old offenses and occasions of stumbling and would publicly confess and lament his negligence and every other form of public offense, confessing how little you have done for souls, crying out, "Oh, how wickedly I have lived in this matter, but I must reform, confess, repent, and completely change the course of my life." If you were all to do this and then set yourselves each in your place to lay your hand in all earnestness upon your neighbor and pluck him out of the fire – how glorious would be the result!

However, to neglect the souls of others and think you will still be saved yourself is one of sin's worst mistakes, for unless you live to save others, how can you hope to be saved yourself? *If any man have not the Spirit of Christ, he is none of his* (Romans 8:9).

# Chapter 21

# People Often Highly Esteem
# What God Abhors

Ye are they which justify yourselves before men, but God
knoweth your hearts; for that which is highly esteemed
among men is abomination in the sight of God.
—Luke 16:15

C hrist had just told the parable of the unjust steward, in which He
presented the case of someone who unjustly used the property of
others entrusted to him for the purpose of placing them under obligation
to provide for him after expulsion from his position. Our Lord represents this conduct of the steward as being wise in the sense of foresight
and providing for himself – a wisdom of the world, void of all morality.

He uses the case to illustrate and recommend the use of wealth in
such a way as to make friends for ourselves who at our death will welcome us into *everlasting habitations* (Luke 16:9). Then going deeper,
even to the foundational principle that should control us in all our use
of wealth, He teaches that no one can serve both God and riches. Rich
and covetous people who were serving wealth did not need to think
that they could also serve God at the same time. The service of the one
is not to be reconciled with the service of the other.

The covetous Pharisees heard all these things, and they mocked Him, as if they would say, "Indeed, You seem to be very sanctimonious to tell us that we do not serve God acceptably! When has there ever been a tithe of mint that we did not pay?" Those Pharisees did not admit that His teaching was correct, by any means. They thought they could serve both God and riches. Let whoever would say they serve riches say that they knew they also served God, and they would have nothing but scorn for those teachings that showed the inconsistency and the absurdity of worshipping two opposing gods and serving two opposing masters.

Our Lord replied to them in the words of our text, *Ye are they who justify yourselves before men, but God knoweth your hearts; for that which is highly esteemed among men is abomination in the sight of God.*

In pursuing this subject, I will show how and why it is that people highly esteem that which God abhors.

They have a different rule of judgment. God judges by one standard, and they judge by another. God's standard requires universal benevolence; their standard is satisfied with an amount of selfishness that is sufficiently suited to meet the times. God requires people to devote themselves not to their own interest, but to His interest and to those of His great family. He sets up only one great purpose – the highest glory of His name and kingdom. He asks them to become divinely patriotic, devoting themselves to their Creator and to the good of His creatures.

> God requires people to devote themselves not to their own interest, but to His interest and to those of His great family.

The world adopts an entirely different standard, allowing people to set up their own happiness as their purpose. It is curious that some pretended philosophers have laid down the same rule – that people should pursue their own happiness and only take care not to infringe on the happiness of others too much. Their doctrine allows people to pursue a selfish course, only not in a way to infringe too noticeably on the rights and interests of others.

God's standard, however, is to not seek one's own wealth (1 Corinthians 10:24). His law is clear: *Thou shalt love [not thy self, but] the Lord thy God with all thy heart* (Mark 12:30). *Love is the fulfilling of the law* (Romans 13:10). *Charity [this same love] . . . seeketh not her own*

(1 Corinthians 13:5). This is characteristic of the love the law requires – it does not seek its own. *Let no man seek his own, but every man another's wealth* (1 Corinthians 10:24). *Look not every man on his own things, but every man on the things of others* (Philippians 2:4). *For all seek their own, and not the things which are Jesus Christ's* (Philippians 2:21). Paul regards it as an entire departure from the standard of true Christianity to seek one's own interest rather than the interest of Jesus Christ.

God regards nothing as virtue except devotion to the proper purpose. The proper purpose is not one's own good, but the general good. Therefore, God's standard requires virtue, while man's standard at best only restrains sin. All human governments are founded on this principle, as all who study the subject know. They do not require compassion, but they only restrain selfishness. In the foundational principles of our government, it is affirmed that people have certain inalienable rights, one of which is the right for each person to pursue his own happiness. This is affirmed to be an inalienable right, and it is always assumed to be right in itself as long as it does not infringe on others' rights of happiness. But God's standard requires positive compassion and regards nothing else as virtue except devotion to the highest good. Man's standard condemns nothing as long as man so restrains himself as not to infringe on others' rights.

Moral character is the result sought. It cannot be based upon forceful action, but must always depend upon the result that the mind has in view. People always really assume and know this. They know that the moral character is really the same as the purpose to which man devotes himself. Therefore, with God's law and man's law being as they are, to obey God's is holiness, while to obey only man's law is sin.

People very inconsiderately judge themselves and others not by God's standard, but by man's. They do this to an extent truly astounding. Look into people's real opinions, and you will see this. Often without being at all aware of it, people judge themselves by their own standard instead of God's.

Here I must notice some proof of this and provide some illustrations. For example, a mere negative morality is highly esteemed by some people. If a person lives in a community and does no harm, defrauds no one, does not cheat or lie, does no obvious harm to society, and transacts his business in a way that is considered honorable and virtuous, then this person stands in high repute according to the standard of the world. But what does all this really amount to? The person is just taking care of himself; that is all. His morality is entirely of this negative form. All you can say of him is that he does no harm, yet this morality is often spoken of in a manner that shows that the world highly esteems it. But does God highly esteem it? No, but it is an abomination in His sight.

For another thing, a religion that is merely negative is often highly esteemed. People of this religion are careful not to do wrong – but what is doing wrong? It is thought not to be wrong to neglect the souls of their neighbors. What do they consider wrong? Cheating, lying, stealing. They will admit that these and similar things are wrong, but what are they doing? Look around you even here and see what people of this type are doing. Many of them never try to save a soul. They are highly esteemed for their inoffensive lives. They do no wrong, but they do nothing to save a soul. Their religion is a mere negation. Maybe they would not take a ferry across a river on the Lord's Day, but they would never save a soul from death. They would let their own employees go to hell without one earnest effort to save them. Must not such a religion be an abomination to God?

> All their religion consists in keeping up their forms of worship. If they add nothing to these, their religion is only an abomination before God.

It is the same of a religion that at best consists of forms and prayers and does not add to these the power of benevolent effort. Such a religion is all hollow. Is it serving God to do nothing except ask favors for oneself?

Some people keep up Sabbath duties, as they are termed, and family prayer, but all their religion consists in keeping up their forms of worship. If they add nothing to these, their religion is only an abomination before God.

There are still other facts that show that people loosely set up a false standard that they highly esteem, but that God abhors. For example, they will require true Christianity only of ministers, but not of anyone else. All people agree that ministers should be really pious. They judge them by the right standard. For example, they require ministers to be compassionate. They must enter upon their profession for the high purpose of doing good, and not for the mere sake of a living – not for *filthy lucre's sake* (Titus 1:11), but for the sake of souls and from unselfish love. Otherwise, they will have no confidence in a minister.

But turn this over and apply it to people of business. Do they judge themselves by this standard? Do they judge each other by this standard? Before they will have Christian confidence in a merchant or a mechanic, do they insist that these people will be as much above the greed for gain as a minister should be, that they should be as willing to give up their time to the sick as a minister, and that they must be as ready to do without a better salary for the sake of doing more good as they insist a minister should be?

Who does not know that they do not demand of people of business any such conditions of Christian character as those that they impose on gospel ministers? Let us see. If a person of business does any service for you, he makes out his bill, and if need be, he collects it. Now suppose I would go and visit a sick man to give him spiritual counsel. Suppose I would visit him from time to time for counsel and for prayer until he died, and then I would attend his funeral. Then, after this, I would make up my bill and send it in, and even collect it; would there not be some talk? People would say, "What right has he to do that? He should perform that service for the love of souls without charging for it."

This applies to those ministers who are not under salary to perform this service, of whom there are many. Let any one of these men go and labor ever so much among the sick or at funerals, and they must not take pay. But let one of these ministers send his saw to be filed, and he must pay for it. He may send it to that very man whose sick family he has visited by day and by night, and whose dead he has buried, without charge, and "for the love of souls," but no such "love of souls" binds the mechanic in his service. The truth is, they call that religion in a layman that they call sin in a minister. That is the fact. I do not complain that people take pay for labor, but that they do not apply the same principle to a minister.

Again, the business goals and practices of people of business are almost universally an abomination in the sight of God. Almost all of these are based on the same principle as human governments are – namely, that the only restraint imposed will be to prevent people from being too selfish, allowing them to be just as selfish as they can be while leaving others an equal chance to be selfish too.

Shall we go into a long list of the principles of people of business regarding their purposes and methods of doing business? What would it all amount to? It would amount to them seeking their own ends – doing something, not for others, but for self. As long as they do it in a way regarded as honest and honorable among people, no further restriction will be imposed.

Take the Bible society for an illustration. This institution is not a risky business venture entered upon for the good of those who print and publish, but the goal aimed at is to furnish Bibles as cheap to the purchaser as possible so as to put a Bible into the hands of every human being at the lowest possible price. It is easy to see that any other course and any different principle from this would be universally condemned. If Bible societies would become merely a moneymaking business, they would cease to be benevolent institutions at all, and to claim such a designation would bring down on them the curses of men.

However, all business should be operated as benevolently as the making of Bibles; why not? If it is not, can it be a benevolent business? And if it is not benevolent, how can it have the approval of God? What is a benevolent business? A benevolent business is one that does the utmost good – that which is undertaken for the one and only purpose of doing good, and that simply intends to do the utmost good possible. In just this sense, people should be patriotic and benevolent and should have a single eye to God's glory in all they do, whether they eat or drink or whatever they may do (1 Corinthians 10:31).

Yet where do you find the person who holds his fellow men to this standard in practice as a condition of their being esteemed Christians – that is, that in all their business, they should be as benevolent as Bible societies are? What would we say of a Bible society that would enter upon an obvious plan to make as much money as they can from their Bibles instead of selling at the lowest living price? What would you say of such a Bible society? You would say, "Horrible hypocrite!" I must say the same of every Christian who does the same thing. Ungodly people do not profess any Christian benevolence, so we will not accuse them of this hypocrisy, but we will try to get this light before their mind.

Now think of a minister and ask if you judge yourself in the same way that you judge him. Do you say of yourself that you should do for others for free everything and whatever you require him to do for free? Do you judge yourself by the same standard by which you judge him?

Apply this to all people of business. No matter what your business is, whether high or low, small or great, filing saws, or counting out bank bills – you call the Bible society benevolent. Do you make your business as much so and as truly so in your purposes and goals? If not, why not? What right do you have to be less benevolent than those who print, publish, and sell Bibles?

Another thing that is highly esteemed among people, yet is an abomination before God, is selfish ambition. How often we see this highly esteemed! I have been amazed to see how people form judgments on this matter. A young man might be a good student in the sense of making great progress in his studies (a thing the devil could do), yet for this only, he is spoken of in the highest terms. Provided they do well for themselves, nothing more seems to be asked or expected in order to entitle them to high praise.

It is the same with professional people. I am thinking of the case of a lawyer who was greatly esteemed and admired by his fellow men. He was often spoken of well by Christians, but what was he? He was nothing but an ambitious young lawyer, doing everything for advancement, ready at any time to travel across the whole country and promote his cause – and for what? To get some good for himself. Yet he is praised and admired by Christian families! Why? Because he is doing well for himself!

Think of Daniel Webster. How lauded – almost canonized! Perhaps he will be yet. Certainly the same spirit we now see would canonize him if this were a Catholic country. But what has he done? He has just played the part of an ambitious lawyer and an ambitious statesman; that is all. He has sought great things for himself, and having said that, you have said all. Yet how people have praised Daniel Webster! When I came to Syracuse, I saw a vast procession. "What," I said, "is there a funeral here? Who is dead?"

"Daniel Webster."

I said that he has been dead a long time. "Yes, but they are acting out his funeral because he was a great man." What was Daniel Webster? He was not a Christian, not a benevolent man; everybody knows this. What have Christians to do in praising and exalting a merely selfish ambition? They might esteem it highly, yet let them know that God abhors it as utterly as they admire it.

The world's entire morality, as well as that of a large portion of the church, are only a false benevolence. You see a family very much united, and you think how they love one another! So they do, but they may be very exclusive. They may exclude themselves and shut off their affection almost entirely from all other families, and they may consequently exclude themselves from doing good in the world. The same kind of a morality can be seen in towns and in nations. This makes up the entire morality of the world.

Many have what they call humanity, but without any piety – and this is often highly esteemed among people. They pretend to love others, but do not honor God, nor even try to. In their love of people, they fall below some animals. I doubt whether many people who are not truly pious would do what I knew a dog to do. His master wanted to kill him, and for this purpose took him out into the river in a boat and tied a stone around his neck. In the struggle to throw the dog and stone overboard together, the boat tipped over. The man was in the river, and the dog, by extra effort, released himself from his weight, seized his master by the shirt collar, and swam with him to land.

> The world's entire morality, as well as that of a large portion of the church, are only a false benevolence.

Few people would have had humanity enough, without piety, to have done this. Indeed, people without piety are not often half as kind to each other as animals are. Humans are more degraded and more depraved. Animals will make greater sacrifices for each other than the human race does. Go and ask a whaler what he sees among the whales when they allow themselves to be murdered to protect a school of their young. Yet many mothers think they do most honorable things simply because they take care of their children.

Humans, as compared with animals, should act from higher motives than they. If they do not, they act wickedly. Knowing more by having the knowledge of God and of the dying Savior as their example and rule, they have greater responsibilities than animals can have.

People often make a great virtue of their opposition to slavery, even though it is only done without any thought of God. Possibly there is no virtue in this, or only a tiny bit more than a mere animal might have. Whoever understands the subject of slavery and is a good person at heart will certainly be an abolitionist. However, a person may be an abolitionist without the least virtue. There may not be the least regard for God in his abolitionism, nor even any honest regard to human well-being. He may stand on a principle that would make him a slaveholder himself if his circumstances favored it. Such people certainly do act on slaveholding principles. They develop principles and adopt practices that show that if they had the power, they would enslave the human race. Some people not only lord it over the bodies of their fellow humans, but also over their minds and souls – their opinions and consciences – which is much worse oppression and tyranny than simply to enslave the body.

There is often a bitter and angry spirit, which is not by any means the spirit of Christ, for while Christ no doubt condemns the slaveholder, He does not hate him. This biting hatred of evildoers is only animosity, after all, and though people may ever so highly esteem it, God abhors it.

On the other hand, many people call piety that which has no humanity in it. They treat others unfairly to get money to give to the Bible Society! This is piety (so called) without humanity. I abhor a piety that has no humanity with it and in it as deeply as I condemn its opposite – humanity without piety. God loves both piety and humanity. How greatly, then, must He abhor either when unnaturally separated from the other!

All those so-called religious efforts that people make, having only self for their goal, are an abomination to God. There is a wealthy man who agrees to give five thousand dollars toward building a splendid church. He thinks this is a very benevolent offering, and it may be highly esteemed among men. But before God approves of it, He will look into the motives of the giver – and so may we, if we want to. We learn that the man owns a good deal of real estate in the village that he expects will rise in value on the very day that will see the church building decided upon, enough to put back into his pocket two or three times what he gives.

Besides this, he has other motives. He thinks of the increased respectability of having a fine house and himself the best room in it. Even more, he has some interest in having good morals sustained in the village, for iniquity is troublesome to rich men and is also somewhat dangerous. Then he has an unspeakable sort of expectation that this new church and his large donation to build it will somehow improve his prospects for heaven. Inasmuch as these are rather dim at best, the improvement, though unclear, is certainly an objective. Now if you examine these motives, you will see that from first to last they are entirely selfish. Of course, they are an abomination in God's sight.

The motives for obtaining a popular minister are often of the same type. The objective is not to get a man sent from God, to labor for God and with God, and one with whom the people may labor and pray for souls and for God's kingdom, but the objective, being something other than this, is an abomination before God.

The highest forms of the world's morality are only abominations in God's sight. The world has what it calls good husbands, good wives, and good children – but what kind of goodness is this? The husband loves his wife and seeks to please her. She also loves and seeks to please him.

But do either of them love or seek to please God in this relationship? By no means. Nothing can be farther from their thoughts. They never go beyond the narrow circle of self. Take all these human relationships in their best earthly form, and you will find they never rise above the morality of the lower animals. They embrace and hold each other, and they seem to take some interest in the care of their children. So do your domestic fowls – not less, and possibly even more. Often these fowls in your poultry yard go beyond the world's morality in these qualities that the world calls good.

Should not human beings have vastly higher aspirations than these? Can God regard their highly esteemed qualities any other than an abomination if, in fact, they are even below the level of the domestic animals?

An unsanctified education comes into the same category. A good education is indeed a great good, but if not sanctified, if it is not used for God, it is all the more abhorrent to God. Yes, let me tell you, if it is not refined for God, it is only the more abhorrent to Him in proportion as you get light on the subject of duty, and sin against that light even more. Those very achievements that will give you higher esteem among men will, if unsanctified, make your character more entirely abhorrent before God.

You may be a polished writer and a beautiful speaker. You stand at the head of the college in these important respects. Your friends look forward with hopeful interest to the time when you will be heard of on the floor of the Senate, moving them to admiration by your eloquence. But sadly, you have no piety! When we ask how God looks upon such talents that are not devoted to Him, we are compelled to answer that God sees them only as an abomination. The eloquent young student is only the more abhorrent to God by reason of all his unsanctified powers.

The very things that give you the more honor among people will make you only the ridicule of hell. The spirits of the lower pit will meet you as they did the fallen monarch of Babylon, tauntingly saying, "What, are you here? You who could shake kingdoms by your eloquence are brought down to the sides of the pit? You who could have been an angel of light, you are a selfish doomed sinner. Go away and get out of our company! We have nobody here as guilty and as deeply damned as you!"

It is the same with all unsanctified talents, beauty, education, and accomplishments. All of these, if unsanctified and not used for God, are an abomination in His sight. All of those things that could make you more useful in the sight of God are, if misused, only greater abomination in His sight.

It is the same in regard to a legal religion, a religion of law and works, with which you serve God only because you must. You go to church, yet not because of love to God or to His worship, but from regard to your reputation, to your hope, or to your conscience. Must not such a kind of Christianity be of all things most abominable to God?

## Remarks

The world has mainly lost the true idea of Christianity. This is too obvious from all I have said to need more examples. To a large extent, the same is true of the church. Professed Christians judge themselves falsely because they judge by a false standard.

One of the most common and fatal mistakes is to employ a merely negative standard. There are people complaining of a lack of conviction. Why don't they take the right standard and judge themselves by that? Suppose you had let a house burn down and made no effort to save it. What would you think of the guilt of foolishness and laziness there? Two women and five children are burned to ashes in the fire. Why did you not give the alarm when you saw the fire? Why did you not rush into the building and drag out the unconscious residents? Oh, you felt sluggish that morning, just as people talk of being sluggish in religion! Well, you hope not to be judged too harshly since you did not set the house on fire. You only let it alone. All you did was to do nothing! That is all many people plead as to their Christian duties. They do nothing to rescue sinners out of the fire, and they seem to think this is a very admirable kind of religion! Was this the religion of Jesus Christ or of Paul? Is it the religion of real compassion – or of common sense?

You see how many people who have a Christian hope indulge it on merely negative grounds. I often ask people how they are getting along in religion. They answer that they are getting along pretty well, and yet they are doing nothing that is really Christian. They are making no effort to save souls. They are doing nothing to serve God. What are they doing? Oh, they say that they regularly pray! Suppose you would hire an employee and pay him each week, yet he does nothing all day but pray to you!

Christianity is very straightforward and is easily understood. It is a warfare. What is a warrior's service? He devotes himself to the service of his country. If need be, he lays down his life. He is expected to do this. In the same way, a Christian is to lay down his life on God's altar, to be used in life or death, as God may please, in His service.

> Christianity is very straightforward and is easily understood. It is a warfare.

The things most highly esteemed among people are often the very things God most abhors (Luke 16:15). Take for example, the legalist's religion. The more he is bound in conscience and enslaved, by so much the more, usually, does his respect as a Christian rise. The more thoroughly he groans under his bondage to sin, the more certainly he says:

> Reason I hear, her counsels weigh,
>     And all her words approve;
> Yet still I find it hard to obey,
>     And harder yet to love.

By so much the more does the world esteem, and God abhor, his religion. The good man, they say, was all his lifetime subject to bondage! He was in doubts and fears all his life. But why did he not come by faith into that liberty with which Christ makes His people free (Galatians 5:1)?

A morality that is based on the most cultured selfishness stands in the highest esteem among people. "He is such a good man of the world," they say, "almost a saint;" yet God must regard him in complete abomination.

The good Christian in the world's esteem is never rude or aggressive, yet he is greatly admired. He has a selfish devotion to pleasing people, and nothing is more admired. I heard of a minister who did not have an enemy in the world. He was said to be most like Christ among all the people they knew. I thought it strange that a man so like Christ would have no enemies, for Christ, who was more like Himself than any other person can be, had a great many enemies, and very bitter enemies too. Indeed, it is said, *All that will live godly in Christ Jesus shall suffer persecution* (2 Timothy 3:12). But when I came to learn the facts of the case, I understood the man. He never allowed himself to preach anything that could displease even Universalists. In fact, he had two Universalists in his congregations. He also had some Calvinists in his congregation, and he must by no means displease them. His preaching was indeed a model of its kind. His motto was "Please the people." He did nothing but please the people. In the midst of a revival, he would leave the meetings and go to a party. Why? To please the people. This may be highly esteemed among people, but does not God abhor it?

It is a light thing to be judged by man's judgment, and all the lighter since they are so inclined to judge by a false standard. What does it matter to me that people condemn me if God approves of me? The longer I live, the less I think of human opinions on the great question of right and wrong as God sees them. They will judge both themselves and others falsely. Even the church sometimes condemns and excommunicates its best people. I have known cases, and could name them, in which I am confident they have done this very thing. They have cut people off from their communion, and now everybody sees that the men excommunicated were the best men of the church.

It is a blessed thought that the only thing we need to care for is to please God. The only inquiry we need to make is, What will God think of it? We have only one mind to please, and that is the Great Mind of the universe. Let this be our single desire, and we will not fail to please Him. However, if we do not aim at this, then everything we can do is only an abomination in His sight.

# Chapter 22

# Victory over the World through Faith

> For whatsoever is born of God overcometh the world: and this is the victory that overcometh the world, even our faith.
>
> —1 John 5:4

The discussion of this text naturally leads us to ask four questions:

    I.   What is it to overcome the world?

    II.  Who are they who overcome?

    III. Why do they overcome the world?

    IV. How do they do it?

These are the natural questions that a serious mind would ask upon reading this text.

## I. What is it to overcome the world?

1. To overcome the world is to get above the spirit of covetousness that possesses the people of the world. The spirit of the world is eminently the spirit of covetousness. It is a greediness after the things of the world. Some worldly people covet one thing, and some another, but all classes

of worldly people are living in the spirit of covetousness in some of its forms. This spirit has supreme possession of their minds.

The first thing in overcoming the world is that the spirit of covetousness in respect to worldly things and objects must be overcome. The person who does not overcome this spirit of rushing and scrambling after the good that this world offers has by no means overcome it.

2. Overcoming the world implies rising above its attraction. When a person has overcome the world, his thoughts are no longer absorbed and swallowed up with worldly things. A person certainly does not overcome the world unless he gets above being preoccupied and absorbed with its concerns.

We all know how exceedingly pr‹ some form of worldly good. One is c‹ politics, a third with getting money, and with pleasure; but each in his ch all-consuming object.

The person who gains the victory just one form of its pursuits, but every itself and all that it has to present as

3. Overcoming the world implies overcoming the fear of the world. It is a sad fact that most people, and indeed all people of worldly character, have so much regard to public opinion that they dare not act according to the dictates of their consciences when acting in such a way would incur the popular disapproval. One person is afraid that his business might suffer if his course runs counter to public opinion. Another person is afraid that standing up for the truth will injure his reputation, and he strangely imagines and tries to believe that supporting an unpopular truth will diminish and possibly destroy his good influence – as if anyone could exert a good influence in any possible way besides maintaining the truth.

It must be admitted that great multitudes of people are under this influence of fearing the world, yet many of them are not aware of this fact. If you or they could thoroughly state the reasons of their reluctance in duty, fear of the world would be found among the main reasons. Their fear of the world's displeasure is so much stronger than their fear of God's displeasure that they are completely enslaved by it.

Who does not know that some ministers dare not preach what they know is true, and even what they know is important truth, afraid that they would offend some people whose good opinion they seek to retain? The institution might be weak, and the favor of some rich person in it seems indispensable to its very existence. Therefore, the fear of these rich people is continually before their eyes when they write a sermon, or preach, or are called to take a stand in favor of any truth or cause that may be unpopular with people of more wealth than piety or conscience. This bondage to man is sad! Too many gospel ministers are so troubled by it that their overall policy is virtually renouncing Christ and serving the world. Overcoming the world means to completely overcome this bondage to men.

4. Overcoming the world implies overcoming a state of worldly concern. You know there is a state of great care and concern that is common and almost universal among worldly people. It is perfectly natural if the heart is set upon securing worldly good and has not learned to receive all good from the hand of a great Father and trust Him to give or withhold according to His own unerring wisdom. However, he who loves the world is the enemy of God, and therefore can never have this filial trust in a parental Benefactor, nor the peace of soul that it gives.

This is why worldly people are almost always in a high state of anxiety for fear that their worldly plans would fail. They sometimes get momentary relief when all things seem to go well, but some misfortune is certain to happen to them at some point soon, so that hardly a day passes that does not bring with it some gnawing anxiety. Their hearts are like the troubled sea that cannot rest, whose waters stir up mire and dirt. However, the person who rises above the world gets above this state of ceaseless and gnawing anxiety.

5. The victory under consideration implies that we cease to be enslaved and in bondage to the world in any of its forms. There is a worldly spirit and there is also a heavenly spirit, and one or the other exists in the heart of every person and controls his whole being. Those who are under the

control of the world, of course, have not overcome the world. No one overcomes the world until his heart is filled with the spirit of heaven.

One form that the spirit of the world assumes is being enslaved to the customs and fashions of the day. It is amazing to see what a goddess fashion becomes. No heathen goddess was ever worshipped with costlier offerings, more devout reverence, or more complete subjection. Certainly no heathen deity since the world began has ever had more universal support. Where will you go to find the man of the world or the woman of the world who does not rush to worship at her shrine of fashion?

Overcoming the world implies that the spell of this goddess is broken. They who have overcome the world are no longer careful either to secure its favor or avoid its displeasure. The good or the bad opinion of the world is to them a small matter. Paul said, *With me it is a very small thing that I should be judged of you, or of man's judgment* (1 Corinthians 4:3). It is the same with every real Christian. His concern is to secure the approval of God. His main concern is to yield himself to God and to his own conscience. No one has overcome the world unless he has attained this state of mind.

Almost no characteristic of Christian character is more noticeable or more decisive than this: indifference to the opinions of the world. Since I have been in the ministry, I have been blessed with the acquaintance of some people who were especially distinguished by this quality of character. Some of you may have known the late Rev. James Patterson of Philadelphia. If so, you know that he was profoundly distinguished in this respect. He seemed to have the least possible desire to secure the approval of men or avoid their condemnation. It did not seem to matter at all to him to gain the approval of man, for it was enough for him if he pleased God.

> Almost no characteristic of Christian character is more noticeable or more decisive than this: indifference to the opinions of the world.

Therefore, you were certain to find him in everlasting war against sin – all sin, no matter how popular and no matter how entrenched it was by custom or sustained by wealth or public opinion. Yet he always opposed sin with a most remarkable spirit – a spirit of inflexible decision, yet of great graciousness and tenderness. While he was saying the most severe things in the most plain language, you might see the big tears rolling down his cheeks.

It is wonderful that most people never complained of his having a bad spirit. As much as they dreaded his rebuke and winced under his strong and daring exposures of wickedness, they could never say that James Patterson had any other than a good spirit. This was a most beautiful and remarkable example of having overcome the world.

People who are not dead to the world in this way have not escaped its bondage. The victorious Christian is in a state where he is no longer in bondage to man. He is bound only to serve God.

## II. Who are those who overcome the world?

Our text gives the quick answer: *Whatsoever is born of God overcometh the world.* You cannot fail to observe that this is a universal premise. All who are born of God overcome the world – all these, and therefore it is obviously implied that it does not include any others. You may know who are born of God by this characteristic – they overcome the world. Of course, that answers the second question.

## III. Why do believers overcome the world?

On what principle is this result achieved? This victory over the world results as naturally from the spiritual or heavenly birth as coming into bondage to the world results from the natural birth.

It might be good to go back for a moment to the law of connection in the latter case, that between coming into the world by natural birth and bondage to the world. This law obviously allows for a rational explanation that is at once simple and apparent to everyone's observation. Natural birth reveals to the mind objects of sense, and these only. It brings the mind into contact with worldly things. Of course, it is natural for the mind to become deeply interested in these objects presented to it through its external senses, especially since most of them sustain such an intimate relation to our conscious nature and become the first and primary sources of our happiness. Therefore, our affections are gradually entwined around these objects, and we become complete lovers of this world before our eyes have been opened upon it many months.

Alongside this universal fact, let another be placed of equal importance and not less universal – namely, that those inherent powers of the mind that were created to become aware of our moral dealings, and therefore to counteract the too great influence of worldly objects, come into action very slowly, and are not developed so as to act vigorously until years are numbered as months are in the case of the external means of sense. The very early and vigorous development of the latter brings the soul so entirely under the control of worldly objects that when the reason and conscience begin to speak, their voice is little heeded. As a matter of fact, we find it universally true that unless divine power intervenes, the bondage to the world brought upon the soul in this way is never broken.

The point that I specifically wanted to explain was simply that natural birth, along with its accompanying laws of physical and mental development, becomes the occasion of bondage to this world.

Right next to this lies the birth into the kingdom of God by the Spirit. By this, the soul is brought into a new relationship, or we might rather say that the soul is brought into intimate contact with spiritual things. The Spirit of God seems to guide the soul into the spiritual world in a manner strictly similar to the result of the natural birth upon our physical being. The great truths of the spiritual world are opened to our view through the illumination of the Spirit of God. We seem to see with new eyes and to have a new world of spiritual objects around us.

As in regard to natural objects, which people not only speculate about, but realize them, so it is in the case of spiritual children, in which spiritual things become not merely matters of speculation, but also of full and practical realization. When God reveals Himself to the mind, spiritual things are seen in their real light and are viewed as realities.

Consequently, when spiritual objects are thus revealed to the mind and believed, they will especially interest that mind. Our mental makeup is such that when the truth of God is completely understood, it cannot fail to interest us. If these truths were clearly revealed to the wickedest man on earth so that he would understand them as realities, it could not fail to stir up his soul to most intense action. He might hate the light, and he might stubbornly resist the claims of God upon his heart, but he could not fail to feel a thrilling interest in truths that so firmly take hold of the great and fundamental things of human well-being.

Let me ask if there is a sinner reading this, or if there can be a sinner on this whole earth, who does not see that if God's presence were made as obvious and as real to his mind as the presence of his fellow humans is to him, it would seriously consume his soul, even though it might not subdue his heart. This revelation of God's presence and character might not convert him, but it would, at least for the time being, deaden his attention to the world.

You often see this in the case of people deeply convicted of sin. You have undoubtedly seen people so fearfully convicted of sin that they cared nothing at all for their food or clothing. They cried out in the agony of their souls, "What do all these things matter to us if, even if we get them all, we must end up in hell?" But these stirring and all-absorbing convictions do not necessarily convert the soul, and I have alluded to them here only to show the controlling power of realizing views of divine truth.

When real conversion has taken place, and the soul is born of God, then realizing views of truth not only awaken interest, as they might do in an unrenewed mind, but they also tend to excite a deep and fervent love for these truths. They draw out the heart. Spiritual truth now takes possession of the person's mind and draws him into its warm and life-giving embrace. Previously, error, falsehood, and death had drawn him under their power, but now the Spirit of God draws him into the very embrace of God. Now he is begotten of God and breathes the spirit of sonship. Now, according to the Bible, the seed of God remains in him (1 John 3:9), and that very truth and that moving of the Spirit, which gave him birth into the kingdom of God, continue still in power upon his mind. Therefore, he continues a Christian, and as the Bible states, *he cannot sin, because he is born of God* (1 John 3:9). The seed of God is in him, and the fruit of it brings his soul deeply into harmony with his own Father in heaven.

Again, the first birth makes us acquainted with earthly things, and the second birth makes us acquainted with God; the first with the finite, the second with the infinite; the first with things correlated with our carnal nature, the second with those great things that stand connected with our spiritual nature – things so lovely and so glorious as to overcome all the entrapments of the world.

The first birth brings about a worldly nature, and the second a heavenly. Under the first, the mind is brought into a snare, while under the second, it is delivered from that snare. Under the first, the conversation is earthly; under the second, *our conversation is in heaven* (Philippians 3:20).

## IV. How is this victory over the world achieved?

The great power is the Holy Spirit. Without Him, no good result is ever achieved in the Christian's heart or life. The text, you notice, says, *This is the victory that overcometh the world, even our faith.* The question might be raised, Does this mean that faith of itself overcomes the world, or is the meaning that we overcome by or through our faith? Without a doubt, the latter is the precise meaning. Believing in God, and having impressions of His truth and character made upon our mind by the Holy Spirit given to those who truly believe, we gain the victory over the world.

> The mind must completely surrender itself up to God.

Faith implies three things: (1) perception of truth, (2) an interest in it, and (3) the committing or giving up of the mind to be immersed in and controlled by these objects of faith.

Perception of the truth must come first in order, for there can be no belief of unknown and unperceived truth. Next, there must be an interest in the truth, which will wake up the mind to fixed and active attention. Third, there must be a voluntary committing of the mind to the control of truth. The mind must completely surrender itself up to God to be governed entirely by His will and to trust Him and Him alone as its own present and eternal portion.

Faith receives Christ. The mind first perceives Christ's character and His relationship to us. It sees what He does for us, and then, deeply feeling its own need of such a Savior and of such a work wrought in and for us as Jesus alone can do, it goes forth to receive and embrace Jesus as its own Savior. This action of the soul in receiving and embracing

Christ is not sluggish. It is not a state of lethargic spirituality. No, for it involves the soul's most strenuous activity. This committing of the soul must become a glorious, living, energizing principle, with the mind not only perceiving, but yielding itself up with the most fervent intensity to be Christ's and to receive all the benefits of His salvation into our own souls.

Faith also receives Christ into the soul as King, in all His dealings, to rule over the whole being, to have our heart's supreme confidence and affection, to receive the entire devotion of our obedience and adoration, and to rule over us and fulfil all the functions of supreme King over our whole moral being. Within our very souls, we receive Christ to live and empower there, to reign forever there as on His own rightful throne.

Many people seem to stop short of this entire and complete commitment of their whole soul to Christ. They might stop short with merely perceiving the truth, satisfied and pleased that they have learned the doctrine of the gospel. Some might go one step further and stop with being interested, with having their feelings stirred up by the things of the gospel, thus going only to the second stage. Maybe they seem to take faith, but not Christ. They resolve to believe, but after that do not warmly and with all the heart welcome Christ Himself into the soul. All these different steps stop short of really taking hold of Christ. None of them result in gaining the victory over the world.

The true Bible doctrine of faith represents Christ as coming into the very soul: *Behold, I stand at the door and knock; if any man hear my voice and open the door, I will come in to him and will sup with him, and he with me* (Revelation 3:20). What could more forcibly and beautifully teach the doctrine that Christ is introduced by faith into the very soul of the believer to dwell there by His gracious presence?

Since my mind was first drawn to the subject, I have been amazed to see how long I have been in a blind state of understanding in respect to this particular view of faith. For a long time, I had scarcely seen it, but now I see it beaming forth in lines of glory on almost every page of the Bible. The Bible seems to blaze with the glorious truth – Christ in the soul, *the hope of glory* (Colossians 1:27) – God, Christ, dwelling in our bodies as in a temple (1 Corinthians 6:19).

I am amazed that a truth so rich and so blessed would have been seen so dimly when the Bible reveals it so clearly: Christ received into the very soul by faith, and thus brought into the nearest possible relationship to our heart and life; Christ Himself becoming the all-sustaining Power within us, and thus securing the victory over the world; Christ, living and empowering in our hearts. This is the great central truth in the plan of sanctification, and no Christian should fail to understand this as he values the victory over the world and the living communion of the soul with its Maker.

## Remarks

1. It is in the very nature of the case impossible that if faith receives Christ into the soul, it would not overcome the world. If the new birth actually brings the mind into this new state and brings Christ into the soul, then of course Christ will reign in that soul. The greatest affections will be surrendered most delightfully to Him, and the power of the world over that mind will be broken. Christ cannot dwell in any soul without absorbing the supreme interest of that soul. Of course, this is equivalent to giving the victory over the world.

2. He who does not regularly overcome the world is not born of God. In saying this, I do not intend to claim that a true Christian may not sometimes be overcome by sin, but I do say that overcoming the world is the general rule, and falling into sin is just the exception. This is the least that can be meant by the language of our text, as well as by similar declarations that often occur in the Bible. Just as in the passage, *Whosoever is born of God doth not commit sin, . . . and he cannot sin, because he is born of God* (1 John 3:9), nothing less can be meant than that he cannot sin regularly – he cannot make sinning his business, and if he can sin at all, it is only occasionally and aside from the general course of his life. In the same manner, we should say of someone who is in general truthful that he is not a liar.

I will not push for more than this respecting either of these passages, but for this much I must contend – that the newborn souls here spoken of do in general overcome the world. The general fact regarding them is that they do not sin and are not in bondage to Satan. The affirmations of Scripture respecting them must at least embrace their general character.

3. What is a religion good for that does not overcome the world? What is the benefit of being born into such a religion if it leaves the world still exercising its dominion over our hearts? What good is a new birth that fails to bring us into a likeness to God, into the affection of His family and of His kingdom, and that still leaves us in bondage to the world and to Satan? What can there be of such a religion more than the name? With what reason can anyone suppose that such a religion trains his heart for heaven if it leaves him earthly minded, carnal, and selfish.

> What is the benefit of being born into such a religion if it leaves the world still exercising its dominion over our hearts?

4. We see why unbelievers have proclaimed the gospel of Christ to be a failure. You may not be aware that lately unbelievers have taken the ground that the gospel of Christ is a failure. They maintain that it professes to bring people out from the world, but fails to do so, and therefore is clearly a failure. You must observe that the Bible does indeed claim, as unbelievers say, that those who are truly born of God do overcome the world. We cannot deny this, and we do not want to deny it. If the unbeliever can show that the new birth fails to produce this result, he has carried his point, and we must yield ours. This is perfectly plain, and there can be no escape for us.

However, the unbeliever is in fault in his premises. He assumes that the current Christianity of the age is an example of real religion, and he builds his estimate upon this. He proves, as he thinks, and possibly truly proves, that the current Christianity does not overcome the world.

We must object to his assuming that this current Christianity is real religion, for this religion of nominal professors of Christianity does not answer the descriptions given of true piety in the Word of God. Moreover, if this current type of religion were all that the gospel and the divine Spirit can do for lost man, then we might as well give up the point in controversy with the unbeliever, for such a religion could not give us much evidence of coming from God, and would be of very little value to man – so little as hardly to be worth contending for.

Certainly if we must accept the professedly Christian world as Bible Christians, who would not be ashamed and perplexed in attempting to confront the unbeliever? We know only too well that the great multitude of professed Christians do not overcome the world, and we would be quickly disconcerted if we were to maintain that they do. Those professed Christians themselves know that they do not overcome the world. Of course, they could not testify concerning themselves that in their own case the power of the gospel is demonstrated.

In view of facts like these, I have often been astonished to see ministers trying to persuade their people that they are really converted, trying to calm their fears and support their uncertain hopes. What a vain effort! It would seem that those same ministers must know that they themselves do not overcome the world, and they must equally well know that their people do not. How fatal, then, to the soul must be such efforts to heal the hurt of God's professed *people slightly, saying, Peace, peace, when there is no peace* (Jeremiah 6:14; 8:11).

Let us get to the bottom of this matter, asking, Do the great majority of professed Christians really overcome the world? It is a fact beyond question that with them the things of this world are the realities, and the things of God are mere theories. Who does not know that this is the real state of large multitudes in the nominal church?

Let the searching inquiry run through you now. What are those things that set your soul on fire, that stir up your warmest emotions and deeply stir your heart? Are these the things of earth or the things of heaven? Are they the things of time or the things of eternity? Are they the things of self or the things of God?

How is it when you enter your private place to pray? Do you go there to seek and find God? Do you in fact find there a present God, and do you hold communion there as a friend with a friend? How is this?

You should certainly know that if your condition is such that spiritual things are mere theories and opinions, then you are entirely worldly and nothing more. It would be blatant absurdity and falsehood to call you spiritually minded, and for you to consider yourself spiritual would be the most fatal and foolish self-deception. You give none of the appropriate proofs of being born of God. Your condition is not that of one who is personally acquainted with God and who loves Him personally with supreme affection.

5. Until we can put away from the minds of people the common error that the current Christianity of the church is true Christianity, we can make only little progress in converting the world. In the first place, we cannot save the church itself from bondage to the world in this life, nor from the dreadful doom of the hypocrite in the next. We cannot unite and arm the church in vigorous assault upon Satan's kingdom so that the world may be converted to God. We cannot even convince intelligent people of the world that our religion is from God and that it brings to fallen people a remedy for their depravity. If the common Christianity of the age is the best that can be, and this does not give people victory over the world, what is it good for? And if it really is of little worth or of no value at all, how can we hope to make thinking people esteem it as of great value?

6. There are only a very few unbelievers who are as much in the dark as they claim to be on these points. There are very few of that class of people who are not acquainted with some humble Christians whose lives commend Christianity and condemn their own ungodliness. Of course, they know the truth – that there is a reality in the religion of the Bible, and they blind their own eyes selfishly and most foolishly when they try to believe that the religion of the Bible is a failure and that the Bible is therefore not true.

Deep in their hearts lies the conviction that here and there are people who are real Christians, who overcome the world and live by a faith unknown to themselves. In how many cases does God set some burning examples of Christian life before those wicked, skeptical people to rebuke them for their sin and their skepticism? This might even be their own wife or their children, their neighbors or their employees. By such means, the truth is lodged in their minds, and God has a witness for Himself in their consciences.

I might have mentioned before a fact that occurred in the South, and was told to me by a minister of the gospel who was acquainted with the circumstances of the case. There resided in that region a very worldly and a most ungodly man who held a large slave property and was also much inclined to horse racing. Unmindful of all religion and admittedly an unbeliever, he fully embraced every evil inclination. But wicked people must one day see trouble, and this man was taken sick and brought to the very gates of the grave. His weeping wife and friends gathered around his bed and began to think of having some Christian called in to pray for the dying man's soul.

"Husband," said the anxious wife, "should I not send for our minister to pray with you before you die?"

"No," he said, "I have known him for a long time, and I have no faith in him. I have seen him too many times at horse races. He was my friend there, and I was his, but I don't want to see him now."

"Then who can we get?" continued the wife.

"Send for my slave Tom," he replied. "He takes care of my horses. I have often overheard him praying, and I know he can pray. Besides, I have watched his life and his character, and I never saw anything in him inconsistent with Christian character. Call him in. I would be glad to hear him pray."

Tom entered slowly and modestly, dropped his hat at the door, and looked at his sick and dying master. "Tom," said the dying skeptic, "do you ever pray? Do you know how to pray? Can you pray for your dying master and forgive him?"

"Oh, yes, with all my heart," Tom said, and he dropped to his knees and poured out a prayer for his soul.

The moral of this story is obvious. Place the skeptic on his dying bed, let that solemn hour arrive and the inner convictions of his heart be revealed, and he knows of at least one person who is a real Christian. He knows one person whose prayers he values more than all the friendship of all his former associates. He knows now that there is such a thing as Christianity, and yet you cannot think that he has never known this before. No, he knew just as much before, but an honest hour has brought the inner convictions of his soul to light. Unbelievers generally know more than they have honesty enough to admit.

7. The great error of those who profess Christianity but are not born

of God is that they are trying to be Christians without being born of God. They need to have that done to them what is said of Adam, that God breathed into him the breath of life, and he *became a living soul* (Genesis 2:7). Their religion has in it none of the breath of God. It is a cold, lifeless doctrine. There is none of the living vitality of God in it. It might be a heartless doctrine, and they might be convinced in their hearts that their creed is sound, but do they love that truth that they profess to believe?

They think that they might possibly have zeal, and they think that their zeal is right and their hearts are right, but are their souls on fire for God and His cause? Where are they, and what are they doing? Are they discussing some sentimental theory, or are they defending it at the point of the sword? Do they care for souls? Do their hearts tremble for the interests of Zion? Do their very nerves quiver under the mighty power of God's truth? Does their love for God and for souls set their doctrine and their creeds on fire so that every truth burns in their souls and glows forth from their very faces?

> Brethren, it cannot be too strongly impressed on every mind that the definitive characteristic of true Christianity is power, not apathy.

If so, then you will not see them absent from the prayer meetings and neglecting to speak to others about Christ, but you will see that divine things take hold of their souls with overwhelming interest and power. You will see them as living Christians – burning and shining lights in the world. Brethren, it cannot be too strongly impressed on every mind that the definitive characteristic of true Christianity is power, not apathy, and its indispensable element is life, not death.

# Chapter 23

# Death to Sin through Christ

Likewise reckon ye also yourselves to be dead indeed unto
sin, but alive unto God through Jesus Christ our Lord.
—Romans 6:11

The connection of this passage will help us to understand its meaning. Near the end of the previous chapter, Paul had said, *The law
entered that the offence might abound; but where sin abounded, grace
did much more abound, that as sin hath reigned unto death, even so
might grace reign through righteousness unto eternal life by Jesus Christ
our Lord* (Romans 5:20-21). He speaks here of sin as being a reigning
principle or monarch, and of grace also as reigning. Then in chapter 6,
he says, *What shall we say then? Shall we continue in sin that grace may
abound? . . . Likewise reckon ye also yourselves to be dead indeed unto
sin, but alive unto God through Jesus Christ our Lord* (Romans 6:1, 11).

You observe here that Paul speaks of the man, the old sinner, as
being crucified with Christ – so destroyed by the moral power of the
cross that he who was once a sinner shall no longer serve sin. When he
speaks of our being planted or buried with Christ, we must, of course,
understand him as using figures of speech to teach the great truth that
the gospel redeems the soul from sin. Just as Christ died for sin, so by
a general analogy we die to sin. On the other hand, just as He rose to a

new and infinitely glorious life, so the convert rises to a new and blessed life of purity and holiness.

But referring specifically to our text, let me say that the language used in our translation would seem to mean that our death to sin is precisely analogous to Christ's death for sin, but this is not the case. We are dead to sin in the sense that it is no longer to be our master, implying that it has been in power over us. But sin was never in power over Jesus Christ. It was never His master. Christ died to abolish its power over us, not to abolish any power of sin over Himself, for it had no power over Him.

The analogy between Christ's death in relation to sin and our dying to sin goes to this extent and no farther: He died for the sake of making an atonement for sin and of creating a moral power that should be effective to kill the love of sin in all hearts. However, the Christian dies unto sin in the sense of being divorced from all sympathy with sin and set free from its control.

I will now proceed to comment upon the text itself, and will consider the following questions:

I.   What does it mean to be dead unto sin in the sense of the text?

II.  What does it mean to be alive unto God?

III. What does it mean to consider ourselves to be dead unto sin, but alive unto God through Jesus Christ our Lord?

IV.  What does it mean to be alive unto God through Jesus Christ?

V.   What is implied in the exhortation of our text?

## I. What does it mean to be dead unto sin in the sense of the text?

Being dead to sin must obviously be the opposite of being dead in sin. Being dead in sin must undeniably be a state of entire sinfulness – a state in which the soul is dead to all good through the power of sin over it. However, being dead to sin means to be indifferent to its attractions, beyond the reach of its influence, as fully removed from its influences as the dead are from the objects of the senses in this world. Just as he who is dead in the natural sense has nothing more to do with earthly things, so he who is dead to sin has nothing to do any more with sin's attractions or with sinning itself.

## II. What does it mean to be alive unto God?

To be alive unto God means to be full of life for Him. It means to be entirely active and on the alert to do His will. It means to make our whole lives a ceaseless offering to Him, constantly delivering up ourselves to Him and His service so that we may glorify His name and serve His interests.

## III. What does it mean to consider ourselves dead indeed unto sin?

The word translated as "reckon" is sometimes translated as "count" or "consider." Abraham's faith was *counted unto him for righteousness* (Romans 4:3). In this passage, then, "reckon" must mean to believe, or consider yourselves dead indeed unto sin. Count this to be the case. Regard this as truly your relation to sin. You are completely dead to it. It will have no more dominion over you.

A careful examination of the passages where this original word is used will show that this is its usual and natural sense. This also gives us the true idea of gospel faith – embracing personally the salvation that is by faith in Jesus Christ. But more about this later.

## IV. What does it mean to be alive unto God through Jesus Christ?

To be alive unto God through Jesus Christ simply means that you are to expect to be saved by Jesus Christ and to depend on this salvation as your own. You are to consider yourself as completely dead to sin and as a result, brought into life and peace in Christ Jesus.

## V. What is implied in the exhortation of our text?

It is implied that there is an adequate provision for this expectation and for realizing these blessings in fact. If there were no basis for realizing this, the command would be most absurd. A command requiring us to consider ourselves dead indeed unto sin and alive unto God would be completely illogical if there were no probability of the thing – if no provision were made for our coming into such a relationship to sin on the one hand, and to God through Christ on the other. If these blessings could not be reasonably expected, there could be no rational basis for the expectation. If it were not reasonable to expect it, then to command us to expect it would be plainly unreasonable. Who does not see that the very command implies that there is a foundation laid and adequate provision made for the condition required?

What is implied in complying with this command?

1. We must believe such a thing to be possible. We must believe that it is possible that through Christ we can live in the required manner, that we can avoid sin, that we can desist from sinning – give it up and abandon it altogether, and put it away from us forever. There can be no such thing as an intelligent compliance with this command except as it is supported by this belief that it is possible.

2. It implies that the mind regards the state required as a possible one – not merely as true in theory, and not just as good philosophy – but as actually made possible by adequate grace that is adapted to the laws of mind and to the actual moral condition of lost men.

3. It implies that we cease from all expectation of attaining this state of ourselves and by our own independent, unaided efforts. We do not begin to receive by grace until we renounce all expectation of attaining by natural works. It is only when empty of self that we begin to be filled with Christ.

4. It implies that there is a present willingness to be saved from sin. We must actually renounce all sin as such; that is, we must renounce sin because it is sin and for what it is. The mind must take this position:

I can have nothing more to do with sinning, for God hates sin, and I am to live from this moment on and forever to please and glorify Him. My soul is committed with its strength of purpose to please God and do His will.

5. It implies also an entire commitment of your whole situation to Jesus Christ, not only for present salvation, but for all future salvation from sin. This is absolutely essential. It must always be the vital step – the central act in this great work of salvation from sin.

6. It also implies the closing of the mind against temptation in such a sense that the mind truly expects to live a life purely devoted to God. This is the same sort of closing of the mind that takes place under a faithful marriage contract. The Bible everywhere keeps this representation prominent. Christians are represented as the bride of Christ. They stand in a relationship to Him that is closely similar to that of a bride to her husband. Therefore, when they commit their whole hearts to Him, placing their affections in Him and trusting Him for all good, their hearts are strongly closed against temptation.

We see this principle illustrated in the merely human relationship. When a man and a woman are solemnly betrothed in mutual honest devotion, there is no longer any thought of letting the eye wander or the heart go abroad for a fresh object of interest and love. The heart is settled – willingly and by pledged faith determined, and this fact shuts out the power of temptation almost entirely. It makes it comparatively an easy matter to keep the heart safely above the influence of temptation to unfaithfulness.

Before the sacred vows are taken, individuals may be excused for looking around and making any observations or enquiries, but never after the solemn vow is made. After the parties have become one by vow of marriage, never to be broken, there is to be no more question as to a better choice – no further thought about changing the relationship or withdrawing the heart's affections. No wavering is acceptable now. The pledge is made for everlasting faithfulness, settled once and forever!

This is God's own illustration, and certainly none can be more appropriate or more powerful. It shows how the Christian should look upon sin and upon all temptation to sin. He must say, "Get away from my heart forever! I am married to Jesus Christ. How, then, can I pursue other lovers? My mind is forever settled. It rests in the deep peace of one whose affections are promised and settled – to wander no more! Sin? I cannot think of yielding to its temptations any longer. I cannot consider the question for a moment. I can have nothing to do with sinning. My mind is settled. The question is forever closed, and I can no more allow the temptation to small sins than to great sins. I can no longer consent to give my heart to worldly idols than to commit murder! I did not enter upon Christianity as upon an experiment to see how I might like it – no more than a wife or husband take on themselves the marriage vow as an experiment. No; my whole soul has committed itself to Jesus Christ with as much expectation of being faithful forever as the most faithful husband and wife have of fulfilling their vows in all faithfulness until death will part them."

Christians in this state of mind no more expect to commit small sins than great sins. Hating all sin for its own sake and for its hatefulness to Christ – any sin, no matter how small – is to them as murder. Therefore, if the heart is ever afterward seduced and overcome by temptation, it is entirely contrary to their expectation and purpose. It was not embraced in their plan by any means, but was distinctly excluded. It was not deliberately indulged in, but broke in on them unexpectedly through the perspective of old habits or associations.

Again, the state of mind in question implies that the Christian knows where his great strength lies. He knows it does not lie in works of fasting, giving alms, making prayers, or doing public or private duties – nothing of this sort, not even in resolutions or any self-originated efforts – but only in Christ received by faith. He no more expects spiritual life of himself apart from Christ than a man in his senses would expect to fly by swinging his arms in the air. Deep in his soul lies the conviction that his whole strength lies in Christ alone.

When people are so enlightened as truly to understand this subject, then to expect less than this from Jesus Christ as the result of committing the whole soul to Him for full salvation is practically to reject Him as a revealed Savior. It does not honor Him for what He is. It does not honor the revelations He has made of Himself in His Word by accepting Him as He is presented there.

Consider what the first element of this salvation is. It is not being saved from hell, but being saved from sin. Salvation from punishment is quite a secondary thing in every sense. It is only a result of being saved from sin, and is not the main element in the gospel salvation. Why was the infant Messiah to be called Jesus? Because He would save His people from their sins (Matthew 1:21). The Bible does not anywhere teach any other or any different view than this.

## Remarks

1. This text alone, *Reckon ye also yourselves to be dead indeed unto sin, but alive unto God through Jesus Christ*, most fully justifies the expectation of living without sin through all-abounding grace. If there were no other passage pertaining to this point, this alone is enough, and for a Christian to offer only this as a reason for such a hope in Him is to offer as good a reason as needs to be given. There are indeed many other passages that fully justify this belief.

> Salvation from punishment is only a result of being saved from sin, and is not the main element in the gospel salvation.

2. To teach that such a belief is a dangerous error is to teach unbelief. Imagine if the apostle Paul had added to this command that requires us to consider ourselves dead indeed unto sin but alive unto God, this one statement: "Yet let me warn you that nobody can rationally hope to be free from sin in this world. You must remember that to entertain

such an expectation as God commands in this language is a dangerous error." What would be thought of this if it were attached to Romans 6:11?

No one can deny that the passage deals with sanctification. The whole question is whether Christians will *continue in sin* (Romans 6:1) after having been forgiven and accepted in their Redeemer. Paul labors to show that they should, and of course that they may die to sin – even as Christ died for sin, and they may also live a new life, a spiritual life (through faith in His grace), even as Christ lives a higher and more glorious life.

Let me refer here to another passage in which it is said, *Be ye not unequally yoked with unbelievers. . . . What agreement hath the temple of God with idols? For ye are the temple of the living God. . . . Wherefore come out from among them, and be ye separate, saith the Lord, and touch not the unclean thing, and I will receive you, and will be a Father unto you, and ye shall be my sons and daughters, saith the Lord Almighty. Having therefore these promises, dearly beloved, let us cleanse ourselves from all filthiness of the flesh and spirit, perfecting holiness in the fear of God* (2 Corinthians 6:14, 16-18; 7:1). This is a very remarkable passage. Notice how the command and promise are intermingled, and how finally, upon the basis of a most glorious promise, the precept calling us to perfect holiness is established.

Now what would we think of Paul and of the divine Spirit who spoke through Paul, if he had immediately added, "Be careful that none of you will be led by these remarks to indulge the very dangerous and erroneous expectation that you can 'perfect holiness' or cleanse yourselves from any sin, either of flesh or spirit, in this world." Would not this have been fooling with the intelligence and Christian sense of every reader of his words through all time? Should we not account it as considerably blasphemous?

It so happens that the Bible never contradicts its own teachings, but I ask, What if it had? What if the Bible had solemnly asserted, "No mere human, either of himself or by any grace received in this life, has ever kept or will ever keep the commandments of God fully, but daily breaks them in thought, word, and deed"?

To teach that such an expectation is dangerous is a great deal worse than no teaching at all. It is much better to leave people to their own unaided reading of God's Word, for this could hardly in any case so sadly mislead them, no matter how inclined they might be to the misconception. Is it dangerous to expect salvation from sin? Dangerous? What does this mean? Is it dangerous to expect victory over any sin? If so, what is the gospel worth? What gospel do we have that can be considered good news at all?

Many people have the very opposite expectation. Far from expecting any such thing as the apostle Paul authorizes them to expect, they know they have no such expectation. Other people even believe it is true to expect themselves to always be in sin. They depend on considering themselves not to be dead indeed unto sin, but to be somewhat alive to it through all their earthly life, and somewhat alive to God through Jesus Christ. The result is that since they do not expect any such thing as complete victory over sin, they will not use any appropriate means since faith stands foremost among those means, and faith must include at least a belief that it is possible to attain that which is sought.

> Is it dangerous to expect victory over any sin? If so, what is the gospel worth?

In this and the following chapters of Romans, we have the essence of the good news of the gospel. Anyone who has been wounded and hurt by sin, with its bitter shafts sinking deep into his moral being – one who has known its bitterness and felt its poison drink up his spirit – such a person will see that there is glory in the idea of being delivered from sin. He will surely see that this deliverance is by far the greatest need of his soul and that nothing can be compared with escaping from this body of sin and death.

Look at Romans chapter 7. There you have the state of a man who is more than convinced, but is really convicted. It is one thing to be convinced, and it is an even further stage of progress in the right direction to be convicted. This term implies the instrumentality of another party. The criminal on trial may be quite convinced of his guilt by the view he was compelled to take of his own case, but his being convicted is a still further step. The testimony and the jury convict him.

Some of you know what it is to see yourself a sinner, and yet the sight of the fact brings with it no pain – no sting. It does not cut deep into your very soul. On the other hand, some of you may know what it is to see your sins all armed like an armed man ready to pierce you through with daggers. Then you cry out as here, *O wretched man that I am! Who shall deliver me from the body of this death?* (Romans 7:24). You feel a piercing sting as if your soul were filled with poison – with horrible, painful venom diffusing the very agonies of hell through the depths of your soul! This is what I mean by being convicted as being a state of mind beyond being merely convinced. The darts and the strikes of sin seem really like the piercings of an arrow, as if arrows from the Almighty really did empty your spirit. When you experience this, then you can understand what the good news of the gospel is. A remedy for such anguish must be good news beyond all dispute. To know that the blood of Christ can save is indeed a salve of life to the weary soul.

Place someone in this state of sharp, piercing conviction, and then let him feel that there is actually no remedy, and he sinks under the iron shafts of despair. See his agony! Tell him there can never be any remedy for his guilty soul, that he must lie there in his misery and despair forever! Can any state of mind be more awful?

> To know that the blood of Christ can save is indeed a salve of life to the weary soul.

I remember a case that occurred in Reading, Pennsylvania, many years ago. There was a man of hard heart and iron frame – a strong, burly man who had stood up against the revival as if he could shake off all the arrows of the Almighty, even as the mastodon of which the tradition of the Native American says shook off all the arrows of the warriors from his brow and felt no harm. So he stood. But he had a praying wife and a praying sister, and they gathered their souls in the might of prayer close about him as a party of men would close in a wild bull in a net. Soon it was apparent that an arrow from the quiver of the Almighty had pierced between the joints of his harness and had taken hold of his innermost heart. He was in agony then! It was night – dark and intensely cold. It seemed that he absolutely could not live.

They sent for me to come and see him. I went. While yet a few hundred yards from his house, I heard his screams and wailings of woe. It made me feel dreadfully solemn. It seemed so much like the echoes of the pit of hell! I reached the house and saw him there on the floor rolling in his agony and wailing as is rarely heard on this side of the pit of despair. As cold as the weather was, he was sweating like rain, every part of his frame being in a most intense perspiration. Oh, his groans – and to see him gnaw his tongue because of the pain! This gives us some idea of the doom of the damned. I thought that if this is only conviction of sin, what must hell be like?

But he could not bear to hear anything about sin. His conscience was already full of it and had brought out the dreadful things of God's law so as to leave nothing more to be done in that direction. I could only put Christ before him and simply hold his mind to the view of Christ alone. This soon brought relief. Suppose, though, that I had nothing else to say except, "Mr. B., there is no help possible for your case! You can wail on and on, but no being in the universe can help you." He has fire enough in his burning soul already. It seems to him that no hell of fire can possibly be worse than this.

How perfectly chilling and horrible for people to oppose the idea of expecting deliverance from sin, and yet talk calmly of continuing in sin all the rest of their earthly days! An elder I knew once rose in a meeting and told the Lord he had been living in sin so far and expected to continue in sin as long as he lived. He said that he had sinned today and would undoubtedly sin tomorrow and so on, yet he talked as calmly about it all as if it were foolish to make any fuss, as well as impossible to attempt any change for the better. Think of that – to talk of all this calmly! How horrible to talk quite calmly of living alone in sin all the rest of his days!

Suppose a wife would say to her husband, "I love you some, but you know that I love many other men, too, and that I find it pleasant to indulge myself with them. You certainly must be aware that all women are frail creatures and are likely to fall continually, and indeed you know that I expect to fall more or less as it may happen every day that I live. Certainly you will not expect from me anything as unrealistic and extreme as flawless virtue! You know that none of us have any idea of being perfect in this life. We don't believe in any such thing!"

Let me ask you to look at this woman and hear what she has to say. Can you hear her talk this way without having your soul filled with horror? What! Is this woman a wife, and does she think and talk this way about marital fidelity?

Yet this is not to be compared in shocking sin and treason with the case of the Christian who says, "I expect to sin every day I live," and who says this with indifferent unconcern. You expect to be a traitor to Jesus each day of your life, to crucify Him again each day, to put Him each day to an open shame, to every day dishonor His name, grieve His heart, and bring sorrow and shame upon all who love Christ's cause – yet you talk about having a good hope through grace! Every true Christian should say, "Do not let me live at all if I cannot live without habitual sin, for how can I bear to go on day after day sinning against Him whom I so much love!"

Those who are really opposed to this idea are either very ignorant of what the gospel is, or they are unrepentant and do not care to be delivered from their sins. At best, they are guilty of great unbelief. Into which of these classes those who oppose this doctrine may fall is a question for themselves to settle between their own consciences and God.

There are two distinct views of salvation held among professed Christians, and correspondingly there are two distinct classes of professing Christians – often embraced within the same church. The one class of people regard the gospel as salvation from sin. They think more of this and value it more than the hope of heaven, or of earth either. The most important thing with them is to realize the idea of deliverance from sin. This constitutes the charm and glory of the gospel. They seek this more than to be saved from hell. They care more by far to be saved from sin itself than from its punitive consequences. Of the latter they think and pray only a little. It is their glory and joy that Christ is sent to deliver them from their bondage in iniquity – to lift them up from their miserable condition and give them the liberty of love. They labor to realize this. To them, this is the good news of gospel salvation.

The other class of people are mostly anxious to be saved from hell. The punishment due for sin is the thing they mainly fear. In fact, fear has been mainly the spring of their religious efforts. The gospel is not thought of as a means of deliverance from sin, but as a great system of indulgences – a great comfort to remove the fear and danger of damnation while still leaving them in their sin. I do not by any means imply that they will call their system of gospel faith a system of indulgences; the name will undoubtedly be an offense to them. They may not have distinctly considered this point, and they may have failed to notice that in fact it is such and nothing better.

They do not seem to notice that a system of salvation that removes the fear of damnation for sin, yet leaves them in their sins to live for themselves to please themselves, and that concludes that Christ will at last bring them to heaven despite their having lived in sin all their days, must be a vast system of indulgences. Indeed, it is a compromise on a most magnificent scale. By virtue of it, the whole church is expected to trudge on in sin through life, and be no less sure of heaven at last.

These opposite views are so prevalent and so apparent that you will see them everywhere as you go around among the churches. You will find many in the church who are completely worldly and selfish. They live conformed to the world in various neglects of duty, and they expect to indulge themselves in sin more or less all the way through life. You may ask them if they think that is right, and they answer, "No." If you ask them why they do it, then, they answer, "Oh, we are all imperfect, and we can't expect to be any better than imperfect while here in the flesh."

Yet they expect to be saved from hell and to have all their sins forgiven – but how? It is not on condition of sincerely turning away from all their sins, but on the assumption that the gospel is a vast system of indulgences – far more vast than Pope Leo X ever used and worked to comfort sinning professors in his day. In the pope's system, the indulgences were merely for those who sinned occasionally, but this current system is for those who live in sin and know they do, and expect to live in sin as long as they live, yet expect to be saved without fail at the end.

The other class of professed Christians have no expectation of being saved unless they have a pure heart and live above the world. If you talk to them about living in sin, you quickly learn that they hate and dread the very thought. To them, the poison of asps is in it. Sin is bitter to their souls. They dread it as they dread death itself.

No one can go around within the church without finding these two classes as distinct in their idea of the gospel as I have described them to be. The one class of people are in agony if they find themselves even slipping, and they are especially cautious against exposing themselves to temptation. It is not so with the other class.

Two ministers of the gospel were together, and one strongly urged the other to take part in a certain activity. The other declined. "Why not?" said the first.

"Because I do not think myself justified in exposing myself to that and to so much temptation."

"But why stop for that? We expect to sin more or less always, and all we have to do is to repent of it afterward."

Horror-struck, the other could only say, "I hold to a completely different gospel from that."

Suppose a wife should say to her husband, "I am determined to go to the theater."

"But, my dear," he said, "you know bad people gather there, and you may be tempted."

She replied, "That does not matter. If I sin, I will repent of it afterward."

The real Christian may be known by this – that the very thought of being drawn into sin drives him to agony. He cannot bear the idea of living in sin, not even for one moment.

You who are truly Christians, be careful about this. Be on your guard, for you may be ensnared into sin. I do not mean that you need to fear to go where God calls you, but it is a terrible thing to be ensnared into sin, and you cannot help but to feel that this is so. If you know what it is to be wounded by the arrows of sin in your soul, you will go out into apparent danger, walking softly and with caution, and with much prayer. You will certainly be much on your guard. But if you say, "Oh, if I sin I will repent," what will I say of you? You will repent, will you? And do you think this will make everything right again so easily?

> A Christian who repents of sin, repents of it as sin. He makes no such discriminations as between a little secret sin and a big sin such as a murder.

Suppose you knew that in going away for a vacation, you would get drunk a few times, and would commit one or two murders. Would you say, "Oh, nevertheless, I may be a good Christian. I will be careful to repent of it after it is all over." That is horrible! And you think of yourself as a good Christian!

Let me tell you that a Christian who repents of sin, repents of it as sin. He makes no such discriminations as between a little secret sin and a big sin such as a murder. He knows no such distinction between sins that will allow him to commit the one kind without guilt and to shy away from the other. With him, anything that grieves God is a horrible thing. Regarding anything that displeases God, he cries out, "Ah, God will see it; it will grieve His heart!" How it will affect God – this is all that matters to him.

Someone who knows what it is to appear guilty of sin before God, and then who knows also what it is to be delivered from this condition, will understand how the Christian should feel in circumstances of temptation when he feels himself in danger of sinning. His hair all stands on end! How awful to sin against God! Therefore, anything that seems likely to bring him into danger will stir up his soul within him and put him on his guard.

The unbelief of the church as to what they may receive from Christ is the great stumbling block hindering themselves and others from experiencing deliverance from sin. Not only is this a great curse and a great hardship to professing Christians, but it is also a great heartache to Jesus Christ.

Many people seem to have hardened their hearts against all expectation of being delivered from sin. They have heard the doctrine preached. They have seen some profess to be in this state of salvation from sin, but they have also seen some of this group fall again, and now they willingly reject the entire doctrine.

But is this consistent with really embracing the gospel? What is Christ to the believer? What was His errand into the world? What is He doing, and what is He attempting to do? He has come to break the power of sin in the heart and to be the life of the believer, working in him a continual salvation from sin and wanting to bring him in this way, and only in this way, to heaven at last. What is faith except the actual giving of yourself up to Christ that He may do this work for you and in you! What are you to believe of Christ if not that He is to save His people from their sins? Can you tell of anything else? Does the Bible tell you to expect something different and less than this?

The fact is that it has been the great stumbling block to the church that this has not been well understood. The common experience of nominal Christians has misrepresented and twisted the truth. The multitudes forming their views much more from this experience than from the

Bible, or at best applying this experience to interpret the Bible, have adopted exceedingly defective, even false, opinions as to the nature and design of the gospel. They seem to completely forget that Paul writing to Christians at Rome assures them that if they are under grace, sin will not have dominion over them (Romans 6:14).

When Christians do not expect this blessing from Christ, they will not get it. While they expect as little as they usually do, it is no wonder they get so little. According to their faith, and not ever very much beyond it, do they need to expect to receive.

It is often the case that sanctification is held as a theory, while the mind does not yet by any means embrace the truth in love. The situation is similar to that of unrepentant sinners who hold in theory that they must have a new heart. They profess to believe this, but do they really understand it? No. Suppose it were revealed to their minds so that they would really see it as it is; would they not see a new thing? Would they not be startled to see how completely far they are, while unrepentant, from being acceptable to God, and how great the change they must experience before they can enter the kingdom?

It is the same regarding sanctification. Although this class of people profess to believe it in theory, yet the passages of Scripture that describe it do not enter into their experience. They do not see the whole truth. If they were to see the whole truth, and would then reject it, I believe it would be in them the unpardonable sin. When the Spirit of God discloses to them the real meaning of the gospel, and they deliberately reject it, how can the sin be less than what the Scriptures represent as the unpardonable sin? Having once been enlightened and having received the knowledge of the truth that they might be saved, but then turning back, is it not impossible from then on for them to be renewed again to repentance (Hebrews 6:4-6)?

One thing, at least, must be said. There is a danger that many professing Christians of our day do not seem to realize. Having so much light before the mind as they actually have in regard to the provisions made in the gospel for present sanctification, they then reject this light practically and live still in sin as if the gospel made no provision to save the Christian from his sins. Into this terrible danger, many people rush blindly to their own destruction!

# Chapter 24

# The Essential Elements of Christian Experience

Blessed are they who hunger and thirst after righteousness, for they shall be filled.
—Matthew 5:6

There are a great many things in the experience of Christians that are exceedingly interesting when traced out in their natural history. I have been amazed to notice how very commonly what is unique to Christian experience drops out of the mind, while that which is merely subordinate remains and constitutes the mind's entire conception of what Christianity is. Their way of talking of their experience leaves you very much in the dark as to its genuineness, even when they intend to specifically give you the reasons of their hope.

I want to first state some of the facts that belong to the life of God in the soul.

1. Hunger and thirst are states of mind and do not belong to the body. They are of two kinds: natural and spiritual. The objects on which the natural state of mind depends are food and drink. By our very constitution, these are necessary to our well-being in the present world. These appetites are natural and depend on their appropriate objects.

There are also spiritual hunger and spiritual thirst, which are as truly natural as physical hunger and thirst. It is no more a figure of speech to use these terms in this case than in the other.

The appetites that demand physical food and drink are facts and experiences. Everybody knows what it is to have them, and everybody knows in general what those things are that are so related to the human constitution as to meet those demands. So also the spiritual appetites are not less matters of fact and experience, and they stand in a similar manner related to the objects that are adapted to the demand.

2. Sin is a fact in the natural history of the human race. That it is so must be attributed to the fall of our first parents. Yet whatever explanation is given of the introduction of sin into the human family, it now exists as an undeniable fact. Some attention to the manner in which sin is first developed may serve to show its relationship to what I have called the natural history of the human race.

We all know it to be a fact that the natural appetites begin their development immediately after the natural birth. The first awakening to a conscious existence in this world seems to be, if not occasioned by, yet closely connected with, a physical demand for food. The repeated changes of demand and supply begin and continue while health continues, developing the strength of this class of appetites the entire time. The natural commonly make their development far in advance of the spiritual.

> Sin is a fact in the natural history of the human race.

Not much is said in the Bible as to the method in which sin entered our world and acquired such a relationship to the human soul, but it distinctly refers to Adam's first sin, and it is asserted to be in some way connected with that event. Facts show that sin has become in a most significant sense natural to the human race, so that they all instinctively, not of necessity, but instinctively, if no special grace intervenes, begin to sin as soon as they begin to act morally – or in other words, as soon as they become capable of moral action.

It is not that people are born sinners, nor that they sin before they are born, nor that sin is born in them, nor even that they are born into sin beyond their control, but still the nature of the man – body and mind – is such, and the law of development is such, that people sin naturally (although voluntarily, consistently, and shamefully), but they all sin of free choice. The temptations to sin are developed before those intellectual and moral powers are developed that could counteract the excessive demands of the physical senses.

Observe the developments of the newborn child. Some pain or appetite awakens his consciousness of existence, and by this is created a demand for the things the child perceives himself to need. Then the little infant begins to struggle for good – for that particular good which its newly developed sensibility demands. Need, the struggling demand for supply, and the gratification form a process of development that gives such power to the sensibility that before long generates an intense selfishness – and before the conscience and reason are perceptibly developed, they have laid the foundation for spiritual death.

If the Spirit of God does not inspire spiritual needs and stir up the mind to efforts in obtaining them, the mind becomes so preoccupied and its sensibilities acquire such habits of control over the will that when the idea of right and wrong is first developed, the mind remains dead to its demands. The appetites have already gained the upper hand. The mind seems to act as if it were hardly aware that it has a soul or any spiritual needs.

The spiritual consciousness is at first not developed at all. The mind does not seem to know its spiritual relationship. When this knowledge first forces itself upon the mind, it finds the ground preoccupied, the habits established, and the soul too much engaged for earthly good to be called off. The tendency of this law of development is completely downward. The appetites become more and more controlling and domineering. The mind has less and less regard for God. The mind comes into a state in which spiritual truth bothers and angers it, and of course it thoroughly leans toward spiritual coldness – choosing apathy, even though aware of its danger, before the continual annoyance of unwelcome truths. This tends toward a state of dead coldness to spiritual need.

The first symptom of change is the soul's awaking to spiritual consequences. Sometimes this is weak at first, or sometimes it may be more strongly awakened to its spiritual relationship, position, and needs. This brings on concern, desire, and a deep sense of what the soul truly needs. From this arises an influence that begins to counteract the power of physical appetite. It begins to operate as a balance and check to those long-unrestrained demands.

You might notice here that in the same proportion as the spiritual consciousness is developed, the mind becomes distressed, for in this proportion, the struggle becomes intense and violent. Previously, the man was dead. He was like an animal as to the unrestrained indulgence of appetite – above the mere animal in some things, but below in others. He continues without that counteracting influence that arises from the spiritual awareness.

You see some people who live a careless, aimless life. They do not seem at all aware that they have a spiritual nature or any spiritual needs. When they awake to spiritual consciousness and reflection, conviction produces remorse and agony. This spiritual struggle, at whatever age it may occur, is in its general character the same that occurs in the infant when its physical awareness is first awakened.

It is only natural that when the spiritual instincts are awakened, people will begin to pray and struggle under a deep sense of being wrong and guilty. At first, this may be entirely selfish, but before conversion takes place, there will be a point in which the counterinfluences of the selfish against the spiritual will balance each other, and then the spiritual will gain the upper hand. The physical and the selfish must relatively decline as the spiritual gains strength, until victory moves to the side of the spiritual powers.

How commonly you can observe that when the mind becomes convicted of sin, the attractions of the world fade away. All it can give looks small. Sinners can no longer take pleasure in worldly things as they once had done. Indeed, this is a most extraordinary and remarkable struggle. How rapid and great are the changes through which the sinner passes!

Today he quenches the light of God in his soul and gropes on in darkness; tomorrow the light may return and reveal yet greater sin. One day he relapses back to worldliness and gives up his soul to his own thoughts and pleasures, but before another day has past, there is bitterness in this cup and he abhors it, and from his soul cries out, "This can never satisfy an immortal mind!"

Now he begins to try to reform outwardly, but before long he finds that this utterly fails to bring peace to his soul. He is full of trouble and anxiety for salvation, yet all his struggles so far have been entirely selfish, and before he is converted, he must see this to be the case. He is in a horrible pit of miry clay. The more he struggles, the deeper he sinks and the more desperate his case becomes. Selfish efforts for spiritual relief are just like a quagmire of thick clay. Each struggle plunges the sinking man deeper in the pit.

The convicted man is ready to put himself to hard labor and mighty effort. At first he works with great hope of success, for he does not at first understand why selfish efforts will not be successful. He prays, but all in a selfish spirit. By this I mean that he thinks only of himself. He has no thought of honoring or pleasing God, and he has no thought of any benefit to his fellow beings. He does not inquire whether God can bless his course of life and state of heart without disservice to the rest of His great family. In fact, he does not think of caring for the rest of that family nor for the honor of its great Father. Of course, such selfish praying brings no answer, and when he finds this to be the case, he agonizes and struggles more than ever.

Now he tries to add to his works and efforts. He attends more meetings, reads his Bible more, and tries new forms of prayer. All is in vain. His heart is still selfish. "What can I do?" he cries out in agony. "If I pray, I am selfish, and if I stop praying, this too is selfish. If I read my Bible or neglect to read it, each is likewise selfish, and what can I do? How can I help being selfish?"

He has no idea how to act from any other or higher motive than his own interests. It is his darkness on this very point that makes the sinner's struggle so long and so unprofitable. This is the reason why he cannot be converted at once and why he needs to sink and flounder so much longer in the quagmire of unavailing and despairing works. It is only when he at last realizes that all this avails nothing that he begins to take some proper views of his situation and of his actions.

When he learns that indeed he cannot work out his own salvation by working at it in this way, he begins to consider whether he is not all wrong at heart – whether his motives of heart are not radically corrupt. Looking around and elsewhere, he begins to ask whether God may not have some claims and some rights as well as himself. Who is God, and where is He? Who is Jesus Christ, and what has He done? What did He die for? Is God a great King over all the earth, and should He not have due honor and reverence? Was it this great God who so loved the world as to give His Son to die for it?

He begins to understand. "Oh, I see I have quite neglected to think of God's rights and honor! Now I see how infinitely vile and wicked I have been! It is plain enough that I cannot live this way. No wonder God did not hear my selfish prayers. There was no hope in that sort of effort, for I had, as I now plainly see, no regard for God in anything I was then doing. How reasonable it is that God would ask me to cease from all my selfish efforts and to put away this selfishness itself – and to surrender myself entirely and forever to do or suffer all His blessed will!"

It is done, and now this long-troubled soul sinks into deep peace. It settles itself down at Jesus' feet, content if only Christ is honored and God's throne is made glorious. The final result, whether saved or lost, seems to give him no longer that agonizing uneasiness. The case is submitted to the Great Disposer in trustful humility. God will do all things well. If He takes due care of His own interests and glory, there will be no complaining – nothing but deep and peaceful satisfaction.

> This state of peaceful trust in God is subject to interruptions. The natural appetites have been denied but they are not dead.

In the case of most young converts, this state of peaceful trust in God is subject to interruptions. The natural appetites have been denied and their dominion over the will has been refused, but they are not dead. By and by they rise to assert their influence. They cry out for gratification, and sometimes they get it. Sadly, the young convert has fallen into sin! His soul is again in bondage and sorrow. Oh, how deeply he is ashamed to think that he has again given in to temptation and pierced the heart on which he loved to rest! He had promised himself he would never sin, but he has sinned, and it is good for him if he finds no heart to conceal or deny the fact.

It is better to admit it all, and most freely, although it wounds his heart more than all his former sins. Observe his agony of spirit! His tears of repentance were never before so bitter! He feels disappointed, and it almost seems to him that this failure must shatter all his plans and hopes of leading a Christian life. It does not work as he thought it would. He feels ashamed before God, for he says, "How can God ever trust me again after such occasions of unfaithfulness?" He can hardly get himself to say a word to God or to Christ. He is almost sure that he has been deceived, but finally he reminds himself of the cross of Calvary and catches a faint ray of light – a beam of the light of love. He says, "There may be mercy for me yet! I will at least go to Jesus and see." Again he goes, and again he falls into those arms of love and is made purposely welcome. The light of God shines on his soul again, and he finds himself once more an accepted son in his Father's presence.

But now a new form of desire is awakened. He has learned something of his own weakness and has tasted the bitterness of sin. With an agony of interest never known before, he asks, "Can I ever become deeply rooted in holiness? Can I have righteousness enough to make me stand in the evil day?" (Ephesians 6:13). This is a new form of spiritual desire, such as our text expresses in the words *hunger and thirst after righteousness.*

These extended remarks are only an introduction to my general subject, and they are intended to get before your mind the true idea of hungering and thirsting after righteousness. This state of mind is not merely conviction. It is not remorse or sorrow or a struggle to obtain a hope or to get out of danger. All these feelings may have preceded this, but the hungering after righteousness is none of these. It is a longing desire to realize the idea of spiritual and moral purity. He has in some degree appreciated the purity of heaven, along with the necessity of being himself as pure as the holy ones there, in order to enjoy their joy and breathe freely in their atmosphere.

This state of mind is not often expanded upon by writers, and it seems rarely to have engaged the attention of the church as its importance demands. When the mind gets a right view of the atmosphere of heaven, it sees plainly that it cannot breathe there, but must be suffocated unless its own spirit is in harmony with the purity of that world. I remember the case of a man who relapsed into sin after living a Christian life for a season. Eventually, God reclaimed His wandering child. When I next saw this man and heard him speak of his state of relapse, he suddenly turned away and burst into tears, saying, "I have been living in sin, almost choked to death in its atmosphere. It seemed as if I could not breathe in it. It almost choked the breath of spiritual life from my system."

Have not some of you known what this means? You could not bear the cursed atmosphere of sin – it is so much like the very smoke of the pit! After you get out of it, you say, "Let me never be there again!" Your soul agonizes and struggles to find some refuge against this awful relapsing into sin. You long for a pure atmosphere and a pure heart that will never hold fellowship with darkness or its works again.

The young convert, like the infant child, may not at first distinctly understand its own condition and needs, but such experience, as I have been explaining, develops the idea of perfect purity, and then the soul longs for it with longings irrepressible. The now-enlightened convert says, "I must be drawn into living union with God as revealed in Jesus Christ. I cannot rest until I find God and have Him revealed to me as my everlasting refuge and strength."

Some years ago, I preached a sermon for the purpose of developing the idea of the spiritual life. The minister for whom I preached said to me, "I want to show you a letter written many years ago by a lady now advanced in age that details her remarkable experience on this subject. After her conversion, she found herself exceedingly weak, and she often wondered if this was all the stability and strength she could hope for from Christ in His gospel. 'Is this,' she said, 'all that God can do for me?' With much time and prayer, she examined her Bible. At last she found that beneath what she had ever read and examined before, there lay a class of passages that revealed the real gospel – salvation from sinning. She saw the provisions of the gospel in full relief. Then she closed herself up, determined to seek this blessing until she would find it. Her soul went forth after God, seeking communion with Him and the great blessing that she so deeply felt she needed. She had found the needed promises in God's Word, and now she held on to them as if she could not let them go until they had all been fulfilled in her own joyful experience. She cried mightily to God. She said, 'If You do not give me this blessing, I can never believe You again.'

"During this time and through His Word, the Lord showed her that the provisions were already made, that they were just as full and as glorious as they needed to be or could be, and that she could receive them by faith if she would. In fact, it was plainly the case that the Spirit of the Lord was pressing the blessing upon her acceptance so that she had only to believe – to open wide her mouth that it might be filled (Psalm 81:10). She saw and obeyed; then she became firm and strong. Christ had made her free. She was no longer in bondage. Her Lord had absolutely enlarged her soul in faith and love, and triumphantly she could exclaim, 'Glory be to God! Christ has made me free.'"

The state of mind expressed by hungering and thirsting is a real hunger and thirst, and the hunger and thirst is fully satisfied with the Bread and Water of Life. These types (if indeed they are to be regarded as types at all) are kept up fully throughout the Bible, and all true Christians can testify to the appropriateness of the language to express the idea.

I have said that this state of mind implies conversion, for although the awakened sinner may have agonies and convictions, he has no clear idea of what this union with Christ is, nor does he clearly understand the need of a cleansed heart. He needs some experience of what holiness is, and he often also seems to need to have tasted some of the exceeding bitterness of sin as felt by one who has been near the Lord before he will fully comprehend this great spiritual need of being made a partaker indeed of Christ's own perfect righteousness.

By righteousness here, we are not to understand something imputed, but something real. It is imparted, not imputed. Christ draws the souls of His people into such union with Himself that they become *partakers of the divine nature* (2 Peter 1:4), or as elsewhere expressed, *partakers of his holiness* (Hebrews 12:10). The troubled Christian longs for this. Having had a little taste of it, and then having tasted the bitterness of a relapse into sin, his soul is stirred to most intense struggles to realize this blessed union with Christ.

A few words should now be said on what is implied in being filled with this righteousness. Worldly people incessantly hunger and thirst after worldly good, but attainment never overtakes desire. Therefore, they are never filled. There is always a conscious desire that no obtaining of this kind of good can satisfy. It is most remarkable that worldly people can never be filled with the things they seek. Well do the Scriptures say that this desire enlarges itself as hell and is never satisfied (Habakkuk 2:5). They really hunger and thirst even more according to how much more they obtain.

Let it be especially noted that this being filled with righteousness is not perfection in the highest sense of this term. People often use the term "perfection" of that which is absolutely complete, a state that has no room for improvement and beyond which there can be no progress. There can be no such perfection among Christians in any world – earth or heaven. It can pertain to no being except God. He, and He alone, is perfect beyond possibility of progress. All else except God are making progress – the wicked from bad to worse, and the righteous from good to better.

Instead of making no more progress in heaven, as some suppose, the law of progress is probably in a geometrical ratio; the more they have, the farther they will advance. I have often wondered whether this law that seems to prevail here (what I refer to as impulsive progression) will operate there. Here we notice that the mind from time to time gives itself to most intense exertion to make attainments in holiness. Once the attainment has been made, the mind rests for a season, as if it had taken its meal and was waiting for the natural return of its appetite before it would put forth its next great effort. Could it not be that the same law of progress is at work even in heaven?

> There can be no such perfection among Christians in any world. It can pertain to no being except God.

We see here the operations of this law in the usual Christian progress. Intense longing and desire produce great struggling and earnest prayer. At last, the special blessing desired is found, and for a time, the soul seems to be filled to overflowing. It seems to be fully satisfied and to have received all that it supposed possible, and possibly even more than was ever asked or thought. The soul cries out before the Lord, "I did not know there was such fullness in store for Your people. How wonderful that God should grant it to someone such as myself!"

The soul finds itself swallowed up and lost in the great depths and riches of such a blessing. Oh, how the heart pours itself out in the one most expressive petition, *Thy will be done in earth, as it is in heaven* (Matthew 6:10). All prayer is swallowed up in this. And then the praise, the fullness of praise! All struggle and agony are interrupted. The soul seems to demand a rest from prayer so that it may pour itself out in one mighty tide of praise. Some suppose that people in this state will never again experience those longings after a new baptism, but in this they are mistaken. The meal they have had may last them a considerable time – maybe even longer than Elijah's meal that strengthened him for forty days (1 Kings 19:8), but the time of comparative hunger will come around again, and they will prepare themselves for a new struggle.

This is what is sometimes expressed as a baptism, an anointing, an unction, a sealing of the Spirit (Ephesians 1:13), or an earnest or the promise of the Spirit (2 Corinthians 1:22). All these terms are applicable and beautiful to signify this special work of the divine Spirit in the heart. So truly does the soul seem to live on Christ that those who experience it know how well and appropriately it is described as eating the flesh and drinking the blood of the Lord Jesus (John 6:53-57).

The bread and the water of life are also promised freely to those who are thirsty. These terms may seem very mystical and meaningless to those who have had no experience, but they are all plain to those who have known in their own souls what they mean. If you ask why figures of speech are used at all to signify spiritual things, you have the answer in the difficulties of the human mind in regard to comprehending spiritual things. Christ's language must have seemed very mystical to His hearers, yet it was the best He could use for His purpose.

If any man will do His will, he will know of His doctrine (John 7:17), but how can a selfish, depraved, foolish, and disobedient mind expect to enter into the spiritual meaning of this language? How strangely must Christ's words have sounded to the ears of Jewish priests: God in us (John 14:23), the Holy Spirit dwelling in you (John 14:17), You shall abide in Me (John 15:7), etc. How could they understand these things? *The living bread that came down from heaven* (John 6:51) – what could this mean to them? They thought they understood about the manna from heaven, and they idolized Moses, but they did not know how to understand what this Nazarene said about giving them the true bread from heaven that would be for the life of the world. No wonder they were perplexed, having only legal ideas of religion, and not having even the most remote speculation about the idea of a living union with the Messiah for the purposes of spiritual life.

What are the conditions of receiving this fullness? The soul must hunger and thirst for it, and this is the only condition specified in this passage. We know that it is very common to have promises made in the Bible, and yet not have all the conditions of the promise stated in the same connection. If we find them elsewhere, we are to regard them as definitive conditions, and they are to be understood as implied where they are not expressed.

In other places, we are told that faith is a fundamental condition. People must believe for it and receive it by faith. This is as naturally necessary as receiving and eating wheat bread is for the nourishment of the body. Ordinary food must be taken into the system by our own voluntary act. We take and eat, and then the body makes use of it. In the same way, faith receives the Bread of Life, which is then made use of for our good.

In general, it is found true that before Christians will sufficiently understand the relationship of this supply to their needs and to the means of supplying them, this hunger and thirst becomes very intense so as to overpower and cast into insignificance all their other appetites and desires. As by a general law, one master passion takes precedence over all minor ones and may sometimes entirely suspend them for a season. That is what we find in this case, when a soul intensely hungering and thirsting after righteousness almost forgets to hunger and thirst even after its common food and drink.

Place before him his study books, and he cannot bring his mind to enjoy them now. Invite him to a singing concert, and he has no desire to go at this time. Ask him to attend a gathering of people, and his mind is headed in another direction. He longs to find God, and he can take little interest in any other friend at present. Offer him worldly society, and you will find that he takes the least possible interest in it. He knows that such companions will not understand what his soul so intensely craves, and of course it were vain to look for understanding there.

It is an important condition that the mind should have a somewhat clear understanding of the thing needed and of the means of obtaining it. Effort cannot be well directed unless the subject is in some good measure understood. What is that sealing of the Spirit? What is this baptism? I must by all means see what this is before I can intelligently seek it and hope to gain it. It is true that no one can know as well before experience as he can and will know afterward, but he can learn something before, and often much more after, the light of experience shines in upon his soul. This is no more of a mystery than it is in hungering for a good dinner and being refreshed by it after you have eaten it.

If we would have this fullness, we must be sure to believe this promise and all similar promises. We must regard them as truly promises of God – all yea and amen in Christ Jesus (2 Corinthians 1:20), and as good for our souls to rely upon as the promise of pardon to the repentant and believing.

We must ask and insist upon the fulfillment of these promises to our souls. We are authorized to expect it in answer to our faith. We should first be certain that we ask in sincerity, and then we should expect the blessing just as we always expect God to be faithful to His Word. Why not? Has He said and will He not do it? Has He promised and will He not follow through (Numbers 23:19)?

We must believe that the promise implies a full supply. Our faith must not limit the power or the grace of Christ. The Christian is not impoverished in God; let him take care, therefore, that he does not impoverish himself by his narrow understanding of what God can do and loves to do for His hungering and thirsting children. Often there is need of great perseverance in the search for this blessing. Because of the darkness of the mind and the smallness of its faith, the way may not be prepared for the full bestowment of this great blessing for a long time.

> Our faith must not limit the power or the grace of Christ.

## Remarks

1. The Antinomian perfectionists mistook the meaning of this and of similar passages. They supposed that whoever believes gets so filled as to never thirst anymore. The fact is, though, that the mind may rise

higher and higher, making still richer attainments in holiness at each rising grade of progress. It may indeed find many resting places, just as John Bunyan gives to his pilgrim in *Pilgrim's Progress* – here at the top of the hill Difficulty, there on the Delectable Mountains – where he passes through scenes of great triumph, great faith, and great joy in God.

After these scenes, other periods of intense desire will occur for new baptisms of the Spirit and for a new ascent upon the heights of the divine life. This is to be the course of things at least as long as we remain in the flesh, and perhaps forever. It might be that the blessed spirits in heaven will never reach a point beyond which there will not be the same experience – new developments of God made to the mind, and by this means, new stages of progress and growth in holiness. With what amazement we will then study these stages of progress and delight to look abroad over the new fields of knowledge successively opened, along with the corresponding developments of mental power and of a holy character, all which stand related to these expressions of God as effects to their cause!

What new and glorious views have been bursting upon us, as fast as we could bear them, for countless ages! Looking back over the past, we will say, "Oh, this everlasting progress – this is indeed the blessedness of heaven! How far this surpasses our highest thought when we looked forward to heaven from the dim distance of our earthly pilgrimage! Here there is no end to the discoveries to be made or to the truths to be learned."

If there was to be no more food, how could there be any more spiritual thirst and spiritual hunger? How, indeed, could there be more spiritual joy? Suppose that somewhere in the passage of heaven's eternal ages we would reach a point where nothing more remains to be learned, not another thing is left to be inquired after, and not another fact remains to be investigated or truth to be known. What a blow to the joy of heaven!

We are told that the angels are desiring to look into the things of salvation (1 Peter 1:12). Oh, yes, when they saw our Messiah born, they were allowed to come so near us with their joyous outbursts of praise that even humans could hear. Do you not suppose that those angels, too, are growing in grace and advancing in knowledge? No doubt they are, most wonderfully, and have been ever since they came into existence.

How much more they must know of God now than they did before our world was created! How much more they still have to learn from God's rule over the human race! Do you think that they have no more desires after the knowledge of God? Have they no more desire to rise to still higher conformity of heart and character to the great Model of heaven? If this is how it is with angels, it is certainly not less so with their younger brethren – the holy who are redeemed from among men.

You might think that you could learn all human science by studying in a great university for a few days. This would be a great mistake. You can master many sciences and still have other heights to ascend – other vast fields of knowledge to explore. You might have the best of human teachers and the best possible opportunities for learning, yet still it would be enough to fill many lifetimes to master all there is in even human science. The mind is not made to be so filled to saturation that it desires no more or can receive no more. Like the trees planted on the rivers of the waters of life that bring forth twelve manner of fruits and whose roots go deep and drink largely of those blessed waters (Revelation 22:1-2), so is the mind that God has blessed with the functions of immortal progress.

As our ideal becomes elevated and we see higher points to which we may arise, we will have more stirrings of desire and more intense struggles to advance. What Christian does not find, as he reads the Bible over, new and deeper levels of meaning never seen before – new truths revealed and new beauties displayed. Old father O. used to say, "I am reading the Word of God. It is deep and rich, like the great heart of its Author. I have read now for two hours, and have only gotten over two verses. It will take me all eternity to read it through." So it was. He really found more in the Bible than other people did. He went deeper, and the deeper he went, the richer he found its precious ores of gold and silver.

The psalmist says, *Open thou mine eyes that I may behold wondrous things out of thy law* (Psalm 119:18). Have you not been so enraptured with love to this blessed Book that you wanted to hold it to your heart and become purified with its spirit? As you go down into its depths and find in each successive level of its deep thoughts new beauties and new fields of truth to explore, have you not been filled with intense desire to live long enough and have time and strength enough to see, to learn, and to enjoy it all? Like the successive landscapes as you ascend the lofty mountain's side and see them spreading out in grander beauty and broader range at each stage, so, as you really study the great and rich things of God's spiritual kingdom, there is no limit to this breadth of the knowledge of God, for the fields only become broader and more delightful as you ascend. Do you not think that the soul of the person who eats and drinks and fills his soul with divine righteousness must be truly blessed?

2. I am strongly impressed with the belief that some of you need new growth in your spiritual life. You need to go deeper into the knowledge of God as revealed in the soul. You need to hunger and thirst more intensely, and by this means to be filled as you have not often been as yet. Even though you may have tasted that the Lord is gracious, you still need to eat and drink abundantly at His table. It will not benefit you to live on those old dinners, long past and long since digested. You need a fresh meal. It is time for you to say, "I must know more about being filled with righteousness. My soul yearns for this heavenly food. I must come again into this banqueting house to be feasted again with His love" (Song of Solomon 2:4).

3. The full soul cannot be satisfied to enjoy its rich spiritual provisions alone. If well fed himself, he will be only more concerned to see others also fed and blessed. The spirit of Christ in his heart is a spirit of love, and this can never rest except as it sees others reaching the same standard of fulfillment and enjoyment that is so delightful to itself.

4. Real Christians should be, and in general they will be, growing better and holier as they get nearer to heaven. On the other hand, how great and fearful is the contrast between an older growing Christian and an older sinner who is growing in depravity and sin. The one is advancing toward heaven, and the other toward hell. The one goes on praising and loving, laboring and suffering for God and for his generation according to the will of God, but the other goes on his downward course, scolding and cursing as he goes, abhorred by men and disowned by his Maker.

> Real Christians should be, and in general they will be, growing better and holier as they get nearer to heaven.

You have seen the dreadful contrast. You could hardly believe that two people so unlike were both raised in the same township, attended the same school, attended the same religious assembly, and heard the same gospel – yet see how clearly the one is saved and the other damned. Each bears the sign in advance – the clear, unmistakable evidence of the destiny that awaits him.

5. Is it not time that each one of you who has any spiritual life should stand out before the world and put on your beautiful garments? Let all the world see that there is a power and a glory in the gospel such as human philosophy has never even approached. Show that the gospel produces purity and peace. Show that it enlarges the heart and opens the hand for the good of all humankind. Show that it conquers selfishness and transforms the soul from hate to love.

Sinners, you who have earthly hunger and thirst enough, let your ears be opened to hear the glad tidings of real salvation. You whose hearts have never known solid peace; you who are forever desiring, yet never satisfied; you who cry in your inmost souls, "Oh, for position, for honor, for wealth!" – look! Here is that which is better far than all you seek. Here are lasting riches and righteousness. Here are the first installments of pleasures that flow forever at God's right hand (Psalm 16:11). Here is heaven offered and even urged upon you to consider and choose. Choose life before death, and you will be wise for your eternal well-being.

# Charles G. Finney – A Brief Biography

One of the men most greatly used by God during America's Second Great Awakening was Charles Grandison Finney. He was born in Warren, Connecticut, on August 29, 1792, and died in Oberlin, Ohio, on August 16, 1875. Finney was a devoted evangelist, revivalist, and abolitionist.

Finney, being human, was certainly not perfect, yet he was greatly used by God to lead thousands to the Savior. Those who actually read his writings learn to love and appreciate him as a man surrendered to God and a servant of Jesus Christ.

Charles Finney began his career as a lawyer, but after his conversion on October 10, 1821, he left his law practice and began preaching the gospel of Jesus Christ. He was ordained as a Presbyterian minister in 1824 and began missionary work in western New York. Finney did not usually fit in well with the Old School Presbyterians, but often won his opponents over after discussing his beliefs with them personally and explaining his beliefs from the Bible. As is still true today, many who opposed Finney at first did so based upon hearsay rather than upon actually knowing the man and his teachings.

Charles Finney began preaching and seeing great results. Entire families and communities were changed by the power of God. He often opposed Universalism, which was a common belief of his day. While knowing that salvation comes only through faith in Jesus, Charles Finney preached that people needed to seek God and choose to follow Jesus.

Charles Finney was opposed by many, both sinners and religionists, yet he continued to preach and see spiritual fruit. He was opposed by some of the strict Presbyterians for some of his non-Presbyterian methods, such as allowing women to pray in meetings and adopting the then-Methodist practice of having a bench up front in meetings where those who were concerned about their souls could come up and sit and be dealt with about their souls.

Finney spent much time preaching in towns in western New York. One of his most well-known times of revival occurred in Rochester, New York, in 1830-1831. Finney continued preaching as a traveling revivalist/evangelist, and he saw thousands and thousands of lives changed by God, believers who remained faithful to God even decades later. Finney also preached about social issues, including the evils of alcohol and worldliness. He wrote much against Freemasonry, and he fiercely promoted the abolition of slavery. Finney also travelled to England twice during the 1850s to preach.

He became the minister of a Presbyterian church in New York City for a little while, but then moved on to preach at the Broadway Tabernacle that had been built for him. After about a year, Finney left to become the pastor of a Congregational church in Oberlin, Ohio, as well as to teach theology at Oberlin College. In 1851, Charles Finney became the college's second president, serving in that role until 1866.

Charles Finney was married three times. He married Lydia Root Andrews in 1824, with whom he had six children. After Lydia died in 1847, Charles married Elizabeth Ford Atkinson, who died in 1863. In 1865, he married Rebecca Allen Rayl, who outlived him, dying in 1907. All three of Finney's wives travelled with him as he preached.

Some of Charles Finney's well-known writings include his *Lectures on Systematic Theology, Lectures on Revivals of Religion*, and his *Autobiography.* He has been called the "Father of American Revivalism," and is thought to have led tens of thousands or even hundreds of thousands of people to the Lord Jesus Christ. He is known as one of America's most influential preachers.

Charles Finney did not always fit the traditional religious mold. His past as a lawyer was often seen in his sermons as he reasoned with people and made a case as to why they should follow Christ. He did not just go along with the traditional methods of the strict religionists of his day, but adapted methods to the needs of the people and spoke to them in common language. He did not fit in with the strict Calvinists, nor with the Arminians. Some have referred to his beliefs as "arminianized Calvinism." Nevertheless, he was a man who led many thousands of people from a life of sin to new life in Christ. Charles G. Finney was devoted to God, used by God, and admired and respected by many. He influenced individuals, families, communities, and the entire nation for God.

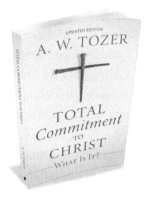

*Total Commitment to Christ,* by A. W. Tozer

*I am the Light of the world; he who follows Me will not walk in the darkness, but will have the Light of life.* – John 8:12

Christians ought to be so totally committed to Christ that it is final. Of looking back over your shoulder to see if there is something better – let that never again be your experience.

A short but inspiring booklet on how to follow Christ with your whole heart.

*Available where books are sold.*

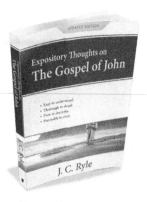

## *Expository Thoughts on the Gospel of John,*
## by J. C. Ryle

*In the beginning was the Word, and the Word was with God, and the Word was God.* – John 1:1

Wisdom, encouragement, and exhortation is contained in these pages. Not because of the author's brilliance, but because of the words of truth contained in the gospel of John. And just as the Apostle John didn't draw any attention to himself, so also J. C. Ryle clearly and wonderfully directs his words and our thoughts towards the inspired words of scripture. If we truly love God, we will love His word; and the more study His word, the more we will love God.

*Available where books are sold.*

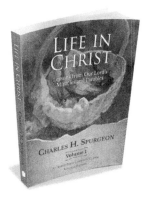

*Life in Christ (Vol. 1-4)*,
by Charles H. Spurgeon

Men who were led by the hand or groped their way along the wall to reach Jesus were touched by his finger and went home without a guide, rejoicing that Jesus Christ had opened their eyes. Jesus is still able to perform such miracles. And, with the power of the Holy Spirit, his Word will be expounded and we'll watch for the signs to follow, expecting to see them at once. Why shouldn't those who read this be blessed with the light of heaven? This is my heart's inmost desire.

    – Charles H. Spurgeon

*Available where books are sold.*

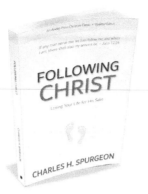

## *Following Christ,* by Charles H. Spurgeon

You cannot have Christ if you will not serve Him. If you take Christ, you must take Him in all His qualities. You must not simply take Him as a Friend, but you must also take Him as your Master. If you are to become His disciple, you must also become His servant. God-forbid that anyone fights against that truth. It is certainly one of our greatest delights on earth to serve our Lord, and this is to be our joyful vocation even in heaven itself: *His servants shall serve Him: and they shall see His face* (Revelation 22:3-4).

*Available where books are sold.*

Made in the USA
Monee, IL
06 February 2023

27230197R00221